D0900871

全 两册
中英双语

The Gay Genius

苏东坡传

上

林语堂 著

张振玉 译

湖南文艺出版社
HUNAN LITERATURE AND ART PUBLISHING HOUSE

博集天卷
CS-BOOKY

THE GAY GENIUSBy Lin Yutang

This edition arranged with Curtis Brown Group Ltd.

through Andrew Nurnberg Associates International Limited

著作权合同登记号：图字18-2016-126

图书在版编目（CIP）数据

苏东坡传 = The Gay Genius：全两册：汉、英 / 林语堂著；张振玉译. —长沙：湖南文艺出版社，2017.6（2022.7重印）

ISBN 978-7-5404-8086-8

Ⅰ.①苏… Ⅱ.①林… ②张… Ⅲ.①苏轼（1037-1101）—传记—汉、英 Ⅳ.①K825.6

中国版本图书馆CIP数据核字（2017）第095667号

上架建议：名家经典·人物传记

SU DONGPO ZHUAN: QUAN LIANG CE: HAN、YING

苏东坡传：全两册：汉、英

作　　者：林语堂
译　　者：张振玉
出 版 人：曾赛丰
责任编辑：薛　健　刘诗哲
监　　制：蔡明菲　邢越超
特约策划：王　维
特约编辑：蔡文婷
版权支持：辛　艳　张雪珂
营销支持：文刀刀　周　茜
封面设计：棱角视觉
版式设计：李　洁
出　　版：湖南文艺出版社
　　　　　（长沙市雨花区东二环一段 508 号　邮编：410014）
网　　址：www.hnwy.net
印　　刷：三河市百盛印装有限公司
经　　销：新华书店
开　　本：875mm×1230mm　1/32
字　　数：651 千字
印　　张：26.5
版　　次：2017 年 6 月第 1 版
印　　次：2022 年 7 月第 5 次印刷
书　　号：ISBN 978-7-5404-8086-8
定　　价：88.00 元（全两册）

苏	THE GAY GENIUS:	目
东坡	THE LIFE AND TIMES OF	录
传	SU TUNGPO	CONTENTS

卷二 壮年
BOOK TWO **Early Manhood**

卷三 老练
BOOK THREE **MATURITY**

卷四 流放岁月
BOOK FOUR **YEARS OF EXILE**

自序

　　我写苏东坡传并没有什么特别理由，只是以此为乐而已。给他写本传记的念头，已经存在心中有年。1936年我全家赴美时，身边除去若干精选的排印细密的中文基本参考书之外，还带了些有关苏东坡的以及苏东坡著的珍本古籍，至于在行李中占很多地方一事，就全置诸脑后了。那时我希望写一本有关苏东坡的书，或是翻译些他的诗文，而且，即便此事我不能如愿，我旅居海外之时，也愿身边有他相伴。像苏东坡这样富有创造力，这样守正不阿，这样放任不羁，这样令人万分倾倒而又望尘莫及的高士，有他的作品摆在书架上，就令人觉得有了丰富的精神食粮。现在我能专心致志写他这本传记，自然是一大乐事，此外还需要什么别的理由吗？

　　元气淋漓富有生机的人总是不容易理解的。像苏东坡这样的人物，是人间不可无一难能有二的。对这种人的人品个性作解释，一般而论，总是徒劳无功的。在一个多才多艺，生活中多彩多姿的人身上，挑选出他若干使人敬爱的特点，倒是轻而易举。我们未尝不可说，苏东坡是个秉性难改的乐天派，是悲天悯人的道德家，是黎民百姓的好朋友，是散文作家，是新派的画家，是伟大的书法家，是酿酒的实验者，是工程师，是假道学的反对派，是瑜伽术的修炼者，是佛教徒，是士大夫，是皇帝的秘书，是饮酒成癖者，是心肠慈悲的法官，是政治上的坚持己见者，是月下的漫步者，是诗人，是生性诙谐爱开玩笑的人。可是这些也许还不足以勾绘出苏东坡的全貌。我若说一提到苏东坡，在中国总会引起人亲切敬佩的微笑，也许这话最能概括苏东坡的一切了。苏东坡的人品，具有一个多才多艺的天才的深厚、广博、诙谐，有高度的智力，有天真烂漫的赤子之心——正如耶稣所说，具有蛇的智慧，兼有鸽子的温柔敦厚，在苏东坡这些方面，其他诗人是不能望其项背的。这些品质之荟萃于一身，是天地间的凤毛麟角，不可多见的。而苏东坡正是此等人！他保持天真淳朴，终身不渝。政治上的钩心斗角与利害谋算，与他的人品是格格不入的；他的诗词文章，或一时即兴之作，或是有所不满时有感而发，都是自然流露，顺乎天性，刚猛激烈，正如他所说的"春鸟秋虫之声"；也未尝不可比作他的诗句："猿吟鹤唳本无意，不知下有行人行。"他一直卷在政治旋涡之中，但是他却光风霁月，高高超越于狗苟蝇营的政治勾当之上。他不伎不求，随时随地吟诗作赋，批评臧否，纯然表达心之所感，至于会招致何等后果，与自己有何利害，则一概置之度外了。因是之故，一直到今天，读者仍以阅读他的作品为乐，因为像他这一等人，总是关心世事，始终亢言直论，不稍隐讳的。他的作品之中，流露出他的本性，亦庄亦谐，生动而有力，虽需视情况之所宜而异其趣，然而莫不真笃而诚恳，完全发乎内心。他之写作，除去自得其乐外，别无理由，而今日吾人读其诗文，别无理由，只因为他写得那么美，那么遒健朴茂，那么字字自真纯的心肺间流出。

　　一千年来，为什么中国历代都有那么多人热爱这位大诗人，我极力想分析出这种缘故，现在该说到第二项理由，其实这项理由，和第一项理由也无大差别，只是说法不同而已。那就是，苏东坡自有其迷人的魔力。就如魔力之在女人，美丽芬芳之在花朵，是易于感觉而难于说明的。苏东坡主要的魔力，是熠熠闪灼的天才所具有的魔力，这等天才常常会引起妻子或极其厚爱他的人为他忧心焦虑，令人不知应当因其大无畏的精神而敬爱他，抑或为了使他免于旁人的加害而劝阻他、保护他。他身上显然有一股道德的力量，非人力所能扼制，这股力量，由他呱呱落地开始，即强而有力地在他身上运行，直到死亡封闭上他的嘴，打断了他的谈笑才停止。他挥动如椽之笔，如同儿戏一般。他能狂妄怪僻，也能庄重严肃；能轻松玩笑，也能郑重庄严。从他的笔端，我们能听到人类情感之弦的振动，有喜悦，有愉快，有梦幻的觉醒，有顺从的忍受。他享受宴饮、享受美酒，总是热诚而友善。他自称生性急躁，遇有不惬心意之事，便觉得"如蝇在食，吐之方快"。一次，他厌恶某诗人之诗，就直说那"正是东京学究饮私酒，食瘴死牛肉，醉饱后所发者也"。

　　他开起玩笑来，不分敌友。有一次，在朝廷盛典中，在众大臣之前，他向一位道学家开玩笑，用一个文辞将他刺痛，后来不得不承担此事的后果。可是，别人所不能了解的是，苏东坡会因事发怒，但是他却不会恨人。他恨邪恶之事，对身为邪恶之人，他并不记挂于心中，只是不喜爱此等人而已。因为恨别人，是自己无能的表现，所以，苏东坡并非才不如人，因而也从不恨人。总之，我们所得的印象是，他的一生载歌载舞，深得其乐，忧患来临，一笑置之。他的这种魔力就是我这鲁拙之笔所要尽力描写的，他的这种魔力也就是使无数中国的读书人所倾倒、所爱慕的。

本书所记载的是一个诗人、画家与老百姓之挚友的事迹。他感受敏锐、思想透彻、写作优美、作为勇敢，绝不为本身利益而动摇，也不因俗见而改变。他并不精于自谋，但却富有民胞物与的精神。他对人亲切热情、慷慨厚道，虽不积存一文钱，但自己却觉得富比王侯。他虽生性倔强、絮聒多言，但是富有捷才，不过也有时口不择言，过于心直口快；他多才多艺、好奇深思，深沉而不免于轻浮，处世接物，不拘泥于俗套，动笔为文则自然典雅；为父兄、为丈夫，以儒学为准绳，而骨子里则是一纯然道家，但愤世嫉俗，是非过于分明。以文才学术论，他远超过其他文人学士，他自然无须心怀忌妒，自己既然伟大非他人可及，自然对人温和友善，对自己亦无损害，他是纯然一副淳朴自然相，故无须乎尊贵的虚饰；在为官职所羁绊时，他自称局促如辕下之驹。处此乱世，他犹如政坛风暴中之海燕，是庸妄官僚的仇敌，是保民抗暴的勇士。虽然历朝天子都对他怀有敬慕之心，历朝皇后都是他的真挚友人，但苏东坡还是屡遭贬降，甚至遭到逮捕，忍辱苟活。

有一次，苏东坡对他弟弟子由说了几句话，话说得最好，描写他自己也恰当不过：

"吾上可陪玉皇大帝，下可陪卑田院乞儿。眼前见天下无一个不好人。"

所以，苏东坡过得快乐，无所畏惧，像一阵清风度过了一生，不无缘故。

苏东坡一生的经历，根本是他本性的自然流露。在玄学上，他是个佛教徒，他知道生命是某种东西刹那间的表现，是永恒的精神在刹那间存在躯壳之中的形式，但是他却不肯接受人生是重担、是苦难的说法——他认为那不尽然。至于他本人，是享受人生的每一刻时光。在玄学方面，他是印度教的思想；但是在气质上，他却是道地的中国人的气质。从佛教的否定人生、儒家的正视人生、道家的简化人生，这位诗人在心灵识见中产生了他的混合的人生观。人生最长也不过三万六千日，但是那已然够长了；即使他追寻长生不死的仙丹妙药终成泡影，人生的每一刹那，只要连绵不断，也就美好可喜了。他的肉体虽然会死，他的精神在下一辈子，则可成为天空的星、地上的河，可以闪亮照明，可以滋润营养，因而维持众生万物。这一生，他只是永恒在刹那显现间的一个微粒，他究竟是哪一个微粒，又何关乎重要？所以生命毕竟是不朽的、美好的，所以他尽情享受人生。这就是这位旷古奇才乐天派的奥秘的一面。

　　本书正文并未附有脚注，但曾细心引用来源可证之资料，并尽量用原来之语句，不过此等资料之运用，表面看来并不明显易见。因所据来源全系中文，供参考之脚注对大多数美国读者并不实用。资料来源可查书后参考书目。为免读者陷入中国人名复杂之苦恼，我已尽量淘汰不重要人物的名字，有时只用姓而略其名。此外对人也前后只用一个名字，因为中国文人有四五个名字。原文中引用的诗，有的我译英诗，有的因为句中有典故，译成英诗之后古怪而不像诗，若不加冗长的注解，含义仍然晦涩难解，我索性就采用散文略达文意了。

　　　　　　　　　　　　　　　　　　　　　　　林语堂

PREFACE

There is really no reason for my writing the life of Su Tungpo except that I want to do it. For years the writing of his biography has been at the back of my mind. In 1936, when I came to the United States with my family, I brought with me, along with a carefully selected collection of basic Chinese reference books in compact editions, also a few very rare and ancient editions of works by and about this poet, for which all considerations of space were thrown overboard. I had hoped then to be able to write a book about him, or translate some of his poems or prose, and even if I could not do so, I wanted him to be with me while I was living abroad. It was a matter of sustenance of the spirit to have on one's shelves the works of a man with great charm, originality, and integrity of purpose, an enfant terrible, a great original mind that could not conform. Now that I am able to apply myself to this task, I am happy, and this should be an all-sufficient reason.

A vivid personality is always an enigma. There had to be one Su Tungpo, but there could not be two. Definitions of a personality generally satisfy only those who make them. It would be easy to pick out from the life and character of a man with such a versatile talent and colorful life a conglomerate of the qualities that have endeared him to his readers. One might say that Su Tungpo was an incorrigible optimist, a great humanitarian, a friend of the people, a prose master, an original painter, a great calligraphist, and experimenter in wine making, an engineer, a hater of puritanism, a yogi, a Buddhist believer, a Confucian statesman, a secretary to the emperor, a confirmed winebibber, a humane judge, a dissenter in politics, a prowler in the moonlight, a poet, and a wag. And yet that might miss the sum total of what made up Su Tungpo. I can perhaps best sum it up by saying that the mention of Su Tungpo always elicits an affectionate and warm admiring smile in China. For more than other Chinese poets', Su Tungpo's personality had the richness and variety and humor of a many-sided genius, possessing a gigantic intellect and a guileless child's heart—a combination described by Jesus as the wisdom of the serpent and the gentleness of the dove. Admittedly, this is a rare combination, shared only by a few born upon this earth. Here was a man! All through his life he retained a perfect naturalness and honesty with himself. Political chicanery and calculation were foreign to his character; the poems and essays he wrote on the inspiration of the moment or in criticism of something he disliked were the natural outpourings of his heart, instinctive and impetuous, like "the bird's song in spring and the cricket's chirp in autumn," as he put it once; or again they may be likened to the "cries of monkeys in the jungle or of the storks in high heaven, unaware of the human listeners below." Always deeply involved in politics, he was always greater than politics. Without guile and without purpose, he went along singing, composing, and criticizing, purely to express something he felt in his heart, regardless of what might be the consequences for himself. And so it is that this readers today enjoy his writings as those of a man who kept his mind sharply focused on the progress of events, but who first and last reserved the inalienable right to speak for himself. From his writings shines forth a personality vivid and vigorous playful of solemn, as the occasion may be, but always genuine, hearty, and true to himself. He wrote for no other reason than that he enjoyed writing, and today we enjoy his writing for no other reason than that he wrote so beautifully, generously, and out of the pristine innocence of his heart.

As I try to analyze the reasons why for a thousand years in China each generation has a crop of enthusiastic admirers of this poet, I come to the second reason, which is the same as the first, stated in a different way. Su Tungpo had charm. As with charm in women and beauty and fragrance in flowers, it is easier to feel it than to tell what elements it is composed of. The chief charm of Su Tungpo was that of a brilliant genius who constantly caused worries to his wife or those who loved him best—one does not know whether to admire and love him for his valiant courage, or stop him and protect him from all harm. Apparently there was in him a force of character that could not be stopped by anyone, a force that, started at the moment of his birth, had to run its course until death closed his mouth and stopped his laughing chatter. He wielded his pen almost as if it were a toy. He could be whimsical or dignified, playful or serious, very serious, and from his pen we hear a chord reflecting all the human emotions of joy, delight, disillusionment, and resignation. Always he was hearty and enjoyed a party and a good drink. He described himself as impatient in character and said that when there was something he disliked, he had to "spit it out like a fly found in one's food." When he disliked the verse of a certain poet, he characterized it as "the composition of a Shantung schoolteacher after sipping bad liquor and eating spoiled beef."

He made jokes on his friends and his enemies. Once at a great court ceremony, in the presence of all the high officials, he made fun of a certain puritanical neo-Confucianist and stung him with a phrase which made the victim smart, and for which he suffered the consequences. Yet what other people could not understand was that he could get angry over things, but never could hate persons. He hated evil, but the evil-doers did not interest him. He merely disliked them. Since hatred is an expression of incompetence, he never knew personal hatred, because he did not know incompetence. On the whole, we get the impression that he played and sang through life and enjoyed it tremendously, and when sorrow came and misfortune fell, he accepted them with a smile. That is the kind of charm which I am trying to describe in my lame and halting fashion and which has made him the favorite poet of so many Chinese scholars.

This is the story of a poet, painter, and friend of the people. He felt strongly, thought clearly, wrote beautifully, and acted with high courage, never swerved by his own interests or the changing fashions of opinion. He did not know how to look after his own welfare, but was immensely interested in that of his fellow men. He was warm, generous, never saved a penny, but felt as rich as a king. He was stubborn, garrulous but witty, careless of his speech, one who wore his heart on his sleeve; versatile, curious, profound, and frivolous, romantic in manners and classicist in letters, a Confucianist as a father, brother, and husband, but a Taoist under his skin, and a hater of all shams and hypocrisy. He was so much better a writer and scholar than others that he never had to be jealous, and he was so great he could afford to be gentle and kind. Simple and unaffected, he never cared for the trappings of dignity; when he was shackled with an office, he described himself as harnessed deer. Living in troublous times, he became the stormy petrel of politics, an enemy of a fatuous, selfish bureaucracy and a champion of the people against their oppressors. With the successive emperors as his personal admirers and the empresses as his friends, Su Tungpo managed to be demoted and arrested, and to live in disgrace.

The best saying of Su Tungpo and the best description of himself was what he said to his brother Tseyu:

"Up above, I can associate with the Jade Emperor of Heaven, and down below I can associate with the poor folks. I think there is not a single bad person in this world."

So he had reason to be joyous and unafraid, and went through life like a whirlwind.

The story of Su Tungpo is essentially the story of a mind. He was a

Buddhist in metaphysics, and knew that life was a temporary expression of something else, an eternal spirit in a temporary carcass, but he could never accept the thesis that life was a burden and a misery—not quiet. At least for himself, he enjoyed every moment he lived. Metaphysically he was Hindu, but temperamentally he was Chinese. Out of the Buddhist faith to annihilate life, the Confucian faith to live it, and the Taoist faith to simplify it, a new amalgam was formed in the crucible of the poet's mind and perceptions. The maximum span of human life was only "36,000 days," but that was long enough; if his search for the elixir of immortality was in vain, still every moment of life was good while it lasted. His body might die, but his spirit in the next incarnation might become a star in heaven, or a river on earth, to shine, to nourish, and to sustain all living. Of this living, he was only a particle in a temporary manifestation of the eternal, and it really did not matter very much which particle he happened to be. So life was after all eternal and good, and he enjoyed it. That was part of the secret of the gay genius.

I have not burdened the text with footnotes, but have taken care to make only statements which can be backed by sources, and have as far as possible used the original words, though this may not be apparent. As all the sources are in Chinese, footnote references would be of no practical value to the great majority of American readers. A general statement of the sources will be found in the Bibliographical Appendix. To prevent readers from floundering in Chinese names, I have eliminated those of the less important persons, or sometimes indicated only their family names. It is necessary also to refer to a person consistently by one name only, where a Chinese scholar had four or five. In spelling Chinese names, I have abolished the atrocious "hs" and substituted "sh," because this is the only sensible thing to do. Some of the poems I have translated into English verse, and some I have had to paraphrase into prose on account of the literary allusions which would make the translation grotesque and unpoetic, and the meaning obscure without lengthy comments.

Lin Yutang

苏
东坡
传

THE GAY GENIUS:

THE LIFE AND TIMES OF

SU TUNGPO

卷一

童年与青年

（一〇三六——一〇六一）

BOOK ONE **CHILDHOOD AND YOUTH**
(1036—1061)

第一章　文忠公

　　要了解一个已经死去一千年的人，并不困难。试想，通常要了解与我们同住在一个城市的居民，或是了解一位市长的生活，实在嫌所知不足，要了解一个古人，不是有时反倒容易吗？姑就一端而论，现今仍然在世的人，他的生活尚未完结，一旦遇有危机来临，谁也不知道他会如何行动。醉汉会戒酒自新；教会中的圣人会堕落；牧师会和唱诗班的少女私奔……活着的人总会有好多可能的改变。还有，活着的人总有些秘密，他那些秘密之中最精彩的，往往在他死了好久之后才会泄露出来。这就是何以评论与我们自己同时代的人是一件难事，因为他的生活离我们太近了。论一个已然去世的诗人如苏东坡，情形便不同了。我读过他的札记、他的七百首诗，还有他的八百通私人书简。所以知道一个人，或是不知道一个人，与他是否为同代人没有关系。主要的倒是是否对他有同情的了解。归根结底，我们只能知道自己真正了解的人，我们只能完全了解我们真正喜爱的人。我认为我完全知道苏东坡，因为我了解他；我了解他，是因为我喜爱他。喜爱哪个诗人，完全是出于一种癖好。我想李白更为崇高，而杜甫更为伟大——在他伟大的诗之清新、自然、工巧、悲天悯人的情感方面更为伟大。但是不必表示什么歉意，恕我直言，我偏爱的诗人是苏东坡。

在今天看来，我觉得苏东坡伟大的人格，比中国其他文人的人格，更为鲜明突出，在他的生活和作品里，显露得越发充分。在我的头脑里，苏东坡的意象之特别清楚明显，其理由有二：第一个理由是，由于苏东坡本人心智上才华的卓越，深深印在他写的每一行诗上，正如我所看见的他那两幅墨竹上那乌黑的宝墨之光，时至今日，依然闪耀照人，就犹如他蘸笔挥毫是在顷刻之前一样。这是天地间一大奇迹，在莎士比亚的创作上，亦复如此。莎翁诗句的遒健，是来自诗人敏感的天性与开阔豁达的胸襟，至今依然清新如故。纵然有后代学者的钻研考证，我们对莎士比亚的生活所知者仍极稀少，可是在他去世四百年之后，由于他的作品中感情的力量，我们却知道了他的心灵深处。

第二个理由是，苏东坡的生活资料较为完全，远非其他中国诗人可比。有关他漫长的一生中多彩多姿政治生涯的那些资料，存在各种史料中，也存在他自己浩繁的著作中。他的诗文都计算在内，接近百万言；他的札记，他的遗墨，他的私人书信，在当时把他视为最可敬爱的文人而写的大量的闲话漫谈，都流传到现在了。在他去世后百年之内，没有一本传记类的书不曾提到这位诗人。宋儒都长于写日记，尤以司马光、王安石、刘挚、曾布为著名；勤奋的传记作者如王明清、邵伯温。由于王安石的国家资本新法引起的纠纷，和一直绵延苏东坡一生的政坛风波的扰攘不安，作家都保存了那一时代的资料，其中包括对话录，为量甚大。苏东坡并不记日记，他不是记日记那一类型的人，记日记对他恐怕过于失之规律严正而不自然。但是他写札记，遇有游山玩水、思想、人物、处所、事件，他都笔之于书，有的记有日期，有的不记日期。而别人则忙于把他的言行记载下来。爱慕他的人都把他写的书简题跋等精心保存。当时他以杰出的书法家出名，随时有人恳求墨宝，他习惯上是随时题诗，或是书写杂感评论，酒饭之后，都随手赠予友人。此等小简偶记，人皆珍藏，传之子孙后代，有时也以高价卖出。在这些偶记题跋中，往往有苏东坡精妙之作。如今所保存者，他的书简约有八百通，有名的墨迹题跋约六百件。实际上，是由于苏东坡受到广泛的喜爱，后来才有搜集别的名人书札题跋文字印行的时尚，如黄山谷便是其一。当年成都有一位收藏家，在苏东坡去世之后，立即开始搜集苏东坡的墨迹书简等，刻之于石的，拓下拓片出卖，供人做临摹书法之用。有一次，苏东坡因对时事有感而作的诗，立刻有人抄写流传，境内多少文人竞相背诵。苏东坡虽然发乎纯良真挚之情，但内容是对政策表示异议，当时正值忠直之士不容于国都之际，当权者之愤怒遂集于他一人之身，情势严重，苏东坡几乎险遭不测。他是不是后悔呢？表面上，在他贬谪期间，对不够亲密的朋友他说是已然后悔，但是对莫逆之交，他说并无悔意，并且说，倘遇饭中有蝇，仍须吐出。由于他精神上的坦白流露，他也以身列当时高士之首而自伤，在与心地狭窄而位居要津的政客徒然挣扎了一番之后，他被流放到中国域外的蛮荒琼崖海岛，他以坦荡荡之胸怀处之，有几分相信是命运使然。

像苏东坡这样的人，生活中竟有如此的遭遇，他之成为文人窃窃私语的话柄、尊重景仰的话题，尤其是在他去世之后，乃是自然之事。若与西方相似之人比较，李白，一颗文坛上的流星，在刹那间壮观惊人地闪耀之后，而自行燃烧消灭，正与雪莱、拜伦相近。杜甫则酷似弥尔顿，既是虔敬的哲人，又是仁厚的长者，学富而文工，以古朴之笔墨，写丰厚之情思。苏东坡则始终富有青春活力。以人物论，颇像英国的小说家萨克雷（Thackeray）；在政坛上的活动与诗名，则像法国的雨果；他具有的动人的特点，又仿佛英国的约翰逊。不知为什么，我们对约翰逊的中风，现在还觉得不安，而对弥尔顿的失明则不然。倘若弥尔顿同时是像英国画家庚斯博罗，也同时像以诗歌批评英国时事的蒲柏，而且也像英国饱受折磨的讽刺文学家斯威夫特，而没有他日渐增强的尖酸，那我们便找到一个像苏东坡的英国人了。苏东坡虽然饱经忧患拂逆，但他的人性更趋温和厚道，并没变得尖酸刻薄。今天我们之所以喜爱苏东坡，也是因为他饱受了人生之苦的缘故。

中国有一句谚语，就是说一个人如何，要"盖棺论定"。人生如梦，一出戏演得如何，只有在幕落之时才可以下断语。不过有这种区别——人生如同戏剧，但是在人生的戏剧里，最富有智慧与最精明的伶人，对于下一幕的大事如何，也是茫然无知的。但是真正的人生，其中总包含有一种无可避免的性质，只有最好的戏剧才庶乎近之。因此在给过去的人写一本传记时，我们能把一场一场已经完成的戏，逐一观看，观看由人内在的气质与外在的环境所引起的必要的发展，这自然是一项重大的方便。在我将《苏东坡传》各章的资料钻研完毕之后，并且了解了为什么他非要有某些作为不可，为什么非要违背他弃官归隐的本意。我觉得自己好像一个中国的星相家，给一个人细批终身，预卜未来，那么清楚，那么明确，事故是那么在命难逃。中国的星相家能把一个人的一生，逐年断开，细批流年，把一生每年的推算写在一个折子上，当然卦金要远高出通常的卜卦。但是传记家的马后课却总比星相家的马前课可靠。今天，我们能够洞悉苏东坡穷达多变的一生，看出来那同样的无可避免的情形，但是断然无疑的是，他一生各阶段的吉凶祸福的事故，不管过错是否在他的星宿命运，的确是发生了、应验了。

苏东坡生于宋仁宗景祐三年（一〇三六），于徽宗建中靖国元年（一一〇一）逝世——是金人征服北宋的二十五年之前。他是在北宋最好的皇帝（仁宗）当政年间长大，在一个心地善良但野心勃勃的皇帝（神宗）在位期间做官，在一个十八岁的呆子（哲宗）荣登王位之时遭受贬谪。研究苏东坡传记，同时也就是研究宋朝因朋党之争而衰微，终于导致国力耗竭，小人当政。凡是读《水浒传》的人都知道当时的政治腐败，善良的百姓都因躲避税吏贪官，相继身入绿林而落草为寇，成了梁山上的英雄好汉了。

在苏东坡的青年时期，朝廷之上有一批淳儒贤臣。到北宋将亡之际，此等贤臣已悉数凋零，或是丢官去位。在朝廷第一次迫害儒臣，排除御史台的守正不阿之士，而由新法宰相王安石安排的若干小人取而代之，此时至少尚有二十余位纯良儒臣，宁愿遭受奸宄之毒手，不肯背弃忠贞正义。等到第二次党争祸起，在愚痴的童子帝王统治之下，忠良之臣大多已经死亡，其余则在流谪中弃世。宋朝国力之削弱，始自实行新法以防"私人资本之剥削"，借此以谋"人民"之利益，而由一个狂妄自信的大臣任其事。对国运为害之烈，再没有如庸妄之辈大权在握、独断独行时之甚的了。身为诗人、哲人之苏东坡，拼命将自己个人之平实常识，向经济学家王安石的逻辑对抗。王安石鼓吹的那套道理与中国当时所付出的代价，至今我们还没有弄清楚。

王安石在热衷于自己那套社会改革新法之下，自然为达目的而不择手段，自然会将倡异议之人不惜全予罢黜，一项神圣不可侵犯的主张，永远是为害甚大的。因为在一项主张成为不可侵犯之时，要实现此一目的的手段，便难免于残忍，乃是不可避免之事。当时情况如此，自然逃不出苏东坡的慧眼，而且兹事体大，也不是他可以付之轻松诙谐的一笑的。他和王安石是狭路相逢了，他俩的冲突决定了苏东坡一生的宦海生涯，也决定了宋朝帝国的命运。

苏东坡和王安石，谁也没活到亲眼看见他们相争的结果，谁也没看到北方异族之征服中国，不过苏东坡还活到亲眼看见那广事宣传的新政的恶果。他看见了王安石那么深爱的农民必须逃离乡里，并不是在饥馑旱涝的年月，而是在五谷丰登的年月，因为他们没能清还被逼他们向官家借的款项与利息，因此若胆敢还乡，官吏定要捕之入狱的。苏东坡只能为他们呼天求救，但是却无法一施援手。察访民情的官员，奸伪卑劣，以为对此新政新贵之缺点，最好装聋作哑，一字不提，因为当权诸公并非不知；而对新政之优点，乃予以粉饰夸张，锦上添花。说漫天之谎而成功（倘若那些谎言漫天大，而且又说个不停），并不是现代人的新发明。那些太监也得弄钱谋生。在这种情形之下，玩法弄权毫不负责之辈，就以国运为儿戏，仿佛国破家亡的后果他们是可以逃脱的。苏东坡勉强洁身自全，忍受痛苦，也是无可奈何了。皇帝虽有求治的真诚愿望，但听而不聪，误信人言，终非明主，焉能辞其咎？因为在国家大事上，他所见不明，他每每犯错，而苏东坡则料事无误。在实行新政神圣不可侵犯的名义之下，百姓只有在朝廷的高压政治之下辗转呻吟。在疯狂的争权夺利之中，党派的狂热，竟凌驾乎国家的利益之上。国家的道德力量、经济力量，大为削弱，正如苏东坡所说，在这种情形之下，中国很容易被来自西伯利亚的敌人征服了。群小甘心充当北方强邻的傀儡，名为区域独立，而向金人臣服。在此等情形之下，无怪乎朝廷灭亡，中国不得不迁往江南了。宋室宫阙在北方铁蹄之下化为灰烬之后，历史家在一片焦瓦废墟中漫步之时，不禁放目观望、低头沉思，以历史家的眼光、先知者的身份，思索国家百姓遭此劫难的原因，但是时过境迁，为时已迟了。

苏东坡去世一年，在当权的宵小尚未把长江以北拱手奉送与来自穷沙大漠的他们那异国的君王时，一件历史上的大事发生了。那就是有名的元祐党人碑的建立，也是宋朝朋党之争的一个总结。元祐是宋哲宗的年号（一○八六——一○九三），在这些年间，苏东坡的蜀党当权。元祐党人碑是哲宗元祐年间当政的三百零九人的黑名单，以苏东坡为首。碑上有奉圣旨此三百零九人及其子孙永远不得为官，皇家子女亦不得与此名单上诸臣之后代通婚姻，倘若已经订婚，也要奉旨取消。与此同样的石碑要分别在全国各县竖立，直到今天，中国有些山顶上还留有此种石碑。这是将反对党一网打尽、斩尽杀绝的办法，也是立碑的宵小蓄意使那些反对党人千年万载永受羞辱的办法。自从中国因王安石变法使社会衰乱，朝纲败坏，把中国北方拱手让与金人之后，元祐党人碑给人的观感，和立碑的那群小人的想法，可就大为不同了。随后一百多年间，碑上人的子孙，都以碑上有他们祖先的名字向人夸耀。这就是元祐党人碑在历史上出名的缘故。实际上，这些碑上的祖先之中，有的并不配享有此种荣耀，因为在立碑时要把反对党赶尽杀绝，那群小人便把自己个人的仇敌的名字也擅自列入了，所以此一黑名单上的人是好坏兼而有之的。

在徽宗崇宁五年（一一○六）正月，出乎神意，天空出现彗星，在文德殿东墙上的元祐党人碑突遭电击，破而为二。此是上天降怒，毫无疑问。徽宗大惧，但因怕宰相反对，使人在深夜时分偷偷儿把端门的党人碑毁坏。宰相发现此事，十分懊恼，但是却大言不惭地说道："此碑可毁，但碑上人名则当永记不忘！"现在我们知道，他是如愿以偿了。

雷电击毁石碑一事，使苏东坡身后的名气越来越大。他死后的前十年之间，凡石碑上刻有苏东坡的诗文或他的字的，都奉令销毁，他的著作严禁印行，他在世时一切官衔也全予剥夺。当时有作家在杂记中曾记有如下文句："东坡诗文，落笔辄为人所传诵。崇宁大观间，海外苏诗盛行。是时朝廷禁止，赏钱增至八十万。禁愈严而传愈多，往往以多相夸。士大夫不能诵东坡诗，便自觉气索，而人或谓之不韵。"

雷击石碑后五年，一个道士向徽宗奏称，曾见苏东坡的灵魂在玉皇大帝驾前为文曲星，掌诗文。徽宗越发害怕，急将苏东坡在世时最高之官爵恢复，后来另封高位，为苏东坡在世时所未有。在徽宗政和七年（一一一七）以前，皇家已经开始搜集苏东坡的手稿，悬价每一篇赏制钱五万文。太监梁师成则付制钱三十万文购买颍州桥上雕刻的苏东坡的碑文（早已经被人小心翼翼地隐藏起来），这笔钱在当时的生活来说，是够高的价钱。另外有人出五万制钱购买一个学者书斋上苏东坡题匾的三个字。这时苏东坡的诗文字画在交易上极为活跃，不久之后，这些宝贵的手稿不是进入皇宫成了御览之宝，便成了富有的收藏家手中的珍品。后来金人攻下京师，特别索取苏东坡和司马光的书画，作为战利品的一部分，因为苏东坡的名气甚至在世时已经传到了塞外异族之邦。苏东坡的手稿书画中的精品，有一部分，敌人用车装运到塞外，同时徽、钦二帝也随车北掳，竟至客死番邦（当时徽宗已让位于儿子钦宗）。苏东坡遗留下的文物未遭毁灭者，也由收藏家运到了江南，始得以保存于天地之间。

苏东坡业已去世，有关时政的感情冲动的争斗风暴也已过去，南宋的高宗皇帝坐在新都杭州，开始阅读苏东坡的遗著，尤其是他那有关国事的文章，越读越敬佩他的谋国之忠，越敬佩他的至刚大勇。为了追念苏东坡，他把苏东坡的一个孙子苏符赐封高官。所有这些举动，都使苏东坡身后的名气地位达到巅峰。到孝宗乾道六年，赐他谥号文忠公，又赐太师官阶。皇帝对他的天才写照，至今仍不失为最好的赞词。到今天，各种版本的苏文忠公全集上的卷首，都印有皇帝的圣旨和皇帝钦赐的序言。兹将封他为太师之位的那道圣旨转录于后：

敕。朕承绝学于百圣之后，探微言于六籍之中。将兴起于斯文，爰缅怀于故老。虽仪刑之莫觏，尚简策之可求。揭为儒者之宗，用锡帝师之宠。故礼部尚书、端明殿学士、赠资政殿学士、谥文忠苏轼，养其气以刚大，尊所闻而高明；博观载籍之传，几海涵而地负；远追正始之作，殆玉振而金声。知言自况于孟轲，论事肯卑于陆贽？方嘉祐全盛，尝膺特起之招；至熙宁纷更，乃陈长治之策。叹异人之间出，惊谗口之中伤。放浪岭海，而如在朝廷；斟酌古今，而若斡造化。不可夺者，峣然之节，莫之致者，自然之名。经纶不究于生前，议论常公于身后。人传元祐之学，家有眉山之书。朕三复遗编，久钦高躅。王佐之才可大用，恨不同时。君子之道暗而章，是以论世。倘九原之可作，庶千载以闻风。惟而英爽之灵，服我衮衣之命。可特赠太师。余如故。

　　由此观之，苏东坡在中国历史上的特殊地位，一则是由于他对自己的主张原则，始终坚定而不移；二则是由于他诗文书画艺术上的卓绝之美。他的人品道德构成了他名气的骨干，他的风格文章之美则构成了他精神之美的骨肉。我不相信我们会从内心爱慕一个品格低劣无耻的作家，他的文字再富有才华，也终归无用。孝宗赐予《苏东坡集》的序言就盛赞他浩然正气的伟大，这种正气就使他的作品不同于那些华丽柔靡之作，并且使他的名气屹立如山，不可动摇。

　　但是，现在我们不要忘记苏东坡主要是个诗人、作家。他当然是以此得名的。他的诗文中有一种特质，实在难以言喻，经过翻译成另一种文字后，当然更难以捉摸。杰作之所以成为杰作，就因为历代的读者都认为"好作品"就是那个样子。归根结底，文学上万古不朽的美名，还是在于文学所给予读者的快乐上，但谁又能说究竟怎样才可以取悦读者呢？使文学作品有别于一般作品，就在于在精神上取悦于人的声韵、感情、风格而已。杰作之能使历代人人爱读，而不为短暂的文学风尚所淹没，甚至历久而弥新，必然具有一种我们称之为发自肺腑的"真纯"，就犹如宝石之不怕试验，真金之不怕火炼。苏东坡写信给谢民师时说："文章如精金美玉，市有定价，非人所能以口舌论贵贱也。"

可是，使作品经久而不失其魔力的"真纯"又为何物？苏东坡对写作与风格所表示的意见，最为清楚。他说做文章"大略如行云流水，初无定质，但常行于所当行，常止于不可不止。文理自然，姿态横生。孔子曰：言之不文，行之不远。又曰：词达而已矣。夫言止于达意，则疑若不文，是大不然。求物之妙，如击风捕影，能使是物了然于心者，盖千万人而不一遇也，而况能使了然于口与手乎？是之谓词达。词至于能达，则文不可胜用矣。扬雄好为艰深之词，以文浅易之说。若正言之，则人人知之矣，此正所谓雕虫篆刻者"。在此为风格作解释，苏东坡很巧妙地描写了他自己的为文之道，其行止如"行云流水"，他是把修辞作文的秘诀弃之而不顾的。何时行、何时止是无规矩法则可言的。只要作者的情思美妙，他能真实精确地表达出来，表达得够好，迷人之处与独特之美便自然而生，并不是在文外附着的身外之物。果能表现精妙而能得心应手，则文章的简洁、自然、轻灵、飘逸，便能不求而自至，此处所谓文章的简洁、自然、轻灵、飘逸，也就是上好风格的秘诀。文章具有此等特性，文章便不至于索然无味，而我们也就不怕没有好文章读了。

不管怎么说，能使读者快乐，的确是苏东坡作品的一个特点。苏东坡最快乐就是写作之时。一天，苏东坡写信给朋友说："我一生之至乐在执笔为文之时，心中错综复杂之情思，我笔皆可畅达之。我自谓人生之乐，未有过于此者也。"苏东坡的文字使当代人的感受，亦复如此。

欧阳修说每逢他收到苏东坡新写的一篇文章，他就欢乐终日。宋神宗的一位侍臣对人说，每逢皇帝陛下举箸不食时，必然是正在看苏东坡的文章。即便在苏东坡被贬谪在外时，只要有他的一首新作的诗到达宫中，神宗皇帝必当诸大臣之面感叹赞美之。但是皇上对苏东坡的感叹赞美就正使某些大臣害怕，必使神宗在世一日，使苏东坡一直流放在外，不能回朝。

有一次，苏东坡写文章力辩文章本身使人感到快乐的力量，就是文学本身的报酬。在世的最后一年，他有时曾想抛弃笔墨根本不再写作，因为他一辈子都是以笔买祸。他在给刘沔的回信中说："轼穷困，本坐文字。盖愿刳形去皮而不可得者。然幼子过文更奇。在海外孤寂无聊，过时出一篇见娱，则为数日喜，寝食有味。如此知文章如金玉珠具，未易鄙弃也。"作者自由创作时，能自得其乐，读者阅读时，也觉愉悦欢喜，文学存在人间，也就大有道理了。

苏东坡天赋的才气，特别丰厚，可以说是冲破任何界限而不知其所止。他写诗永远清新，不像王安石的诗偶尔才达到完美的境界。苏诗无须乎获得那样完美。别的诗人作诗限于诗的辞藻，要选用一般传统的诗的题材，而苏东坡写诗不受限制，即便浴池内按摩筋骨亦可入诗，俚语俗句用于诗中，亦可听来入妙。往往是他在作诗时所能独到而别的诗人之所不能处，才使他的同道叹服。他在文学上的主要贡献，是在从前专限于描写闺怨相思的词上，开拓其领域，可以谈道谈禅，谈人生哲理，而且在冒极大之危险在几乎不可能的情形之下成功了。因为他经常必须在饭后当众作诗，通常他比别人写起来快，也写得好。他的思想比别人清新，类比典故也比别人用得恰当。有一次在黄州为他送行的筵席上，一个歌伎走到他面前，求他在她的披肩上题诗。但是苏东坡从来没听说有此一歌伎，立即吩咐她研墨，拿笔立即开头写道：

> 东坡四年黄州住，
> 何事无言及李琪。

至此停下，接着与朋友说话。在座的人以为这是很平淡无味的起头，而且仅仅两句，全诗尚未完稿。东坡继续吃饭谈笑。李琪上前求他把诗写完。东坡又拿起笔来，将此首七绝的后两句一挥而就：

> 却似西川杜工部，
> 海棠虽好不吟诗。

此诗音韵谐和，犹如一粒小宝石，有轻灵自然之美。对李琪的恭维恰到好处，因而使此一黄州歌伎的芳名也永垂不朽了。中国诗的韵律很严，在用典故时需要高度的技巧，在和别人的诗时，也要用同样的字，押同样的韵。不知何故，苏诗的韵，总比别人的用韵自然，并且他的用典，经仔细看来，含义更深。在写散文时，他笔力所及，至为广阔，自庄严纯正的古文风格，至轻松曼妙扣人心弦的小品，无所不能，各臻其妙。东坡之以大家称，不无故也。

因此之故，苏东坡在中国是主要的诗人和散文家，而且他也是第一流的画家、书家，善谈吐，游踪甚广。天生聪慧，对佛理一触即通，因此，常与僧人往还，他也是第一个将佛理入诗的。他曾猜测月亮上的黑斑是山的阴影。他在中国绘画上创出了新门派，那就是文人画，而使中国艺术增加了独特的优点。他也曾开凿湖泊河道，治水筑堤。他自己寻找草药，在中国医学上他也是公认的权威。他也涉猎炼丹术，直到临去世之前，他还对寻求长生不死之药极感兴趣。他曾对神恳求，与妖魔争辩，而且有时他居然获胜。他想攫取宇宙间的奥秘，不幸未竟全功，只成功了一半，乃一笑而逝。

倘若不嫌"民主"一词今日用得太俗滥的话，我们可以说苏东坡是一个极讲民主精神的人，因为他与各行各业都有来往，帝王、诗人、公卿、隐士、药师、酒馆主人、不识字的农妇。他的至交是诗僧、无名的道士，还有比他更贫穷的人。他也喜爱官宦的荣耀，可是每当他混迹人群之中而无人认识他时，他却最为快乐。他为杭州、广州兴办水利，建立孤儿院与医院，创监狱医师制度，严禁杀婴。在王安石新法的社会改革所留下的恶果遗患之中，他只手全力从事救济饥荒，不惜与掣肘刁难的官场抗争。当时似乎是只有他一个人关心那千里荒旱，流离饿殍。他一直为百姓而抗拒朝廷，为宽免贫民的欠债而向朝廷恳求，必至成功而后已。他只求独行其是，一切付之悠悠。今天我们确实可以说，他是具有现代精神的古人。

Chapter One
LITERARY PATRIOTIC DUKE

It is really not so difficult to know a man dead a thousand years ago. Considering how incomplete our knowledge usually is of people who live in the same city with us, or even of the private life of the mayor, it seems sometimes easier to know a dead man than a living one. For one thing, the living man's life is not completed, and one never knows what he is going to do next when a crisis comes. The drunkard reforms, the saint falls, and the pastor runs away with a choir girl. A living man has always so many "possibilities." Then, too, the living man has secrets, and some of the best secrets usually come out long after the man is dead. That is why it is so difficult usually to judge a contemporary, whose life is too close to us. Not so with a dead poet like Su Tungpo. I read his journals, his seventeen hundred poems, and his eight hundred private letters. The question of knowing or not knowing a man has nothing to do with being his contemporary. It is a matter of sympathetic understanding. After all, one knows only those whom one really understands, and one completely understands only those whom one really likes. I think I know Su Tungpo completely because I understand him, and I understand him because I like him. The question of liking a poet is always a question of taste. I think Li Po reached a greater height of sublimity and Tu Fu reached a greater stature in his total impression as a poet great by all the standards of greatness in poetry—freshness, naturalness, technical skill, and compassions. But without any apology, my favorite poet is Su Tungpo.

For me the great personality of Su Tungpo today stands out more sharply and fully etched against his life and writings than that of any other Chinese writer. There are two reasons for the clearness of the mental portrait of Su Tungpo in my mind. First, it comes from the brilliance of Su Tungpo's own mind, stamped upon every line he wrote, like the black luster of ink in the two original bamboo paintings by Su that I have seen, which still glistens as if it were applied only an hour ago. This is a curious phenomenon, as in the case of Shakespeare, too. The vitality of Shakespeare's lines, coming straight from a sensitive and generous mind, remains fresh today. In spite of the labors of generations of research scholars, we still know extremely little about his external life; yet we feel some four hundred years after his death that we know the recesses of his mind by the power of emotion he injects into his writing.

The second reason is that there is a more complete record of Su Tungpo's life than of other Chinese poets. The material exists in various historical records of a long and colorful political career, in his own voluminous writings, both poetry and prose (close to a million words), in his journals, autograph notes, and private letters, and in the tremendous gossip about him as the most loved and admired scholar of this times, which has come down to this day in the form of journals and memoirs by his contemporaries. For a century after his death, there was not an important book of memoirs which did not have something to say about the poet. The Sung scholars were great keepers of diaries, notably Szema Kuang, Wang Anshih, Liu Chih, and Tseng Pu; or indefatigable writers of memoirs, like Wang Mingching and Shao Powen. Owing to the imbroglio over Wang Anshih's state capitalism and the heat and excitement of the political battles that extended through Su Tungpo's lifetime, the writers preserved the material for the period, including dialogues,[1] in more than usual abundance. Su Tungpo himself kept no diary; he was not the diary-keeping type—it would have been, for him, too methodical, too self-conscious. But he kept a journal, which was a collection of dated and undated items on particular trips, thoughts, men, places, and events. Other people were busy keeping memoirs of what he said and did. His letters and his postscripts were carefully preserved by his admirers. As a first-rate calligraphist very much sought after, he had the habit of writing a poem on the spot or of recording a thought or a comment and giving it away to a friend after a wine dinner. Such brief notes were carefully preserved and handed down to the friend's grandchildren, or, in some cases, parted with for a very handsome sum of money. These casual notes contain admittedly some of Su's best writings. Some eight hundred of his letters and six hundred of his famous autograph notes and postscripts are preserved today. In fact, it was Su's popularity that started the fashion of collecting the postscripts and casual notes of other scholars after him, like Huang Tingchien, and publishing them in a volume. There was an art collector of Chengtu who, soon after his death, began to collect any autograph notes and intimate letters of Su Tungpo, inscribed them on stone, and sold rubbings from them as calligraphy.[2] The poem Su Tungpo wrote on a certain occasion was immediately circularized and repeated by heart among the scholars of the land. Innocent and honest, such poems of protest against the government's doing, at a time when all good scholars were hounded out of the capital, concentrated on him alone the fury of the ruling regime and almost cost him his life. Did he repent? Outwardly, in his banishment, to his less intimate friends he said he did, but to his

---

[1] The dialogues in this book are based on actual records. See Bibliography. Section I.

[2] The *Western Tower Scripts*, in thirty volumes. See page 586.

best friends he said he did not and that he would do it all over again when the necessity came for spitting out a fly in one's food. Through these outpourings of his spirit, he found himself, to his sorrow, at the head of all decent-minded scholars of his time, and after a futile struggle with petty minds but great politicians, he went into his second exile outside civilized China in the island of Hainan, somewhat fatalistically and with great peace of mind.

It is natural, therefore, that the life of this man should be the center of literary gossip and honored with profound reverence, especially after his death. For Western analogies, Li Po may be compared to Shelley or Byron, a literary meteor that burned itself out in a short spectacular display. Tu Fu was like Milton, a devout philosopher and a good old man, writing in a profusion of apt, learned, and archaic metaphors. Su Tungpo was forever young. He was as a character more like Thackeray, in his politics and poetic fame more like Victor Hugo, and he had something of the exciting quality of Dr. Johnson. Somehow Dr. Johnson's gout is exciting to us even today, while Milton's blindness is not. If Johnson were a Gainsborough at the same time, and also a Pope making criticism of current politics in verse, and if he had suffered like Swift, without the growing acidity of Swift, we would have an English parallel. The human spirit in Su Tungpo was mellowed, not soured, by his many troubles, and we love him today because he suffered so much.

There is a current Chinese saying that final judgment upon a man is possible only when the cover is nailed on his coffin. A man's life is like a drama, and we can judge a drama only when the curtain drops. There is this difference—a man's life is a drama in which the wisest and shrewdest actor does not know what comes in the next act. But real human life always evolves with an inevitability which only the best drama approaches. There is, therefore, a great advantage in writing the biography of a man of the past, where we can review scene after scene already completed, watching the inevitable development of events arising out of the necessity of outward events and inner temperament. After I had completed research on the chapters of Su Tungpo's life and understood why he had to do what he did, against his deep and sincere urge to forsake politics and retire, I felt as if I were reading the predictions of a man's entire life by a Chinese astrologist, clear, definite, inescapable. Chinese astrologists are able to plot the course of a person's entire life year by year, and are willing to put the whole prediction down in writing for a substantially higher sum than usual. But the hindsight of biographers is always better than the foresight of astrologers. Today, we are able to discern a clear pattern in Su's life with its many ups and downs, perceiving the same inevitability, but with the certainty that the different phases all came to pass, whether or not the fault was in the stars.

Su Tungpo was born in 1036 and died in 1101, twenty-five years before the conquest of northern China by the Kins and the end of the Northern Sung Dynasty. He grew up under the best emperor of that dynasty, served under a well-meaning but overambitious one, and fell into disgrace when an eighteen-year-old idiot ascended the Dragon Throne. The study of Su Tungpo's life is, therefore, at the same time a study of national degeneration through party strife, ending in the sapping of national strength and the triumphant misrule of the petty politicians. Readers of *All Men Are Brothers* are acquainted with the quality of this misrule when good, honest men, in order to avoid tax-gatherers or evade the "justice" of rapacious officials, one by one took to the woods and became the much-beloved forest heroes of that novel.

At the time of Su Tungpo's youth there was a brilliant galaxy of scholars gathered at the court of the Chinese emperor. At the end of the dynasty there was none left. During the first persecution of scholars, and the purging of the censorate and packing it with underlings by the illustrious state capitalist Wang Anshih, there were at least two dozen distinguished scholars and men of integrity who were willing to suffer for their convictions. During the second persecution, under the idiotic boy emperor, the good men were mostly dead or soon died in exile. This sapping of national strength had started in the name of "social reform" to prevent "exploitation by private capital," "for the benefit" of the always lovable common people of China, by an ardent believer in himself. Nothing is so dangerous to a nation's destiny as a misguided but opinionated idealist. Su Tungpo the poet and human philosopher pitted his common sense against the logic of Wang Anshih the economist, and the lesson he taught and China paid for we still have not learned today.

In such ardent zeal for social reform Wang Anshih inevitably regarded any means as justifiable by the end, including purging of all dissenting opinion. A holy cause is always a dangerous thing. When a cause becomes holy, the means used to achieve it inevitably becomes vile. Such a trend of things could not escape Su Tungpo's perspicacious mind and was a little too much even for his sense of humor. His path and Wang Anshih's crossed; their clash determined his whole career and the fate of the Sung Dynasty.

Neither Su nor Wang lived to see the outcome of their struggle and the conquest of China by barbarian hordes from the north, although Su lived long enough to see the terrible results of the widely publicized "social reforms." He lived to see that the "peasants" whom Wang had so "loved" had to flee their homes, not during famine or flood, but *in years of good crops*, when the officials put them in jail if they dared return to their villages, for failure to pay the loans and interest which the socialist regime had forced upon the peasants. And his voice cried to high heaven; he could not help himself. There were dishonest reporters who thought it expedient to maintain a strict silence on the bad features of the socialist regime, of which they could not be unaware, and to glamorize its virtues. The success of telling big lies, if the lies are big enough and repeated often enough, is not a modern invention. Then eunuchs had to make their living. In such a way did irresponsible men play with a nation's destiny, as if they themselves could escape its consequences. Su Tungpo could at least keep his own soul and pay the price for it. The honest intentions of the Emperor were no excuse for his gullibility, for he was wrong, and Su Tungpo right, on the main issue. An iron rule was clapped over the people in the holy name of social reform. In the mad struggle for power, party fanaticism overruled patriotic interests, and the moral and economic fiber of the nation was consumed and weakened, as Su Tungpo foretold, making the country an easy prey to a conqueror from the direction of Siberia. When petty men were ready to serve as puppets of a powerful neighbor from the north in the name of a "regional independent China" which owed allegiance to a foreign power, it was but right that the imperial dynasty should be extinguished and China should retreat south of the Yangtse River. When the Sung house had burned down, historians, walking among the charred ruins, began to survey the field and ponder, with self-important historical perspective, but a little too late, the causes of the catastrophe.

One year after the death of Su Tungpo, when the petty partisans were in power before they handed North China over to His foreign Majesty from across the Mongolian wilds, a historically important episode occurred. This was the establishment of the famous Yuanyu Partisan's Tablet, a symbol and a summing up of the struggles of the whole period. "Yuanyu" is the name of the reign (1086—1093)under which Su Tungpo's own party was in power, and the tablet was a blacklist of 309 men, headed by Su Tungpo, of the Yuanyu regime. It banned forever by imperial order these persons and their children from assuming office in the government. Descendants of the royal family were forbidden to marry children of the "Yuanyu partisans," and if there had been a betrothal, it was to be broken off by imperial order. A tablet containing the blacklist was to be set up in all districts of the country; some of these still exist today on China's mountaintops. It was a method for weeding out all opposition forever, and, in the authors' minds, of committing these men to eternal infamy. Since China was turned over to the conquerors from the north by the social reformers, the effect achieved by these tablets was very different from what the authors had intended. For over a century, the children of the blacklisted men boasted that their ancestors' names were included in the tablet. That is why the Yuanyu Partisans' Tablet became so famous in history. Actually, some of these ancestors did not deserve the honor, for in the zeal to weed out all opposition, the authors of the tablet included all their personal enemies, and blacklisted some bad men as well as the good ones.

As the gods had decreed it, however, in January 1106 a comet appeared in the sky and the tablet established on the east wall of the Wenteh Palace was struck by lightning and split in two. There could not be a clearer indication of Heaven's displeasure. Emperor Huitsung was frightened, and in fear of the objection of the premier had the other tablet at the Tuan Gate secretly destroyed at night. On finding this out, the premier was greatly chagrined, but righteously exclaimed, "The tablet may be destroyed, but the names of these men shall be remembered forever!" We know today that his wish was fulfilled.

The striking of the tablet by lightning started Su Tungpo's steadily increasing fame after his death. During the first decade all stone inscriptions bearing his handwriting or composition were ordered destroyed, his books were banned, and he was deprived of every rank he had held in his lifetime. A writer of this time noted down in his journal, however, that "the poems he wrote in exile are very popular. Although the court has increased the fine for possession of Su's works to 800,000 cash [or $ 800], the stronger the ban, the wider the poems spread. Scholars feel disgraced and are considered uncultured when they cannot recite his poems in company."

Five years after the lightning had struck, a Taoist priest reported to the Emperor that he had seen the spirit of Su Tungpo serving as the minister of literature at the gods' court in Heaven. The Emperor was still more frightened and hastily restored to Su the highest rank he had obtained in his lifetime, and later conferred one higher than he had ever possessed. By 1117 the imperial household, under the same emperor, was itself collecting Su Tungpo's manuscripts, offering as much as 50,000 cash apiece. The eunuch Liang Shihcheng paid 300,000 cash, a high price according to the then standard of living, for the inscription on the Stone Bridge of Ingchow (which had been discreetly hidden), and another man paid 50,000 cash for three words written by Su on the tablet of a scholar's studio. A brisk business was going on, and soon these precious manuscripts were in the palace or in the homes of rich collectors. When the Kin (Manchurian)barbarians captured the capital, they specifically demanded as part of the booty the works of Su Tungpo and Szema Kuang, for Su's name had spread to the northern tribes beyond China's border even in his lifetime. Some of the best of Su's paintings and manuscripts were carted north to enemy territory, together with two emperors who died there in captivity. (Huitsung had resigned in favor of his son.)Still hundreds of Su's manuscript items survived and were brought by their owners to the south.

Now that Su Tungpo was dead and the storms of passion over current politics were over, the emperors in the Southern Sung Dynasty, sitting in the new capital of Hangchow, began to read his works, particularly his state papers, and the more they read, the more they admired the intrepid patriotism of the man. One of his grandchildren, Su Fu, was given a high office in consideration of his illustrious grandfather. All this leads to the final culmination of Su Tungpo's posthumous fame and position. By 1170 the filial emperor Shiaotsung conferred upon him the posthumous title of "Literary Patriotic Duke" and gave him the rank of Grand Imperial Tutor. The Emperor wrote what remains to this day the best tribute to his genius. The imperial decree and the Emperor's own preface to his *Works* stand at the beginning in all editions of Su's *Complete Works*. The imperial decree conferring upon him the title of Grand Imperial Tutor reads:

By Imperial Order: We come after the tradition of the hundred sages and seek wisdom in the Six Classics. While desiring to promote the culture of ideas, our thoughts turn back to the great one of the past. Although it is no longer possible to see him in person, we have the works of this great man before us. We desire to confer upon him the honor of an Emperor's teacher and exalt him to leadership among the scholars.

The deceased, Su Shih, formerly Minister of Education, Scholar of the Tuanming Palace, subsequently made Scholar of the Tsecheng Palace and posthumously titled Literary Patriotic Duke, cultivated the noble and upright spirit born in man and elevated to a higher level of understanding the tradition of the past. His scholarship was all-embracing, like the sea and the earth, and his words of advice were like the striking of jade and bells. In literary eloquence he can be compared to Mencius, and in political criticism he was not second to Lu Chih. At the nation's height of literary prosperity during Chiayu [reign of Jentsung] he was exalted to fame; during the confusing changes of Shining [reign of Shentsung] he submitted the principles for a lasting national prosperity. We sigh at the appearance of such a rare genius and are shocked at his suffering from his detractors. He was banished across the seas and mountains, but he remained the same man as if he were holding power at the court; he studied the past and the present and his mind comprehended the laws of the universe. What could not be taken away from him was his sturdy integrity, and what no man could confer upon him was his popular fame. In his lifetime he had no consideration for his own good, and posterity gave him his fair due after his death. So today everyone continues to speak of the scholar of Yuanyu, and every home possesses a copy of the works of Meishan. Three times over we have read his bequeathed works, and for a long time we have admired his high principles. We regret not being born at the same time with him in order to make full use of his talents as a counselor of kings, but from generation to generation, the superior man's teachings ever grow from obscurity to popular acceptance.

We wish that your spirit could rise from the underground springs, so that the world might pay homage to your fame, and we pray that your talented soul will accept our Imperial favor. Su Shih is hereby specially given the title of Grand Imperial Tutor. His other titles may be kept as before.

Su Tungpo's peculiar position in China's history was, therefore, based on his courageous stand for his principles and opinions, as well as upon the charm of his poems and prose. His character and principles constitute the "bones" of his fame, while the charm of style and language forms the "flesh and skin" that embody the beauty of his spirit. I do not think that we can, at heart, admire a writer lacking in integrity, however brilliant and charming his writings may be. The imperial preface to Su's *Collected Works* emphasizes the greatness of his "spirit," which distinguishes his works from mere "fine writing" and gives solidity to his fame.

But let us not forget that Su was principally a poet and writer. On this his reputation rests. His writings have a quality that is difficult to explain, much less feel in translation. A classic becomes a classic because the people in all ages recognize "good writing" as such. Ultimately, lasting fame in literature rests on the pleasure the writing gives to the readers, and who shall say in what way a reader is pleased? What separates literature from ordinary writing is the charm of sound and sense and manner which pleases the spirit. That a classic pleases all men in all ages and survives temporary literary fashions must come of a quality that we may call *genuineness*, like that of precious gems which survive all tests. "Literature is like genuine gold and good jade," Su wrote to Shieh Minshih. "They have an intrinsic value independent of fluctuating prices."

Yet what is that "genuineness" which accounts for its quality of wearing well? Su expressed his opinion on writing and style as clearly as anyone ever put it. "Roughly, [good writing]is like the sailing of clouds or flowing of water, moving forward where it is natural to move forward, and stopping where it must stop. From the natural flow of thoughts and language arises its wayward, abundant charm. 'An expression lacking literary beauty cannot survive very long,' said Confucius. Again he said, 'All you ask of writing is that it *expresses* well.' One may think that if the aim of writing is merely to express something well, it may be lacking in literary beauty. That is not so. Only one person in a thousand or ten thousand can appreciate an intangible, elusive idea, or the essence of a given situation, and make it clear to himself It is still more difficult to communicate it by hand or mouth to others, which is what we mean by expressing it well. When one can do this, he can do anything with his pen. Yang Shiung loved to clothe a simple, insipid thought in high-flown, difficult phraseology, just because he knew that if he did not, the thought itself would be shown to be quite commonplace. That is the trick of the so-called petty journeyman writers." In this definition of style, Su Tungpo aptly describes his own process of literary composition, moving and stopping like "sailing clouds and flowing water," and he gives away all the mysteries of composition and rhetoric. There are no rules on when to go on and when to break off. The charms and wayward beauty come by themselves if the writer's thoughts are beautiful and he only can express them truthfully, genuinely, and well. They are not something laid on the writing. Simplicity, naturalness, and a certain freedom which comes from mastery of expression are the secrets of a good style. When such qualities are present, and the writing is not insipid, we have genuine literature.

Anyway, pleasure given was a characteristic of all Su's writings. Most pleased of all was the author himself in the act of writing. "The happiest moments of my life," Su said to his friend one day, "are when, at the time of writing, my pen can express all the intricacies of my thoughts. I say to myself, 'There is no greater pleasure in this earthly life than this.'" Much the same was its effect on his contemporaries. Ouyang Shiu said that whenever he received a new composition by Su, he remained happy for the whole day. An attendant upon Emperor Shentsung told people that whenever the Emperor's chopsticks stopped in the middle of his eating, it was sure to be Su Tungpo's memorandum that he was reading. Always whenever a new poem reached the court, even during the period of Su Tungpo's exile, the Emperor would praise it before the other ministers with sighs of admiration. But it was also these sighs of admiration on the part of the Emperor that frightened the ministers and kept Su in exile so long as this emperor lived.

Once the poet defended the power of giving pleasure as literature's own reward. In the last years of his life he sometimes wanted to throw away his brush and stop writing entirely, since it was writing that had brought him all his trouble. A friend and admirer, Liu Mien, edited his works and wrote to him about it. In his reply to Liu Mien he said, "I have fallen upon evil days because of my writing, and sometimes I wish to black out my intelligence, which unfortunately cannot be done. My youngest son, Kuo, is beginning to write more beautifully than ever. During my hours of boredom, living overseas, sometimes Kuo shows me one of his compositions and I am happy for days and enjoy my food and my sleep better. This shows that literature is like gold and jade or precious stones, which have an intrinsic value of their own that cannot be denied." In the pleasure it gives to the author during his free creative activity, and in the happiness it gives to its readers, literature justifies its own existence.

Su possessed an unusually generous talent, which broke all boundaries and seemed to know no limitations. His poems were always fresh, not like Wang Anshih's, which occasionally attained perfection. Su did not have to attain such perfection. Where other poets were limited by poetic diction and conventional themes, Su could write a poem on massage at a bathhouse, and he could incorporate slang and make it sound well in a poem. Always it was that extra something which others could not do that compelled admiration from his fellow craftsmen. His chief contribution to a special form of poety, the *tse*, confined hitherto to yearnings of the lovelorn, was that he could turn the meter into a vehicle for discourse on Buddhism and philosophy, and he succeeded in this almost impossibly risky task. Usually he wrote a little better and a little faster than others, for he often had to compose poems after dinner with people looking on. His thoughts were fresher and his analogies and allusions more appropriate than those of other poets. Once at a farewell dinner given him at Huangchow, a female entertainer came up and asked him to write a poem on her shawl. Now he had not heard of this entertainer, Li Chi, during his stay at Huangchow. He asked her to grind the ink and took up the brush and wrote a simple beginning:

Four years has Tungpo lived at Huangchow,
Strange that he never mentioned Li Chi.

Then he stopped and went on talking with his guests. It was, in the opinion of those present, a rather flat beginning, and besides, the poem was not finished. Su went on eating, chatting and laughing. Li Chi came up again and asked him to finish it. "Oh, I almost forgot," said Su. He took up the brush again and dashed off the second half of the quatrain:

Exactly like Tu Fu of the West River;

Of the best flower, begonia, he sang the least.

It fitted perfectly in rhyme and tone, and in effect the poem was like a little gem, written as usual with the poet's effortless grace. It gave a very subtle compliment to the girl, and Li Chi thereby became immortal in literature. The technical restrictions in Chinese poetry were many, requiring a high skill in the use of allusions and in the writing of a poem with the same rhyme words as those used in a poem written by a friend. Somehow, Su's rhyming was more natural, and his allusions, upon close examination, were found to suggest deeper implications. In prose his pen commanded a wide range of powers, from the most dignified pure prose in the simple style of the ancient classics to charming chatter in the style of the familiar essayists. It is difficult to choose between the two. That is why he was acknowledged a master.

Su Tungpo, therefore, ranks as a major poet and prose writer of China. In addition he was a painter and calligraphist of the first order, a distinguished conversationalist, a great traveler. Quick to comprehend Buddhist philosophy, he constantly associated with monks, and was the first poet to inject Buddhist philosophy into Confucianist poetry. He made a good guess that the dark spots on the moon were the shadows of mountains. He pioneered in a new school of painting, the "scholar painting" which makes Chinese art unique. He opened up lakes and canals, fought floods, built dams. He picked his own herbs and was a recognized authority in medicine. He dabbled in alchemy and was interested almost to his last days in his search for the elixir of immortality. He pleaded with the gods and argued with the devil—and sometimes won. He wanted to wrest the secrets of the universe, was half defeated, and died with a laugh.

Were the word not so much abused today, we would say he was a great democrat, for he associated with all manner of men and had for his friends emperors, poets, cabinet ministers and retired farmers, pharmacists, wineshop keepers, and illiterate peasant women. His best friends were poetic monks, unknown Taoists, and those poorer than himself. He loved official honor and yet was happiest when the crowds did not recognize him. He established good water systems for Hangchow and Canton, founded orphanages and hospitals, instituted prison physicians, fought infanticide. During the aftermath of the social reforms he worked passionately and singlehandedly at famine relief, against the colossal obstruction of bureaucracy. It almost seems he was the only man concerned over the widespread famine and the roaming refugees. Always he was the champion of the people against the government and worked for the forgiveness of debts to the poor until he got it. He wanted only to be himself. Today it may be said that he was truly a modern man.

第二章　眉山

　　自长江逆流而上，经汉口，过名满天下的三峡，便进入了中国西南的一大省份——四川。再沿江上行，过重庆，直到水源，便可看见一尊大石佛，其高三百六十英尺，是由江边一个悬崖峭壁雕刻而成。在此四川省西部的边界，在雄伟高耸的峨眉山麓，就是乐山，当年在苏东坡时名为嘉州，岷江就在此处流入长江。岷江自大西北原始部落聚居的山岭上，汹涌澎湃奔流而至，与来自峨眉的另一河流汇合后，直向乐山的大石佛奔腾而来，洪流渐渐折向东南，然后向东，便一直流入中国海。在千年万古为阴云封闭的峨眉山的阴影中，在乐山以北大约四十英里之外，便是眉州的眉山镇。在中国文学史上，这座小镇便以当地一个杰出的文学世家出了名。这一家便是苏家，亦即人所周知的"三苏"。父亲苏洵，生有二子，长子苏轼，字子瞻，号东坡；次子苏辙，字子由，父子三人占唐宋八大家中的三席之地。

　　在乐山，当年也和现在一样，旅客可以乘一小舟自玻璃江逆流而上直到眉山。玻璃江因其水色而得名，因为在冬季，水色晶莹深蓝；夏季之时，急流自山峦间奔流而至，水色深黄。玻璃江为岷江一支流，因眉山位于乐山与四川省会成都两地之间，凡欲赴省会之旅客，必须经过眉山。若坐帆船上行，可以看见蟆颐山临江而立。山势低而圆，与江苏之山形状相似。此处即是眉山，即"三苏"的故乡。幸亏战国时代李冰的治水天才，当地才有完整的水利灌溉沟渠，千余年来，在良好维护之下，始终功能完好，使川西地区千年来沃野千里，永无水患。蟆颐山的小山丘下，稻田、果园、菜圃，构成广漠的一带平原，竹林与矮小的棕树则点缀处处。自南方进入眉山镇，沿着整洁的石板路走，便可到达城镇的中心。

眉山并非一个很大的城市，但住家颇为舒适。一个现代诗人曾描述眉山，他说眉山镇上街道整洁，五六月间荷花盛放，最为有名。当地种植荷花已成一项庞大行业，因为邻近各市镇的荷花贩子都来此地采购荷花。人在街上步行之时，会见到路旁许多荷花池，花朵盛开，香气袭人。在纱縠巷，有一座中等结构的住宅。自大门进入，迎面是一道漆有绿油的影壁，使路上行人不至于看见住宅的内部。影壁之后，出现一栋中型有庭院的房子。在房子附近，有一棵高大的梨树，一个池塘，一片菜畦。在这个小家庭花园之中，花和果树的种类繁多，墙外是千百竿翠竹构成的竹林。

宋仁宗景祐三年（一〇三六）十二月十九日，在这栋房子里，一个婴儿脚踢着襁褓的包布，发出了啼声。自从第一个儿子夭折之后，这个初生的婴儿便成了这家的长子。现在在这儿趁着这个婴儿并没有什么特别的活动，也可以说只像其他的婴儿一个样地活动之时，我们利用这段时光把这一家大略看一下吧。不过关于这个孩子的生日先要说一说，不然会使海外中国传记的读者感到纷乱。在中国，小儿初生便是一岁，这是由中国人历来都愿早日达到受人尊敬的高龄的缘故。第一个新年一到，人人都长了一岁，那个婴儿就是两岁。根据中国的计算法，一个人在他生日前来算，他总比实际年龄大两岁，在生日之后算，总是大一岁。在本书里，年龄是按西方计算的，不再精确估计生日。不过在论到苏东坡，还是要顾到一点儿精确。因为他一降生就是一岁大，那是十二月十九日，再新年来临，他就已经两岁大——实际上他还不足半个月。因为他的生日是在年终，按中国年岁计算，他总是比实际年龄小两岁。

关于他的生日要说的第二件事，他的降生是在天蝎宫之下。照他自己的话说，这就是为什么他一生饱经忧患的原因，不管是好谣言、坏谣言，他总是谣言的箭垛，太好的谣言，他当之有愧；太坏的谣言，他无端受辱。这种命运和韩愈的命运相似。韩愈降生也是属于同样的星座，韩愈也是因固执己见而被朝廷流放。

在那栋宅院中，一间屋子墙的正中，挂着一张仙人的画像，画的是八仙中的张果老。婴儿的父亲苏洵，现年二十七岁，正是一生中精神上多灾多难的岁月。他在市场上看见这张画像，乃用一只玉镯子换来的。在过去的七年之中，每天早晨他向这幅张果老像祷告。数年前他妻子已经生了一个女孩儿，再生的就是那个夭折的孩子。他过去一直盼望生个儿子，现在是如愿以偿了。他必然是非常快乐的，并且我们也知道，当时他正在饱受屈辱折磨，痛苦万分。

苏家总算是个小康之家，自己有田产，也许比一般中产之家还较为富有。家中至少有两个使女，并且家里还能给苏东坡和在他之前的姐姐各雇用一个奶妈。等弟弟辙生下时，家中还能再雇一个奶妈。这兄弟二人的两个奶妈，按照中国的习惯，要一直跟她们照顾到成年的孩子过活一辈子。

苏东坡一降生，祖父仍然健在，正是六十三岁。他祖父以前年轻时，生得高大英俊，身体健壮，酒量极大，慷慨大方。后来苏东坡已经成为当代公认的文坛泰斗，官居翰林学士知制诰之职，家已移居在开封城皇宫附近。一天，几个至交与仰慕他的人前去拜访，正好那天是他祖父的寿诞之期，他就开始向来客述说这位怪老汉的几件趣事。老人不识字，但是人品不凡。那时他们正住在乡间，自己广有田地。他祖父不像别家那样储存食米，却以米换谷，在自家谷仓中存了三四万石之多。别人不知道他何以如此。随后荒年歉收，他祖父乃开仓散粮，先给他自己的近族近亲，然后才轮到他妻子的娘家人，再后给他家的佃农，最后给同村的贫民。这时别人才知道他当初为什么广存稻谷——因为稻谷可藏数年，而稻米天潮时则易霉坏。他祖父衣食无忧，优哉游哉，时常携酒一樽，与亲友在青草地上席地而坐，饮酒谈笑，以遣时光。大家饮酒高歌，令规矩拘谨的农人都大为吃惊。

一天，老汉正在喝酒取乐，重要消息来到了。他的二儿子，苏东坡的叔父，已赶考高中。在邻近还有一家，儿子也是同样考中。那是苏东坡的外祖母程家。因为苏程联姻，所以可以说是双喜临门。程家极为富有，算得上有财有势，早就有意大事铺张庆祝，而苏家的老汉则无此意。知父莫如子，苏东坡的叔叔亲自派人由京中给老人家送上官家的喜报，官衣官帽，上朝用的笏板，同时还有两件东西，就是太师椅一张，精美的茶壶一个。喜信到时，老汉正在醺醺大醉，手里攥着一大块牛肉吃。他看见行李袋里露出官帽上的红扣子，一下子就明白了。但是当时酒力未消，他拿起喜报，向朋友们高声宣读，欢乐之下，把那块牛肉也扔在行李袋里，与那喜报官衣官帽装在一处。他找了一个村中的小伙子为他背行李袋，他骑着驴，往城里走去。那是他一生中最快乐的日子。街上的人早已听到那个考中的消息，等一看见酩酊大醉的老汉骑在驴背上，后面跟着一个小子扛着一件怪行李，都不禁大笑。程家以为这是一件令人丢脸的事，而苏东坡则说只有高雅不俗之士才会欣赏老人质朴自然之美。此老汉也是一个思想开通的人。一天，他在大醉之下，走进一座庙里，把一尊神像摔得粉碎。原来他早已对那尊像怀有恶感，并且那尊神像全村人都很惧怕，更可能的理由是对那庙里的庙祝存有敌意，因为他常向信徒们勒索钱财。

苏东坡的酒量倒不是由祖父那里继承而来的，但是他的酒趣则是得自祖父，以后不难看出。这位不识字的老汉的智慧才华，原是在身上深藏不露的，结果却在他儿子的儿子的身上光荣灿烂地盛放了。身心精力过人的深厚，胸襟气度的开阔，存心的纯厚正直，确都潜存在老人的身上。苏家在当地兴起，和别的望族世家之兴起一样，也是合乎无限的差异变化与物竞天择的自然规律的。对于苏东坡外婆家的才智如何，我们尚无明证，但是苏程两家血统的偶然混合，不知在何种情形之下，竟产生了文学天才。

此外，祖父对他孙子的文学生活并无什么大的影响，只是一点，祖父的名字是"序"。当年对一个作家而言，这确是最为难的事，因为苏东坡是个名作家，必须写很多序。苏东坡若用"序"这个字，便是对祖先失去尊敬。于是他只好把他作品中所有的"序"，都改称之为"引"。不称父母与祖父母的名讳，在中国是很古老的风俗，有时候十分麻烦，尤其父亲的名字是很普通的字时为甚。在中国最伟大的史学家司马迁皇皇巨著中，我们找不到一个"谈"字，因为"谈"是他父亲的名字。有一个人名叫"赵谈"，司马迁竟擅自改为"赵通"。同样，后汉书的作者范晔必须避开他父亲的名字"泰"，所以今天我们在他那一百二十卷的大作中找不到一个"泰"字。诗人李翱的父亲名"今"，于是此位诗人必须用一个古字代替现代这个普通字"今"。这种禁忌是由禁写当朝皇帝名字的禁忌而起。科举考试时，考生的名字之中若有一个字与当朝已驾崩的皇帝的名字相同，则被逐出考场。可是皇帝通常总是称年号或谥号，而不称名，所以就有不少考生忘记了皇帝的名字，而真被逐出考场。有时一个皇帝也会在这方面犯了禁忌，因为谁也不易随时记着十代祖先的名字。一次，一个皇帝一时没记清楚，在给一座亭子起名字时用错了字，忽然想起来犯了禁忌，误用了祖先之名，于是，刚为那个亭子颁赐了名字，立刻又改换。

苏东坡的父亲苏洵，天性沉默寡言，就其政治上的抱负而言，他算是抑郁终身，不过在去世之前，他想追求的文名与功名，在他的两个儿子身上出现了。苏洵秉赋颖异，气质谨严，思想独立，性格古怪，自然不是易于与人相处的人。直至今日，人人都知道他到二十七岁时，才发愤读书。大人常举这件事来鼓励年轻人，告以只要勤勉奋发，终会成功的。当然，聪明的孩子也许会推演出相反的结论，那就是孩童之时不一定非要专心向学。事实上，苏洵在童年并非没有读书作文学习的机会，而似乎是，苏洵个性强烈，不服管教，必又痛恨那个时代的正式教育方式。我们都知道好多才气焕发的孩子确是如此。若说他在童年时根本没读书写字做文章，恐非事实。他年轻之时，必然给程家有足够好的印象，不然程家不会愿意把女儿嫁给他。另外，同样令人惊异的是，他晚到二十七岁才发愤读书，而能文名大噪，文名不为才气纵横的儿子的文名所掩，这究属极不寻常之事。

大约他得了长子之后，自己的态度才严肃起来，追悔韶光虚掷，痛自鞭策。他看到自己的哥哥、自己的内兄，还有两个姐丈，都已科考成功，行将为官做吏，因而觉得含羞带愧，脸上无光。此等情事，即便平庸之才，都会受到刺激，对一个天赋智力如此之高的人，当时的情形一定使他无法忍受，今日由他的文集中所表现的才智看，我们对此是不难了解的。在苏洵给他妻子（苏东坡的母亲）的祭文里，他表示妻子曾激励他努力向学，因为那位程家小姐是曾经受过充分的良好教育的。祖父对他儿子并没有说什么，也没有做什么，在他眼里，他这个儿子，无论从哪方面看，只是一个倔强古怪的孩子，虽有天才却是游手好闲不肯正用。有朋友问他，为什么他儿子不用心读书而他也不肯管教，他很平静地回答说："这个我不发愁。"他的话暗示出来他那才气焕发而不肯务正的儿子总有一天会自知犯错、会痛改前非，他是坚信而不移的。

四川的居民，甚至远在宋代，就吃苦耐劳，机警善辩，有自持自治的精神，他们像偏远地区的居民一样，依然还保持一些古老的风俗文化。由于百年前本省发明了印刷术，好学之风勃然兴起。在苏东坡的时代，本省已经出了不少的官员学者，其学术的造诣都高于当时黄河流域一带，因为在科举时，黄河一带的考生都在作诗方面失败。成都是文化中心，以精美的信笺、四川的锦缎、美观的寺院出名。还有名妓、才女，并且在苏东坡出世百年以前，四川还出了两个有名气的女诗人。那些学者文人在作品上，不同于当时其他地区文章浮华虚饰的纤丽风格，仍然保有西汉朴质遒健的传统。

在当年，也和如今一样，四川的居民都耽溺于论争，酷爱雄辩的文章。甚至在中等社会，谈话之时都引经据典，富有妙语佳趣，外省人看来，都觉得充满古雅精美的味道。苏东坡生而辩才无碍，口舌之争，决不甘拜下风。他的政论文章，清晰而有力，非常人可望其项背，数度与邪魔鬼怪的争辩，自然更不用提了。东坡和他父亲，被敌人攻击时，都比之为战国诡辩游说之士，而友人则誉之为有孟轲文章的雄辩之风，巧于引喻取譬，四川人为律师，必然杰出不凡。

就因为这种理由，眉州人遂有"难治"之称。苏东坡一次辩称：此地居民，不同于教养落后之地，不易为州官所欺。士绅之家，皆置有法律之书，不以精通法律条文为非。儒生皆力求遵守法律，亦求州官为政不可违法。州官若贤良公正，任期届满之时，县民必图其像，悬于家而跪拜之，铭之于心，五十年不能忘。当地人像现代的学生一样，新教师初到任，他们要对他施以考验。州官若内行干练，他们决不借故生非。新州官若但有扰民傲慢之处，以后使他为难棘手之事多矣。正如苏东坡所说，眉州之民难治，非难治也，州官不知如何治之耳。

在眉州那些遗风古俗之外，民间还发展出一项社会的门阀制度。著有名声的世家列为甲等乙等，而称之为"江卿"。江卿之家不与普通人家通婚嫁，只要对方非江卿一等，再富而有势，亦不通融。另外，农民之间有一种完美的风俗。每年二月，农人开始下田工作，四月份以前拔除野草。农人数百之众，共同动手。选出二人管理，一人管钟漏，一人管击鼓。一天的开工收工完全听从鼓声。凡迟到与工作不力者皆受处罚交纳罚金。凡田多而工作人少者，都捐款归公。收割已毕，农民齐来，盛筵庆祝，击破陶土做的钟漏，用所收的罚金与指派的捐款，购买羊肉美酒，共庆丰收。这项典礼开始时，先祭农神，然后大吃大喝，直至兴尽，才各自归家。

Chapter Two
MEISHAN

If you go up the Yangtse River, beyond Hankow, past the famous gorges into the westernmost province of Szechuen, and further follow the river past Chungking to its origins, you will come to a giant stone Buddha, three hundred and sixty feet high, carved out of a mountain cliff on the bank. Here at the western border of the province and at the foot of the giant Omei Mountain, is Loshan, called Kiachow in the days of Su Tungpo. At this point the Min River flows into the Yangtse. The Min River, coming down from the northwestern mountains of the western aborigines, rushes down in a big and deep torrent and, joining another river coming down from the Omei, makes a straight dash for the Giant Stone Buddha of Loshan, where the river then turns gradually southeast and then east to flow directly into the China Sea. Lying in the shadow of the eternally cloud-covered peaks of the Omei, and some forty miles north of Loshan, is the town of Meishan, in Meichow district, made famous in China's literary history as the home of the most distinguished literary family in China. This was the Su family, also known as the "Three Sus." The father was Su Shun, who gave birth to two illustrious sons, Su Shih (Tungpo), and Su Cheh (Tseyu). Together the father and sons account for three of the "Eight Great Prose Master of the Tang and Sung

Dynasties."[1]

At Loshan, then as now, a traveler could go up the Polikiang, or Glass River, in a junk to Meishan. The river received its name from its color, for it was a deep crystal blue in winter, while in summer the torrents coming down from the mountains turned it into a murky yellow. The river was a branch of the Min River, and as Meishan lay halfway between Loshan and the capital of the province, Chengtu, travelers who wanted to go to the capital had to pass through the town. You would go up in the junk until you saw the Moyishan, or Frog's Jowl Hill, standing directly over the stream. It was a low, round hill like those we see around Kiangsu. Here was Meishan, the home town of the Sus. Thanks to the engineering genius of Li Ping, who lived at the end of the third century B.C., there was a perfect water control and irrigation system, maintained and kept working for over a thousand years; it made this whole region of western Szechuen into a perennially fertile plain, free from floods. The little hill stood against a vast plain of rice fields, orchards, and vegetable gardens, dotted here and there with bamboo groves and curiously dwarfed palm trees. You entered the city from the south and went up the clean stone pavements into the heart of the city.

It was not a very big town, but it was comfortable for a place of residence. A poet of the twelfth century reported that the streets were kept very clean and that Meishan was famous for its lotus flowers in May and June. The cultivation of the lotus flower had grown into an industy, for dealers from the neighboring cities obtained their lotus flowers from this place. As one went up the streets, one passed many ponds on the roadside covered with these flowers, whose fragrance filled the air. At Shakuhang one came upon a middle-class home. Entering the gate, one faced a green

---

[1] Of these eight masters, six are important figures in this book. Besides the "Three Sus," the other three are Wang Anshih, Ouyang Shiu, and Tseng Kung.

painted screen which shut out the view of the interior from the passers-by. Behind the screen, a mediumsized house with its courtyards appeared. Somewhere near the house stood a tall pear tree, and there were a pond and a vegetable patch. In the little family garden there was a great variety of flower and fruit trees, while outside the wall stood a grove of hundreds of bamboo trees.

It was the year 1036, a baby boy was crying and kicking in his swaddling clothes. Since the first son had died in infancy, he was the eldest son of the 'family. And here, as the baby was doing nothing in particular or doing what every baby does, we may take time to look around at the family. But first something must be said about this birthday, lest we but add to a certain confusion plaguing Chinese biographies abroad. A Chinese baby is "one year old" the moment he is born, following the general pattern of everyone's desiring to reach venerable age as quickly as possible. On the next New Year's Day, when all people advance their age one year, he is "two years old." According to the Chinese reckoning, therefore, as compared with Western reckoning, a person always counts himself two years older before his birthday and one year older after that date in any given year. In this book, ages are given according to the Western reckoning, without taking into consideration a person's exact birthday. In the case of Su Tungpo, however, a little more exactness is required. As he was "one year old" the day he was born, on December nineteenth, he would be "two years old" already on the following New Year's Day—when he was hardly two weeks old, actually. As his birthday came toward the very end of the year, he was actually always two years younger than he would be according to the Chinese reckoning.

The second thing to be said about the birthday is that he was born under Scorpio. According to the poet himself, this explains why he ran into so many troubles all his life and was a target of rumors, both good and bad, which he did not deserve—a fate similar to that of Han Yu, who was born under the same star, and who was also sentenced to exile for his opinions.

On the central panel of one of the rooms in the house hung a portrait of a certain fairy by the name of Chang. The father of the baby, who was now twenty-seven and going through the greatest spiritual crisis of his life, had seen this portrait at one of the markets and had got it by offering a jade bracelet for it to the dealer. He had prayed to this fairy every morning for the last seven years. His wife had given birth to a girl several years ago and to the boy who died in infancy. He had always wanted a boy, and now his wish was granted. He must have been happy; and yet we know that he was suffering from a sense of terrific shame and torment.

It was a fairly well-to-do family, owning lands and perhaps richer than the average middle-class family. There were at least two maid-servants, and besides, the family was able to afford a wet nurse for Su Tungpo and his elder sister. When the younger brother was born, they were able to hire another wet nurse, and these two nurses remained according to Chinese custom for the rest of their lives with the children they had brought up to maturity.

At this time of Su Tungpo's birth, the grandfather was still living and was sixty-three years old. In this young days he had been a tall, handsome man, hale and hearty, given to drink, big-hearted and generous. One day when Su Tungpo was the acknowledged first scholar of his time and was acting as secretary to the emperor, he moved into a new residence close to the palace. Some of his close friends and admirers came to visit him, and as it happened to be his grandfather's birthday, he began to tell them certain amusing incidents about this curious old man. He was wholly illiterate, but a rather extraordinary personality. At that time they were living out in the country and owned large tracts of land. But instead of storing up rice in the way everybody did usually, he exchanged it for unhusked rice and stored it up to the amount of thirty or forty thousand bushels in his granary. People could not understand why he was doing this. Then a famine came, and the grandfather opened the granary and began to distribute the unhusked rice first to his own immediate family and relatives, then to his wife's relatives, then to the tenant farmers, and then to the poor of the village. Now people understood why he had accumulated the unhusked rice—it would keep for years, whereas husked rice would spoil in wet weather. Being carefree and well provided, he would often pick up a wine jug and go about with his friends to sit on the grass and enjoy himself. They would laugh and drink and sing, to the amazement of the usually quiet and well-behaved peasants.

One day during a carousal an important piece of news arrived. His second son, Su Tungpo's uncle, had passed the imperial examinations. There was another family in the neighborhood whose son had also passed the same examinations. This was the family of Su Tungpo's mother, the Chengs. As the two houses were then connected by marriage, it was a double occasion for joy. The Chengs, however, were a very rich family, belonging to the landed aristocracy, and had long ago prepared for this celebration, while Su's grandfather had not. The son knew his father and had himself sent, along with the announcement, the official cap and gown and the ceremonial hand tablet, together with an armchair and a beautiful teapot. The news arrived when the grandfather was very drunk and was holding a large chunk of beef in his hand. He saw the red button on the official cap peeping out from the luggage bag and knew what it meant. Still under the influence of liquor, he took the official message, read it aloud to his friends, and gaily dumped the chunk of beef into the bag along with the announcement and the cap and gown. Having called a village boy to carry the luggage, he rode on a donkey into town. It was the happiest moment of his life. The people in the streets had heard the news and laughed at the sight of the drunken old man on donkey-back with the curious luggage following behind. The Cheng family thought it a disgrace; but Su Tungpo says only the intelligent scholars appreciated its beautiful simplicity. This grand old man was also a freethinker. One day, in a drunken fit, he went into the temple of a particular god and smashed the idol into pieces. He had developed a special hostility toward this god, who was very much feared by the populace of this district, or more probably a special hostility toward its soothsayer, who extorted money from the believers.

Su Tungpo did not inherit from his grandfather his capacity for wine, but he did inherit his love for it, as we shall have occasion to see later. The intellectual brilliance of this illiterate old man, which lay dormant in his blood, was to blossom forth in all its power and glory in his son's sons. That extra energy of mind and body, that bigness of heart, and underneath it all the strong integrity of purpose were there in the grandfather. The Su family rose from the land, as all other distinguished families rose, by the law of infinite variations and natural selection. We have no indications of the mental qualities of Su Tungpo's mother's family, but a fortuitous combination of the blood of the Sus and the Chengs somehow produced the literary genius.

Apart from this, there was no great influence of the grandfather over the poet's literary life except the fact that his personal name was "Shu." It was most embarrassing for a writer, for this word meant "preface," and Su Tungpo, being a renowned scholar, had to write many prefaces. As it would have been sacrilegious for him to use the word preface, he called his prefaces forewords (*yin*)throughout his works. This taboo against mentioning one's parent's or grandparent's name was a very ancient custom which sometimes produced embarrassing results. It is particularly irritating when personal names of fathers happen to be very common words. In the voluminous tomes of Szema Chien, the greatest historian of China, we cannot find the word *tan*, meaning "talk" or "conversation," because that was the historian's father's personal name. There was a man by the name of Chao T'an—he had arbitrarily to change his name to Chao T'ung. In the same way the author of the *Later Han History* had to avoid the personal mane of his father, T'ai, and today we cannot find that word in all its hundred and twenty volumes of verbiage. The personal name of the father of the poet Li Ao happened to be the common word meaning "now"; thus the poet had always to use an archaic word for the contemporary moment. The same thing resulted from the taboo with respect to the personal names of the emperors of a ruling dynasty. A candidate for the state examinations was expelled if his name contained a word identical with any of the personal names of the preceding emperors of the dynasty. As it happened, the emperors of a dynasty were usually known by their reigns or their posthumous titles, so that many scholars did forget about the emperors' personal names and were expelled. Sometimes an emperor would fail in this way himself, as no one always remembers his ancestor's names back for ten generations. In a moment of forgetfulness an emperor once named a new pavilion and then suddenly realized that he had used a tabooed word—the name of his ancestor. No sooner was the name conferred than it had to be changed.

Su Tungpo's father, Su Shun, was a reticent man, and as far as his political ambitions were concerned, he died disappointed, although his hopes for literary and official honors were realized in the persons of his two sons before he died. Possessing a high intelligence, severe in temperament, independent in mind, and crotchety in character, Su Shun was not a man easy to get along with. He is known to this day as the one great scholar who did not seriously begin to study until he was twenty-seven. This is usually pointed out to young children as an example to prove that with determination and industry, success always awaits a man; though a bright child might deduce the opposite conclusion that one did not *have to* begin to study in childhood. And the fact is, Su Shun had full opportunity to learn to read and write in childhood; it seems that there was enough ruggedness in this individual to resist coercion and resent the formal education of those times. We know that many brilliant children do. It cannot be true that he did not learn to read and write at all in childhood, but rather that he completely wasted his childhood years. Yet, he made enough impression as a young man for the Cheng family to be willing to make him their son-in-law. Equally amazing is the fact that, starting at the late age of twenty-seven, he did achieve such a high literary fame, a fame which was by no means totally eclipsed by his brilliant sons.

About the time when his son was born, he began to take himself seriously, regretting rather late, but with a sharp sense of remorse, the wasted years of his youth. He must have been bitten with shame to see that his own brother and his wife's brother, and his two sisters' husbands, had all passed state examinations and were going out as officials. Such a state of affairs might not affect a mediocre person, but to one gifted with the mental powers that he showed in his *Complete Works*, the situation must have become unbearable. In this sacrificial prayer to his wife on her death, he afterward indicated that she had prodded him along, for the wife, Su Tungpo's mother, was a very well-educated woman. The grandfather, however, had said and done nothing about the son, who to all intents and purposes appeared to be nothing better than a stubborn, erratic, loafing genius. When friends asked him why his son did not study and why he had done nothing about it, he replied placidly, "I am not worried," suggesting an enormous confidence that his brilliant but erring son would himself realize the mistake in due time.

The people of Szechuen were, even in those days, a hardy, argumentative, self-reliant, and largely self-governing race, retaining, as people of remote districts or colonies often do, certain ancient customs and habits and culture. Thanks particularly to the invention of printing in this province a century earlier, a sudden impetus had been given to learning, and in Su Tungpo's day a fairly high percentage of officials, or successful scholars, came from this province. Its general level of scholarship was higher then than that of the provinces now named Hopei and Shantung, for at the imperial examinations candidates from the latter provinces often failed in poetry. Chengtu was the center of culture, famous for its fine letter paper, Szechuen brocade, and beautiful monasteries. There were gifted courtesans and talented beauties, and in the centuries immediately preceding Su Tungpo it had produced at least two famous women poets. In their writings the scholars still held to the early Han tradition of simple austerity of style as against the decadent, ostentatious style prevalent elsewhere at the time.

Then, as now, the people of that province were given to arguments and eloquent disquisitions. Even in middle-class society, conversations were often studded with learned instances and clever allusions, and had an air of archaic refinement to those from the outside provinces. Of this inborn eloquence and this determination not to be worsted in an argument, Su Tungpo had a fair share. Not to mention his arguing several times with the devil, his state papers were distinguished for clarity and forcefulness of presentation. Both Su and his father were attacked by their enemies as resembling the sophists of the Warring Kingdoms, and were praised by their friends as having the style of Mencius, with Mencian eloquence and aptness of analogy. Szechuen people should make good lawyers.

It is for this reason that the people of Meichow acquired the reputation of being "difficult to govern." Su Tungpo once defended it thus: the people here, as different from the people of less cultivated regions, could not be easily bullied by a magistrate. The gentry kept lawbooks in their homes and "did not regard it as wrong" to be thoroughly conversant with the laws and statutes. These scholars tried to live according to the laws and wanted to hold the magistrates to them also. If a magistrate was good and just to the people, they would on his termination of office make a portrait of him and worship him in their homes and remember him for fifty years. But, like modern children at school upon the arrival of a new teacher, they had a game of their own to play. When a new magistrate arrived they would test him, and if he "knew his onions," they would let him alone. But if he was in any way officious or overbearing, he would have a hard time of it. As Su explained, they were hard to govern only when the magistrate did not know how to handle them.

In addition to a certain ancient quaintness in their local customs and habits, the people of Meichow also had developed a kind of social aristocracy. The well-known old families were classified as "A" and "B," and called *chiang ching* or "river squires." The squires would not marry their children to other families, however rich and powerful, if they did not "belong." There was also a well-developed custom of co-operation among the farmers. In the second month of each year the farmers would start work on the fields. By the beginning of April the time came for weeding. The farmers would come together by the hundreds and work collectively at this chore. They chose two leaders for command, one in charge of the hourglass and the other in charge of a drum, and they started and stopped the day's work according to the drum signal. Those who arrived late, or those who were slack, were fined. Farmers who had proportionately more land but fewer farm hands had to make up for it by contributing money to the general fund. At harvesttime, the villagers came together and made a grand festival of it. They broke the earthenware "hourglass" and with the money from the fines and the assigned dues bought mutton and wine to celebrate the harvest. The ceremony was preceded by a sacrificial offering to the god of agriculture, and the people ate and drank and made merry before they dispersed to their homes.

第三章　童年与青年

苏东坡八岁到十岁之间，他父亲进京赶考，落第之后，到江淮一带游历，母亲在家管教孩子。这段时间，家中发生一件事，《宋史》苏东坡的传记与苏辙为他母亲写的长篇碑文里，都有记载。母亲那时正教孩子《后汉书》。书上记载后汉时朝政不修，政权落入阉宦之手，当时书生儒士反抗不阴不阳的小人统治。贪婪、纳贿、勒索、滥捕无辜，是经常有的事。因为地方官都是那些太监豢养的走狗小人，忠贞廉正之士和太学生，竟不惜冒生命之险，上书弹劾奸党。改革与抗议之声，此起彼落；调查与审讯之事，层出不穷。当时学者与太学生辈，在朝廷圣旨颁布之下，或遭皮肉之苦，或遭迫害折磨，或遭谋杀丧命。

在这群正人学者中，有一个勇敢无畏的青年，名叫范滂，而苏洵的妻子正教儿子读的就是《范滂传》：

建宁二年，遂大诛党人，诏下急捕滂等。督邮吴导至县，抱诏书，闭传舍，伏床而泣。滂闻之，曰："必为我也。"即自诣狱。县令郭揖大惊，出解印绶，引与俱亡，曰："天下大矣，子何为在此？"滂曰："滂死则祸塞，何敢以罪累君，又令老母流离乎！"其母就与之诀。滂白母曰："仲博孝敬，足以供养，滂从龙舒君归黄泉，存亡各得其所。惟大人割不可忍之恩，勿增感戚！"母曰："汝今得与李、杜齐名，死亦何恨！既有令名，复求寿考，可兼得乎？"滂跪受教，再拜而辞。顾谓其子曰："吾欲使汝为恶，则恶不可为；使汝为善，则我不为恶。"行路闻之，莫不流涕。时年三十三。

小东坡抬头望了望母亲，问道："母亲，我长大之后若做范滂这样的人，您愿不愿意？"母亲回答道："你若能做范滂，难道我不能做范滂的母亲吗？"

东坡六岁入学。这个私塾不算小，有学童一百多人，只有一个老师，是个道士。苏东坡那副绝顶聪明的幼小头脑，很快就显露出来。在那么多的学童中，苏东坡和另外一个学生是最受老师夸奖的。那个学生是陈太初，后来也考中科举，但是出家做了道士，一心求道成仙去了。陈太初在晚年时，一直准备白昼飞升。一天，他去拜访一个朋友，朋友给他食物金钱。他出门之后，把那食物金钱全散与穷人，自己在门外盘膝打坐，在不食人间烟火之下，就准备脱离此红尘扰攘的人间世。几天之后，他呼吸了最后一口气就不动弹。那位朋友叫仆人把他的尸体移走。但是当时正是新年元旦，在一年如此吉祥的日子，仆人们不愿去搬运尸体。但是死人说了话："没关系，我可以自己搬运。"他立起身来，自己走到野外，在一个更为舒适的地方死去。这就是一般所谓道家修炼之士的"白昼飞升"。

幼年时，苏东坡在读书之外，富有多方面的兴趣。下学后，他就回家往鸟巢里窥探。他母亲已经严格告诫东坡与家中的使女，不得捕捉鸟雀。因此之故，数年之后，鸟雀知道在庭园里不会受害，有的就在庭园的树枝上做巢，矮得孩子们都可以望得见。有一只羽毛极其美丽鲜艳的小鸟，一连数日到他家的庭园去，苏东坡对这只小鸟记得特别清楚。

有时，有官员经过眉山镇，到苏家拜访，因为东坡的叔叔已经做了官。家里于是忙乱一阵，使女就光着脚各处跑，到菜园去摘菜、宰鸡，好治筵席待客。这种情形在孩子眼里，留下了很深的印象。

东坡和堂兄妹等常在母亲身边玩耍。他和弟弟辙也常到村中去赶集，或是在菜园中掘土。一天，孩子们掘出来一块美丽的石板，既晶莹光泽，又有精美的绿色条纹。在他们的敲击之下，发出清脆金属之声。他们想用来做砚台，非常合用。砚台必须用一种有气孔的特别石头，要善于吸收潮湿，并且善于保存潮湿。这种好砚台对书法艺术十分重要。一方上品砚台往往为文人视为至宝。好砚台是文人书桌上的重要物品，因为文人一天大半的生活都与之有密切关系。父亲给孩子一方砚台，他必须保存直到长大成人，他还要在砚台上刻上特别的词句，祝将来文名大噪。

据有些文字记载，苏东坡十岁时，已经能写出出奇的诗句。在他那篇《黠鼠赋》里，我们找到了两句。这篇短文字是描写一只狡猾的小老鼠，掉入一个瓦瓮里，假装已死，等把瓮倒在地上，它便急速逃去，这样把人欺骗过。大约也正在此时，他的老师正读一篇长诗，诗里描写当时朝廷上一群著名的学者。苏东坡这个幼小的学童在老师肩膊后面往前窥探了一下，就开始问到与他们有关的问题。他们都是中国历史上的名人，因为在苏东坡的童年，中国是在宋朝最贤明的君主统治之下，他极力奖励文学艺术。国内太平无事，中国北方与西北的游牧民族如金、辽、西夏，这些部落蛮族本来常为患中国，这时也与宋朝相安无事。在这样的朝廷之下，贤良之臣在位，若干文才杰出的人士都受到恩宠，侍奉皇帝，点缀升平。正是在这个时候，幼童苏东坡首次听到欧阳修、范仲淹等人的大名，当下深受鼓舞。幸好在这位大诗人的童年生活里，我们还有这些对他将来崭露头角的预示。虽然苏东坡记载了不少他成年时代做的梦和梦中未完成的诗句，可是还没有什么无心流露的话，供现代的传记作家使之与解释、直觉、狂想相结合，而捏造出东坡这位诗人下意识中神经病的结构形态。苏东坡倒丝毫没提到尿布和便秘等事呢。

苏东坡十一岁时，进入中等学校，认真准备科举考试。为应付考试，学生必须读经史诗文，经典古籍必须熟读至能背诵。在班上背诵时，学生必须背向老师而立，以免偷看敞开在老师桌子上的文章。肯发愤努力的学生则把历史书上的文字整篇背过。背书时不仅仅注重文章的内容、知识，连文字措辞也不可忽略，因为做文章用的词汇就是从此学来的。用著名的词语与典故而不明言其来源出处，饱学之士读来，便有高雅不凡之乐。这是一种癖好相投者的共用语言。读者对作者之能写此等文章，心怀敬佩，自己读之而能了解，亦因此沾沾自喜。作者与读者所获得的快乐，是由观念的暗示与观念的联想而来的，此种暗示比明白直说更为有力动人，因为一语道破，暗示的魅力便渺不可得矣。

这种背诵记忆实在是艰难而费力的苦事。传统的老方法则是要学生背一整本书，书未加标点，要学生予以标点，用以测验学生是否彻底了解。最努力苦读的学生竟会将经书和正史抄写一遍。苏东坡读书时也是用这种方法。若对中国诗文朴质的经典，以及正史中常见的名称事故暗喻等典故，稍加思索，这种读书方法，自有其优点。因为将一本书逐字抄写之后，对那本书所知的深刻，绝非仅仅阅读多次所能比。这样用功方法，对苏东坡的将来大有好处，因为每当他向皇帝进谏或替皇帝草拟圣旨之际，或在引用历史往例之时，他决不会茫无头绪，就如同现代律师之引用判例一般。再者，在抄书之时，他正好可以练习书法。

　　在印刷术发明之前，此种抄写工作自不可免，但是在苏东坡时，书籍的印刷早已约有百年之久。胶泥活字印刷术是由一个普通商人毕昇发明，方法是把一种特别的胶泥做成单个的字，字刻好之后，胶泥变硬；然后把这些字摆在涂有一层树胶的金属盘子上，字板按行排好之后，将胶加热，用一片平正的金属板压在那些排好的字板上，使各字面完全平正。印书完毕之后，再将树胶加热，各字板便从金属盘上很容易脱落下来，予以清洗，下次再用。

　　苏东坡与弟弟苏辙正在这样熟读大量的文学经典之时，他父亲赶考铩羽而归。当时的科举考试有其固定的规矩形式，就像现代的哲学博士论文一样。当年那种考试，要符合某些标准，需要下过某等的苦工夫，要有记住事实的好记忆力，当然还要一般正常的智力。智力与创造力过高时，对考中反是障碍，并非有利。好多有才气的作家，像词人秦少游，竟而一直考不中。苏洵的失败，其弱点十之八九在作诗上。诗的考试，需要有相当的艺术的雅趣，措辞相当的精巧工稳，而苏洵则主要重视思想观念。因为读书人除去教书之外，仕途是唯一的荣耀成功之路，父亲名落孙山而归，必然是懊恼颓丧的。

　　晚辈高声朗读经典，老辈倚床而听，抑扬顿挫清脆悦耳的声音，老辈认为是人生的一大乐事。这样，父亲可以校正儿子读音的错误，因初学者读经典，自然有好多困难。就好像欧阳修和后来苏东坡都那样倚床听儿子读书，现在苏洵也同样倚床听他两个儿子的悦耳读书声。他的两眼注视着天花板，其心情大概正如一个猎人射了最后一箭而未能将鹿射中，仿佛搭上新箭，令儿子再射一样。孩子的目光和琅琅之声使父亲相信他们猎取功名必然成功，父亲因而恢复了希望，受伤的荣誉心便不药而愈。这时两个青年的儿子，在熟记经史，在优秀的书法上，恐怕已经胜过乃父而雏凤清于老风声了。后来，苏东坡的一个学生曾经说，苏洵天赋较高，但是为人子的苏东坡，在学术思想上却比他父亲更渊博。苏洵对功名并未完全死心，自己虽未能考中，若因此对儿子高中还不能坚信不疑，那他才是天下一大痴呆呢。说这话并非对做父亲的有何不敬，因为他以纯粹而雅正的文体教儿子，教儿子深研史书为政之法，乃至国家盛衰隆替之道，我们并非不知。

对苏东坡万幸的是，他父亲一向坚持文章的淳朴风格，力戒当时流行的华美靡丽的习气，因为后来年轻的学子进京赶考之时，礼部尚书与礼部主试欧阳修，都决心发动一项改革文风运动，便借着那个机会，把只耽溺于雕琢文句卖弄辞藻的华美靡丽之文的学子，全不录取。所谓华美靡丽的风格，可以说就是堆砌艰深难解之辞藻与晦涩罕见的典故，以求文章之美。在此等文章里，很难找到一两行朴质自然的句子。最忌讳指物直称其名，最怕句子朴质无华。苏东坡称这种炫耀浮华的文章里构句用字各自为政，置全篇效果于不顾，如演戏开场日，项臂各挂华丽珠宝的老妪一样。

这个家庭的气氛，正适于富有文学天才的青年的发育。各种图书插列满架。祖父现在与以前大不相同了，因为次子已官居造务监裁，为父者也曾蒙恩封赠为"大理评事"。此等官爵完全是荣誉性的，主要好处是使别的官员便于称呼。有时似乎是，求得这么一个官衔刻在墓志铭上，这一生才不白过——等于说一个人若不生而为士绅，至少盼望死得像个士绅。若不幸赶巧死得太早，还没来得及获得此一荣耀，死后还有一种方便办法，可以获得身后赠予的头衔。其实在宋朝，甚至朝廷正式官员，其职衔与真正职务也无多大关系。读者看苏家的墓志铭，很容易误以为苏东坡的祖父曾任大理评事，甚至做过太傅，而且误以为他父亲也做过太子太傅——其实这些荣耀头衔都是苏辙做门下侍郎时朝廷颁赠的。苏东坡这时有个叔父做官，两个姑母也是嫁给做官的，因此他祖父和外祖父都拥有官衔，一个是荣誉的，另一个是实际的，刚才已经说过。

在苏家，和东坡一起长大一起读书而将来也与他关系最密切的，就是他弟弟辙，字子由。他们兄弟之间的友爱与以后顺逆荣枯过程中深厚的手足之情，是苏东坡这个诗人毕生歌咏的题材。兄弟二人忧伤时相慰藉，患难时相扶助，彼此相会于梦寐之间，写诗互相寄赠以通音信。甚至在中国伦理道德之邦，兄弟间似此友爱之美，也是迥不寻常的。苏子由生来的气质是恬静冷淡，稳健而实际，在官场上竟尔比兄长得意，官位更高。虽然二人有关政治的意见相同，宦海浮沉的荣枯相同，子由冷静而机敏，每向兄长忠言规劝，兄长颇为受益。也许他不像兄长那么倔强任性；也许因为他不像兄长那么才气焕发，不那么名气非凡，因而在政敌眼里不那么危险可怕。现在二人在家读书时，东坡对弟弟不但是同学，而且是良师。他写的一首诗里说："我少知子由，天资和且清。岂独为吾弟，要是贤友生。"子由也在兄长的墓志铭上说："我初从公，赖以有知。抚我则兄，诲我则师。"

走笔至此，正好说明一下"三苏"的名字。根据古俗，一个中国读书人有几个名字。除去姓外，一个正式名字，在书信里签名，在官家文书上签名，都要用此名字。另外有一个字，供友人口头与文字上称呼之用。普通对一个人礼貌相称时，是称字而不提姓，后而缀以"先生"一词。此外，有些学者文人还另起雅号，作为书斋的名称，也常在印章上用，此等雅号一旦出名之后，人也往往以此名相称。还有人出了文集诗集，而别人也有以此书名称呼他的。另外有人身登要职，全国知名，人也以他故乡之名相称的。如曾湘乡、袁项城便是。

老苏名洵，字明允，号老泉，老泉是因他家乡祖茔而得名。长子苏轼，字子瞻，号东坡，这个号是自"东坡居士"而来。"东坡居士"是他谪居黄州时自己起的，以后，以至今日，他就以东坡为世人所知了。中国的史书上每以"东坡"称他而不冠以姓，或称东坡先生。他的全集有时以谥号名之，而为《苏文忠公全集》，宋孝宗在东坡去世后六十年，赠以"文忠公"谥号。文评家往往以他故乡名称而称他为"苏眉州"。小苏名辙，字子由，晚年隐居，自称"颍滨遗老"，因而有人称他为"苏颍滨"。有时又因其文集为《栾城文集》而称之为"苏栾城"。栾城距北平以南之正定甚近，苏姓远祖二百年前，是自栾城迁至眉州的。

一个文人有那么多名字，对研究中国历史者颇以为难。苏东坡在世时，当时至少有八人同叫"梦得"，意思是在母亲怀孕前，都曾梦到在梦中得了儿子。

在东坡十六岁时，发生了一件意外的事情，使他家和他母亲的娘家关系紧张起来，也使他父亲的性格因而略见一斑。事情是，苏东坡的父亲把东坡的姐姐许配给东坡外婆家东坡的一个表兄，在中国家庭里这是常有的事。而今去古已远，我们无法知道详情，但是新娘在程家并不快乐。也许她受程家人折磨，总之，不久去世。经过的情况激起苏洵的恼怒，似乎这个新儿媳的公公是个大坏蛋。苏洵写了一首诗，暗含毒狠的字眼儿，为女儿之死而自责。然后，他露了一手非常之举。他编了一个家谱，刻在石头上，上面立了一个亭子。为庆祝此一盛事，他把苏姓全族请到，他要在全族面前，当众谴责他妻子家。在全族人已经奠酒祭告祖先之后，苏洵向族人说，村中"某人"——暗指他妻子的兄长——代表一个豪门，他已经弄得全村道德沦丧；他已然把幼侄赶走，独霸了家产；他宠妾压妻，纵情淫乐；父子共同宴饮喧哗，家中妇女丑名远播；一家是势利小人，欺下媚上，嫌贫爱富；家中车辆光亮照眼，贫穷的邻人为之侧目而视，他家金钱与官场的势力可以左右官府，最后是，"是三十里之大盗也。吾不敢以告乡人，而私以诫族人焉"。东坡的父亲自然把妻子的娘家得罪到底了，不过他已经准备与这门亲戚根本断绝关系，所以他又告诉两个儿子永远不要和那个表兄来往。这件事发生之后四十多年内，东坡兄弟二人一直没有和那个表兄程之才有往还。不过老泉逝世之后，苏氏兄弟和外婆家别的表兄弟，倒保持了很好的亲戚关系。苏洵对豪门的挑战与当众对豪门的谴责，略微显示出他激烈的性格，他的疾恶如仇，他儿子东坡在晚年时也表现出了这种特性。

东坡的母亲当然为这件事很不快，也为自己的女儿很伤心。在这一场亲戚冲突之中，她究竟是站在娘家那一方，还是站在自己的亡女这一方，这就很难猜测了。前面已经提过，这位母亲是个受过良好教养的，她父亲在朝为官，而且官位不低。据我们所知，她曾经反抗家中那份金钱势力的恶习气，至少反对她哥哥的邪恶败德的行为。她可以说是受了伤心断肠的打击，身体迅速坏下去。

在中国流行一个很美妙的传说，说苏东坡有一个虽不甚美但颇有才华的妹妹。她颇有诗才，嫁了一位词家，也是苏东坡的门下学士，秦观。故事中说，她在新婚之夜，拒绝新郎进入洞房，非要等新郎作好了她出的一副对子才给他开门。那个上联很难对，秦观搜索枯肠，终难如意，正在庭院里十分焦急地走来走去，苏东坡却助了他一臂之力，他才对上了下联。另有故事说这一对情侣曾作奇妙的回文诗，既可以顺着读，又可以倒着读，更可以成为一个圆圈读。在此等故事里，据说苏东坡曾经向他妹妹说："妹若生为男儿，名气当胜乃兄。"这虽然是无稽之谈，人人却都愿相信。但不幸的是，我们找不到历史根据。在苏东坡和弟弟子由数百封信和其他资料之中，虽然多次提到秦观，但是我始终没法找到他们有什么亲戚关系的踪迹。苏东坡当代数十种笔记著作之中，都不曾提到苏东坡还有个妹妹。再者，秦观在二十九岁并且已经娶妻之后，才初次遇见苏东坡。苏东坡的妹妹，即便真有此一位才女，在秦观初次遇见苏东坡时，她已然是四十左右的年纪了。这个故事后来越传越广越逼真，成了茶余酒后最好的趣谈。此等民间故事之所以受一般人欢迎，正是以表示苏东坡的人品多么投好中国人的癖好。

不过，苏东坡倒有一个堂妹，是他的初恋情人，而且他毕生对伊人念念不忘。东坡的祖父去世之后，他父亲远游归来，他的叔叔和家属也回来奔丧。这时堂兄堂妹颇有机会相见，也可以一同玩耍。据苏东坡说，伊人是"慈孝温文"。因为二人同姓，自然联姻无望，倘若是外婆家的表妹，便没有此种困难了。后来，此堂妹嫁与一个名叫柳仲远的青年。以后，苏东坡在旅游途中，曾在靖江她家中住了三个月。在堂妹家盘桓的那些日子，东坡写了两首诗给她。那两首颇不易解，除非当作给堂妹的情诗看才讲得通。当代没有别的作家，也没有研究苏东坡生平的人，曾经提到他们的特殊关系，因为没人肯提。不过，苏东坡晚年流放在外之时，听说堂妹逝世的消息，他写信给儿子说"心如刀割"。在他流放归来途经靖江之时，堂妹的坟就在靖江，他虽然此时身染重病，还是挣扎着到坟上，向堂妹及其丈夫致祭。第二天，有几个朋友去看他，发现他躺在床上，面向里面墙壁，正在抽搐着哭泣。

Chapter Three
CHILDHOOD AND YOUTH

When Su Tungpo was a child of between eight and ten years, his father went to the capital to take his chance at the imperial examinations. After his failure, he traveled abroad as far as the modern Kiangse Province, and the mother took over the personal instruction of the child at home. There is an incident recorded both in the official biography of the poet in the *Sung History* and in the long tomb inscription written by the poet's brother. The mother was teaching the young son a chapter in *Later Han History*. As the result of terrible misrule the government had fallen into the hands of eunuchs; and the scholars rebelled against the rule of the intermediate sex. Corruption and graft and extortion, and arbitrary arrests, were the order of the day, for the local magistrates were all underlings and protégés of the eunuchs. Courting death for themselves, the good scholars time and again impeached the ruling clique. Repeated waves of reform and protest followed repeated inquisitions. The scholars were subjected to bodily torture, persecuted, and murdered by imperial decree.

Among this group of upright scholars was a fearless young man by the name of Fan Pang, and it was his life that the mother and son were reading. The story was that after repeated persecutions and escapes, the end came. The imperial courier bearing the message that sentenced Fan

Pang to death had arrived. As bearer of the unhappy news, the good courier shut himself up in the *yamen* and wept. The magistrate himself was a good man, too, and had high respect for the scholar. He offered to lay down the magistrate's seal and, instead of carrying out the arrest, flee with him, but Fan Pang refused, saying that it would involve his old mother and condemn her to the life of a fugitive form justice. Confiding the care of his mother to his younger brother, he went to say farewell to her. In this decision not to escape the mother concurred, and she said to him, "I had hoped for you a long life and a good name, but since you cannot have both, I prefer that you have a good name." So they parted, and in going, Fan Pang said to his young son: "If I should advise you to do wrong, I know that this would not be right, but if I should advise you to do right, you see I have done no wrong."

The young Su Tungpo looked up to his mother and asked her, "Mother, if I grow up to be a Fan Pang, will you permit it?" And his mother replied, "If you can be a Fan Pang, can I not be Fan Pang's mother?"

The young child entered school at the age of six. It was a fair-sized school with over a hundred pupils, all of whom studied under a Taoist priest. The brilliant young mind quickly distinguished itself, and among the great number of pupils Su and another child were the most praised by the teacher. This other pupil, Chen, later also passed the state examinations but became a Taoist with the ambition to become "an immortal." Quite late in his life, Chen was preparing to go up to Heaven, and he came to pay a visit to one of his friends. The friend gave him food and money. He went out and distributed the food and money to the poor and then sat down in Taoist fashion outside the gate, ready to depart from this earthly life by starvation. Some days later, to all intents and purposes, he had breathed his last. The friend, therefore, called his servants to remove the corpse. However, it was New Year's Day, and the servants complained at having to remove a corpse on such an auspicious day. Thereupon the dead man said, "Never mind, I will carry myself." He got up, walked to the country, and died in a more convenient place. Such is the factual manner in which many of the Taoist recluses were supposed to have "ascended to Heaven."

As a child Tungpo interested himself in other things besides study. After school, he would come home and peep at the birds' nests. His mother had strictly forbidden the boys and maidservants to catch birds, as a result of which, in a few years' time, the birds knew that they would not be molested in this garden and some came to build their nests on a branch low enough for the child to see. Su Tungpo remembered particularly a small bird with wonderful bright plumage that came and visited their garden for days.

Now and then, an official would pass by the town and pay them a visit, since Tungpo's uncle was already an official. There would then be a hullabaloo in the family and the maidservants would run about barefooted to pick vegetables from the garden and kill chickens to prepare a dinner. Such visits of the officials produced a deep impression upon the child.

He played with his cousins on the mother's side. He and his younger brother would visit the village fairs or dig in the vegetable garden. One day the children dug up a beautiful stone slab with a wonderful luster and having delicate green veins in it. They struck it and it gave out a clear metallic tone; they tried using it as an ink slab, and it served the purpose very satisfactorily.

Ink slabs had to be of a special porous stone, absorbing and retaining moisture well; they had a great deal to do with the art of calligraphy. A specially good one was always highly valued by a scholar, since it was an object upon his desk with which he had to do most of the day. The father gave the child this slab, which he kept until he grew up, and upon which he carved a special inscription. This was considered a good omen for his rise in *belles-lettres*.

If we believe the records, he is supposed to have penned some extraordinary lines at the age of ten. Two of these lines are found in his amusing tale of "The Cunning Mouse." It is a short piece describing how a little mouse, when found trapped in a bag, had pretended death, and then worsted his captors when thrown upon the ground. Also at about this time his teacher was reading a copy of a long poem describing the galaxy of illustrious scholars then living at the court. The young pupil looked over the teacher's shoulder and began to ask questions about these scholars. They were names great in China's history, for in Su Tungpo's childhood China was ruled by perhaps the best emperor of the dynasty, who was a patron of literature and the arts. There was peace in the country and peace with the barbarian hordes on the north and northwest, the Kins, the Liaos, and the Shishia Kingdom, which had been a constant source of trouble. Under such a regime, good men held office and a number of literary talents had arisen to grace the court with their presence. It was then that the child first heard of the great names of Ouyang Shiu, Fan Chungyen, and others, and he was deeply inspired. Happily, these are about all the revelations we have of the poet's childhood. Though Su recorded many of his adult dreams and unfinished poems written during his dreams, there are no unwitting remarks for the modern biographer to build, with a mixture of interpretation, intuition, and fantasy, into a fabric of the poet's subconscious neuroses. Su Tungpo mentioned no diapers or constipation.

At the age of eleven he entered the secondary school in serious preparation for the official examinations. To meet the official tests, the students had to cover in their reading all the ancient classics, history, and poetry, and selected prose. Naturally they had to commit the classics to memory, and recitation in class consisted in repeating the passages by heart, with the student's back turned toward the teacher to prevent him from looking at the book lying open on the teacher's desk. The more ambitious ones would memorize whole chapters from the histories. It was not only the contents and information that were important but also the language and phraseology, which were to become elements in a writer's vocabulary. The use of a famous phrase or of an allusion without indicating the source aroused an aristocratic and egoistic pleasure in the learned reader. It was a kind of coterie language; the reader conceived a respect for the writer for writing it and for himself for understanding it. It worked by suggestion and the association of ideas, and was always more effective than an explicit statement that lacked the charm of suggestion.

This memory work was hard and strenuous toil. The traditional method was for the student to go over a printed history book, which was never punctuated, and try to punctuate the passages as a means of making sure that he had completely understood them. But the most ambitious of all would do the really hard thing by copying the whole of the classics and dynastic histories once over by hand. This was actually what Su Tungpo did in his student days. Considering the severe canons of Chinese prose and poetry, and the constant allusions to names and incidents and metaphors used in the standard histories, such a method had distinct advantages. For after copying the whole book word by word, one began to know that book in a way that no amount of reading would give him. This labor served Su Tungpo well in the future, for when pleading with the emperor or drafting an edict for him, he was never at a loss to quote historic examples, used by scholars in those times as "cases" are used by lawyers today. Besides, in copying, he could practice his calligraphy.

Before the invention of printing this copy work was necessary, but in Su Tungpo's time the commercial printing of books had been in existence already for about a hundred years. The invention of printing from movable clay types had been made by a certain Pi Sheng, an ordinary businessman. The method was to have individual types for characters made of a special clay which hardened after carving; these were set on a metal tray prepared with a coating of resin. When the types had been set in line, the resin was heated and a flat sheet of metal was used to press upon the assembled type and give it a perfectly even surface. After printing was done, the resin was heated again; the types came off easily from the metal tray, to be cleaned and put in place for the next job. However, the method of printing from wood blocks, each block representing two pages, continued to be the one in popular use.

While Su Tungpo and his brother Tseyu were storing away this immense knowledge of literature and the classics, their father had failed at the examinations and had come back home. The civil service examinations went by set standards and formulas. Like a Ph.D. thesis, they required conformity to certain standards, a certain amount of drudgery, a good memory of facts, and normal intelligence. Too much intelligence or originality might be a hindrance, rather than an aid, to success at the examinations. Many brilliant writers, such as the poet Chin Kuan, could never pass them. In the case of Su Shun, his weak point may have been versification; tests in poetry required a passable virtuosity and aptness of phraseology, and Su Shun was chiefly interested in ideas. Since, however, an official career was the only road to honor and success and almost the only profession outside teaching open to a scholar, the father must have come home despondent.

It was the custom for young people to read aloud while their father lay on a couch and listened to their voices reciting the classics, said to be one of the most pleasant and musical sounds ever heard upon this earth. In this way the father was able to correct any errors in pronunciation, which was full of traps for the uninitiated. As Ouyang Shiu, and Su Tungpo himself later, lay and listened to their sons' recitation, so Su

Shun lay now on the couch listening to the musical flow of his sons' voices, his eyes fixed on the ceiling, approximately in the state of mind of a hunter who had shot his last arrow and missed the deer, and it was as if he was refashioning new arrows and sending forth his sons to shoot that deer yet. Something in the boys' eyes and their voices, as their tongues rolled so smoothly over the syllables of the classics, told him that they would succeed, and his hope recovered and his wounded pride was healed. The probability is that the adolescent brothers had already outstripped their father, from exact memory of history to excellence of penmanship. One of Su Tungpo's disciples later said that Su Shun had a greater natural talent but that Su Tungpo was the more profound scholar. The father had not yet given up all ambition for an official career, but he would have been an idiot had he not already grasped the certainty that his two sons would pass the examinations though he had failed. This is not said in any disparagement of the father, for we know that he guided his two sons in the direction of purity of style and of a serious concern with history and government, through the study of the laws of prosperity and decay of a period.

It was lucky for Su Tungpo that his father had always stood for simplicity of style in contrast to the precious, ornate manner prevalent at that time; for when later the young scholar went up to the capital to take the examinations, the minister of education and chief examiner, Ouyang Shiu, had determined to start a reform of the literary vogue by failing all candidates who indulged in pedantic nonsense. This pedantic style may be described as a continual piling up of abstruse phrases and obscure allusions in order to "beautify" one's composition. It would be difficult to find one simple natural line in such compositions. The great fear was that things should be called by their right names and a line might be left unadorned. Su Tungpo described such pathetic writing as "building up each sentence by itself and using each word by itself" without reference to the total effect—like the opulent jewels worn on an old lady's arms and neck at an opera *première*.

The home atmosphere seemed just right for the growing up of an adolescent with a strong literary bent. The library was stacked with books of all kinds. The grandfather now was a different person; on the merit of his second son's having become an inspector in the finance ministry, the old man had also received an official rank, that of "counselor" at an imperial court of justice. Such ranks were purely honorary, their chief merit being that of enabling an official to refer to his father as "the Counselor" or "the Commodore," although he might never have seen a court or a ship in his life. It seemed at times that to die with some such title on his epitaph was all that a man lived for—if one could not live as a gentleman, he at least hoped to die like one. And if he happened to die too soon, before securing such honors, there was always the convenient device of posthumous titles. Particularly in the Sung Dynasty, even for the regular officials, one's title had little to do with one's actual post. Readers of the tomb inscriptions of the Su family may be misled into thinking that the poet's grandfather was a counselor at a court of justice and also an imperial tutor, and that his father was a tutor to the prince, honors conferred upon them when Su Tseyu became a vice-premier. As a matter of fact, neither had ever held such an office in his lifetime. Su now had an uncle who was an official and two aunts who were married to husbands holding government offices. Both his paternal and maternal grandfathers held official ranks, one honorary, as we have just pointed out, and the other actual.

But the most important member of his family who grew up and studied with him and with whom his life was to be most closely connected was his younger brother, Tseyu. The love and devotion between these two brothers and their constant loyalty to each other through all vicissitudes of fortune was a theme song of the poet's entire life. They comforted each other in sorrow, helped each other in distress, and dreamed about each other and wrote poems to each other as a form of communication. Even in China the beautiful love between the two brothers was something quite unique. Tseyu was of steady, phlegmatic temperament, with practical sense, and somehow he managed to attain eventually a higher position than his elder brother. Although they shared the same political views and followed the same ups and downs through their entire political careers, Tseyu was the more hardheaded one and often helped his brother with wise counsel. Perhaps he was less headstrong; perhaps, being less brilliant and not enjoying such a singular reputation as his elder brother, he was considered less dangerous by their political opponents. At this period Su Tungpo acted not only as a fellow student but also as a teacher to his brother. He wrote in a poem, "In my youth I knew Tseyu as a child, gentle and bright. I regarded him not only as a junior fellow student, but also as a clever pupil." And the younger brother wrote in Su Tungpo's tomb inscription, "I had knowledge from you, my brother. You cared for me as an elder and guided me as a teacher."

At this point it is convenient to state the various names of the three Sus. In accordance with ancient custom, a Chinese scholar has several names. Besides the family name he has a legal personal name (*ming*)with which he signs his own signature in all letters and official registrations. He has a courtesy name (*tse*)by which he should be addressed orally and in writing by his friends. The usual way of addressing a person formally is by his courtesy name without his family name, with "Mr." added to it. In addition many scholars adopt special poetic names (*hao*)on various occasions as names for their libraries or studies—names that are often used in their seals, and by which they are popularly known once they become famous. Others are sometimes referred to by the names of their collected works. A few who rise to a position of national importance are referred to by the name of their home town. (A Chinese Wendell Willkie might have been known as "Indiana Willkie," and F.D.R. would have been entitled to be called "Hyde Park Roosevelt.")A great many eminent officials received also a posthumous honorific title.

Su senior's personal name was *Shun*; his courtesy name, *Mingyun*; and the poetic name by which he was commonly known, *Laochuan*, which came from the name of his family cemetery. The elder son was *Su Shih*; his courtesy name was *Tsechan*, and his poetic name, *Tungpo*. This last comes from his poetic title, "Recluse of Tungpo," the name he adopted for himself when he was living in banishment on the Eastern Slope (*Tungpo*)of Huangchow. This in time became the name by which he was and is popularly known all over China. Chinese records usually refer to him as "Tungpo," without "Su," or sometimes as "Mr. Tungpo." His complete works sometimes go by his posthumous title of *Wen Chung Kung* or "Literary Patriotic Duke," the title conferred on him by the emperor about seventy years after his death. Poetic critics sometimes refer to him with great respect by his home district: as Su *Meichow*. The younger brother's name was Su *Cheh*, his courtesy name *Tseyu*; in his old age, living in retirement, he styled himself "the Old Recluse on the Bank of the Ying River." He was therefore sometimes referred to in Chinese works as Su *Yingpin*, and sometimes as Su *Luancheng*, Luancheng being the title of his collected works and of the district of the remote ancestry of the Su family, situated near Chengting, south of Peking, whence the family had come to live at *Meichow* two hundred years earlier.

As one Chinese name per person is more than enough for the Western reader to follow, I shall always call the father *Su Shun*, the elder son *Su Tungpo*, and the younger son *Su Tseyu*, following the prevailing Chinese practice. The confusion arising from so many names adopted by one scholar takes up a great deal of the time of a student doing research in Chinese history. In Su Tungpo's time at least eight persons had the same name, *Mengteh*, which meant that the person's mother, before she conceived, had dreamed that she had a boy.

When Tungpo was sixteen, there was an episode which put a heavy strain on the relationship between the father's and the mother's family, and which reveals something of the father's character. As often happens in Chinese families, the father has married Su Tungpo's elder sister to a first cousin in the mother's family. We cannot know details at this late date, but we know that the young bride was unhappy in the Cheng family. Perhaps she was persecuted by her husband's relations. Anyway, she soon died and under circumstances that stirred up Su Shun's indignation. It seems the girl's father-in-law was a thorough scoundrel. Su Shun wrote a poem couched in bitter words and blaming himself for his daughter's death. He then did an unusual thing. He compiled a family genealogy, had it inscribed in stone, and erected a pavilion over it. To celebrate the occasion, he gathered the entire Su clan, before whom he intended to read a public denunciation of his wife's family. After the members of the clan had poured wine offerings to the dead ancestors, Su said to the clansmen that a "certain" person in the village, meaning his wife's brother, represented a powerful family; that he had brought moral chaos into the village; that he had driven out the orphan child of his own brother and monopolized the family property; that he had placed his concubine above his wife and indulged in licentious pleasures; that the father and son caroused together and the women's behavior was scandalous; that they were snobs, "confusing the wealthy with the nice people"; that their beautiful carriages dazzled the eyes of their poor neighbors, and their money and official connections were able to influence the court; and finally, that "they are the scoundrels of the village. I dare not tell this to all the villagers, but I say it to the people of our own clan." The father undoubtedly offended his wife's family forever, but he was prepared to sever all connections with them, and he told his sons never to have anything to do with their brother-in-law. For more than forty years after the incident neither Su Tungpo nor his brother had any contact with their brother-in-law, Cheng Chihtsai, although they maintained cordial relations with the other cousins after their father's death. The challenge to the powerful clan and the tone of the public denunciation show in the father something of the impetuosity and intolerance of evil that were characteristics of the poet in his later career.

The mother was very unhappy over the incident. She, too, felt great sorrow over the loss of her young daughter. It is difficult to surmise whether, in this family conflict, she stood for her own dead daughter or for her maiden family. The mother was, as we have said, a well-educated woman, her father being an official who had risen to a fairly high rank at the capital. For all we know, she may have rebelled against the snobbery of her family, or at least against the debauchery of her brother. She was brokenhearted and her health rapidly declined.

Charming legends very generally accepted in China credit Tungpo with having a very talented, if not beautiful, younger sister. She is reputed to have been a poet, and to have married Chin Kuan, a very well-known poet and a protégé of Su Tungpo. Stories are told of how she kept away the bridegroom from her chamber on the wedding night until he had completed a couplet she had set for him to finish. It was an extraordinarily difficult task and the poet bridegroom was in despair, pacing up and down the courtyard frantically, until Su Tungpo helped him out. Other stories tell of how the two lovers exchanged the most fanciful kinds of poems with words arranged to be read backward and forward and in a circle. In such stories Su Tungpo was reported to have said to his sister, "If you were a man, you certainly would have become more famous than myself." One would like to believe these stories. Unfortunately there is no historic basis for them. In the hundreds of letters and records in Su Tungpo's works and those of his brother, with many mentions of Chin Kuan, I have not been able to find the slightest indication that they were ever related. Nor was it once mentioned in the dozens of memoirs written by scholars of the period that Su Tungpo had a younger sister. Moreover, Chin Kuan never saw Tungpo until he was twenty-nine and married, and Su's younger sister, if she was born at all, would have been around forty when Chin Kuan met Su. The legends grew up very much later and are usually connected with stories which made good after-dinner conversation. But the existence of such popular legends merely shows how the personality of Su Tungpo captured the imagination of the Chinese people.

Tungpo, however, had a younger cousin-sister, who was his first love, and for whom he showed very tender feelings till the end of his days. She was his first cousin on the father's side. When his grandfather died, Tungpo's father returned from his trip abroad, and so also did his uncle with his family, to attend the funeral ceremony. The cousins therefore had much chance of seeing and playing with one another. According to Tungpo she was "good and intelligent and kind." Since they both bore the same family name, marriage was out of the question, as would not have been the case had she been a first cousin on the mother's side—that is, had she borne a different family name. In time, the cousin was married to one Liu Chungyuan. Later, in his travels, Tungpo had occasion to visit her at Chinkiang at her home for three months. During his stay he wrote two poems that are difficult to explain except as love poems addressed to her.[1] No writer of the period and no research student of Su Tungpo's life ever mentioned this special relationship, because no one would. However, when he was

---

[1] See pages 345 ~ 350.

living in exile in his old age and heard of this cousin's death, he wrote to her son that he felt as if "a knife had been thrust into his heart." After his return from exile, when he was passing through Chinkiang where her grave lay, he made an effort, though he was very sick at the time, to go and sacrifice to her spirit and the spirit of her husband. The day after, when some friends went to call on him, he was found to be lying in bed and shaking with sobs, with his face turned toward the wall.[1]

---

[1] See pages 732~733, 809~811.

第四章　应试

在苏东坡兄弟年二十岁左右，已经准备好去赶考之时，不可避免的事，婚姻问题也就来临了。他们若是未婚进京，并且一考而中，必然有女儿长成之家托人向他们提亲。那时有求婚的风俗，京都中有未婚之女的富商都等待着考试出榜，向新得功名的未婚举子提亲。所以科举考试举行的季节，也是婚姻大事进行得活跃的季节。在父母看来，让儿子娶个本地姑娘，他们对姑娘的家庭知根知底，自然好得多。按照当年的风俗，青年的婚姻一向是由父母妥为安排。苏东坡年十八岁时，娶了王弗小姐。王弗小姐那时十五岁，家住青神，在眉山镇南约十五里，靠近河边。次年弟弟子由成家，年十六岁，妻子比他小两岁。当然算是早婚，但是并不足为奇。

在根本道上看，早婚，当然并不一定像苏氏兄弟那么早，在选择与吸引合意的配偶时，可以省去青年人好多时间的浪费和感情的纷扰。在父母看来，年轻人若能把爱情、恋爱早日解决，不妨碍正事，那最好。在中国，父母自然应当养儿媳妇，年轻的男女无须乎晚婚。而且一位小姐爱已经成为自己丈夫的男人，和爱尚未成自己丈夫的男人，还不是一样？不过在拼命讲浪漫风流的社会里，觉得婚前相爱更为惊奇可喜罢了。无论如何，苏家兄弟婚后却很美满。但这并不是说由父母为儿女安排的婚姻不会出毛病，也不是说这样的婚姻大都幸福。所有的婚姻，任凭怎么安排，都是赌博，都是茫茫大海上的冒险。天下毕竟没有具有先见的父母或星相家，能预知自己儿女婚姻的结果，即便是完全听从他们的安排也罢。在理想的社会里，婚姻是以玩捉迷藏的方式进行的，未婚的青年男女年龄在十八岁到二十五岁之间，虽然当地社会伦理和社会生活十分安定，但是幸福婚姻的比例，也许还是一样。男人，十八岁也罢，五十八岁也罢，几乎没有例外，在挑选配偶时，仍然是以自然所决定的性优点为根据的。他们仍然是力图作明智的选择，这一点就足以使现代的婚姻不致完全堕落到动物的交配。婚姻由父母安排的长处是简单省事，容易成就，少废时间，选择的自由大，范围广。所有的婚姻，都是缔构于天上，进行于地上，完成于离开圣坛之后。

次子子由成婚之后，父子三人起程赴京。他们先要到省会成都，拜谒大官张方平，后来张方平对苏东坡几乎如同严父。为父的仍然打算求得一官半职。他现年四十七岁，但自上次科举名落孙山之后，一直苦读不懈。在那段期间，他已经写了一部重要的著作，论为政之道、战争与和平之理，显示出真知灼见，此一著作应当使京都文人对他刮目相看。当时只要有名公巨卿有力的推介，朝廷可以任命官职。苏洵把著作呈献给张方平，张方平对他十分器重，有意立刻任他为成都书院教席。但是老苏意犹未尽。最后，张方平在古道热肠之下，终因情面难却，乃写信给文坛泰斗欧阳修，其实当时张与欧阳相处得并不十分融洽。另外有一位雷姓友人，也写了一封推荐信，力陈老苏有"王佐之才"。怀有致欧阳修与梅尧臣的书信，父子便自旱路赴京，迢迢万里，要穿剑阁，越秦岭，为时需两月有余。

在仁宗嘉祐元年（一○五六）五月，三苏到了汴梁城，寄宿于僧庙，等待秋季的考试。这是礼部的初试，只是选择考生以备次年春季皇帝陛下亲自监督的殿试。在由眉州来京的四十五个考生之中，苏氏昆仲在考中的十三名之内。当时除去等候明春的殿试之外，别无他事，父子三人乃在京都盘桓，在城内游览，参加社交活动，与社会知名人士结交。苏洵将著作向德高望重的欧阳修呈上。欧阳修一副和蔼可亲的样子，两耳长而特别白皙，上唇稍短，大笑时稍露牙龈。欧阳修，看来并非美男子，但是一见这位文坛盟主而获得他的恩宠，却足以使天下士子一慰其梦寐之望。欧阳修之深获学术界敬爱，是由于他总是以求才育才为己任。他对苏洵热诚接待，并经他介绍，老苏又蒙枢密韩琦邀请至家，又转介绍认识一些高官显宦。不过苏洵冷淡自负的态度，在朝廷的领袖人物心目之中，并未留下什么好印象。

苏氏兄弟则游逛华美的街市，吃有名的饭馆子，站在寒冷的露天之下，以一副羡慕的心情注视大官在街上乘坐马车而过。宋朝共有四个都城，河南开封为首，称为东都。开封有外城内城。外城方十三里，内城七里，城周有城门十二座，入城处有两层或三层的城圈，用来围困进犯的敌军。城墙上筑有雉堞，供发炮射箭之用。因为国都地处一低下之平原，无险可守，只有北部黄河绵延约有二百里（今日之陇海铁路即沿河而行），可以拱卫国都，因此拟订了一个设想极为周密的军事防御计划。

在西部洛阳，距开封约一百三十里，建立西都，用以扼制经军事要隘潼关自西北而来的进犯。在东部约八十里以外的商丘，设立另一军事重镇，是为南都，并不怕有敌人自南部而来。在另一方面，唐朝末年，蛮族已自北方侵入中国。当时有一军阀，由于向北番异族一霸主效忠，在其卵翼之下，遂成立朝廷，对抗中国。石敬瑭向契丹王以儿子自称，但自谓深

爱中国并关心国家之太平与百姓之幸福。他自称"儿皇帝"，称契丹王为
"父皇帝"。他在世之时，使中国形成分裂，获取外族之赞美。但是国家应
当慎谋严防有此等情形出现。不论古今，在中国总是有打着爱国旗号的汉
奸，只要自己能大权在握显赫一时，便在救国救民的堂皇名义之下，甘心
充当异族的傀儡。石敬瑭后来以"儿皇帝"之身，为"父皇帝"所废，羞
愤而死，此一事实并不足以阻止十二世纪时另一傀儡张邦昌之出现。而在
张邦昌失去利用价值后，立即被推翻，弃之如敝屣，但并不足以阻止清末
另一个汉奸吴三桂向关外借兵，进入长城，让满洲人毁灭了中国政府。宋
朝因此在河北南部的大名府，建立了北京，遏止北方异族的南侵。

　　开封是中国首都大城，保有皇都的雄伟壮丽，财富之厚，人才之广，
声色之美，皆集于朝廷之上。城外有护城河围绕，河宽百尺，河的两岸种
有榆树杨柳，朱门白墙掩映于树木的翠绿之间。有四条河自城中流过，大
都自西而东，其中最大者为汴河，从安徽河南大平原而来的食粮，全在此
河上运输。河上的水门夜间关闭。城内大街通衢，每隔百码，设有警卫。
自城中流过的河道上，架有雕刻的油漆木桥相通。最重要的一座桥在皇宫
的前面，乃精心设计，用精工雕刻的大理石筑成。皇宫位于城市之中央。
南由玄德楼下面的一段石头和砖建的墙垣开始，皇宫的建筑则点缀着龙凤
花样的浮雕，上面是光亮闪烁的殿顶，是用各种颜色的琉璃瓦建成的。宫
殿四周是大街，按照罗盘的四角起的街名。皇宫的西面为中书省和枢密
院。在外城的南部，朱雀门之外，有国子监和太庙。街上行人熙来攘往，
官家的马车、牛车、轿子——轿子是一般行旅必需的——另外有由人拉的
两轮车，可以说是现代东洋车的原始型，这些车轿等在街上川流不息。坐
着女人的牛车上，帘子都放了下来。在皇城有个特点，就是必须戴帽子，
即使低贱如算命看相的，也要打扮得像个读书人。

殿试的日子到了。皇帝任命欧阳修为主试官，另外若干饱学宿儒为判官。在读书人一生这个紧要关头到来之际，大家心中都是紧张激动，患得患失。过去多年来三更灯火五更鸡的苦读力学，都是为了这一时刻。考生必须半夜起身，天甫黎明就要来到皇宫之外，身上带着凉的饭食，因为没考完是不许出考场的。在考试时，考生要各自关闭在斗室之中，有皇宫的侍卫看守。朝廷有极严厉的规定，借以防止纳贿或徇私。考生的试卷在交到考试官之前，先要由书记重抄一遍，以免认出试卷的笔迹。在重抄的试卷上，略去考生的名字，另存在档册里。考生在考完放出之时，考试官则关入宫中闱场，严禁与外界有任何接触，通常是从正月底到三月初，直到试卷阅毕呈送给皇上为止。考生首先考历史或政论，次考经典古籍，最后，在录取者的试卷已阅毕，再在皇帝陛下亲自监察之下考诗赋，然后再考策论。宋仁宗特别重视为国求才，对这种考试极为关注。他派贴身臣仆把题目送去，甚至有时为避免泄露，他还在最后一刹那改变题目。

苏氏兄弟都以优等得中。苏东坡的文章，后来欧阳修传给同辈观看，激赏数日。那篇文章论的是为政的宽与简，这正是苏东坡基本的政治哲学。不过，不幸有一个误会。欧阳修对此文章的内容与风格之美十分激赏，以为必然是他的朋友曾巩写的。为了避免招人批评，他把本来列为首卷的这篇文章，改列为二卷，结果苏东坡那次考试是名列第二。在仁宗嘉祐二年（一〇五七）四月八日，苏东坡考中，在四月十四日，他那时才二十岁，成为进士，在三百八十八人之中几乎名列榜首。得到此项荣誉，于是以全国第一流的学者知名于天下。

苏东坡这个才气纵横的青年，这次引用历史事例，却失之疏忽，而且在试卷上杜撰了几句对话。他发挥文意时说，在赏忠之时，宁失之宽厚；在罚罪之时，当恻然有哀怜之心，以免无辜而受戮。他写道："当尧之时，皋陶为士，将杀人。皋陶曰杀之，三。尧曰宥之，三。"这几句对白读来蛮好，显示贤君亦肯用不肖，使之有一展长才之日，这种史实颇可证实明主贤君用人之道。判官梅圣俞阅卷至此，对尧与皋陶有关此事之对白，不敢公然提出查问，因为一经提出，即表示自己对年久湮没的古籍未曾读过。苏东坡因此才得以混过。考试过去之后，梅圣俞一天问苏东坡：

"可是，尧和皋陶这段话见于何书？我一时想不起在何处读过。"

苏东坡这位年轻学者承认说："是我所杜撰。"

梅圣俞这位前辈宿儒大惊："你所杜撰！"

东坡回答说："帝尧之圣德，此言亦意料中事耳。"

主考官录取一学生，即表示自己克尽其职发现了真才，二人彼此之间即形成了"老师"与"门生"终身不渝的关系。考中的门生要去拜谒主考老师致敬，并修函感谢恩德。欧阳修为当时文学权威，一字之褒，一字之贬，即足以关乎一学人之荣辱成败。当年一个作家曾说，当时学者不知刑罚之可畏，不知晋升之可喜，生不足欢，死不足惧，但怕欧阳修的意见。试想一想，欧阳修一天向同僚说的话，那该有何等的力量啊！他说："读苏东坡来信，不知为何，我竟喜极汗下。老夫当退让此人，使之出人头地。"这种话由欧阳修口中说出，全京都人人都知道了。据说欧阳修一天对儿子说："记着我的话。三十年后，无人再谈论老夫。"他的话果然应验，因为苏东坡死后的十年之内，果然无人再谈论欧阳修，大家都谈论苏东坡。他的著作在遭朝廷禁阅之时，有人还暗中偷读呢。

苏东坡的宦途正要开始，母亲病故。根据儒家之礼，这当然是极其重大之事，甚至官为宰相，也须立即退隐，守丧两年三个月之后，才能返回复职。东坡的姐姐已于数年前去世，因此苏家全家三个男人进京应试之后，家中只有母亲和两个儿媳妇。母亲死时还没听到京都的喜讯。苏家父子三人急忙返家，到家只见母亲已去，家中一团纷乱，篱墙倾倒，屋顶穿漏，形如难民家园。

正式办完丧礼之后，他们在一山坡之下名为"老翁泉"的地方，挑选一处作为苏家的茔地。这个泉之所以得此名，是因为当地人说月明之夜，可见一白发俊雅老翁倚坐在堤防之上，有人走近时，老翁则消失于水中。后来苏洵也葬埋于此，因为那片地方的名称，苏洵通常亦称为"苏老泉"。

苏洵在祭妻文里说：

> 非官实好，要以文称。……嗟余老矣，四海一身。自子之逝，内失良朋……昔余少年，游荡不学，子虽不言，耿耿不乐。我知子心，忧我泯没。感叹折节，以至今日……有蟠其丘，惟子之坟。凿为二室，期与子同。我归旧庐，无有改移。魂兮未泯，不日来归。

居丧守礼之下的一年又三个月的蛰居生活，是苏东坡青年时期最快乐的日子。兄弟二人和年轻的妻子住在一起。东坡常到青神岳父家去。青神位于美丽的山区，有清溪深池，山巅有佛寺，涉足其间，令人有游仙寻异超然出尘之感。东坡常与岳父家叔伯表兄弟等前往庙中游历，坐在瑞藻桥附近的堤防上，以野外餐饮为乐。在夏季的夜晚，他坐在茅屋之外，吃瓜子和炒蚕豆。岳父家为大家庭：有岳父王杰，两个叔叔及其妻子儿女。在岳父家约三十个人之中，有一个小姐，名唤"二十七娘"，是命定与苏东坡一生不可分的。

这时，老苏正在等待京中的任命消息。这时他接受官职并无不当，因为妻丧和母丧不同。京师已经有巨官显宦答应提拔他，但是他已等了一年有余，尚无消息到来。最后，终于有圣旨下降，要他赴京参加一种特殊考试。这一来，使此翁着了慌。因为这时他已经有了一种惧怕考试的心理。他给皇帝上一奏折，谢绝前去，以年老多病为辞。但是在给朋友的信里则说："仆固非求仕者，亦非固求不仕者……何苦乃以衰病之身，委曲以就有司之权衡，以自取轻笑哉……向者权书论衡几策，乃欧阳永叔以为可进而进之。苟朝廷以为其言之可信，则何所事试？苟不信其平居之所云，而其一日仓卒之言又何足信耶？"给梅圣俞的信里说："惟其平生不能区区附和有司之尺度，是以至此穷困……自思少年尝举茂林，中夜起坐，裹饭携饼，待晓东华门外，逐队而入，屈膝就席，俯首据案。其后每思至此，即为寒心……"

第二年，仁宗嘉祐四年（一○五九）六月，他又接到朝廷的圣旨，仍是上一次的内容。并未言及免除任何考试，自然不足餍足老泉之望。朝廷主其事者当对他前所呈奏信而不疑才是——相信固好，否则即搁置亦可。他是不肯像学童一样去接受考问的，所以他又再度辞谢。他的奏折上说他已年近五十。五十之年又何以能报效国家？身为读书人之所以愿居官从政，欲有以报效国家也，否则为一寒士足矣。倘若他此时再入仕途，既无机会以遂报国之志，又不能享隐逸贤达之清誉。他最后结束说，时已至夏季，下月妻子之居丧将满，他将随子入都一行，届时当一谒当道，细叙情由。全信中之语气显示他在五十之年，实已无意入朝为官，除非有力人士能使他不再如童子之受考试。

事实上，苏洵的妻子已死，他已准备远离家乡而不复返。非常明显，他是适于住在京都的。他的两个儿子既然已中进士，下一步就看朝廷何时有缺可以派儿子去任职，他自己倒也罢了。在居丧期满之后刚过两个月，父子三人又再度起程入京。这一次有两个儿媳同行，出发之前，已经把亡母之灵柩安派妥当。苏洵使人请了六尊菩萨像，安放在两个雕刻好镀金的佛龛中，供在极乐寺的如来佛殿里。那六尊菩萨是：观世音菩萨、势至菩萨、天藏王、地藏王、解冤王者、引路王者。出发之前，苏洵正式把这些佛像供在庙里，并且去向亡妻灵前告别。祭文的结语是："死者有知，或升于天，或升于四方，上下所适如意，亦若余之游于四方而无系云尔。"

Chapter Four
THE EXAMINATIONS

When Su Tungpo and his brother were adolescents and almost ready to take their examinations, inevitably the marriage question came up. If they went up to the capital unmarried and if they passed the examinations, they would be spoken for by families having grown-up daughters anyway. At this time there was the custom of *chuo-bun* ("catch marriage"): rich merchants at the capital with unmarried daughters were on the lookout for the announcement of the results of the examinations, and were ready to negotiate financial settlements on successful bachelor candidates. The time of the civil service examinations was also the busy season of the matrimonial market. It was far preferable, from the parents' point of view, to have their sons married to girls of their own town, born of families they knew. As was the general custom, it was all properly arranged by the parents. Tungpo was going on his eighteenth year when he married Miss Wang Fu, aged fifteen, of a family living at Chingshen, some fifteen miles to the south, on the river. His younger brother was married the following year at the age of sixteen to a girl two years younger. These were early marriages, though not uniquely so.

In principle, early marriages, though not quite as early as those of the Su brothers, tend to save the young people a great waste of time and energy and emotional confusion in trying to select and attract a desirable match. It was most desirable for the young people to have their love and romance settled and out of the way. In China, the system of parents' support of daughters-in-law made it unnecessary for young people to postpone marriage, and it was perhaps just as well for a girl to love a man who was already her husband as to love one who was not yet married to her, though to an incurably romantic society, the latter seems more exciting. Anyway, the Su brothers were happily married. It is not by any means implied that mistakes were not made by parents in arranging their children's marriages, or that a higher percentage of happy marriages ensued; all marriages, however arranged, are a gamble and an adventure upon an uncharted sea. The prescient parent or fortuneteller who knows exactly how his son's marriage is going to turn out, even if arranged by him, does not exist. In an ideal society where marriages are made in a blindfold game in a dark forest, participated in by unmarried men and women between the ages of eighteen and twenty-five, but where social ethics and community life are stable, the percentage of happy marriages may still be the same. Men, whether at the age of eighteen or fifty-eight, select their mates, with rare exceptions, still on the basis of sexual selection designed by nature, while women attract, but do not select, on the same basis. They make more of an attempt to approach an intelligent choice, and this alone prevents a modern marriage from completely resembling the amorous mating of animals. The advantages of the system of arrangement by parents are merely that it is simpler, more efficient, less wasteful of time, and allows a much greater freedom and wider range of choice. All marriages are contracted in heaven but made on earth and by the men and women who have to make it *after* they come away from the altar.

Soon after the younger son's marriage, therefore, the brothers and father set out for the capital. They had first to go to Chengtu, the capital of the province, where they came into contact with Chang Fangping, a very high official who later was almost like a father to Su Tungpo. Their father also hoped to obtain a position of some kind. He was now about forty-seven, but he had worked hard since his return after his failure at the examinations. In that period he had produced an important work on the principles of government, war, and peace, showing great depth and originality, which should bring him the attention and respect of the scholars at the capital. There were at the time possible channels for one to receive an office on special recommendation of some high minister of state. He submitted his works to Chang Fangping, who thought very highly of them and was ready to appoint him a teacher at the district college of Chengtu. But Su senior was not content with a "mere post as a college teacher." Eventually, overcome by his enthusiasm, Chang was persuaded to write a letter of introduction to Ouyang Shiu, the first writer of the land, although he was not on very good terms with him. Another friend, by the name of Lei, also wrote a letter of introduction, speaking of the eldest Su as having the "talent of a counselor of kings." Armed with these letters to Ouyang Shiu and Mei Yaochen, the father and sons went up to the capital by a land journey of over two months, passing through the high mountain ranges of northern Szechuen and Shensi.

In May of 1056 the three Sus arrived at the capital and put up at a Buddhist temple, awaiting the tests that were to come in the autumn. These were the preliminary tests given by the ministry of education selecting candidates for the spring examinations to be held under the personal supervision of the emperor. Of the forty-five candidates from Meichow, both brothers were among the successful thirteen. Having nothing more to do than to wait for the palace examinations in spring, the father and sons stayed to look over the city and get an introduction to society. Su Shun now submitted his works to Ouyang Shiu, the highly respected and loved leader of the scholar class. The genial-mannered

Ouyang Shiu had unusually white long ears and a short upper lip which revealed his gums when he laughed. He was not particularly handsome to look at, but to meet this dean of letters and receive his favor was the dream of all aspiring scholars. Ouyang Shiu had won the love of the *literati* because he had always regarded it as his duty to discover and encourage young talent. He received Su Shun cordially, and through him Su senior was invited to privy councilor Han Chi's home and introduced to the high-ranking officials. But with his aloof and somewhat self-important manner, Su Shun failed to make a good impression on the government leaders.

The young brothers spent their time looking at the gay streets, eating at the famous restaurants, and standing in the cold watching with great admiration the renowned ministers passing by in their carriages. The Sung Dynasty had four capitals, of which Kaifeng, in modern Honan, was the chief. Kaifeng, then called the Eastern Capital ("Tungking," which in Japanese would be pronounced "Tokyo"), consisted of an outer city, thirteen miles in circumference, and an inner city seven miles in cirmumference. The city had twelve gates, provided with double and triple traps against enemies, and on top of the city wall, "horse heads" resembling gun emplacements were constructed at regular intervals. As the capital was situated on a low-lying plain without strategic protection, save that on the north it was protected by the long stretch of some two hundred miles of the Yellow River, along which the modern Lunghai Railway now runs, a well-thought-out plan of military defense had been devised.

On the west at Loyang, about a hundred and thirty miles away, was the Western Capital, which was established as a bulwark guarding the approach from the northwest through the strategic Tungkuan Pass. On the east, at Shangchiu, some eighty miles away, was established another military anchor, the Southern Capital. There was no fear of invasion from the south. On the other hand, during the first half of the tenth century, barbarian tribes from the north had invaded China. There was a war lord then who had set up a separate government and was able to defy the rest of China by pledging allegiance to a strong dictatorial foreign power lying in the direction of Mongolia. Shih Chingtang became the son of the Siberian emperor, though he declared that he loved China and was concerned for the peace and welfare of the people. He called himself the "Sonny Emperor," while he addressed the Siberian as "Daddy Emperor." While he lived and broke up China's unity, he won the plaudits of foreigners. Particular care, therefore, was taken to prevent a repetition of such a separatist regime, because whether in ancient or in modern China, there are always enough "patriots" willing to serve as puppets of a foreign government in the name of the common people of China so long as they can keep themselves in power. The fact that the "son" of a foreign dictator was thrown out of power and died of shame and frustration did not prevent the rise of another puppet, Chang Pangchang, in the twelfth century; and the fact that Chang was thrown out when he had served his purpose did not prevent still another "patriot" in the sixteenth century, Wu Sankuei, from leading his army, armed by a foreign power, inside the Great Wall to crush the Chinese government. The Northern Capital, therefore, was established at Tamingfu in southern Hopei, guarding against the approach of Mongol potentate from the north.

The city was the metropolis of China, kept in imperial grandeur, where the wealth and talent and beauty of the nation gathered about the court. All around the city ran a moat a hundred feet wide, planted on both banks with elms and willows, revealing the white parapeted walls and vermilion gates behind. Four rivers flowed through the city, running mainly east and west, the most important being the Pien River, which carried all the river traffic and food supplies to the capital from the southeast plains of Anhuei and Honan. Water gates on these rivers were closed at night. Inside the city, the great avenues were provided with guard posts every hundred yards. Painted and carved wooden bridges spanned the rivers running through the city, while the most important one in front of the palace was built of carved marble, elaborately designed. The palace occupied the center of the city, beginning in the south with a long stretch of stone and brick wall below the Shüanteh Tower, with an elaborate bas-relief of dragons and phoenixes, while above showed the glittering roofs of the palaces, made with glazed tiles of variegated colors. Around the palace on four sides were the main streets, named by the four points of the compass. On the west of the palace stood the premier's office, and the office of the military privy council. In the southern outer city, outside the Red Sparrow Gate, stood the national college and imperial temples. The streets swarmed with pedestrians, officials' horse carriages, bull carts, and sedan chairs, which were the general mode of travel, while a few small two-wheeled carts were pulled by men—prototypes of the modern rickshaw. The women in the bull carts traveled with their screens let down. It was the peculiarity of the imperial city that no one was allowed to go about bareheaded, and even the humblest fortuneteller tried to dress like a scholar.

The time for the palace examinations came. Ouyang Shiu was nominated by the emperor to be chief examiner, together with a number of distinguished scholars as judges. The approach to this most critical moment of a scholar's life was always filled with keen excitement, tense hope, and a nervous fear of failure. It was the moment to which all his years of grinding labor and hours of burning the midnight oil were supposed to lead. The candidates had to get up in the middle of the night and come to the palace at dawn, bringing their cold meals with them, for they would not be able to leave until the examinations were over. During the examinations, they were shut up in cubicles under the supervision of palace guards. There was a rigorous system to prevent bribery or favoritism. The candidates' papers were recopied by official clerks before they were submitted to the examiners, to avoid recognition of their identity by their handwriting. In the recopied papers the writers' names were taken out and kept on file. While the candidates were let out after the examinations, the judges themselves were shut up within the palace and forbidden to have any contact with the people outside, usually from late January till early March, until the papers were properly graded and submitted to the emperor. The candidates were examined first on questions of history or principles of government. There was a second examination on the classics, and finally, after the successful ones had been graded, there was one—under the direct supervision of the emperor— on lyrics, descriptive poetry (*fu*), and again, essays on politics. Emperor Jentsung was especially anxious to recruit good talent for his government and took a personal interest in these tests. He sent out the subjects for the papers by his own personal servants, and sometimes, to avoid leakage, changed them at the last moment.

Both the Su brothers passed with high honors. Tungpo wrote a paper which Ouyang Shiu later showed to his colleagues and admired for days. It dealt with the principle of simplicity and leniency in the administration of a country, which was Su Tungpo's basic philosophy of government. However, there was an unfortunate mistake. Ouyang Shiu was so delighted with the brilliant style and content of the paper that he thought it must have been written by Tseng Kung, his friend. In order to avoid criticism he shifted it from the first to the second place, and thus Su Tungpo came out second in the examinations. On April 8, 1057, Su passed the examinations, and on April 14, at the age of twenty, was officially decorated a *chinshih*, almost at the head of 388 successful candidates. To obtain such an honor meant that one became at once nationally known as one of the first scholars of the land.

It was typical of the brilliant young man, however, that he took some liberties with history and invented a dialogue in his paper. He was developing the theme that in giving rewards the one should rather err on the side of generosity, and in punishment one should give every benefit of the doubt to an offender lest an innocent man be killed. In the time of Emperor Yao, he wrote, a man was about to be condemned to death. "Three times the minister of justice said, 'Let him be killed!' and three times Emperor Yao said, 'Let him be pardoned!'" The dialogue read very well, and it seemed to support an authentic story that the sage emperor was willing to use a bad man and give him a chance to prove his talent. The judges read the story, but dared not question it, because it amounted to their admitting not having read it somewhere in one of the obscure ancient texts. So Su Tungpo was passed. After the examinations one day Mei Yaochen, one of the judges, said to him:

"By the way, where does that story occur about Emperor Yao and the minister of justice? I can't quite recall where I read it."

"I invented it," the young scholar confessed.

"You did!" said the old judge.

"Well, that was what the sage emperor would have done, wasn't it?" replied Su Tungpo.

To pass an examination under a certain examiner was to place a scholar under heavy obligation to him for recognition of his talent, and establish a permanent relation between the two as "master" and "disciple" (*mensbia*). The candidates went up to pay their respects to their master and the chief judges and wrote them letters of gratitude. Ouyang Shiu was the authority on literature. He could make or unmake a scholar by a word of praise or blame. A writer of the time said that the scholars did not know the fear of punishments or the joy of promotions, nor did they value the gift of life or fear the doom of death, but they did fear the opinion of Ouyang Shiu. Imagine, therefore, the effect on the young poet when Ouyang Shiu said to one of his colleagues, "On reading Su Tungpo's letter, somehow I perspired all over with joy. My old person must give place to this young man and let him rise to the top." When such a statement was made by Ouyang Shiu, the whole capital heard about it. Ouyang Shiu was also reported to have said to his own sons, "Mark my word, thirty years from now nobody will talk about me." This prediction came true, for in the first decade after Su Tungpo's death, nobody was talking about Ouyang Shiu but everybody was talking about Su Tungpo and reading him in secret, when his works were banned.

Just as he was about to begin his official career, Tungpo's mother died. It was such an important event according to Confucian custom that even a premier had immediately to retire and go into a twenty-seven months' period of mourning before he could return to office. Tungpo's eldest sister had died several years earlier, and thus when all the men of the family went away to the examinations, the mother was left alone with the daughters-in-law. She died without hearing the good news from the capital. Hurriedly the father and brothers set out for home, to find the mother gone and the house in very bad condition, with the fences broken down and the roof leaking, "like the home of a refugee."

After the proper ceremonies they selected a site for the family cemetery at Old Man's Spring, at the foot of a mountain slope. The spring was so named because, according to the people of the district, on clear moonlight nights an old man with white hair and a beautiful face could be seen sitting or reclining on the bank; but upon the approach of people he would disappear into the water. Later Su Shun was buried in the same grave, and it was from the name of this place, Old Man's Spring, that he was popularly known as "Laochuan."

In his sacrificial prayer to his wife's spirit Su Shun said: "I know your heart as a mother did not wish your children high official honors, but that they might be renowned in literature. When I was young I wasted my talent; I knew that in your heart you were concerned lest I should die unknown. With a sigh, I decided to reform, and it is thanks to you that

I have this day... In your grave I have opened two chambers that I may share the tomb with you when I die... Alas, I am old and alone in this wide world; after your death, who will give me good advice? I am going back to our old home to make improvements and alterations in our house. If your soul has not perished, come and visit us."

The twenty-seven months of compulsory hibernation were the happy days of Su Tungpo's youth. The brothers were living with their young wives. Tungpo often visited his wife's home at Chingshen, which was in beautiful mountain country with streams and deep ponds and Buddhist temples on high mountaintops. An air of mystery and romance and legends hung over the region. Su Tungpo often visited the temples or enjoyed picnics and drinking parties on the banks of the river near the Juitsao Bridge with his wife's uncles and cousins. On summer evenings he sat outside their cottage eating melon seeds and hard fried beans. It was a big household: there were his wife's father, Wang Chieh, and her two uncles and their families. Among the cousins in the Wang family, some thirty in number, there was one girl, known as "Miss Number Twenty-Seven," who was destined to become a part of his life.

Meanwhile Su senior was waiting for his appointment. He was eligible to office at this time because mourning for a wife was not an impediment to holding an office, as mourning a mother was. High officials at the capital had promised help, but he had been waiting for over a year and no news had arrived. Finally an imperial edict came, asking him to go up to the capital and submit himself to special examinations. This threw the old man into consternation. By that time he had developed a phobia about all examinations. He wrote a reply to the emperor declining to go, giving old age and poor health as his excuse. But in his letter to a friend he said, "I do not necessarily want to be an official, nor do I decline on principle to be one... Why should I, at this dignified old age, submit myself to the disgrace of being judged by official examiners and become a laughingstock of others? ... I have already submitted my works to Ouyang Shiu. If he considers them good, why should there be further examinations? If he cannot believe the best that I have written, how can he rely upon the tests of a day?" In another letter, to a high official, Mei, he said, "I have never been able in my life to conform to the standards of the judges, and that is why I have not succeeded to this day... I remember how when I was young and preparing to go into the examination hall, I got up at midnight, packed up my rice and cakes, and stood at dawn before the Eastern Palace Gate. Then we filed in together and sidled up to our respective seats and cowered over our desks. Every time I think about that scene, my heart shudders..."

By June of the following year, 1059, he received another order from the government, a repetition of the first. There was no mention of any special exemption from examinations; but nothing else would satisfy him. The government leaders should believe in him—take it or leave it. He was not going to be quizzed like a schoolboy. So a third time he declined. He was already about fifty, he wrote to say. What could he do at this age for the country? A scholar, after all, wants to go into the government only to do something for the country, or else he should live as a poor humble scholar. If he should decide to go into the government now, he would neither gain an opportunity of serving the country nor enjoy the distinction of being a great recluse. But, he concluded, it was summer already, and his son's mourning period would be over by the next month; he would go with them to the capital again. He hoped to see the officials then and talk over the situation. The tone of the whole letter suggests that he really did not mind going into the government even at the age of fifty, provided these influential people arranged that his papers would not be graded by the examiners like those of school children.

In fact, Su senior was prepared to leave his Szechuen home forever, now that his wife was dead. It was clear that he belonged at the capital.

His two sons had obtained official degrees and the next step was, therefore, to see what openings there would be in the way of government positions for them, if not for himself. Hardly two months had passed after the regular mourning period when the father and his sons set out once more for the capital, this time with the young wives. Proper preparations had been made for the spirit of the deceased mother. Su Shun had had images of six bodhisattvas made and placed in two carved and gilt wooden niches, to be set up at the Hall of Buddha Julai at the Paradise Temple. These six bodhisattvas were: the Goddess of Mercy; the God of Wisdom; the Ruler of the Skies; the Ruler of the Earth; a saint specially in charge of pacifying souls who were victims of injustice in human life; and a celestial guide for all the wandering spirits. Immediately before their departure, Su Shun formally presented these images to the temple and went to say farewell to the spirit of his dead wife. The prayer ended with the words, "I have done these things in the hope that your soul, if it is still conscious, will either go up to Heaven or float around in the upper or the lower regions in complete comfort and ease, just as I myself am going to roam over the world in complete freedom."

第五章　父与子

　　父子三人和两个儿媳妇，现在已经准备妥当，即将进京。这次和前一次自然不同，三人已是文名大著，宦途成功几乎已确然无疑。这次举家东迁，要走水路出三峡，而不是由陆路经剑门穿秦岭。这次行程全长一千一百余里，大概是七百里水路，四百里旱路，要从十月起程，次年二月到达。用不着太急，因为有女人同行，他们尽可从容自在，在船上饮酒玩牌，玩赏沿途美景。两个姘娌从来没有离开过老家，心里知道这次是与进士丈夫同游，但可没料到她俩是在大宋朝三个散文名家的家庭里，而且其中一个还是诗词巨擘呢。一路上兄弟二人时常吟诗。那时所有读书人都会作诗，借以写景抒情，就如同今天我们写信一样。子由的妻子姓史，出自四川旧家。东坡的妻子的地位年龄较高，她属于实际聪明能干型，所以子由的妻子与她相处，极为容易。并且，老父这一家之长，也和他们在一起，做晚辈的完全是服从柔顺，大家和睦相处。在这位大嫂眼里，三个男人之中，她丈夫显然易于激动，不轻易向别人低头，而说话说得滔滔不绝。子由身材较高而消瘦，不像哥哥那么魁伟，东坡生而颅骨高，下巴颏儿和脸大小极为相配，不但英俊挺拔，而且结实健壮。和他们在一起的，还有东坡的小儿子，是苏家的长孙，就是那一年生的。有这么一个孩子，这家真是太理想，太美满了。倘若这个孩子早生一年，多少有点儿让人不好意思，因为觉得这位年轻才子苏东坡是在母丧期间和妻子太任性，太失于检点。宋朝的道学先生就会说他有亏孝道，要对他侧目而视了。

苏家是在以大石佛出名的嘉州上船，对两对小夫妇而言，这是一次富有希望的水路旅行，有兴致、有热情、有前途、有信心。真是"故乡飘已远，往意浩无边"。四川为中国最大之省份，其大与德国相似，也是和三国的历史密切相关的。走了一个月才到东边的省界，这时三峡之胜才开始，山顶上的城镇庙宇，会令他们想起古代的战将、过去的隐人道士。兄弟二人上岸，游历仙都。据说当年有一个修行的道士，在白昼飞升之前就住在那个地方。东坡这个少年诗人早期写的诗，其中有一首，是关于传说中的一头白鹿的，也就是那个道士身边相伴的那头鹿，这首诗足以证明东坡精神的超逸高士。那首诗是：

> 日月何促促，尘世苦局束。
> 仙子去无踪，故山遗白鹿。
> 仙人已去鹿无家，孤栖怅望层城霞。
> 至今闻有游洞客，夜来江市叫平沙。
> 长松千树风萧瑟，仙宫去人无咫尺。
> 夜鸣白鹿安在哉，满山秋草无行迹。

长江三峡，无人不知其风光壮丽，但对旅客而言，则是险象环生。此段江流全长一百二十余里，急流漩涡在悬崖峭壁之间滚转出入，水下暗石隐伏，无由得见，船夫要极其敏捷熟练，才可通行。三峡之中，每年都有行船沉没、旅客丧生之事，在如此大而深的江流之中，一旦沉下，绝无生望。然而三峡确是富有雄壮惊人之美，在中国境内无一处可与之比拟，在世界之上，也属罕见。四川何以向来能独自成一国家，原因就在自然地理方面，省东界有高山耸立，水路则有三峡之险，敌人无从侵入。

经三峡时如若逆流而上，船夫的操作真是艰苦万分。那时，一只小平底木船，要由六十至七十个纤夫，用长绳子一头拴在船上，一头套在肩上，在势如奔马的狂波中逆流而上，在沿江的岸边一步步俯首躬身向上跋涉而行。顺流而下时，则危险更大，在水流漂浮而下之时，全船的安全全操在一个舵夫之手，他必须有极高的技巧、极丰富的经验，才能使船庶乎有惊而无险。三峡也者，即为四川境内的瞿塘峡、巫峡和湖北省宜昌以上的西陵峡。每一个峡都是一连串危险万分的洪流激湍，其中漩涡急流交互出现，悬崖峭壁陡立水中，达数百尺之高。

惊险之处自瞿塘峡开始，因为水中有若干巨大的岩石，因季节之不同、水面之高低即因之而异，而岩石有时立出水面高达三十尺，有时又部分隐没于水中。当时正是冬季，正是江面航行困难之时。因为水面变窄，夏季洪水泛滥时与冬季水干时，江面水平高低之差，竟达一百尺之多。船夫总是不断注视江心岩石边水的高度。这些岩石叫滟滪堆，是因为惊涛骇浪向巨大岩石上冲击，水花飞散起来，犹如美女头上的云鬟雾鬓，因此而得名。滟滪堆的巨石在完全淹没之时，则形成一片广阔的漩涡，熟练的船夫，亦视之为畏途。当地有个谚语说："滟滪大如马，瞿塘不可下；滟滪大如象，瞿塘不可上。"这两句俗语也不见得有多大用处，只因为河床的变化太大，有的地方水位低时宜于行船，有的地方水位高时便于行船，主要以隐藏于水下的岩石之高低为准。有的地方，偶然降有大雨，船夫就要等候数天，直到水恢复到安全的水位再开船。纵然如此危险，人还是照旧走三峡，或为名，或为利，而不惜冒生命之险，就像现在苏家一样。出外旅行的人，极其所能，也只有把自己的安危委诸天命，因为除此之外，别无办法。行经三峡的人，往往在进入三峡之前焚香祷告，出了三峡再焚香谢神。不管他们上行下行，在三峡危险的地方，神祇准保有美酒牛肉大快朵颐。

自然界有不少奇妙之事，在这里，三峡正好是奇谈异闻滋生之处，这里流传着山顶上神仙出没的故事。在进入瞿塘峡处，有"圣母泉"，是在岸上岩石间有缝隙，能回答人声。每逢有旅客上去向缝隙大呼"我渴了"，泉即出水，正好一杯之量而止。要再喝第二杯还需喊叫。

苏家向神祈求赐福之后，开船下驶。因为船只行驶时相距太近会发生危险，通常都是在一条船往下走了至少半里之后，另一条船才开出。若逢官家有船通过时，有兵丁手持红旗，按距离分立江边，前面的船已然平安渡过险地之后，便挥旗发出平安信号。苏东坡就曾作诗描写道：

入峡初无路，连山忽似龛。
萦纡收浩渺，蹙缩作渊潭。
风过如呼吸，云生似吐含。
坠崖鸣窣窣，垂蔓绿氂氂。
冷翠多崖竹，孤生有石楠。
飞泉飘乱雪，怪石走惊骖。

偶尔他们的船驶过一个孤立的茅屋，只见那茅屋高高在上侧身而立，背负青天，有时看见樵夫砍柴。看那茅屋孤零零立在那里，足可证明居住的人必然是赤贫无疑，小屋顶仅仅盖着木板，并无瓦片覆盖。苏东坡正在思索人生的劳苦，忽然瞥见一只苍鹰在天空盘旋得那么悠然自在，似乎丝毫不为明天费一些心思，于是自己盘算，为了功名利禄而使文明的生活受到桎梏镣铐的夹锁，是否值得？在高空飘逸飞翔的苍鹰正好是人类精神解脱后的象征。

现在他们的船进入巫峡了，巫峡全长五十里，高山耸立，悬崖迫人，江面渐窄，光线渐暗，呈现出黎明时的昏黄颜色，仿佛一片苍茫，万古如斯。自船面仰望，只见一条细蓝，望之如带，那正是天空。只有正值中午，才能看见太阳，但亦转瞬即逝；在夜间，也只有月在中天之际，才能看见一线月光。岸上巨石耸立，巨石顶端则时常隐没于云雾中。因为风高力强，云彩亦时时改变形状，山峰奇高可畏，亦因云影聚散而形状变动不居，虽绘画名家，亦无法捉摸把握。巫山十二峰中，神女峰状如裸女，自从宋玉作《神女赋》以来，独得盛名。此处，高在山巅，天与地互相接触，风与云交互鼓荡，阴阳雌雄之气，获得会合凝聚，是以"巫山云雨"一词，至今还留为男女交欢之称。峡内空气之中，似乎有神仙充盈，而云雾之内亦有精灵飞舞。苏东坡青年的理性忽然清醒，他觉得此等神话悖乎伦理。他说："成年之人也仍不失其童稚之心，喜爱说神道鬼。《楚辞》中的故事神话，全是无稽之谈。为神仙而耽溺于男女之欲者，未之有也。"

这时有一个年老的船夫，开始给他们说故事。他自称年轻时，常攀登那些最高的山峰，在山顶池塘中洗浴，衣裳挂在树枝上晾干。山中有猿猴，但是他爬到那样高处，鸟鸣猿啼之声已渺不可闻，只有一片沉寂与山风之声而已。虎狼也不到那样高处，所以只有他一人，但他并不害怕。神女祠附近有一种特别的竹子，竹枝柔软低垂，竟直触地面，仿佛向神俯首膜拜一样。有风吹拂，竹枝摆动，使神坛随时保持清洁，犹如神女的仆人一般。苏东坡听了，颇为所动，心想："人也许可以成仙，困难就在于难忘人欲耳。"（神仙固有之，难在忘势利）在东坡一生之中，他也和当代其他人一样，很相信会遇到神仙，相信自己也许会成仙。

他们的船进巫峡之时，"神鸟"开始随船而飞。其实这种乌鸦也和其他聪明的鸟一样，因为在神女祠上下数里之内，这些乌鸦发现有船来，就一路追随，从船上乘客那儿啄取食物。乘客往往与乌鸦为戏，他们把饼饵扔到半空中，兴高采烈地看着神鸦自天空俯冲下来，将食物由空中衔起，百无一失。

这一带地方，自然无人居住，也不适于人居住。三苏行经"东濡滩"时，波涛汹涌，船身被打击抛掷，就像一片枯干的树叶在漩涡之中一般。在他们以为已经过了最危险的地方时，谁知又来到"怒吼滩"。这里更为惊险，怪石如妖魔，沿岸罗列，有的直入江心。然后又来到一个地方，叫作"人鲊瓮"，意思是好多旅客在此丧命，就如同一罐子死鱼。这里是一块特别巨大的圆石头，伸入江中，占了水道的五分之四宽度，水道因之变窄，逼得船只经过此处时，必须急转直下。凡是旅客过了人鲊瓮，都觉得那个老船夫，真不啻自己"生身的父母，再造的爹娘"一样。

出了巫峡，他们不久就到了秭归，开始看见沿岸高高低低散布着些茅屋陋舍。此处是一极小的乡镇，居民不过三四百家，坐落在陡峭的山坡上，居民极为贫苦。可是想到这一带令人心神振奋的风光之美，觉得在这个半文明的穷乡僻壤，居然出了两个大诗人，一个著名的皇后，还有另一个历史上著名的女人，也并非无故了。这大概就是奇山异水钟灵毓秀的缘故吧。一般居住山地的人，在风俗上总是把东西装在桶里或筐子里而背在背上，而且大部分是由妇女背着，这很容易使人肌肉疲劳，但是却永远对她们的身段儿有益。处在这里，未嫁的姑娘总是把头发分开，高高梳成两个扁圆的髻儿，以别于已婚的妇人。髻儿上插着六根银簪子，横露在两侧，另外还拢上一个大象牙梳子，有手掌那么大小，在头的后面。

苏家现在才过了巫峡和瞿塘峡，最要命的一个还在下面呢。大约三十年之前，有一次山崩，尖锐的岩石滚落在江心，使船只无法通过。江面的交通在这带断绝了大约二十年，后来才勉强开了一条狭窄的通道。这个地方因之叫作"新滩"。在此处因为风雪甚大，苏家在此停留了三天。苏东坡曾有诗记此事：

缩颈夜眠如冻龟，雪来惟有客先知。
江边晓起浩无际，树梢风多寒更吹。
青山有似少年子，一夕变尽沧浪髭。
方知阳气在流水，沙上盈尺江无澌。
随风颠倒纷不择，下满坑谷高陵危。
江空野阔落不见，入户但觉轻丝丝。
沾裳细看巧刻镂，岂有一一天工为。
霍然一挥遍九野，吁此权柄谁执持？
……
山夫只见压樵担，岂知带酒飘歌儿。
……
冻吟书生笔欲折，夜织贫女寒无帏。
高人著屐踏冷冽，飘拂巾帽真仙姿。
野僧斫路出门去，寒液满鼻清淋漓。
……
舟中行客何所爱，愿得猎骑当风披。
草中咻咻有寒兔，孤隼下击千夫驰。

敲冰煮鹿最可乐，我虽不饮强倒卮。

楚人自古好弋猎，谁能往者我欲随。

纷纭旋转从满面，马上操笔为赋之。

长江在此处有如此自然的危险，本地人却因此落个有利可图。他们打捞沉船，转卖木板用以修理别的船，以此为业。他们也像一般名胜古迹城镇的居民一样，观光客往往因故不得不在本地停留数日，他们就可以和观光客交易而有生意做。此地江流湍急，船上的货物往往需要卸下，而乘客也宁愿在岸上走走，使身体舒服一下。

从秭归再往下走，已然可以在遥远的地平线上望见大牛的背部耸立在较近的山岭顶端。他们现在正在进入的地区，是以庞大的黄牛山为主要景物的。这里的岩石甚为奇怪，在山岭的侧影蚀刻在遥远的天空时看来，黄牛山这头巨牛似乎是由一个穿蓝衣戴斗笠的牧童牵着。本地有个俗语描写这头黄牛蛮横的面貌说："朝发黄牛，暮宿黄牛，三朝三暮，黄牛如故。"本地的女人脸皮细嫩白净，头上包着小黑圆点儿的头巾。风光之美可与巫峡抗衡，在有些乘客看来，甚至会超巫峡之上。那种风景正是在中国山水画上常可见到的。形状令人难以置信的巨石，矗立天际，望之如上帝设计的巨型屏风；又有如成群的石头巨人，或俯首而立，或跪拜于地面向上苍祷告。河边上的岩石，层层排列成阵，似乎是设计出来欲以大自然之壮丽故意向人炫示。此处有一巨大之断崖，表面平坦，竖立如同巨剑，尖端正刺入江岸。再沿江下行不远，危险的航程即将结束之前，来到了"虾蟆培"。"虾蟆培"是一个巨大的扁圆石头，酷似一个青蛙头，口中有水滴入河中，形状极似水晶屏风。此一巨大的扁圆石头，呈苔绿色，背上满是晶莹的小水珠。青蛙尾尽处为一石洞，其中发出清脆的潺湲之声。有些赴京赶考的举子往往在青蛙嘴边接水，带到京中研墨，供做文章之用。

过了"虾蟆培"不远，大自然一阵子的天威怒气，算是消散尽了，岩石江水的洋洋大观也收场了，从宜昌以下，风光一变而为平静安详。夕阳照着一带低平的稻田与炊烟处处的茅舍，提醒旅客们已再度回到人类可以安居的世界。一般习俗是，旅客到此，因为逃过灾难，转危为安，都相向庆祝。旅客以美酒猪肉犒劳船夫，人人快乐，人人感恩。回顾过去，都以为刚刚做了一个荒唐梦。

到了江陵，苏家弃船登陆，乘车起旱，奔向京都。江上航行完毕之日，兄弟二人已然作了诗歌百首。这些诗另集印行，名之为《南行集》。但是，苏东坡最好的几首诗是在陆地上的行程中写的。那几首诗特别注重音韵情调气氛之美，节奏极好，形式多变化。在襄阳他写了几首歌，如《船夫吟》、《野鹰来》，系为追忆刘表而作，《上堵吟》则为追忆孟滔因手下二将不才失去沃土的经过。其诗为：

台上有客吟秋风，悲声萧散飘入宫。

台边游女来窃听，欲学声同意不同。

君悲竟何事，千里金城两稚子。

白马为塞凤为关，山川无人空且闲。

我悲亦何苦，江水冬更深，鳊鱼冷难捕。

悠悠江上听歌人，不知我意徒悲辛。

苏家在二月安抵京城。他们买了一栋房子，附有花园，约有半亩大，靠近仪秋门，远离繁乱的街道。绕房有高大的老槐树和柳树，朴质无华的气氛，颇适于诗人雅士居住。一切安顿之后，父子三人便恭候朝廷任命了，当然那一向是需时甚久的。兄弟二人又经过了两次考试，一是考京都部务；另一种更为重要，名为"制策"，要坦白批评朝政。仁宗求才若渴，饬令举行此种考试，以激励公众舆论的风气，所有读书人经大臣推荐，并凭呈送的专门著述之所长，都可以申请参加。苏氏兄弟经大臣欧阳修的推荐，都申请而蒙通过。苏东坡蒙朝廷赐予的等级，在宋朝只有另一人获得。他又呈上二十五篇策论文章，其中有些篇已经成为后世学校中必读的散文。后来，皇后告诉人，仁宗曾经说："今天我已经给我的后代选了两个宰相。"

万幸的是，苏洵被任命为校书郎，并未经考试，正合他的本意，后来又授以新职，为本朝皇帝写传记。这本来就是作家的事，他自然乐于接受。但是后来出现了问题，就是那些皇帝都是当今天子的先人，他们的传记需忠实到什么程度呢？苏洵决定采取史家的严格写法，史家不应当文过饰非，即使为自己的先人立传，亦当如此。于是有了争论，在今日苏洵的文集里尚保有下列的文句：

洵闻臣僚上言，以为祖宗所行不能无过差。不经之事，欲尽芟去，无使存录……纂集故事……非曰制为典礼而使后世遵而行之也。然则洵等所编者，是史书之类也。遇事而记之，不择善恶，详其曲折，而使后世得知而善恶自著者，是史之体也。若夫存其善者，而去其不善，则是制作之事，而非职之所及也……班固作汉志，凡汉之事悉载而无所择也。欲如之，则先世之小有过差者，不足以害其大明，而可以使后事无疑之。

苏氏父子的文名日盛。他们与当代名家相交往，诗文为人所爱慕，一家皆以文坛奇才而知名于时。兄弟刚二十有余，年少有时也会成为天才的障碍。苏东坡这时轻松愉快，壮志凌云，才气纵横而不可抑制，一时骅骝长嘶，奋蹄蹴地，有随风飞驰、征服四野八荒之势。但是弟弟则沉默寡言。父亲则深沉莫测，对事对人，一概不通融假借，因此处世则落落寡合，将身旁这两匹千里之驹，随时勒抑，不得奋鬣奔驰。

Chapter Five
FATHER AND SONS

The father and sons and sons' wives were now ready to set out for the capital. It was to be a different journey from the one they had taken previously. Their literary ambitions had been vindicated, their success in official careers was almost assured. As they were moving their home to the capital, they took the voyage down the Yangtse instead of going by land through the northwest. It would be a journey of eleven hundred miles, about seven hundred miles by water and four hundred by land, beginning sometimes in October and ending in February of the next year. There was no great hurry, and as the women were with them, they took their time, drinking and playing cards while on the boat and enjoying the beautiful scenery on the way. The brothers' wives had never been outside their hometown. They knew they were traveling with *chinshin* scholars for their husbands, but they could hardly be aware that they were in a family of three prose masters of the dynasty, one of them a major poet. The brothers made verses all the way—but all scholars versified in those days, to record a scene or a sentiment, as we write letters today. Tseyu's bride came from an old family of Szechuen, the Shihs. Young Mrs. Su Tungpo was by position and age the senior. She was the practical, sensible, able sort, with whom it was easy for her sister-in-law to get along. Besides, the old father, the head of the family, was with them; nothing short of obedience and complete harmony would be considered good form. She saw that of the three men, her husband was decidedly the excitable, irrepressible, talkative one. Tseyu was taller, thin, and not as robust as his brother, while Tungpo, born with very prominent cheekbones and a well-proportioned jaw, was handsome and had a more muscular build. With them was her baby boy, the first grandson of the Su family, born within the year. That was all good and proper. It would have been slightly embarrassing if the baby had been born a year earlier, for it would have meant that the young poet had indulged himself during the first year of mourning for his mother. The Sung neo-Confucianists might look askance at such a regrettable lapse from austere filial piety.

Embarking at Kiachow where the Great Stone Buddha was, the young couples set out on a voyage of hope; keen, enthusiastic, confident. "Leaving our hometown far behind, we look forward to the vast horizon beyond." Szechuen was the largest province of China, the size of Germany, and closely connected with the history of the Three Kingdoms. It took them a month to come to the eastern border of the province, where the Yangtse Gorges begin and where cities and towns and temples on mountaintops reminded them of the warriors and Taoist saints of long ago. The brothers went up to visit Shientu, the "Fairies' City," where an ancient Taoist saint had lived before he went up to heaven. One of the earliest poems by the young poet, about a legendary white deer, a companion of the Taoist, already bore witness to the elevation of his spirit.

> The unremitting wheels of time turn round,
> And we to this terrestrial life are bound.
> The fairy went to his celestial home
> And left his deer upon the sainted mound.
> The homeless deer now sadly gazed afar
> At where, cloud-capped, the Elysian City lay.

I hear at night this creature of the forest
Come wandering and cry on river's bay,
While myriad pines are sighing in the wind,
So near the ancient Master's hallowed place!
Oh, where are you, night-crying deer? Alas!
Among the woods I cannot find a trace.

The Yangtse Gorges, majestic in their beauty and exciting in hazards
for the travelers, are a stretch of two hundred and twenty miles of the river
where the torrents swirl in and out through the rocky precipices, with
hidden rocks beneath the water, requiring a great dexterity on the part
of the boatmen. The gorges annually claim their toll of shipwrecks and
travelers' lives, for this is a big, deep river, and those who sink are lost. But
the gorges are also, in their majestic, awe-inspiring beauty, unsurpassed
anywhere in China and by very few places in the world. They are also the
reason why Szechuen has always been considered practically a kingdom by
itself, naturally protected by the gigantic mountains on its eastern border
and by these narrow gorges, impenetrable by an enemy.

While going up the gorges was a strenuous task for the boatmen, with
perhaps sixty or seventy boat hands tugging a little junk against the swift
current by long ropes slung across their shoulders, the voyage down was
always more dangerous, the boat being carried forward by the force of
the current and guided only by the extreme skill of the boatman at the
rudder. This dangerous long stretch is known as the Three Gorges: the
Chutang Gorge and the Wu Gorge in Szechuen, and the Shiling Gorge
above Ichang in Hupeh. Each of these consists of a series of dangerous
rapids alternating with whirlpools and torrents that pass between sharp
cliffs rising several hundred feet high straight from the water.

The thrills and dangers began at Chutang, conveniently indicated by
a group of rocks which sometimes stood up thirty feet above water and

sometimes were partly submerged, as the water rose and fell according to the seasons. It was winter, a difficult time for navigation. Because of the narrow passage, the difference in the level between the summer floodtime and the dry winter could be as much as a hundred feet. The boatmen usually watched the level of the water at this group of rocks in the middle of the river. These rocks, called Yenyu, took their name from the appearance of swirling waters which, breaking against them, formed spray like the misty, tremulous hair of women. When completely submerged, they formed a vortex even more dangerous for the sailors. There was a local proverb, "When Yenyu appears like a horse, down the Chutang do not pass; when Yenyu becomes an elephant, up the Chutang do not ascend." But the saying really did not help much because of the varying nature of the river bed; it was desirable at one place for the water to be low, and at others to be high, all depending on the height of the hidden rocks under the water. At a certain point, if there was a sudden storm, the boatmen would wait for days for the water to recede to its safe level before they proceeded. Still, through these gorges people went and were willing to risk their lives for money or for fame, as the Su brothers were doing now. All a traveler could do was to confide the care of his soul to God, because there was nothing else he could do about it. People usually offered a prayer at the beginning of the gorges and another prayer of thanks at the end, in whichever direction they were traveling, and consequently the gods at the more dangerous sections of the voyage were always well provided with wine and beef.

One of Nature's wonders, the gorges provided the proper setting for strange tales and legends of fairies living on the mountaintops. Just before coming to the entrance to the Chutang Gorge, there was the "Spring of the Holy Mother." This was a small crevice in the rock on the bank, responsive to the sound of human voices. Whenever a traveler went up to this crevice and shouted loud enough, "I am thirsty!" the spring would give forth water to the amount of exactly one cup and then stop. A man who wanted a second cup had to shout again.

The Sus asked the blessing of the gods and proceeded down the river. As it was dangerous for boats to travel too closely together, it was the custom for one boat to pass at least half a mile below before another boat started. When officials were traveling, soldiers were stationed at proper intervals with red flags in their hands to give the signal when the boat in front had safely passed a dangerous point. As Su Tungpo decribed it,

Entering the gorge, the river seemed blocked in front.
The from the cliffs a cleft appeared like Buddha's niche.
The swirling waters began to leave their wide expanse,
And narrow themselves into a deep abyss.
The winds bellowed through the cliffs,
And the clouds spewed forth from the caves.
Overhanging cliffs whistled in the high winds,
And twining vines glistened in resplendent green.
Bamboo groves stood over rocks, dripping with cold verdure,
And rhododendrons dotted the mountainside.
Falling cataracts spread a shower of snowy mist,
And strange rocks sped past like horses in fright.

Now and then they sailed past lone cottages, and saw, silhouetted high up against the sky, some country lads cutting wood. The bare huts of the cottagers bore witness to their extreme poverty; their roofs were made of wooden boards, without tiles. As Su was reflecting on the toil of human life, his attention was arrested by a gray falcon circling at ease and in freedom in the sky without a thought for the morrow, and he wondered whether the honors and emoluments of office were worth the fetters of a civilized life. The falcon became a symbol of the emancipated human spirit.

Now they entered the famous Wu Gorges, a stretch of fifty miles. Here the mountains rose in height, the cliffs closed in, and the river narrowed. The daylight changed into the dusk of an eternal dawn. Gazing up from the boat, the travelers could see only a tiny ribbon of blue which was the sky. Only at high noon could they see the sun for a moment, or at night only get a glimpse of the moon when it was at its zenith. Strange monoliths rose straight from the banks, while the peaks were usually hidden in clouds. As the clouds, driven by the high winds, constantly shifted and changed, the peaks at the awe-inspiring heights changed their shapes also, making a moving picture beyond the power of portrayal by artists. One of these peaks, the Fairy Girl, had the shape of a nude female form and had become the most famous one of the twelve since a poet of the third century B.C. celebrated it in a passionate, imaginative poem. It was clear that here up on the mountaintops where the heaven and the earth met in an eternal interplay of winds and clouds, the *yang* and the *yin*, or the male and the female, principles had achieved a union, and today the "rains and clouds of the Wu Mountains" remain a literary euphemism for sexual union. The air itself seemed filled with fairies and sprites frolicking in the clouds. For a moment, Su Tungpo's young rationalism asserted itself The legends carried a logical contradiction. "People are only little children. They like to talk about spirits and ghosts," he said. "The ancient tale of Ch'u is pure fiction. The fairies do not have a sex life."

But the old boatman began to tell him stories, how in his young days he used to climb the highest peaks, bathe in a mountain pool, and hang his clothes on a branch to dry. There were monkeys on the mountains, but as he went up to the great altitudes, the bird calls and the monkey cries stopped, and there was nothing but silence and the mountain wind. The tigers and wolves did not go up there and he was completely alone and unafraid. At the temple to the Fairy Maiden there was a special variety of bamboo whose soft branches bent low and touched the ground, as if in worship of the fairy spirit. As the wind moved, the branches swayed and kept the stone altar always clean, like a servant of the goddess. Su Tungpo was touched. "Perhaps one can become a fairy after all. The difficulty lies in forgetting human desires." Throughout his life Su Tungpo, like his contemporaries, was quite open-minded about the possibility of meeting fairies and becoming one himself.

When they entered the Wu Gorges, "divine birds" began to follow the boat. These ravens were doing no more than what every bird of sense would do. For several miles above or below the Fairy Girl's Temple, they spotted a boat coming and followed it all the way to pick up food from its passengers. The latter usually made a game of it. They tossed up cakes into mid-air and watched with delight how the ravens swooped down and picked them up without fail.

Naturally, these regions were uninhabited and uninhabitable. The Sus passed through the East Dashing Rapids where the water surged and billowed and tossed the boat about like a dry leaf in a small whirlpool, and when they thought they had gone through the worst, they came upon the even more dangerous Roaring Rapids. Strange monster rocks lined the shore and extended to the middle of the stream. Then they came to a place whose name, to be intelligible, can only be translated as "the Jar of Human Herrings," meaning a place where many travelers had lost their lives, like a kettle of dead fish. This was a giant boulder occupying four fifths of the river, narrowing it down to a small passage and forcing the boat going down to take a precipitous curve. Any traveler surviving the sudden dip around the Jar of Human Herrings would feel toward the old boatman as toward his second father.

Coming out of the Wu Gorges, they soon arrived at Tsekuei and began to see shabby huts dotting the bank at different levels. It was a very small town, with no more than three or four hundred families, situated on the sharp slope of the hillside. The inhabitants were extremely poor, and yet considering the exciting beauty of the place, which must enter into men's souls, it was not altogether unreasonable that this half-civilized remote village should have produced two major poets, a famous queen, and another famous woman in history. As is generally the custom with mountaineers, the men and women carried their loads in a barrel or basket swung on their backs; but it was mostly the women who did the carrying. This was tiring for their muscles, but as we know, was always good for their figures. The unmarried girls distinguished themselves by wearing a high coiffure in two joined buns, decorated with as many as six silver pins sticking out on both sides and a large ivory comb, the size of one's palm, at the back.

But the travelers had passed only two of the gorges, and the worst was yet to come. About thirty years before, there had been a landslide which threw sharp-edged rocks into the middle of the stream, and made it impossible for navigation. River traffic had been stopped at this point for about twenty years until a narrow passage had been opened. This place was, therefore, called "the New Rapids." At this point Su Tungpo and his family were held up for three days by a snow storm.

> Lying huddled in the night, I slept like a frozen turtle,
> But I was the first to know that it was snowing outside.
> In the morning I discovered a vast expanse of white,
> And the cold wind was shaking the treetops.
> The green hills were like a youth transformed,
> Overnight covered with white hair and whiskers.
> The atmosphere of warmth had descended to the river,
> And the gurgle of the stream had been silenced on the bank.
> Up in the air the flakes fluttered without choice of direction,
> And down they came and spread and disappeared

Over the wide river and the empty wastes.

But entering the boat their fluffy footsteps were light;

Like engraved flowers they rested on one's clothing.

Could it be that God had carved these one by one?

Extravagantly these were broadcast and filled the valley;

Alas! Who held this mighty power in his hands? ...

I see the mountaineers carrying their load of fuel;

They would not know of the pleasure of warm wine and song...

The poet's frozen brush is hard and ready to break,

And the peasant girl is weaving at night uncurtained.

A recluse is treading in the icy cold in his sandals,

And the wind blowing at his hood makes him look like one of God.

A poor monk is clearing the snow before his doorstep,

And the cold liquid is frozen below his nose...

What does the traveler in the boat want?

He wants a hunting horse to dash through the winds.

While a cold rabbit is hiding in the grass,

A lone falcon swoops down like a fierce host.

Ah, to boil venison in water from broken ice!

Though I cannot drink, I will raise the cup high.

The people of Ch'u are known for hunting;

I will follow whoever leads the hunt.

Let the snowflakes flutter and swirl round my face;

I will take up my brush and make of them a worthy poem.

The natives of this place profited from the natural hazards. They made a business of salvaging wrecks and selling the boards for repair of other ships. They also profited in the way of all resort towns from trade with the tourists, who were often compelled to remain there for days. The torrents were such at this point that the boat usually had to be relieved of all its load and the passengers preferred to walk on land for their health.

From Tsekuei on, the back of the Giant Buffalo was visible on the distant horizon, towering above the tops of the nearer mountain ridges. For they were now entering a section dominated by the giant Yellow Buffalo Mountain. The rocks here were so strange that the Yellow Buffalo seemed to be led by a cowherd in blue, wearing a farmer's hat on his head, as the silhouette of the mountain was etched against the distant sky. The local saying here described the dominating appearance of the buffalo as follows: "In the morning you start from the Buffalo and at night you stop at the Buffalo. For three mornings and three nights you do not get away from the Buffalo." The women here were of fair complexion and tied scarves with black polka dots on their heads. The landscape vied in its beauty with that of the Wu Gorges, even surpassing it in the opinion of some travelers. It was the kind of landscape that we usually see in Chinese paintings, with monoliths of unbelievable shapes standing against the horizon like a stone screen designed by God, or a group of stone giants, some with bended heads and some on their knees, offering their prayer to heaven. On the riverbanks were formations of rock strata designed to impress men with Nature's grandeur. Here a massive bluff with a flat surface would stand like a giant sword blade sticking its point into the bank. Some distance below, before they were quite finished with the dangerous section of their voyage, they came to the Frog. The Frog was a great flat boulder with a striking resemblance to a frog's head, with water dripping down into the river like a crystal screen from its mouth. The color of the boulder was a mossy green, and the Frog's back was covered with little globules. At the tail end there was a stone cave from which came the clear gurgling sound of a spring. Some scholars, going up to the capital for their imperial examinations, would collect water from the Frog's mouth and use it to grind ink for their examinations.

Not far past the Frog the temporary spell of Nature's fury spent itself, the drama of rocks and water came to an end, and below Ichang the landscape changed into one of peace and quiet. The setting sun shone upon a low plain of rice fields and cottages with chimney smoke, reminding the travelers that they had come back once more to a habitable world. According to custom, the travelers congratulated one another on their narrow escape and their good fortune in remaining alive. The boatmen were rewarded for their labors with pork and wine, and everybody was happy and grateful. Looking back, the travelers felt as if they had lived through an unbelievable dream.

At Kiangling they left the boat and began the land journey by cart toward the capital. By the time they had ended their voyage, the brothers had already composed a hundred poems. These were published in a separate volume entitled *The Southern Voyage.* Yet some of the best poems Su Tungpo wrote were composed on the land journey, which concentrated on music and tone and atmosphere alone, and were rich in rhythm and variety of form. At Shiangyang he wrote "songs" or boatman's ditties, like the "Song of the Eagle," recalling the story of Liu Piao, and the "Song of Shangtu," recalling the story of Meng Ta who lost his control of a rich district through two incompetent officers:

On the wind-swept terrace stands a handsome knight.
His sad song melts into the autumn forest's moan.
Some maidens attentively listen unobserved;
They learn the tune but cannot imitate his tone.
    O knight! what ails you? —Two idiot lads
    Have lost a golden city and silvery plain,
    Well guarded by the White Horse and Phoenix Hill!
    The kingdom's lost, though land and water remain.
To what avail do I distress myself?
The bream are hard to catch in this deep cold.

The people on the bank listen and pass by,
But the burden of my song cannot be told.

The Su family arrived at the capital in February. They bought a house and garden, about half an acre, near the Ichiu Gate, far away from the busy streets. There were tall old locust trees and willows around the house, and the rustic atmosphere suited the family of poets very well. Thus settled, the father and sons waited for official appointments, which usually were a long time in coming. The brothers passed yet two other examinations, one for ministry posts in the capital, and the other, more important, for "frank criticism" of the administration. Emperor Jentsung, anxious to secure good talent, ordered this special examination to encourage the spirit of public criticism, and all scholars could apply upon the recommendation of some minister and upon the merits of special works submitted. On the recommendation of Ouyang Shiu, both the brothers applied and passed, Su Tungpo receiving a grade given to only one other person in the Sung Dynasty. He also submitted a collection of twenty-five historical essays, some of which have remained favorite prose selections for schools. Later, the wife of the Emperor told people that Jentsung had said, "Today I have secured two future premiers for my descendants."

Happily, the father was appointed an examiner of scripts in the department of archives, *without examinations*, according to his wish, and later was given a post in a bureau to compile a history of the lives of the emperors of the dynasty. It was a writer's job and he accepted it gladly. But then the question came up how truthful these lives of the emperors should be, the emperors being ancestors of the reigning ruler. Su Shun took the view that this was strictly a historian's job and a historian should not gloss over the faults even of one's ancestors. There was a dispute. In a paper preserved in his *Collected Works* today, Su Shun said, "I hear that some colleagues have petitioned to Your Majesty, saying that the ancestors may have had personal blemishes, but that if they were no concern of the state, these should be struck off the records... We are not establishing a code of ceremonies or moral conduct for the future generations to follow. It is a historian's duty to record all that they did, regardless of good and bad, to the end that posterity may learn of the truth. If it is the intention of the court to present and preserve idealized, complimentary portraits of the ancestors, I cannot regard this as part of my duty. The author of *Han History* recorded all that happened. If we now emulate his example, we shall be able to show that their personal weaknesses were easily outweighed by the great things that they accomplished, and we shall have a record that the future generations may regard as honest and reliable."

The reputation of the three Sus as scholars and writers had now steadily risen. They were friends of the most famous writers of the land, their poems and essays were greatly admired, and the family was already known as a literary phenomenon. The brothers were just over twenty, and youth sometimes acted as a handicap for a genius. Vivacious, irrepressible, ambitious, Su Tungpo felt like a thoroughbred impatiently pawing the ground, ready to break into whirlwind speed to conquer the world. But he had a silent partner, Tseyu, and an old father, deep in intellectual penetration, uncompromising in spirit, and socially aloof in character, who held the pair of thoroughbreds in check.

苏	THE GAY GENIUS:
东坡	THE LIFE AND TIMES OF
传	SU TUNGPO

BOOK TWO   **Early Manhood**
(1062—1079)

卷二

壮年

（一〇六二——一〇七九）

第六章　神、鬼、人

纵然苏东坡才华熠熠，在仕途上他仍须由低级而上升。在仁宗嘉祐六年（一〇六一），朝廷任命他为大理评事，签书凤翔府判官，有权连署奏折公文。在唐朝，因行地方分权之制，形成藩镇割据，国家颇蒙其害，最后酿成叛乱，陷国家于危亡，而藩镇大员每为皇亲国戚、朝廷诸王。宋代力矫其弊，采用中央集权，武力环驻于国都四周，并创行新制，对各省长官，严予考核节制，其任期通常为三年，因此时常轮调。每省设有副长官连署公文奏议，即为此新制度中之一部分。苏子由也被任为商州军事通官，但是父亲则在京为官，兄弟二人必须有一人与父亲同住京师，因为无论如何，总不可使鳏居的老父一人过活。于是子由辞谢外职不就。子由为兄嫂赴任送行，直到离开封四十里外的郑州，兄弟二人为平生第一次分手，子由随后回京。在此后三年之内，东坡在外，子由一直偕同妻子侍奉老父。东坡在郑州西门外，望着弟弟在雪地上骑瘦马而返，头在低陷的古道上隐现起伏，直到后来再不能望见，才赶程前进。他寄弟弟的第一首诗写的是：

不饮胡为醉兀兀？此心已逐归鞍发。

归人犹自念庭帏，今我何以慰寂寞？

登高回首坡陇隔，惟见乌帽出复没。

苦寒念尔衣裘薄，独骑瘦马踏残月。

路人行歌居人乐，僮仆怪我苦凄恻。

亦知人生要有别，但恐岁月去飘忽。

寒灯相对记畴昔，夜雨何时听萧瑟。

君知此意不可忘，慎勿苦爱高官职。

"风雨对床"之思，在唐人寄弟诗中有之，此种想法成了兄弟二人团聚之乐的愿望，也是辞官退隐后的理想生活。后来有两次弟兄二人又在官场相遇，彼此提醒在诗中曾有此"风雨对床"之约。

由京都到凤翔的函件，要走十天才到，兄弟二人每月经常互寄诗一首。由那些诗函之中，我们可以发现，初登宦途时，苏东坡是多么心神不安。兄弟二人常互相唱和。在唱和之时，要用同韵同字，所以是磨炼写诗技巧的很好的考验。在中国过去，此种写诗方法，是文人必须具备的成就。在这类诗中，可以找到令人惊喜的清新思想，用固定韵脚的字，各行要有自然的层次。犹如在玩纵横字谜一样，韵用得轻松自然时，其困难正足以增加乐趣。在写给弟弟最早的和诗之中，东坡已经显示出他那完美的诗才。他按规定用"泥"和"西"两字做韵脚，写出了下列的诗：

人生到处知何似，应似飞鸿踏雪泥。

泥上偶然留趾爪，鸿飞哪复计东西。

　　这首七绝成了东坡诗的佳作。此处"飞鸿"一词是人心灵的象征。实际上，本书中提到东坡的行动事故，也只是一个伟大心灵偶然留下的足迹，真正的苏东坡只是一个心灵，如同一只虚幻的鸟，这只鸟也许直到今天还梦游于太空星斗之间呢。

　　凤翔位于陕西的西部，离渭水不远。因为陕西为中国文化的发源地，整个渭水流域富有古迹名胜，其名称都与古代历史相关。强邻西夏，位于今之甘肃，时常为患中国，陕西省因而人力财力消耗甚大，故人民生活甚为困苦。苏东坡到任后第一年内，建了一栋庭园，作为官舍，前有水池，后有亭子，另有一上好花园，种花三十一种。

　　苏东坡既已安定下来，判官之职又无繁重公务，他遂得出外遨游，到南部东部山中游历，动辄数日。有一次，他因公须到邻近各地视察，急需结束些悬而未决的罪案，并要尽其可能地将甚多囚犯释放。这件差事对他再适合无比，他于是畅游太白山和黑水谷一带的寺院，以及周文王的故里。有时清闲无事，他到西安附近有名的终南山去，去看珍奇的手稿，或是一个朋友珍藏的吴道子画像。

　　东坡年富力强，无法安静下来，这时是他生平第一次独自生活，只与娇妻稚子在一起。如今他已然尝到做官生活的味道，但并不如他梦想的那么美妙。远离开京都的骚扰杂乱，在外县充任判官，副署公文，审问案件，颇使他感觉厌烦无味。有时难免感觉寂寞，但也有时举杯在手，月影婆娑，又感觉欣喜振奋。

　　在他还不够成熟老练之时，他需要妻子的忠言箴劝。苏夫人在务实际、明利害方面，似乎远胜过丈夫。她对丈夫非常佩服，知道自己嫁的是个年轻英俊的诗人。才华过人的诗人和一个平实精明的女人一起生活之时，往往是显得富有智慧的不是那个诗人丈夫，而是那个平实精明的妻子。在婚姻上所表现的，仍然是男女相辅相成。苏夫人知道丈夫那坦白直爽甚至有时急躁火爆的性格之后，她觉得倒不需急于向他表示什么佩服崇拜，还是要多悉心照顾他，才是尽自己身为贤妻的本分。苏东坡是大事聪明，小事糊涂，但是构成人生的往往是许多小事，大事则少而经久不见，所以苏东坡则事事多听从妻子。夫人提醒他说他现在是初次独自生活，而没有父亲照管。苏东坡把人人当好人，但是太太则有知人之明。苏东坡与来访的客人谈话之时，太太总是躲在屏风后屏息静听。一天，客人走后，她问丈夫："你费那么多工夫跟他说话干什么？他只是留心听你要说什么，好说话迎合你的意思。"

她又警告丈夫要提防那些过于坦白直率的泛泛之交，要提防丈夫认为"天下无坏人"的大前提之下所照顾的那些朋友。总之，苏东坡的麻烦就在看不出人的短处。妻子对他说："提防那些人，速成的交情靠不住。"东坡承认妻子的忠言很对。我想苏夫人的这种智慧是自"君子之交淡如水"得来的——水没有刺激的味道，但是人永远不会对之生厌。真诚的友谊永远不会特别表白的，真正的好朋友彼此不必通信，因为既是对彼此的友情信而不疑，谁也不需要写什么。一年分别后，再度相遇，友情如故。

有的人不忙不快乐，苏东坡就是这一型。那时陕西旱象出现，已经好久不雨，农人为庄稼忧心如焚，除去向神灵求雨，别无他法，而求雨是为民父母官者的职责。苏东坡突然活动起来，心想一定是什么地方出了毛病，不然神不会发怒。现在若不立刻下雨，黎民百姓就要身蒙其害了。苏东坡现在要写一份很好的状子，向神明呈递。在这方面，他是万无一失的。他现在准备立即在神明之前，以他那雄辩滔滔的奇才，为老百姓祈求普降甘霖。

在渭水以南，有一道高大的山脉，通常称之为秦岭，而秦岭上最为人所知、最高、最雄伟的山峰，叫太白峰。太白山上一个道士庙前面，有一个小池塘，雨神龙王就住在其中，这个龙王可以化身为各种小鱼。苏东坡就要到那个道士庙里去求雨。他为农人求雨，但是也像一个高明的律师一样，他想办法叫龙王明白天旱对龙王也没有好处。在奉承了几句话之后，他在那篇祈雨文里说："乃者自冬徂春，雨雪不至。西民之所恃以为生者，麦禾而已。今旬不雨，即为凶岁；民食不继，盗贼且起。岂惟守土之臣所任以为忧，亦非神之所当安坐而熟视也。圣天子在上，凡所以怀柔之礼，莫不备至。下至愚夫小民，奔走畏事者，亦岂有他哉？凡皆以为今日也。神其盍亦鉴之？上以无负圣天子之意，下亦无失愚夫小民之望。"

由太白山下来之后，他继续游历各处，特别是上次漏过的名胜。在当月十一日，他曾求过雨，回到城里，十六日，曾下小雨，但是对庄稼则嫌不足，农民也不满意。他研求原因，人告诉他在太白山的祈求并不是无效，但是神由宋朝一个皇帝封为侯爵之后，再去祈求便不再灵验。苏东坡在唐书上一查，发现太白山神在唐朝原是封为公爵的。山神实际上是降低了爵位，大概因此颇不高兴。苏东坡立刻为县官向皇上草拟了一个奏本，请恢复山神以前的爵位。然后他又与太守斋戒沐浴，派特使敬告神灵，说他们已为神求得更高的封号，又从庙前的池塘里取回一盆"龙水"。

十九日，苏东坡出城去迎"龙水"。全乡下人人振奋，因为这次的成功是他们极为关心的事。乡间早已来了好几千人，当地十分热闹，在"龙水"未到时，已然阴云密布，天空昏黑。老百姓等了好久，雨硬是不肯下。苏东坡又进城去，陪同宋太守到真兴寺去祷告。在路上，他看见一团乌云在地面低低飘过，在他面前展开。他从农夫手里借了个篮子，用手抓了几把乌云，紧紧藏在篮子之中。到了城里，他祷告乌云的诗里有："府主舍人，存心为国，俯念舆民，燃香霭以祷祈，对龙湫而恳望，优愿明灵敷感。"祷告已毕，他又和宋太守出城去。他俩走到郊区，忽然来了一阵冷风，旗帜和长枪上的缨子都在风中猛烈飘动。天上乌云下降，犹如一群野马。远处雷声隆隆。正在此时，一盆"龙水"到来。苏东坡和宋太守前去迎接"龙水"，把"龙水"放在临时搭建的祭台上，随即念了一篇祈雨文，这篇祈雨文和其他的祭文至今还保存于他的文集里。仿佛是有求必应，暴雨降落，乡间各地，普沾恩泽。两天之后，又下大雨，接连三日，小麦、玉蜀黍枯萎的秸茎又挺了起来。

现在欢声遍野，但是最快乐的人却是诗人苏东坡。为纪念这次喜事，他把后花园的亭子改名为"喜雨亭"，写了一篇《喜雨亭记》，刻在亭子上。这篇文章是选苏东坡文章给学生读时，常选的一篇，因为文笔简练，很能代表苏文的特性，又足以代表他与民同乐的精神。

这件事之后，太白山的山神也升了官，又由皇帝封为公爵。苏东坡和宋太守为此事再度上太白山，向神致谢，又向神道贺。次年七月，又有大旱，这次求雨，却不灵验。苏东坡失望之余，到蟠溪求姜太公的神灵。姜太公的神灵直到今天还是受老百姓信仰的。姜太公在周文王时是个贤德有智慧的隐士，据稗官野史上说，他用直钩在水面三尺之上垂着钓鱼。据传说他心肠好、人公正，鱼若从水中跳出三尺吞他的饵，那是鱼自己的过错。常说的"姜太公钓鱼，愿者上钩"便是此意。

苏东坡此次向姜太公求雨是否应验，并无记载。但是不管信仰什么神，信佛也罢，信一棵得道的老树桩子也罢，这并不是怀疑祷告不灵的理由。祷告不灵永远无法证明，因为根据佛经，若出什么毛病，总是祷告的人不对，普通是他的信心不足，所谓"诚则灵"，便是此意。所有的神都必须要显出灵验，否则便无人肯信了。再者，祷告也是人根深蒂固的天性。祷告，或是具有祷告的那种虔诚态度，毕竟是很重要的，至于是否灵验，那倒在其次。

无论如何，后来苏东坡做其他各县的太守，只要事有必要，他还是继续祷告。他知道他的此种行动是正当无疑的，他也就相信神明必然会竭其所能为人消灾造福。因为，倘若明理是人性最高的本性，神明也必然是明理的，也会听从劝告，也会服理。但是在苏东坡几篇论到天灾的奏折里，他也按照中国的传统指出来，朝廷若不废除暴政以纾民困，向神明祷告也无用处。这就是中国凭常识形成的宗教，这种看法就使中国古籍上有"尽人事，听天命"的说法。在知道了中国人所有的愚蠢行为之后，这种谚语又让我重新相信中国人毕竟是伟大的思想家。

我简直不由得要说苏东坡是火命，因为他一生不是治水，就是救旱，不管身在何处，不是忧愁全城镇的用水，就是担心运河和水井的开凿。说他是火性并无不当，因为他一生都是精力旺盛的，简单说来，他的气质，他的生活，就犹如跳动飞舞的火焰，不管到何处，都能给人生命温暖，但同时也会把东西毁灭。

这个跳动飞舞的火苗，据说曾经两度和邪魔外祟争辩。因为他深信，不但是神灵，即使是妖魔鬼怪，也得对他那义正词严的攻击顺服，所以他有所恃而无恐。他痛恨一切悖乎情理的事，甚至妖魔鬼怪也得对他的所作所为，要能判别何者为是何者为非。妖魔等物也许有时会遗忘或分辨不清，可是在苏东坡的雄辩口才之下，他们就会自见其行为的愚蠢，也得立即罢手。

有一次，他在从凤翔回京都的路上，正顺着一条山路行走，经过白华山。侍从之中一个人忽然中邪，在路上就把衣裳一件一件脱下来，直到脱了个精光。苏东坡吩咐人勉强给他穿上，把他缚起来，但是衣裳又掉了下来。大家都说一定触怒了山神，那个兵才中了邪。苏东坡走到庙里，向山神说道：

某昔之去无祈，今之回也无祷。特以道出祠而不敢不谒而已。随行一兵狂发遇祟。而居人曰："神之怒也"，未知其果然否。此一小人如蚁虱耳，何足以烦神之威灵哉。纵此人有隐恶，则不可知。不然人其懈怠失礼或盗服御饮等小罪尔，何足责也，当置之度外。窃谓兵镇之重，所隶甚广，其间强有力富贵者盖有公为奸蠹，神不敢于彼示其威灵，而乃加怒于一卒，无乃不可乎？某小官一人病则一事缺，愿恕之可乎？非某愚，其谅神不闻此言。

祷告完毕，苏东坡刚一离开那座山神庙，一阵山风猛向他脸上扑来，转眼间，风势愈狂，竟而飞沙走石，行人无法睁眼。苏东坡对侍从说："难道神还余怒未息？我不怕他。"他继续向前走，狂风越发厉害。这时只有一个侍从携带他随身的行李在后面跟随，别人和马匹都正在想法避风，因为觉得实在无法前进。有人告诉他回庙去向山神求饶。苏东坡回答说："吾命由天帝掌握，山神一定要发怒，只好由他。我要照旧往前走，山神他能奈我何？"然后，风逐渐减弱，终于刮完，并无事故发生，那个兵也清醒过来。

苏东坡对自己有急智和看不见的精灵相斗，坚具信心。有一次，他和一个邪魔力争不让。那是此后数年，他在京师身为高官之时，他的二儿媳妇（欧阳修的孙女）一天晚上也中了邪，是在产后。年轻的儿媳妇以一老妪的声音向周围的人说："我名清，姓王，因为阴魂不散，在这一带做鬼多年。"苏东坡对儿媳妇说："我不怕鬼。再说，京都有好多驱鬼除妖的道士，他们也会把你赶跑的。不要不识相。显然是你糊涂愚蠢才送了命，现在既然已死，还想闹事！"然后他向女鬼讲了些佛教对阴魂的道理，又告诉她说，"你给我老老实实地走开，明天傍晚我向佛爷替你祷告。"女鬼乃合掌道："多谢大人。"儿媳妇于是霍然而愈。第二天日落后，他给佛爷写了一篇祈祷文，焚香，供上酒肉，把女鬼送走。

此后不久，他次子的小儿子说看见一个贼在屋里跑，看来又黑又瘦，穿着黑衣裳。苏东坡吩咐仆人搜查，结果一无所获。后来奶妈又忽然倒在地板上，尖声嘶喊。苏东坡过去看她，她向东坡喊道：

"我就是那个又黑又瘦穿黑裳的！我不是贼，我是这家的鬼。你若想让我离开奶妈的身上，你得请个仙婆来。"

苏东坡对鬼斩钉截铁地说："不，我不请。"

鬼的声音缓和了点儿说："大人若一定不肯请，我也不坚持。大人能不能给我写一篇祷告文，为我祈祷？"

东坡说："不行。"

鬼的条件越来越低，用更为温和的声音请求可否吃点儿肉喝点儿酒，但是苏东坡越发坚强。鬼被这个不怕鬼的人慑服了，只请求为他烧点儿纸钱便心满意足，东坡仍不答应。最后，鬼只要求喝一碗水。东坡吩咐："给他。"喝完水之后，奶妈跌倒在地上，不久恢复了知觉，但从此断了奶。

苏东坡在凤翔那一段，发生了一件事，使他有点儿不光彩，在他后来的日子里不愿提起。到那时为止，他和上司宋太守处得很融洽，宋太守与他家是世交。此后，来了一位新太守，情形就有了变化。新太守姓陈，是武人出身，严厉刻板，面黑体壮，两眼炯炯有神。他与苏东坡同乡，认为苏东坡少年得意，颇把他看作暴发户。陈太守为官以来，颇负美誉。曾在长沙捕获一恶僧，此一僧人颇与权要交往，他仍将此僧交与有司法办，全境之人，无不惊异。又有一次，他捕获七十余男巫，这些男巫平素皆鱼肉乡民，他将他们强行遣返故乡，耕田为农。那时有些寺庙暗中干些邪污败德之事，他拆除了几座庙。据说他的兵卒奉命站定不动时，敌人的箭从天上稠密飞来，兵卒们仍然屹立不动。

现在苏东坡新来的上司却是这样的一个人。所有的文武官员都向他俯首致敬，但是对苏东坡而言，我们都不难猜测，现在是两个不妥协通融的硬汉碰了面。二人之间遇有争论，便唇枪舌剑，恶语相加。苏东坡年少多才，有才自负的年轻人而要向外在的权威俯首拜服，实在难之又难。也许令苏东坡感到最大的不快是陈太守往往改动拟妥的上奏文稿。陈太守往往在苏东坡造访时不予接见，有时使他久候，久到足够让他睡个午觉的工夫，用以表示不悦之意。二人的龃龉不合，后来竟闹到陈太守向京师上公文，陈明苏东坡的抗命情形。

苏东坡的报复机会不久到来。陈太守在太守公馆里建造了一座"凌虚台"，以便公务之暇，登台观望四野景物之胜。不知何故，陈太守吩咐苏东坡写一篇文字，预备刻在凌虚台的石碑上，作为兴建此台的纪念。这个诱惑对年轻多才的苏东坡，是欲拒不能了：他必得借此机会来玩笑一番。做文章刻石留念，自然是为传之久远，必须庄重典雅，甚至富有诗情画意方为得体。显然是他不得直接攻击陈太守，但是知道向老头子放支玩笑的小箭，总无伤于人，亦无害于己。今天我们还可以读到那篇《凌虚台记》：

台因于南山之下，宜若起居饮食与山接也。……而太守之居，未尝知有山焉。……太守陈公杖屦逍遥于其下，见山之出于林木之上者，累累如人之旅行于墙外，而见其髻也。曰："是必有异。"使工凿其前为方池，以其土筑台，高出于屋之檐而止，然后人之至于其上者，恍然不知台之高，而以为山之踊跃奋迅而出也。公曰："是宜名凌虚。"以告其从事苏轼，而求文以为记。轼复于公曰："物之废兴成毁，不可得而知也。昔者荒草野田，霜露之所蒙翳，狐虺之所窜伏，方是时，岂知有凌虚台耶。废兴成毁，相寻于无穷，则台之复为荒草野田，皆不可知也。尝试与公登台而望，其东则秦穆之祈年、橐泉也，其南则汉武之长杨、五柞，而其北则隋之仁寿、唐之九成也。计其一时之盛、宏杰诡丽、坚固而不可动者，岂特百倍于台而已哉。然而数世之后，欲其求仿佛，而破瓦颓垣无复存者，既已化为禾黍荆棘、丘墟陇亩矣。而况于此台欤？夫台犹不足恃以长久，而况人事之得丧、忽往而忽来者欤？而或者欲以夸世而自足，则过矣。盖世有足恃者，而不在乎台之存亡也。"

倘若苏东坡年龄再大些，文字之间的语调儿会更温和些，讽刺的箭也许隐藏得更巧妙些。这篇记叙文，本为庆祝而作，却在沉静中沉思其将来坍塌毁坏之状，并含有太守不知所住之城外有山之讽刺，在中国志记文中尚属罕见。但是陈太守这个老头子确实肚量够大，竟不以为忤。这一次他对此文一字未予更动，照原作刻在石碑上。

由此可见，陈太守为人心地并不坏。在二人分手之后，东坡也看出此种情形，因而有修好之举。成了名的作家常有的应酬，就是应子侄辈之请为其先人写墓志铭。墓志文字必须赞美亡故者，但多为陈词滥调，而且言不由衷，故无文学价值。写此等文字古人每称之为谄媚死者，但是此等事仍为作家极难避免之社交应酬。在这一方面，苏东坡自己应有极严格的规定，而且确实做到了。他绝不写一篇此种文章，即使王公贵人相求，也是不写。在他一生之中，他只写了七篇墓志铭，皆有特别的理由，他的确有话要说才写的。几年之后，他也为陈太守写了一篇。除去他为司马光写的那篇之外，这篇算是最长的。因为东坡和那位陈太守，最后彼此都对对方十分敬仰。

陈太守的儿子陈慥，后来成了苏东坡毕生的友人，此子不可不在此一提。陈慥喜欢饮酒骑马，击剑打猎，并且慷慨大度，挥金如土。一天，陈慥正在山中骑马打猎，有两个兵卒相随。他前面忽然有一只喜鹊飞起，他的随员没有将此喜鹊击落。这位年轻的猎人咒骂了一声，从丛林中隐藏处一马冲出，嗖的一箭射去，喜鹊应声落地。这个青年的脸上，似乎有什么特别之处吸引住苏东坡。后来有人传言，说陈慥的父亲在他处做官之时曾有纳贿之事，被判处死刑。传闻是这样的，苏东坡正要遭受贬谪之时，陈慥正隐居在黄州，苏东坡的仇人想起苏东坡当年与陈慥的父亲交恶，就把他贬谪到黄州来，好使陈慥对付苏东坡。也许陈慥要为父报仇，这样苏东坡的敌人就可以借刀杀人了。但是事实上，苏东坡与陈慥父亲之死毫无关系，陈慥反成了苏东坡谪居黄州期间最好的朋友。

苏东坡又遇见了一位"朋友"——章惇，章惇命定是苏东坡后半生宦途上的克星。章惇后来成了一个极为狠毒的政客，现在官居太守之职，所治县份距此不远，也在湖北省境。我们手下没有资料可以证明是否苏夫人曾经警告过丈夫要提防章惇，但是章惇确是富有才华，豪爽大方，正是苏东坡所喜爱的那等人。苏东坡曾经预测过章惇的前途，这个故事是人常说起的。是在往芦关旅行的途中，苏章二人进入深山，再往前就到黑水谷了，这时来到一条深涧边，上面架着一条窄木板，下面距有百尺光景，有深流滚翻倾泻，两侧巨石陡峭。章惇是极有勇气之人，向苏东坡提出从木板上走过去，在对面岩石的峭壁上题一行字，一般游客是常在名胜之地题词的。苏东坡不肯过去，章惇以无动于衷的定力，独自走过那条深涧，然后把长袍塞在腰间，抓住一根悬挂的绳索，坠下悬崖，到对面小溪的岸上，在岩石上题了"苏轼章惇游此"六个大字。随后又轻松自如若无其事般由独木桥上走回来。苏东坡用手拍他这位朋友的肩膀说："终有一天你会杀人的。"章惇问："为什么？"苏东坡回答说："敢于玩弄自己性命的人自然敢取别人的性命。"苏东坡的预测是否可靠，且看后文分解。

仁宗驾崩后，苏东坡受命督察自陕西西部山中运输木材供修建陵寝之用的工事。这时他又忙碌了一阵子，此外平时他并不十分快乐，他颇为想家。仁宗嘉祐八年（一○六三），他写信向子由说：

始者学书判，近亦知问因。但知今当为，敢问向所由。士方其未得，唯以不得忧，既得又忧失，此心浩难收。譬如倦行客，中路逢清流。尘埃虽未脱，暂憩得一漱。我欲走南涧，春禽始嘤呦，鞅掌久不决，尔来已徂秋。桥山日月迫，府县烦差抽。王事谁敢愬，民劳吏宜羞……千夫挽一木，十步八九休……对之食不饱，余事更遑求……劬劳幸已过，朽钝不任镂。秋风迫吹帽，西阜可纵游。聊为一日乐，慰此百日愁。

仁宗嘉祐九年（一○六四），他解除官职，内兄自四川来与同居，次年正月，举家迁返京都。当时，凡地方官做官三年之后，朝廷就要考察他政绩如何，叫作"磨勘"。依据考察的结果，再经推荐，另授新职。东坡既然回京，子由获得了自由，不久就外放到北方的大名府去做官，当时大名府也叫"北京"，在今日的北京南方一百里。

新主英宗，早闻苏东坡的名气，要破格拔擢，任以翰林之职，为皇帝司草诏等事。宰相韩琦反对，建议皇帝为苏东坡计，应俟其才干老练，不宜于突然予以如此高位。皇帝又称拟授命他掌管宫中公务之记载。宰相又提出反对，说此一职位与"制诏"性质相近。他推荐苏东坡到文化教育部门去任职，并且苏东坡要经过此等职位所需之正常考试。皇帝说："在不知一人之才干时，方予以考试。现在为何要考苏东坡？"但是终于按照宰相的意见，苏东坡依法考试，考试及格，于是他在史馆任职。在史馆任职的官员，要轮流在宫中图书馆工作，而苏东坡正以有此良机饱读珍本书籍、名人手稿、名家绘画为乐。

那年五月，苏东坡的妻子以二十六岁之年病逝，遗有一子，年方六岁。苏洵对东坡说："汝妻嫁后随汝至今，未及见汝有成，共享安乐。汝当于汝母坟茔旁葬之。"在妻死后的第十周年，苏东坡写了两首词以寄情思，两首小词颇离奇凄艳，其令人迷惘的音乐之美，可惜今日不能唱出了。其词如下：

十年生死两茫茫，不思量，自难忘。千里孤坟，无处话凄凉。纵使相逢应不识，尘满面，鬓如霜。

夜来幽梦忽还乡，小轩窗，正梳妆。相顾无言，惟有泪千行。料得年年断肠处，明月夜，短松岗。

妻子死后，次年四月老父病逝，时为英宗治平三年（一〇六六）。苏洵已完成了《大常因革礼》一百卷。自然如一般预料，兄弟二人立即辞去官职，经过迢迢的旱路水路，把父亲和东坡妻子的灵柩运回四川眉州故里，在祖茔埋葬。朋友们纷纷馈送葬仪。

运送灵柩，他们必须雇船自安徽走水路，然后再顺长江逆流而上。两兄弟不惜多费时日，用以满足沿途畅游之愿，所以到次年四月才安抵故里。父亲的坟墓早在父亲自己营建之下完成，只要将父亲的灵柩安放在母亲墓穴之旁，便算完事。不过苏东坡好大喜功，他在山上种了三千棵松树，希望将来长成一带松林。

现在又要过一段蛰居的生活，要到两年零三个月才居丧期满（神宗熙宁元年七月，一〇六八）。在他们回京之前，必须做两件事。苏东坡要师法父亲为纪念母亲而立两尊佛像的往例，必须立一座庙，以纪念父亲。在庙内，他悬有父亲遗像，另外四张极宝贵的吴道子画的四张佛像，是他在凤翔时物色到的。庙的建造费要白银一千两，苏氏兄弟共出一半，其余由和尚筹募。

居丧期满后，苏东坡要做的第二件大事，就是续弦。新娘是前妻的堂妹，王杰的女儿。十年前，为母亲的葬礼，苏东坡曾经返回故里奔丧，常到妻家青神去。闰之当年只有十岁或是十一岁，多次在她家看见东坡。在大家一同出外游玩野餐之时，她看见东坡那么年轻就在科举考试中得了魁元，心里惊奇赞赏。现在她是二十岁的小姐了，因为东坡父母双亡，他自然可凭自己的意思择偶，而觉得她正合心意。这件婚事大概要归功于闰之哥哥的张罗，因为他已经对东坡感情很深厚。闰之因为比丈夫小十一岁，早就对他佩服得五体投地，似乎是什么事都听从丈夫的心愿。她一直无法叫丈夫节省花费，一直到他在世最后那些年。她不如前妻能干，秉性也比较柔和，遇事顺随，容易满足。在丈夫生活最活跃的那些年，她一直与他相伴，抚养堂姐的遗孤和自己的儿子，在丈夫宦海浮沉的生活里，一直和丈夫同甘共苦。男人一生在心思和精神上有那么奇特难言的惊险变化，所以女人只要聪明解事，规矩正常，由她身上时时使男人联想到美丽、健康、善良，也就足够了。男人的头脑会驰骋于诸多方面，凝注新的事物情况，为千千万万的念头想法而难得清闲，时而欣喜雀跃，时而有隐忧剧痛，因此觉得女人的宁静稳定，反倒能使人生在滔滔岁月之中进展运行而不息，感到纳闷难解。

　　在神宗熙宁元年（一〇六八）腊月，在把照顾父母的坟茔等事交托给堂兄子安和一个邻人杨某之后，苏氏兄弟乃携眷自陆路返回京都。此后兄弟二人谁也没再返归乡里，因为抵达京都之后，二人都卷入政坛的旋涡之中。后来虽然宦游四方，但迄未得返里一行。

Chapter Six
GODS, DEVILS, AND MEN

In spite of Su Tungpo's brilliant record, he had to start from the bottom. Late in 1061, the sixth year of the reign of Chiayu, he was given the rank of a councilor of justice and the office of an assistant magistrate at Fengshiang, with the power of countersigning reports and official communications with the court. In the previous Tang Dynasty, the country had suffered from decentralization, and at the end the dynasty had fallen as a result of rebellion among the provincial governors, who were often princes of royal blood. The Sung Dynasty, therefore, tried to correct this evil by centralization, concentrating its army around the capital and devising a system of checks and controls for the magistrates in the provinces. Magistrates' terms of office were usually three years, so that they were constantly shifted around. The system of having assistant magistrates with the power of countersigning official memorandums was a part of this setup. Tseyu also had been appointed to an assistant magistracy at Shangchow; but their father's work was at the capital, and one of the brothers had to stay, as it was unimaginable to leave the widowed father living alone. Tseyu therefore declined the appointment. After he had seen Tungpo and his family as far on their way to his post as Chengchow, a distance of forty miles, the two brothers parted for the first time in their lives, and Tseyu returned to live with his wife and father for the three years while Tungpo was away. Tungpo watched his brother riding on a thin horse in snow outside the West Gate of Chengchow, his head bobbing up and down above the sunken road, until he could see him no more. And in his first poem letter to his brother Su Tungpo wrote:

"Why is it that I feel like being drunk without wine? When your horse turned back home, my heart went home with it. I knew you were thinking of our parent, but now what am I to do with myself? I went up the slope and turned back for a last look, and saw your black hat bobbing up and down beyond the ledge. I was sorry that you were so thinly clad in this weather, riding on a skinny horse in that declining moonlight. A few passersby came my way singing and laughing, and the servants wondered why I look so sad. I know that there must be parting in this life, and I fear the months and years will too quickly pass over us. Remember, my brother, whenever you sit in the lamplight on a cold evening, how we promised each other that one day we shall sleep in opposite beds and listen to the rain in the night. Keep this in mind, and don't let us be carried away by our official ambitions."

This idea of "sleeping in opposite beds listening to a storm at night" was found in the poem of a Tang poet to his brother, and it became a pledge between these brothers and an ideal of the happy life that they planned to live together when they were able to retire. Twice later, when the brothers met together in their official careers, they reminded one another of this promise in their poems.

Mail from the capital to Fengshiang took only ten days, and the brothers sent each other regularly one poem a month. From these poem letters we are able to read Su Tungpo's restlessness of spirit during the beginning of his official career. The brothers often *ho*, or "echoed" each other's poems; to "echo" a poem is to answer it with another one using the same thyme words. It was a good test of poetic skill, for the rhyming had to be natural, and this was one of the accomplishments of all scholars in ancient China. People looked for surprising, or delightful, or refreshing turns of thought, expressed with the prescribed rhyme words, and the lines had to have natural sequence. As in a crossword puzzle, the difficulty increased the delight when the rhyming was done with ease and without effort. In one of these earliest "echo" poems, written to Tseyu, Tungpo revealed already a complete mastery. Having to write a poem where the first two rhyme words had to be "snow" and "west," Tungpo wrote:

"To what can human life be likened?
Perhaps to a wild goose's footprint on snow;
The claws' imprint is accidentally left,
But carefree, the bird flies east and west."

It remained one of Tungpo's best poems. The flying bird was a symbol of the human spirit. In truth, the events and doings of Su Tungpo we are reading about in this book are but the accidental footprints of a great spirit, but the real Su Tungpo is a spirit, like a phantom bird, that is even now perhaps making dream journeys among the stars.

Fengshiang is near the Wei River in the western part of Shensi province. The whole Wei valley is filled with historic sites and names connected with ancient history, for Shensi is the cradle of Chinese civilization. Owing, however, to constant troubles with a very strong neighboring kingdom, the Shiahia, situated in what is now northern Kansuh, there was a heavy drain on the manpower and wealth of the people, and the country was very poor. In the first year after his arrival Su Tungpo built a little house and garden as the deputy magistrate's official residence, with a pond in front, a very good garden planted with thirty-one varieties of flowers, and a pavilion at the back.

Now he was well settled and without too much official responsibility as an assistant magistrate. He was free to travel, and he made trips to the mountains east and south for days. Once his official duty called for extensive travel in the neighboring district on an inspection tour to settle outstanding cases of crime quickly and to release as many prisoners as he could. Nothing could have suited him better, and he roamed through the mountains of Taipo, the temples of the Black Water Valley, and the birthplace of the founder of the Chou Dynasty. Sometimes there was nothing to do, and he would go as far as the famous Chungnan Hills near Sian, to look at a precious manuscript or an original painting by the famous portrait painter Wu Taotse, owned by one of his friends.

Su Tungpo was young and restless. For the first time he was completely on his own, living with his young wife and baby. Now that he had tasted the first flavor of official life, it did not seem so wonderful as he had pictured and dreamed. Living away from the excitement of the capital, the position of a deputy magistrate in an outlying district countersigning documents and trying lawsuits rather bored him. Now and then he would feel very lonely, but at other times, seeing the moonbeam in his wine goblet, he would be elated.

In his years of immaturity, he had need of the advice of his wife. Mrs. Su seems to have had far better practical sense than he. She admired her husband, it is true, for she realized that she had married a famous, young, handsome poet. When a brilliant poet lives with a woman of plain common sense, however, it usually turns out that the wife rather than the husband shows superior wisdom. Always in marriage there is the continual play of the opposite and complementary forces of man and woman. Knowing Tungpo's very forthright and sometimes impetuous nature, she felt not so much the need of admiring him as the duty of taking care of him. Su Tungpo had sound sense in big things and no sense in little things; but life usually consists of the many little things and the big things are usually few and far between, and Tungpo the husband listened to his wife. Mrs. Su reminded him that he was now living for the first time without the guidance of his father. Su believed in everybody, but his wife was a better judge of men. She would stand behind the screen and listen to the conversations between her husband and his visitors. One day, after a guest had left, she said to him, "Why did you waste your time talking with that man? He was always watching what you were going to say in order to agree with you."

She warned him against superficial friends who were a little too demonstrative, and whom he had befriended on his famous theory that there was not a bad person in this world. To the end this seemed to be his trouble; he could not see faults in others. His wife said to him, "Be careful of those people. A friendship which is too quickly formed never lasts." Tungpo admitted that her advice turned out to be true. She had learned this wisdom, I think, from the accepted Chinese saying, "The friendship between gentlemen is mild, like the taste of water"—it has no exciting flavor, but one never grows tired of it. Sincere friendship is never demonstrative. Really good friends don't write letters to each other, for in the complete trust of each other's friendship, no one needs to write. And after a few years of parting, they meet again and find the friendship as true as ever.

Su Tungpo was the type that was unhappy and bored when he had nothing to do. A drought, however, was threatening to come over the land there. It had not rained for a long time, and the farmers were desperately worried over their crops. There was nothing to do except to pray for rain, and it was the magistrate's duty to do it. Su Tungpo was suddenly aroused into activity. Something was wrong somewhere, for the gods were angry, and the farmers were going to suffer if rain did not come immediately. He had a very good case to present to the gods. In this he could not possibly fail and he was ready to plead for the farmers before the gods with all the eloquence in his command. And he did.

One the south of the Wei River there is a high mountain range, generally known as the Tsinling Mountains, and in this range the highest and best-known peak is the majestic Taipo. On top of the Taipo Mountain, in front of a Taoist temple, there was a little pool where lived the God of Rain, a "dragon" who could disguise himself in the form of any small fish. Su Tungpo went up to this temple and prayed. He pleaded for the farmers, but, like a good lawyer, he tried to make the Dragon God see that a drought or famine was not to the god's own interests. After flattering the god a little, he said in the official prayer, "There has been no rain or snow since last winter. Thou knowest well that the people's lives depend upon their crops. If it doesn't rain now, there will be a famine; the people will starve and be forced to become bandits. This is not only my personal duty as a magistrate to prevent; as a spirit, thou shouldst not stand quietly by and do nothing about it. His Imperial Majesty has conferred upon thee the different honors, and we have kept up the sacrifices, all for this day when we may need thee. Wilt thou please listen and fulfill thy obligation to His Majesty?"

Coming down from the Taipo Mountain, he went on to visit various places, particularly one that he had missed on his previous trip. He had offered the prayer on the seventh day of the month, and, returning to the town, he found that there was a slight shower on the sixteenth, but not enough to satisfy the crops or the farmers. He searched for the reason and was told that prayer at the Taipo Mountain had never failed, but that since the god had been made a count by a Sung emperor, prayers to him no longer worked. Su looked up a volume of *Tang History* and discovered that in the previous dynasty the Mountain Spirit of Taipo had been created a duke. The spirit had been in fact degraded in rank and was probably displeased on this account. Immediately, he drafted for the chief magistrate a memorial to the Emperor asking that the Mountain Spirit of Taipo be restored to his previous rank as a duke. Then he and the chief magistrate took a ceremonial bath and sent a special messenger to inform the spirit of what they had done in the way of securing a higher rank for him, and also to bring back a basin of the "dragon water" from the pool.

On the nineteenth, Su Tungpo went out of the city to welcome the arrival of the basin of "dragon water." The whole country population was excited, for in the success of this venture they were all concerned. Several thousand people had come from all over the countryside and there was a great hubbub. The "dragon water" had not yet arrived. But a huge sheet of dark clouds had overcast and darkened the sky. The people waited a long time and still it did not rain. Su Tungpo went into town again and prayed at Chenshing Temple with the chief magistrate, Sung. On his way, he saw a column of cloud coming very low over the ground and spreading in his direction. Borrowing a basket from one of the farmers, he caught some of this cloud in the basket and shut it as tightly as he could. The poem prayer he addressed to this cloud when in the city says, "Now I am going to let you return to the mountaintops. Pray do not embarrass us, the officials." After the prayer, he and Sung came out of the city again. As they reached the suburb there was a sudden gush of cold wind. The flags and pennants and tassels of spears waved violently in the air, and from up in the heights the clouds descended like a herd of wild horses. There was a rumble of distant thunder. At this point, the basin of "dragon water" arrived. Su and Sung went up to receive the basin and after setting it up on a temporary altar, said a prayer to it, which is preserved along with his other prayers in his *Works*. As if in answer to the prayer, the showers came and spread all over the countryside. Two days after, there came another heavy rain lasting three days, and the wilting stalks of wheat and corn stood up again.

Now there was great joy all over the country, but the poet was the happiest of all. To commemorate this joyful occasion, he gave the pavilion at the back of his official residence a new name, the "Pavilion of Joyful Rain," and wrote an inscription on it. This inscription is one of the favorite prose selections from Su Tungpo for use in schools because it is simple in language and typical of Su Tungpo's character, happiest when he was sharing the happiness of the common people.

A sequel to this episode was that the god on the Taipo Mountain was promoted and appointed a duke by the Emperor. Both Su and Sung went up again to the mountain on this occasion and offered their thanks and their congratulations. In July of the following year there was another drought, but this time the prayer was not answered. Disappointed, Su Tungpo went to Panchi to pray to the spirit of a famous man, Chiang Taikung, who is still a very popular god among the common people of China today. He had been a great and wise old man, living in the twelfth century B.C., who, in legend, was reputed to have fished with a hook and line three feet above the water. What the beautiful legend seems to say is that Chiang was a kind and fair person, and if a fish jumped three feet out of the water to be caught by his hook, it was the fish's own fault.

There is no record whether the prayer to Chiang Taikung was answered. But that is no reason for believers in any god, whether it be Buddha or a magic old stump, to doubt the efficacy of prayer. It can never be proved that prayer is not efficacious because, according to Buddhist teachings, something can always be wrong with the man saying the prayer, usually his lack of complete faith. All gods must answer prayers, or humanity would not be interested in them. Besides, prayer is based upon one of the deepest instincts in man. To pray, or to have the attitude of prayer, is, after all, the important thing; whether it is answered or not is secondary.

Anyway, Su Tungpo, as a magistrate in different districts, continued to pray for rain whenever the occasion required it. He knew he was doing the right thing. He believed in the essential justice of the Creator and in His reasonableness. Since he believed in the existence of spirits, he could not but believe also that a spirit would do its best to help relieve suffering and bring happiness and justice into human life. For if reasonableness is the highest human attribute, surely God must be reasonable too, and open to persuasion and a fair argument. But in some of his later memorandums on natural calamities, Su pointed out also, in the orthodox Chinese fashion, that prayers were useless unless at the same time the government gave the people relief from its own oppressive measures. Such is the Chinese religion of common sense which made a writer in the earliest classic say, "Consult the oracles after you have made up your mind what to do." After knowing all the stupid things the Chinese have done, such sayings as this restore my confidence that the Chinese are, after all, truly great thinkers.

I am almost tempted to say that the spirit of Su Tungpo represents the Element of Fire, for all his life he was fighting floods and drought and was always preoccupied with a city's water supply and with canal systems and drinking wells wherever he went. The symbol of fire is also appropriate because it was a life distinguished by an expansive spirit, or *esprit*; in simple words, his temperament and his whole life were like a leaping flame, giving life and warmth wherever it went and also destroying certain things on its way.

This leaping flame, according to the record, twice argued with the devil. For Su went safely upon the assumption that not only the gods, but also the devil, should be open to a forceful onslaught of his logic. He hated anything that did not make sense, and even the devil should be made to see the sense or nonsense of what he was doing. Devils may be sometimes forgetful or confused, but if by Su Tungpo's eloquence they could be made to see the folly of what they were doing, they could also be stopped.

Once, walking along a mountain road on his return from Fengshiang to the capital, he was passing Paihua Mountain. One of his guards was suddenly possessed of the devil and began to take off his clothes one by one while on the road, until he was completely naked. Su Tungpo ordered that they put his garments on him by force and have him bound, but the clothing came off again. Everybody said that the Mountain Spirit must be angry and that the soldier was possessed. Su, therefore, went up to the temple and addressed the spirit as follows:

"Dear Mountain Spirit, I am paying thee a visit because I happen to be passing this way. When I passed here last time, I did not ask anything of thee and now when I am returning, I am asking nothing for myself. I have, however, a guard who is possessed of the devil and the people say that thou art angry. I do not know whether this is true or not. He is only a small, insignificant being in thine eyes, not worthy of the manifestations of thy spirit. If this man had committed some great crime unknown to others, I would not know what to say. But if he has committed only small offenses, such as negligence of duties or discourtesy, or perhaps if he has stolen food or dress, thou shouldst not bother thyself with these small things. It seems to me that thou, the spirit of a mountain, dost control a vast district, and in this vast district there are a great many rich and powerful persons who commit much greater offenses and violations of the law. Is it not preposterous that thou darest not to manifest thyself against the rich and powerful, but showest thy anger against a humble soldier? I am only a small official, dependent upon the service of my little retinue, and when one of them is ill, there is nobody to do his work. Wilt thou not please forgive him? I am a stupid and straightforward person, and am therefore telling thee frankly all this."

As soon as Su Tungpo left the temple after finishing this prayer, a gust of wind blew right into his face. Soon it developed into a squall blowing up pebbles and sand into the air and blinding the travelers. Su Tungpo said to his followers, "Is the spirit getting angrier still? I am not afraid of him." He went ahead on his journey and the storm blew fiercer than ever. Only one man with his immediate luggage followed him, while the others and the horses tried to seek shelter, for they found it impossible to proceed. Someone advised him to go back to the temple and to apologize to the Mountain Spirit. "My fate is controlled by God in high heaven," Su Tungpo replied. "If the Mountain Spirit chooses to be angry, let him be angry. I shall proceed. What can the spirit do to me?" Then the storm abated and blew over, nothing else happened, and the soldier was cured.

Always believing in matching his wits against the unseen spirits, Su Tungpo once drove a sharp bargain with the devil himself Years later, when he was a high official living at the capital, the wife of his second son, who was a granddaughter of Ouyang Shiu, one night was also possessed of the devil, after childbirth. The young daughter-in-law assumed the personality of a dead woman and said to those present, "My name is Tsing and my surname, Wang. My coagulated spirit has not been able to disperse and I have remained a ghost around this place for a long time." Su Tungpo said to the possessed woman, "I am not afraid of ghosts. Besides, there are plenty of priests at the capital who can drive out an evil spirit, and they can drive you out, too. Don't be so stupid! Apparently you died because you were a stupid woman, and now that you have died, you still want to create trouble." Then he explained to the ghost some Buddhist ideas about human spirits, and told her, "Now go quietly away, and tomorrow at dusk I shall say a prayer to Buddha on your behalf." The ghost then put her palms together and said, "Thank you, Your Excellency," and the daughter-in-law recovered. The next day after sunset he wrote a prayer to a buddha and prepared an offering of incense and wine and meat and sent the ghost away.

Soon after, however, a child of his second son said that he had seen a thief running about the house, looking very dark and thin, and clad in a black dress. Su told his servants to search the house but could fine nobody. Then the wet nurse suddenly fell on the floor and screamed. Su went to see her and the wet nurse shouted,

"I am that dark, thin person in a black dress! I am not a thief, I am the house ghost. If you want me to depart from the person of the maidservant, you must invite a sorceress."

Addressing the ghost, Su said firmly, "No, I won't do it."

"If Your Excellency won't do this, I will not insist," replied the ghost in a modified tone, "but can I have a prayer in my favor?"

"No," Su said.

The ghost began to come down in her terms and asked in a still softer tone if she might have a little wine and meat, but Su Tungpo was still adamant. Overawed by the infidel, the ghost would now be satisfied with the burning of a little prayer money. The poet still refused. Finally the ghost asked only for a glass of water and Su Tungpo said, "Give it to her." After drinking the water, the wet nurse fell upon the ground again and soon recovered her consciousness. But her breasts dried up thereafter.

There was an episode during his Fengshiang period of which Su Tungpo seemed a little ashamed and which he did not like to talk about in later life. So far, he had got along beautifully with his superior, Sung, who was an old friend of his family. When a new chief magistrate arrived, however, there came a change. The new magistrate, one Chen, was an old soldier and a stern disciplinarian, dark and muscular and with a sharp glint in his eyes. He came from Su Tungpo's home district and was inclined to look upon him as a young upstart. Chen had an unusual and creditable official record. Once he arrested a corrupt monk of Changsha with many powerful connections and handed him over to justice, to the amazement of the people of the district. Another time he arrested more than seventy sorcerers who preyed upon the ignorant populace, and he compelled them to return to their homes as farmers. At the same time he demolished certain temples given over to immoral practices. It was said that when his soldiers were commanded to stand still, they would do so even when arrows from the enemy were falling thick from the sky.

It was such a person that Su Tungpo now had for his superior. All the military and civil officials bowed their heads in his presence, but in the case of Su Tungpo, as we can well surmise, two uncompromising characters were brought face to face. Often in an argument hot words were exchanged. Su Tungpo was both young and brilliant, and it was difficult for a brilliant young man who had very definite ideas of his own to bow to external authority. Probably the chief annoyance to Su Tungpo as a writer was the fact that the chief magistrate again and again would correct and mutilate Su's drafts of official communications. As a means of showing his displeasure, Chen often would not receive him when he called, and sometimes kept him waiting long enough for Su to take a nap. The quarrel between the two eventually went so far that Chen sent a report to the capital on Su Tungpo's insubordination.

The opportunity soon came for Su Tungpo to have his revenge. The chief magistrate had erected an open terrace inside the official residence where, in his leisure hours, he could go up and get a better view of the surrounding country. For what reason we do not know, Chen asked Su Tungpo to write a piece, to be inscribed on stone, in commemoration of this terrace. It was too good a temptation for the young poet to resist: he had to have his fun. A text prepared for stone inscription was meant for posterity; it should be solemn, elegant, and even poetic. Obviously he could not make direct attacks on Chen, but he knew he could aim little shafts of fun at the old man and get away with it. And so today, the "Record on the Terrace for Stepping on the Void" reads:

"Since the terrace is situated at the foot of the southern hills, it would seem that every day one would eat and sleep and live in close association with the hills, but His Honor the Chief Magistrate was unaware of their existence. When His Honor Sire Chen was walking around in the garden one day, he saw hilltops showing above the trees like the knotted hair of passengers walking outside the wall, and he declared, 'This is strange indeed!' His Honor ordered a square pond to be dug in the front part of the garden, and with the dug-up earth he built a terrace to the level of the house roof, so that future visitors of this terrace would not be aware that they were standing on a high place but the hills would seem to meet their eyes on the level. 'Let this terrace be called the Terrace for Stepping on the Void,' said His Honor. He told this to his junior colleague, Su Shih [Su Tungpo], and asked the latter to write an inscription for the terrace. Su Shih replied to His Honor and said: 'Who can tell how and when the things of this life rise and decay? When this place was a stretch of wild country, exposed to the dew and frost, and foxes and snakes made their homes therein, who would suspect that one day the Terrace for Stepping on the Void would be erected at this place? Since the laws of rise and decay go on in a continual cycle, who can tell but one day this terrace may once more become a stretch of wasteland and barren fields? Once I went up to the terrace with His Honor and looked around. On the east we saw the prayer temple and springs of Emperor Mu of Chin, on the south we saw the halls and terraces of Emperor Wu of Han, and looking to the north we saw the Jenshou Palace of Sui and the Chiucheng Palace of Tang. I thought of the days of their glory, their magnificence and everlasting solidity, greater a hundred times than this terrace. Yet, after a few centuries, travelers over these ruins found only broken tiles and rubble, and mounds covered with brambles and fields of corn. How much more must this be true of the present terrace? And, if even the solid structure of a terrace cannot last long, how much more deceptive are the successes and failures and the ever changing fortunes of human affairs? It would indeed be a mistake for some people to pride themselves on their present good fortune. For we know that there are things in this life which last forever, but this terrace is not one of them.' "

If Su Tungpo had been older, his tone would have been mellower and his shafts better concealed. As it is, the inscription, containing such a calm contemplation of the ruin of the terrace it was supposed to celebrate and the innuendos about an old man never hearing of the hills outside the city where he lived, is certainly unique in the literature of inscriptions. But the old man was also big enough to take it. This time he ordered the text inscribed on stone without any corrections.

As may be seen, Chen was really not a bad person at heart. After the two parted their ways, Su came to see this and made amends. One of the constant obligations of a writer who became famous was to write a tomb inscription for a man upon the request of his sons or relatives. Tomb inscriptions containing expected and rather hackneyed eulogies of the deceased were of no literary value, besides always bordering on dishonesty. The writing of such a tomb inscription was sometimes called by the ancients "flattering the dead." Still, it was a social obligation that a writer often found hard to decline. On this point Su Tungpo made a rigorous rule for himself and carried it out; he would not write a tomb inscription even upon the request of a prince. In all his life he wrote only seven tomb inscriptions, each for a very special reason, when he really wanted to say something. He also wrote one for this chief magistrate years later. It was the longest he ever wrote except that for Szema Kuang. For in the end the two men gained a high respect for each other.

One must mention here Chen Tsao, the chief magistrate's son, who became Su Tungpo's friend for life. Chen Tsao loved drinking, riding, fencing, and hunting, and was a great spendthrift. Su Tungpo met him one day in the mountains when Chen Tsao was hunting with two soldiers on horseback. A magpie had suddenly appeared in front of him and his horsemen failed to shoot it down. With a curse the young hunter dashed out from his hiding place in the thicket and brought the bird down with his first arrow. Something in the face of that young man attracted Su Tungpo to him. Later, Chen's father was sentenced to death on account of allegedly receiving a bribe when serving in another place. The story goes that when Su Tungpo was about to be banished, Chen Tsao was at the time living in retirement in Huangchow. Remembering the quarrel Su Tungpo had had with Chen's father, Su's enemies banished him to this place with the idea of placing him at Chen Tsao's mercy. Perhaps Chen Tsao might want to avenge his father, and Su's enemies would be technically guiltless. As a matter of fact, Su had nothing to do with the father's death, and Chen Tsao turned out to be Su Tungpo's best friend during his long years of banishment at Huangchow.

Another "friend" Su Tungpo met, Chang Chun, was destined to blight his later career. Chang Chun, who later became a vicious political enemy, was then a young magistrate serving in a district near by in the same province. We have no record whether Mrs. Su had advised him against Chang Chun, but the latter was brilliant, hearty, of the type Su Tungpo liked. The story has often been told how Su Tungpo predicted Chang Chun's future. On a trip to Loukuan, the two friends went deep into the mountains and on to the Black Water Valley, where they came to a chasm. A small wooden plank served as a bridge across the chasm, with a deep current churning perhaps a hundred feet below, enclosed by the straight rocks of the canyon. A very courageous man himself, Chang Chun made a bow to Su and proposed that he go over the wooden plank and leave a writing on the wall of the cliff on the opposite side, as tourists often do. Su Tungpo declined, but Chang Chun went over the bridge alone with great nonchalance. Gathering up his gown, he took hold of a suspended rope and descended the sheer cliff to the bank of the stream, where he wrote five big characters on the rock: "Su Shih and Chang Chun visited this place." Then he returned in as leisurely a fashion as if nothing had happened. Patting his friend on the back, Su Tungpo said, "One day you are going to commit murder." "Why?" asked Chang Chun, and Su Tungpo replied, "One who can take his own life in his hands can also kill others." Whether Su Tungpo's prediction was correct or not, we shall see later in the story.

Except for a brief period when he was aroused to great activity again when Emperor Jentsung died, and was put in charge of supervising the transportation of timber from the mountains of western Shensi to build the Emperor's mausoleum, Su was not particularly happy with himself. He grew very homesick. In the autumn of 1063 he wrote to Tseyu: "When I first came, I learned to countersign the signatures, and now I have learned even to preside at a law court. Every day I carry on the daily duties, without asking what they are for. Before a scholar obtains an office, he worries about obtaining it, and if after obtaining it he worries about losing it, what is to be the end of such a life? Now I feel like a tired traveler on a journey, coming upon a clear stream midway. Though I cannot shake off the dust of the road, I would like to have a dip in the stream. I was going away to the southern brooks, where I could hear the bird's song in spring, but official duties tied me down, and now already autumn begins. Every day I receive rush orders for timber, and as a magistrate I have to draft ever more farm hands. Who would dare to complain about service to the Emperor? But the people's hard life is an official's shame. I see hundreds of workmen lugging one piece of lumber, and yet at every step forward they have to pause for rest. The rations are barely enough to keep their stomachs filled. That leaves no time to worry about other things. I am glad that the work is now over, and I wish my vessel were made of better clay. Soon there will be high winds in September, and I am going to roam on the western hills, to let one day of happiness make up for a life of toiling days."

In December 1064 he was relieved of his post. His wife's elder brother had come from Szechuen to stay with them, and the family returned to the capital in January of the following year. Usually, at the end of three years' service, a local official was put through a review of his records, called *mokan*, literally meaning "the grind." On the basis of such a review an official would receive recommendations for other appointments. Now that Tungpo was back, Tseyu could be relieved and he very soon departed to serve as a magistrate at Tamingfu up in the north, then called the Northern Capital or "Peking," but actually over a hundred miles south of the present Peiping.

The new emperor, Ingtung, had heard of Su Tungpo's fame and wanted to make an exception of him and promote him at once to the post of a *banlin* serving as secretary to the Emperor in charge of drafting edicts. Premier Han Chi opposed this step and advised the Emperor that for the good of Su Tungpo, the young poet should be allowed to mature his talents and not suddenly come into a position of such high eminence. The Emperor then suggested that perhaps he might be put in charge of recording the official proceedings of the palace. Again the premier objected, saying that such a post was too close to that of an imperial secretary. He recommended some post in the cultural and educational departments and suggested that Su Tungpo be submitted to the regular tests for such a post. "We give a test," said the Emperor, "only when we do not know a person's real talents. Why should we test Su Tungpo?" But the premier had his way, Su was put to the tests, and again he passed and was given a post in the department of history. In this department, officials took turns working in the imperial library, and Su Tungpo was delighted at the opportunity of looking at the rare books, manuscripts, and paintings in the imperial collection.

That year in May, Su Tungpo's wife died at the age of twenty-six, leaving him a son six years old. His father said to him, "Your wife has followed you and lived with you without being able to enjoy success with you. You should bury her together with her mother-in-law." On the tenth anniversary of his wife's death, Su wrote an exquisite poem revealing his sentiments about her, full of a strange, ghostly beauty and a haunting music which unfortunately cannot be reproduced.

Ten years have we been parted:
The living and the dead—
    Hearing no news,
    Not thinking
    And yet forgetting nothing!
I cannot come to your grave a thousand miles away
To converse with you and whisper my longing;
And even if we did meet
    How would you greet
        My weathered face, my hair a frosty white?
                Last night
I dreamed I had suddenly returned to our old home
And saw you sitting there before the familiar dressing table,
We looked at each other in silence,
With misty eyes beneath the candle light.
May we year after year
    In heartbreak meet,
    On the pine-crest,
    In the moonlight!

His wife's death was followed by that of his father in April of the next year, 1066. Su Shun had completed his work on the *Lives of the Emperors* of that dynasty. As was expected, both brothers immediately resigned from their offices. They carried the father's and Mrs. Su Tungpo's coffins home a thousand miles by land and water to be buried at their hometown in Meichow. Their friends showered them with funeral gifts.

With the coffins, they had to take a boat down the rivers of Anhuei and then go up the Yangtse. The brothers took a long time going home, trying perhaps to satisfy their yearning for travel on the way, and they did not arrive at Meichow till April of the following year. The construction of their father's tomb had been completed by the father himself, and all they needed to do was to lay the coffin in the chamber provided for it next to that for his wife. However, Su Tungpo liked to do big things, and on the mountain slope he planted thirty thousand pine seedlings, hoping that one day they would grow into a great pine forest.

Again a period of compulsory hibernation followed until the twenty-seven months of mourning were over, in July 1068. Before they returned to the capital, two things had to be done. Following his father's example in setting up Buddhas in honor of his mother, Su Tungpo had a temple erected in his father's honor. In this temple he placed a portrait of his father and four extremely precious paintings of Buddhas by an old master, Wu Taotse, which he had acquired at Fengshiang. The temple was erected at the cost of one thousand dollars, of which the Su brothers contributed fifty, the rest being provided by the monk.

The second important thing Su Tungpo did after the mourning was over was to remarry. The bride was his wife's first cousin, daughter of Wang Chieh. Ten years earlier, in the period of his mother's mourning, Su Tungpo had returned home and had often visited his wife's home at Chingshen. Junchi, then a girl of ten or eleven, frequently saw him in her house. On their outings and picnics she was excited about this young man who had gained the highest honors in the imperial examinations. Now she was a girl of twenty, and she was Su Tungpo's choice, since his parents were dead. The match was probably instigated by her brother, who had become devoted to the poet. Being eleven years her husband's junior, and adoring him with complete surrender, she seems to have let her husband have everything pretty much his way. She was unable to make him save money to the end of his days. Less capable than the first wife, she was also of a gentler disposition, yielding and always content. She was to be the poet's companion during the most active period of his life, bringing up her cousin's son and her own sons, and sharing with him all the ups and downs of fortune that came in alternate succession in his life. Against the man's curious adventures of the mind and spirit, it was enough that a woman remained sane and normal and stood as a constant reminder of beauty, health, and goodness. With his mind darting about in all directions, absorbed in new interests and occupied with a world of ideas, with his leaps of high gaiety and deep anguish, many times did he wonder at the serenity of woman that enabled human life to be carried on.

In December 1068 the Su brothers with their families returned to the capital by land, after entrusting the care of their parents' cemetery to their cousin Tse-an and a good neighbor, one Yang. Neither of the brothers ever visited their home again, for soon after their arrival at the capital they were swept into the center of a political storm. Their later official duties took them to almost every province of China except their own.

第七章　王安石变法

苏氏兄弟在神宗熙宁二年（一〇六九）到达京师。从那年起，中国则在政潮汹涌中卷入新社会的实验里，而此一政治波浪所引起的冲击震荡不绝，直到宋朝灭亡而后已。这是中国最后一次的国家资本主义的实验，绝不是第一次。在中国四千年的历史上，有四次变法，结果都归于惨败。最成功的一次是法家商鞅的法西斯极权主义，因为商鞅的学说由秦始皇——万里长城的筑造人，认真地实行出来。这个早期法西斯学说有两大特色，一为崇武，一为重农。但是这两项仍是合而为一的，因为商鞅坚信有勤苦之农民乃有勇武之精兵，中产阶级的商人贸易者，应当力予制压。但是，尽人皆知，那个威力强大的军事组织，依照此一学说已经建立，随后发展起来，且已使秦朝的专政之君统一了全中国。正当这样的政治学说要应用于全中国之时，一个庞大无比的帝国，真是出人意料，竟在数年之内崩溃了。

另外有两次激进的改革，一次是汉武帝时，一次是在王莽当政时。第一次是按照桑弘羊的国家资本财政论，虽然战争绵延，国库赖以增富，但是终以几乎招致叛乱而废止。第二次则因王莽被推翻而新政亦成泡影。所以，如今王安石变法成为第四次失败，固不足为奇。但是在此四次新的实验之中，每一次都是由一个具有创新力的思想家的观点出发，其人宁愿把过去全予摒弃，凭其信念与决心，全力以赴。王安石对商鞅极为钦佩，曾经写过一首诗吁请大家对他当有正确的了解，此一事颇具重要意味。同时，我们必须注意，凡有极权主义提出来，不论古时或现代，基本上的呼声，都是为了国家和人民的利益。在历史上，多少政治上的罪恶都是假借"人民"的名义而犯下的，现代的读者自然不难明白。

王安石是个怪人，思想人品都异乎寻常。学生时代很勤勉，除去语言学极糟糕之外，还算得上是个好学者，当然是宋朝一个主要的诗人。不幸的是，徒有基督救世之心，而无圆通机智处人治事之术，除去与他本人之外，与天下人无可以相处。毫无疑问，他又是一个不实际的理想主义者。倘若我们说理想主义者是指的不注意自己的饮食和仪表的人，王安石正好就是这等人。王安石的衣裳肮脏，须发纷乱，仪表邋遢，他是以此等恶习为众所周知的。苏洵在《辨奸论》那篇文章里刻画王安石说："衣臣虏之衣，食犬彘之食。"又说他"囚首丧面而谈诗书"。王安石是否喜欢以这样特点异乎常人，我们无从知道，但是一个人把精力完全倾注在内在的思想上，自然会忽略了他的外表，这话倒不难相信。有一个故事流传下来，说他从来不换他的长袍。一天，几个朋友同他到一个寺院里的澡堂。在他由浴池出来之前，朋友们特意偷偷地留在外头一件干净的长袍，用以测验他是否知道衣裳已经被换了。王安石洗完出来，把那件新袍子穿上，朋友动了手脚，他完全不知道。不管怎么样，他总是身上穿了件衣裳就行了。

又有一天，朋友们告诉王安石的胖太太，说她丈夫爱吃鹿肉丝。

胖太太大感意外，她说："我不相信。他向来不注意吃什么，怎么会突然爱吃鹿肉丝了呢？你们怎么会这样想？"

　　大家说："在吃饭时他不吃别的盘子里的菜，只把那盘鹿肉丝吃光了，所以我们才知道。"

　　太太问："你们把鹿肉丝摆在了什么地方？"

　　大家说："摆在他正前面。"

　　太太明白了，向众人说："我告诉你们，明天你们把别的菜摆在他前面，看会怎么样。"

　　朋友们第二天把菜的位置调换了，把鹿肉丝放得离他最远，大家留意他吃什么。王安石开始吃靠近他的菜，桌子上照常摆了鹿肉丝，他竟然完全不知道。

　　还有一个故事说王安石在做扬州太守幕府时，彻夜读书。那时的太守是韩琦，他后来做了宰相。王安石总是苦读通宵，天将黎明之时才在椅子中打盹。等睡醒时，已然晚了，来不及洗脸梳头发，便连忙跑到办公室上班。韩琦一看他那副样子，以为他彻夜纵情声色，就向他劝导几句。

　　韩琦说："老弟，我劝你趁着年轻，多用功念点儿书吧。"

　　王安石立在那儿未作分辩。在去职之时，他告诉朋友说韩琦不赏识他。后来，王安石的学者名气日大，韩琦对他的看法也有了改变，也愿把他看作自己的属下，王安石却很恼怒。事情赶巧是，王安石在京师接受朝廷一项高位那一年，正好韩琦罢相。王安石记日记甚勤，竟写了七十巨册，他曾有这样批评韩琦的话："韩琦别无长处，惟面目姣好耳。"

　　但是王安石这个怪人，除去邋遢的外表之外，尚有不止此者。在他得势之前大约二十年之中，他之所以使人谈论者，是他屡次谢绝朝廷的提升。这倒很难相信他之如此是纯系沽名钓誉之意，因为从他二十一岁考中进士，到他四十六岁得势——那是他壮年最活跃的时期，共二十五年——他一直谢绝任命，宁愿在一个偏远的省份当一小吏。那是仁宗在位之时，国家太平，才俊之士咸荟萃于京都。王安石越谢绝朝廷授予高位之意，他的声誉越高。最后，朝廷上的官员皆急欲一睹此人的真面目，此时因为他除去以文章出名之外，他位居太守，治绩斐然，行政才干之优，堪称能吏。他建堤筑堰，改革学校，创农民贷款法，把他的新社会理想，实施了数项。政绩确实不错，也深得百姓爱戴。他对入朝为官的引诱一直视若无睹，直到仁宗嘉祐五年（一〇六〇），朝廷任命他为三司度支判官，他才来到京师。很显然，此人的兴趣是在经济财政方面，只有在这方面他才会对国家有最大的贡献。后来他母亲去世，他必须辞官守丧；但是甚至于守丧期满，他又被召入朝之时，他又谢绝在京为官，宁愿留在金陵。

他这一段自己韬光养晦的历程，颇难了解，因为此人一定深信一旦时机到来，他必可为国家做大事。若说他壮年这段时间已经建立了他政治生涯的基础，是合乎情理的说法。也许当时朝廷名臣重儒之间的竞争，他觉得不能胜任，因为那时朝中有年高德劭学识渊博的文臣，如范仲淹、司马光、欧阳修、曾公亮等人，这些人都会对锐意的改革侧目而视，都深得人望，足以使抱有新见解的后起之辈无从发展。王安石是在坐以待时。但是，从心理上看，恐怕另有一个理由。王安石那样气质的人，不管身居何处，总愿自为首领，而在偏远的外县身为太守，仍不失小池塘中的大青蛙。他在京师担任一项官职，那一段短短的时间，他曾和同僚争吵不和，使事事错乱失常。他想变动成规，照自己的想法办事。吴珪和张方平都记得与他为同僚或为属下之时，遇事都极难与人合作。

在仁宗嘉祐五年他来到京师时，时人都视之为奇才。他已经写过些好诗文，他有创见，也善于言谈。老一辈的名公巨卿如富弼和文彦博对他颇有好评，甚至欧阳修也对他有好感。在他那古怪的仪表之下，暗藏着当时那些官员所不能窥测的才干和品格，他这个奇特之士就曾与那些大员周旋。在能看穿王安石的品格并认为他将会成为国家一大害的寥寥数人之中，有苏洵和他的老友张方平。张方平曾与王安石为同僚，共同监督地方考试，因相处不洽而将他峻拒之后，便不再与他交往。他一定把早年与王安石共事的经验告诉过苏洵。于是二人对王安石极为厌恶，更因为他穿着习惯的矫揉造作不近人情，而对他反感更深。欧阳修曾经把王安石介绍给苏东坡的父亲，而王安石也愿意结识苏氏父子，但是老苏对他拒而不纳。王安石母亲去世时，在所有经邀请参加丧礼之人当中，只有苏洵拒绝前往，并且写了那篇著名的文章《辨奸论》，这一篇成了后来历代学生常读的文章。

在这篇文章里，苏洵开头儿就说了解人的性格很难，甚至聪明人也常会受骗，只有冷静的观察者才能看透人的性格而预知他将来的发展。他引证古代的一个学者山巨源预言王衍的将来，那时王衍仅仅是聪颖秀逸的书生；还引证名将郭子仪预测卢杞的将来，后来卢杞对唐代的灭亡多少负有责任。卢杞为人阴险而富有才干，但其容貌极丑。郭子仪在接见卢杞时，必须把歌女舞姬等斥退，恐妇女辈见其丑陋而受惊，或因一时嗤笑而开罪于他。但是苏洵说，当时若不是有昏庸之主，这两个人还不足单独有亡国的才干。现在一个具有卢杞的阴险与丑陋，兼有王衍的辩才的人出现了。"今有人，口诵孔老之言，身履夷齐之行，收召好名之士、不得志之人，相与造作言语，私立名字，以为颜渊孟轲复出，而阴贼险狠，与人异趣。"此人如一旦得势，足以欺英明之王，为国家之大害。"夫面垢不忘洗，衣垢不忘浣，此人之至情也。今也不然，衣臣虏之衣，食犬彘之食，囚首丧面而谈诗书，此岂其情也哉！凡事之不近人情者，鲜不为大奸慝。"苏洵希望他的预言不应验才好，这样他就可比为"善战者无赫赫之功"的名将了。但是他说："使斯人而不用也，则吾言为过，而斯人有不遇之叹。孰知祸之至于此哉！不然，天下将被其祸，而吾获知言之名，悲夫！"

王安石的奇怪习惯，是否是矫揉造作，无法断言；但每逢一个人对某一事做得过度，人总容易怀疑他是沽名钓誉。我们若是相信邵伯温的记载，仁宗皇帝也曾有此怀疑。一天大臣等蒙恩宠召，盛开御宴。客人须在池塘中自己捕鱼为食。在用膳之前，做成小球状的鱼饵，摆在桌子上的金盘子里。王安石不喜欢钓鱼，便将金盘子里的鱼饵吃光。第二天，皇帝对宰相说："王安石为伪君子。人也许误食一粒鱼饵，总不会有人在心不在焉之下把那些鱼饵吃完的。"由这个故事可以看出，为什么仁宗不喜欢王安石了。在王安石的日记里，他对仁宗也挑剔得特别苛酷。由后来的发展看，苏洵的话没说错。但是不知何故，在世界各国，怪人、狂想家、精神分裂者，总是相信邋遢脏乱才是天才的标志，而最能使自己获有千秋万岁名的办法，就是拒绝正人君子般的装束。还有一种怪想法，就是，肮脏污秽就表示轻视物质环境，因此也就是精神崇高，于是合理的结论必然是：天堂者，恶臭熏人的天使集中处也。

老苏写《辨奸论》时，苏东坡说他和弟弟子由都认为责骂得太重，只有张方平完全赞同。可是，事过不久，苏东坡的同代人就看到老苏的所见太对了。那篇文章至今流传，足以显示苏东坡老父的真知灼见。

王安石接任三司判官不久，他就企图试探一下自己的政治基础。当时仁宗在位，他就上书论政，长达万言。在此万言书中，陈明他对改革财政的基本原则，"因天下之力以生天下之财，取天下之财以供天下之费"。他说自宋开国以来，政府即感财力不足之苦，此皆因缺乏一良好之财政经济政策。此等政策之所以未为人所想到，只因为无伟大而有力者谋其事。他说当时有其权位者，却无此大才。在全国之中，他亦不知何人具有此等才干足以出任斯职。他很巧妙地指出若从事基本改革，必使之与古圣先生之道相联系，要使庶民相信不悖乎先王之道。他又说，在顺乎古代传统之时，切勿师先王之法，但仅师先王之意，政策无论如何不相同，但皆以人民之利益为依归。总之，那是一篇结构谨严、文字老练的政论文章，论到政府的每一方面，财政、官制、教育，无不在内。

倘若王安石打算试探他的政治基础，他发现他的政治基础还在松软下陷。仁宗皇帝把他的万言之书看完，就置诸高阁了。在随后英宗皇帝短短的四年当政之中，王安石又蒙恩召，但是他仍然辞谢不就。历史家往往举出的理由是，因为仁宗无子，仁宗驾崩后，他曾奏请免立英宗为帝，因此他心中感觉不安之故。

这时，英宗之子，将来要继承帝位，现今正以王储之身，居于京都，后来即位为神宗，王安石那时才因宠得势。神宗为太子时，韩维为太子司文书事，而韩维对王安石则极为佩服。韩维常对朝政表示意见，每逢太子赞同那些意见，韩维就说："此非臣之意见，乃王安石之意见耳。"于是，太子对王安石渐渐器重，希望将来要借重王安石的政治大才。在英宗四年（一〇六七），神宗年二十岁，即帝位，立即任王安石为江宁知府，九月又将他擢登翰林之位。王安石与他的好友韩维不断联系，深信他的机会终于到来。他这次违背了以前的老习惯，圣命一到，立即拜受了官职。但是延迟晋京，七个月后才成行。

神宗皇帝说："先王之时，王安石一向谢绝任命，不肯来京都。有人以为他冒失无礼，现在他仍然不来，称病为借口。是真有病在身，还是冀图高位？"

这一时期，朝中有两位元老重臣，互相嫉恨：一为曾公亮，一为韩琦。韩琦在三朝继续担当宰相与枢密之职，已有权责太重之势。曾公亮在企图动摇韩琦之时，希望拉王安石为有力的同党。他向皇帝力保王安石真有宰相之才具，皇帝应当对他的话信而不疑。另一方面，大臣吴珪深知王安石之为人，他警告皇帝说，若使王安石得权，必致天下大乱。

最后，在神宗熙宁元年（一〇六八），王安石已然深知皇帝对他的态度，乃自外地来京，奉召入朝，奉准"越级进言"，不受朝仪限制。

皇帝问："朝政当务之急为何？"

王安石回奏道："以决定政策为要。"

皇帝又问："卿以唐太宗为如何？"

"陛下当以尧舜为法，固不仅唐太宗而已。尧舜之道行之亦甚易。后世儒臣并不真了解先王之道，认为尧舜之政，后世不可复见。"

皇帝听了颇觉称心，但谦谢道："卿之所望于寡人者过奢，恐怕寡人无以符贤卿之望。"

后来王安石得到一次单独召见的机会，别的官员已全退去。那是王安石的千载良机。

皇帝说："坐下。我要和你长谈。"皇帝陛下开始问他为什么过去两个明君（其中一个是唐太宗）一定要获得贤臣为相以辅佐朝政。皇帝提出的两个贤相之一并非别个，正是诸葛亮，可以说是历史上最贤能的宰相。王安石又使谈话不离三千年前的尧舜之治这一题目，他说他愿谈尧舜的贤相。他说诸葛亮在高人心目之中，无足多论。诸葛亮的政治才干，也不过是按部就班，循序渐进，以达到一个明确的目标，此种做法决不适于像他这等急躁自信的财政经济的鬼才。

王安石接着说："陛下如今御临一个地大民多的国家。国家升平百年之久，全国才智之士如此之多，竟无贤德才智之臣佐陛下以为善政？其故恐在陛下无明确之政策与用人不专故耳。今日虽有非常之才，一如当年辅佐尧舜之贤臣，如受小人之阻挠，亦必弃职而罢。"

皇帝道："每朝皆有小人。即使尧舜时代，尚有恶迹昭彰的四凶。"

王安石道："诚如陛下所说，正因尧舜知道此四奸臣之劣迹而杀之，尧舜才能有其成就。倘若此四奸臣在朝不去，仍逞其阴谋而妒贤害能，贤良之臣亦必弃官而去。"

神宗听了，颇为感动。他年方二十，像一般年轻人一样，雄心万丈，极愿国富兵强。他为人善良而公正，圆脸盘，五官端正，和祖宗长相相似。宋朝的皇帝，到神宗以后，才明白显出了精力衰颓的样子。王安石心想年轻皇帝对远大可期的热望，终于点燃起来。自从那次密谈之后，神宗皇帝就决定不惜赴汤蹈火也要完成王安石的变法计划，即便牺牲其他所有大臣也无不可——结果竟不幸而如此。不知为何缘故，每逢贤德的老臣进谏反对王安石的新法之时，这位年轻皇帝的头脑中便浮现出那"四凶"的影子来。

在神宗熙宁二年（一〇六九）苏氏兄弟回到京师之时，王安石被任为参知政事（副宰相）。随后两年之中，但见稳重的老臣纷纷离朝，御史台遭到清肃排斥，继之身为谏官的都是王安石的一群小人。王安石就职不久，就开始大刀阔斧在政府各部门大事清除异己。抗争之事此起彼落，整个官场闹得乌烟瘴气。贤德干练深孚众望的大臣，对王安石公开反对。这位年轻的皇帝反倒不明白究竟是何缘故。王安石想尽方法，使皇帝觉得这场混乱纷争，是皇帝和胆敢反对皇帝的那批奸邪的大臣之间的殊死之战。

皇帝问道："为什么会闹得这么人仰马翻？为什么所有的大臣、御史，全朝的读书人，都群起反对新法呢？"

王安石回奏说："陛下要知道，陛下是要师法先王之道，为了事功，不得不清除这些反对旧臣。在反动的旧臣与陛下之间的夺权之争，是不可免的。倘若他们获胜，朝廷大权将落在他们之手；若陛下获胜，朝廷的大权则仍将在陛下之手。那些自私的大臣，全都是存心阻挡陛下行先王之道。就是因此才闹出这一番纷乱。"

有年轻好胜志在国富兵强的皇帝在上，有对自己的财政经济学说坚信不移的宰相在下，实行王安石激进的政治财政改革已经如箭在弦了。实行新政的动机是不容置疑的。宋朝承五代残唐纷争杀戮的五十年之后，一直没有强盛起来。而且，西夏、契丹（后来称辽）、金，不断侵略中国的边境。中国与这些北方部落短期交战之后，遂订约言和。和约的条款对中国皇帝也是忍垢蒙羞的条款，因为那些番邦虽然承认中国的皇帝，但那是中国皇帝按年赐予他们金银绸缎换来的，每年付出的财帛要十万到二十五万缗，这自然使国库财力大量外流。国内行政一向松弛泄沓！政府经费则捉襟见肘。王安石自命为财务奇才，能凭耍弄纳税征兵制度便可以给国库筹集款项。我相信借在中国西北用武而恢复国威，是王安石政策中打动君心的要点，因为王安石当政时曾在西北由中国发动战争数次，其中有数次胜利，一次惨败。为继续作战，皇帝需要金钱，为了筹款，国家财政制度必须改变。可是，我们不必怀疑力主新政者真纯的动机，我们先看看那些财政经济改革的严重后果吧。

王安石到达京都不久，司马光就和他在神宗面前争论起来，这次争论就总括了双方基本的歧见。这时国库已到真正空虚的地步，到了春季的祭天大典，皇帝竟想免去赐予臣子的银两绸缎，这样可以给皇家节省一笔钱。这件事引起司马光和王安石之间一次争论。王安石认为国库空虚完全为朝臣不知理财之道的结果。

司马光反驳他说："你之所谓财政，只是在百姓身上多征捐税而已。"

王安石回答说："不是。善于理财者能使国库充裕而不增加捐税。"

司马光说："多么荒唐！总之，一国有其固定量的财富。这笔财富不是在百姓手中，便是在政府手中。不论你实行什么政策，或给此政策什么名称，你只是把百姓手中的钱拿过一部分交给政府罢了。"

皇帝有几分持司马光的说法，于是在随后一两个月内把新政暂行搁置。

不必身为经济学家，尽可放心相信一国的财富方面的两个重要因素只是生产与分配，谅不致误。要增加国家的财富，必须增加生产，或是使分配更为得当。在王安石时代，增加生产绝无可能，因为那时还没有工业化的办法。所以一个财政天才之所能为，只有在分配方面。因为王安石基本上关心的，是充裕国库，而增加国家财富的意思，也就是提高政府的税收。王安石看得很清楚，富商与地主正以自由企业方式获利，他不明白政府为什么不应当把他们的利润抢过来而由政府自己经商，自己获利。那结论是可想象而知的。他用的名称的确很够新奇，他要用资本削减垄断，叫"钱平"；他要取之于富归之于贫以求均富；他要阻止农民向地主高利贷款。在春耕期间由政府借款予农民，在收割后由农民归还政府，自然是仁善之举。王安石能使皇帝深信所有这些措施都是为了人民的利益；但是历史上记载，经过了一段踌躇，王安石才决定实行借款予农民的理论，这理论是一个小吏提出的，就是：投资五十万两白银，每年政府可赚二十五万缗，因为一年两收，则百分之二十或三十的利息可以一年收两次。

我们无须把这些新政的细节详予说明，总之新政是由神宗熙宁二年（一〇六九）开始，大约八年之后闹得天怒人怨，王安石自己本人和皇帝都十分心烦，二人彼此之间也不愉快。现在仅略述其大要于后。

最重要与最为人所熟知者共有九项，为方便计，今归纳为三组。有三种国营企业、三种新税、三项管制人民的登记制度。三种国营企业是均输法（国营贸易局）、市易法（国营零售店管理局），以及利息二分实收三分（加上申请和登记费）的青苗法。三项新税收是免役税、国产消费税、所得税。登记制度是把国民组织起来，编成十家为一组的征兵单位，亦即保甲；重新登记土地和马匹（方田均税法与保马法）。大体说来，这些方案近乎现代的集体经济政策。

国营企业自神宗熙宁二年（一〇六九）以首先设立全国或省际的批发机构开始。深信政府有厚利可图，神宗皇帝拨了五百万缗现款、三千万石谷子作为由政府接收省际贸易的货品和原料的经费。但是这套办法立刻遇到了困难。当年二月，朝廷先创立制置三司条例司，负研究条款之责并予以公布。在条例司的官员之中就有苏子由。苏子由上奏折指出，朝廷若接收全国贸易，自由企业会立即瘫痪，只因各地的批发商人无力与官家竞争。政府与商人必将互相掣肘，而且他否认国库会有利可图。私人商业有相沿已久的信用关系及其他办法，政府经营时则无此种便利。必须先成立庞大机构以高薪雇用大批官员，并建筑美轮美奂的官衙。结果不是从事以供与求为基础的商业经营，而是视佣金多寡来处理，按私人交情厚薄而分配利润，照亲疏远近而订立合同。子由力陈，由于官僚作风的无能，官方无力压低物价，只能以高价买入，远比正常商人购货时价钱高，所以自然失败无疑。

所谓官营的均输法，亦即政府批发生意，因此搁置了一年，从长计议。后来朝廷用一个新名称提出一项修正计划。批发与零售的分界不是一个呆板硬性的规定，主管大公营商店的贸易局分设在大城市，如成都、广州、杭州。为了这些贸易机构的发展，朝廷又由国库拨出一百万缗，由京都地方的货币中拨出八十七万缗。为成立这些机构所举出的理由为："富商大贾因时乘公私之急，以擅轻重敛散之权。""宜收轻重敛散之权，归之公上，而制其有为，以便转输，省劳费，去重敛，宽农民。"领导者是一个极为能干的官员。他向政府所呈报的利润越厚，则上级认为他越干练。这个能干的官员名叫吕嘉问，成了全国的市易务官，全权控制全国的小商人。京都市易务的规矩是，小贸易商必须做该机构的会员，可以把货物与该处的资财联合经营，或由官方出钱收买他们店铺的存货。商人若想歇业，可把存货售与官家；也可用部分存货作为抵押向官方借钱，半年付息一分，或一年付两分。非该处会员，也可把货物卖与官家，价格由官家规定；最后是，不论官家需用何等货物，统由该处办理。

政府吸收小商家，为此一制度最弱的一点，而私人营业几乎完全停顿。数年后，贸易和商业大为减少，按理论朝廷获利甚大，而实际上朝廷税收受损却到惊人的程度。皇帝在百姓心目中已经降低为与小民争利的贩夫走卒，皇帝知道后，大为不悦。最后，京都市易务和商税的丑闻传到了皇帝耳朵里，皇帝下令停止新法中最为人厌恶的几项。

但是变法中最为人所知的是青苗法。直到今日，每逢人谈到王安石的变法时，先想到的是这一项。这一项措施影响到全国每一个村庄，也是引起朝中轩然大波的主要原因。这一项措施本身确实不错，有些近似现代的农民银行。王安石年轻时做太守，曾在春耕时贷款予农民，收割时本利收回。他觉得这个办法对老百姓确实有帮助，因为他任职地方政府，能知道借款确有其需要，并且还要经官方适当的调查。在陕西省，官方亦曾试办，也颇为成功。而且由于这项办法由陕西春耕时开始，所以农民借款仍叫"青苗"贷款。

在年成好时，当局知道必然会丰收，就贷款与农人购买农具和麦苗；一经收割，官方就去收麦子以供军需，且有利息可赚。据制置三司条例司所说："诸路常平、广惠仓钱谷，略计贯石可及千五百万以上，敛散未得其宜，故为利未博。今欲以见在斛斗，遇贵量减市价粜，遇贱量增市价籴。可通融转运司苗税及钱斛，就便转易者，亦许兑换。仍以见钱，依陕西青苗钱例，愿预借者给之。随税输纳斛斗，半为夏料，半为秋料。内有请本色或纳时价贵愿纳钱者，皆从其便。如遇灾伤，许展至次料丰熟日纳。非惟足以待凶荒之患，民既受贷，则兼并之家不得乘新陈不接以邀倍息。又常平、广惠之物，收藏积滞，必待年俭物贵，然后出粜，所及者不过城市游手之人。今通一路有无，贵发贱敛，以广蓄积，平物价，使农人有以赴时趋事，而兼并不得乘其急。凡此皆以为民。而公家无利其入，是亦先王散惠兴利、以为耕敛补助之意也。"

这项美丽纯正的计划原本是为农民之利益而设，结果竟一变而为扰民，弄得农民家败人亡，到底何以演变至此一地步，我们到后面再看。不过我们应当说明的是，这个新措施本乃常平仓古法的延续，但后来渐渐把古法取而代之。由宋朝开国始，政府在各县一直保持此类谷仓，用以稳定谷价。谷贱伤农，政府则收买剩余的稻谷；在歉年时，正相反，稻谷之价高涨时，官方则将稻谷抛售，用以平抑粮价。诚然，主管粮政的当局不见得行政效率能永远很好，因为不少官吏在谷价低贱时，不见得愿意收买。甚至在英宗治平三年（一〇六六）常平仓公布的数字显示，官家一年内收购五百零一万四千一百八十石谷物，卖出为四百七十一万一千五百七十石。现在，仓廪的财货都已变为青苗贷款的本金，常平仓的正常功用自然终止了。

青苗法的基本问题是，这种贷款必然会变成强迫贷款。王安石不容许人有异议，如今必须成功不可。他必须向神宗表示此种贷款极为成功，深受农民欢迎。他不容许属下放款松懈。他不能了解农民不需要此项贷款，每逢预备贷出的款项不能如数贷出时，他就暴跳如雷。他开始把办理贷款成绩好的官员提升，把他认为懈怠者处罚。每一个官员无不注意自己的成绩，最关心的就是由报表上显出好成绩。此等对众官吏竞赛的刺激办法，很像现代的推销政府公债。主办贷款的官员一旦知道自己若不能将款如数贷出，便会因"阻碍变法"的罪过行将革职或降职时，被王安石称之为能吏的官员，便将款项开始在官方压力之下强行分配。每家都得向官家借债，每一期三个月，每个人在一期得交付百分之三十的利息。也有善良的官吏深知这种贷款对贫民为害之大，也知道若本利不能缴还，必难免牢狱之灾。因此依照朝廷的明文规定，正式向民众宣布，此等贷款，依据圣旨，纯属自愿；心里对会因"阻挠变法"而降级，早有准备了。

免役法亦复如此。官方的本意与实施情形，也是大相径庭。但是这一项措施，可以说是王安石变法中最好的一项。后来苏东坡的"蜀党"当权时，他一派中所有的人都打算把王安石的新法全予推翻，苏东坡所支持新法中唯一的一种，就是免役法。

在宋以前，中国实行征兵制已经很久。王安石提出的就是老百姓要付税以代替兵役。换言之，这条措施就是以募兵组成常备军代替征兵制。不过，仔细研究一下免役法的规定，其结论恐怕难逃政府从税收以裕国库的目的，至于使人民免于征兵之利益，则已由实行保甲制度而化为泡影，而保甲制度较之征兵制弊害更多。免役法慎重研讨一年之后，条文终于公布了。条文中规定凡过去免于征兵之家仍须付免役税，例如，寡妇，家中无子女或只有独子，或虽有子女而尚未成年者，尼姑与和尚道士，都须纳一种税，名之为"助役金"。各地区在免役配额之外，须多缴纳百分之二十，以供荒年百姓无力缴纳时应用。由此种税征集的款项，则充政府雇兵与雇用其他人员之用。正如苏东坡在青苗贷款措施上所说,百姓将因拖欠而入狱,而受鞭笞之苦,也正如司马光当时所指出将来必然发生之情况——凡无现款以缴纳春秋之免役税者,必强迫而出售食粮,杀其耕牛,伐其树木,方可以缴纳此项捐税。再者,在前项征兵法中,民家只不过轮流服役数年,而在新实行之免役法中,常常须为免役而年年缴税,连不需服役之年,亦须照常缴税。

免役法以及新商税与所得税法,必须看作向民征税的一项新方法,而并非免于征兵,因为人民在保甲法之下仍须接受征调而接受军事训练的。新商事法是根据商人账目在商人的利润上征取捐税的。所得税,并非现代意义上的所得税。我之所以要在此称之为所得税,是因为官方强迫人民登记其收入与财产,据此以做分配其他捐税之用。此税之所以像所得税,就是人民必须要报其收入与财产之所得,煞费心机去欺骗政府。在这项新政的争论上,据说此项措施公布之后,"民家尺椽寸土,检括无遗,至鸡豚亦遍抄之",无一不登记报官的。最后一项措施于神宗熙宁七年(一〇七四)历时不久而废,因王安石不久失势之故;甚至在此项措施停止实施之前,苏东坡称其不合于法,在他治下地区拒予推行。

王安石在免役法中表明意在解除人民在征兵法中之苦,结果保甲法证实了他是言不由衷。事实至为明显。他的新保甲法与免役法是同时公布的,在神宗熙宁三年(一〇七〇)十二月。朝廷用免役法的法宝,一只手从人民身上解除了征兵的重担,却用另一只手把那个重担又放回人民身上。保甲是邻居连保制度,每十家为一保,每五十家为一大保。一保中如有人窝藏贼犯,保内各家要负连带责任;如有谋杀、强奸等罪,保中必须报告官府。每一大保之壮丁必须组队接受军事训练,一家有壮丁二人者抽其一,如超过二壮丁,则依比例多抽。凡抽去者每五天离田受训,此五天相当于现今之一星期，一个月分为六节。家有壮丁者，不必如古代征兵制度下只身赴外乡，而是使军队深入村中。但是王安石善于宣传，他知道给旧事物一个新名称，此旧事物便不复存，所以"征兵制已废"。

在集中登记管理人民之外，还有一种农民田地强迫登记，作为征收新税的依据，以及另一种将政府的马匹寄养在民家的制度，也就是方田均税法及保马法。像所有集体制度一样，王安石的新法是不放人民自由生活的。政府在妥为照顾人民的焦虑之下，这个新政权必须确知人民做些什么，有些什么。也像其他集体制度一样，这个新政权也认为缺少了特务人员是不能统治的，因而其特务制度在神宗熙宁五年（一○七二）成立，幸而苏东坡已经离开京都了。这个新政权若不把御史台（相当于现代的报章杂志界）控制住，而以甘心效忠的同党手下人填满，这个新政权也是无法发挥效能的。王安石也觉得有控制学者文人的思想观念之必要。他以前像王莽，往后则像希特勒，因为他一遇到别人反对，则暴跳如雷——现代的精神病学家，大概会把他列为患有妄想狂的人。

显出王安石的妄想狂性格，以及所有历史家和批评家共同认为他一个不可饶恕的行为，倒不是他的政治社会的冒险改革，而是他自命为经典的唯一解释人一事。他也像王莽那样篡改古籍，所以王安石也写他自己的《三经新义》，使之成为思想的官定标准，用以代替所有过去经典的名家疏解。以一个学者而论，王安石还算不错，但还不足以把郑康成、马融、陆德明等鸿儒取而代之。他此种行为，既是官权的滥用，又是对学术的污辱。中国科举考试，一般都是以经书的一段为题，而应考者的发挥题意也要依据经书。这个王氏新制度的建立，就是说国内的考生必须在每个题意上，要研究并且吸收王安石所说的话，自为政之道、佛教色彩的儒学，一直到"鹑""枭""雉"等字的语源。苏东坡离开京都之后，一次在地方考试时监考，曾写过一首诗，表示对考生试卷上所表现的思想观念之呆板雷同的厌恶感。

王安石的《三经新义》也和他的语言学一样，往往带有佛教思想，新思想创见多，而学术根基浅。但是他却相信，在解释古籍的思想和政治观念时，他之认为如何就必然如何。他的《三经新义》糟不可言，他死之后就完全为人所遗忘，而且也一本无存了。可是在他当权之时，则是科举考生人人所必读的经典；考生的意见如与宰相的见解小有出入，便因之落第而有余。最为人所厌恨者，是此《三经新义》是在两年之内仓促编成的；此书之正式开始编纂是在神宗熙宁六年（一〇七三）三月，在他的小儿子和一个政治走狗帮助之下编成，后两年出版。这本急就章，就定为儒家思想的标准疏解，但每逢王安石对疏解有所改变，为应天下考生之需，新版本立即出现。考生人人知道，他们的前途是全系于能做这个修正本的应声虫与否而定。

这里不讨论王安石学问如何，苏东坡觉得实在难以容忍，因为苏东坡的学问胜过他实在太多。不过现在也可以提一提，王安石的字源学之荒唐可笑，简直跟外行人一样。在他的《三经新义》之外，在当代学人之中，大家最愤怒的事，就是王安石所引起的讨论字源学的怪风气。他的字源学，只是字的结构与来源的研究，不是用比较方法，而是凭个人的幻想。王安石相信这是独得之秘，是对学术上不朽的贡献，至老年时犹苦研不辍，成书二十五卷。西方的学者会了解，一旦学者任凭想象力纵情驰骋而不予以科学方法的限制，就是不用汉人的说经与清儒的朴学方法，那他写二十五卷字源学真是易如反掌的事。若施用幻想，则这部"幻想字源学"一天可写十部。像王安石这样研究一个字构成的各种理由，为什么一个字由某些偏旁组织起来就表示某种意义，那倒是容易而有趣的。王安石的字源说有五十条左右流传下来，都是供茶余酒后的笑谈。苏东坡和王安石之间的许多笑话，都是以此等字源学为关键的。

苏东坡喜用"反证论法"。中文里有一个"鸠"字，是"九""鸟"合成，显然"九"字是表音。王安石不管语音学的道理，只想从意义上找点趣谈。一天，苏东坡和他闲谈时，忽然问王安石："可是，为什么'鸠'字由'九''鸟'二字合成呢？"王安石语塞。苏东坡说："我能告诉你为什么。《诗经》上有：'鸣鸠在桑，其子七兮。'七只小鸟加上父母两个，不是九个吗？"

"波"字是由"水"加"皮"而成，"皮"此一偏旁表音。这个"波"字触动了王安石丰富的想象，他说"波"者"水"之"皮"也。一天苏东坡遇见他，向他戏谑道："'波'若是'水'之'皮'，则'滑'就是'水'之'骨'了。"王安石违反中国字构成的基本原则，有时他割裂字根为二，再另与一个部首相接，像"富"字一例，真会使语言学家啼笑皆非的。

有些中国后代的学者，在西方集体主义的观点上看，打算为王安石洗刷历史上的污点，说他的观念基本上符合现代的社会主义，打算这样恢复他的名誉。在为王安石辩护的学者之中，中国现代一个伟大的学者梁启超，便是其一。主张王安石的社会主义观念为是为非，自无不可，但是他那社会主义的政权必须凭其政绩去判断才是。事实是，王安石使国家的垄断取私人的垄断而代之，弄得小生意人失业；农人在无力付强迫的青苗贷款和利息之下，卖妻儿而逃亡，为他担保的邻居，或与之共同逃亡，或把财产典卖。县镇监狱有人满之患，每一县政府都有查封的抵押品和没收的财产，衙门也讼案充斥。朝廷这样失政之下，即使没有外族侵入，任何朝代也会灭亡的。在神宗熙宁七年（一〇七四），一道圣旨说商业停顿，百姓失业；过了两年，另一道圣旨停止了青苗贷款，其中说很多百姓因无力归还贷款而遭监禁鞭笞。在哲宗元祐五年（一○九○），已是二十年左右之后，苏东坡在设法挽救乡间的经济破产，请求政府归还没收的财产，宽免贫民的欠债，他的奏折中说：

> ……籍纳拘收产业……除已有人承买交业外，并特给还；未足者，许贴纳收赎，仍不限年。四方闻之，莫不鼓舞歌咏……以谓某等自失业以来，父母妻子离散，转在沟壑，久无所归。臣即看详，元初立法，本为兴置，市易以来，凡异时民间生财自养之道，一切收之公上。小民既无他业，不免与官中首尾胶固，以至供通物产，召保立限，增价出息，赊贷转变，以苟趋目前之急。及至限满，不能填偿，又理一重息罚。岁月益久，逋欠愈多。科决监锢，以逮妻孥。

在实行新法的前几年，王安石还能把惨况巧为掩饰，使神宗不明真相，坚称他的土地政策颇获农民支持，将一个极权政治渲染成民主政治，那种巧立名目，令人觉得犹如今日一样。那时，也和现在一样，人民对一个政权是否爱戴，只有在那个政权失势之后才能知道。皇帝诚心要明白真相，自己派人去察访。但是太监和那些诡诈的调查官吏，知道皇帝赞成变法，于是总是向皇帝报告百姓喜爱新政，说税吏一到，人民欢呼，若照预先布置好的欢迎会的情况说，这话当然不错。王安石在当政数年之后，可怕的情况终于在皇帝驾前泄露出来，是经由一个地位卑微的宫廷门吏的几幅画，皇帝才知道的。

那个皇宫的门吏名叫郑侠，他看见成群的农民从东北逃到京都，充塞在街道之上。他知道绘画比文章力量更大，想画几幅灾民图呈献给皇上。

一幅难民图上画的是农民身上一半裸露，忍受着饥饿，在狂风暴雨使人无法睁眼之下，在阳关大道上挣扎跋涉。另一幅画上是半裸的男女正在吃草根树皮，还有别人戴着铁链，扛着瓦砖薪柴去卖了缴税。皇帝一见，掉下泪来。这次出奇的献图（容后再叙），继之以惊人的彗星出现，中岳嵩山崩陷，神宗才废止了多项王安石的新法。

Chapter Seven
EXPERIMENT IN STATE CAPITALISM

The Su brothers arrived at the capital in 1069, in the second year of Shining, in the reign of Shentsung, the "Divine Emperor." From that year on, China was to be plunged into a wave of new social experiments amid political storms whose concussions were felt to the very end of the Sung Dynasty. This was the last of China's experiments in state captalism, though by no means the first. In the four thousand years of China's history, four great political experiments in totalitarianism, state capitalism, socialism, and drastic social reforms were attempted, and each of these failed miserably. The most successful one was the fascist totalitarianism of the philosopher Shang Yang, whose theories were effectively carried out by the first emperor of Chin, the builder of the Great Wall (third century B. C.). The outstanding two principles of this early fascist theory were the glorification of war and soldiery and the promotion of agriculture, but the two were really one because Shang Yang believed that peasants made the best soldiers and that all businessmen and traders of the bourgeois class should be suppressed as far as possible. As is well known, the powerful military machine built up and developed according to these doctrines enabled Chin to establish a dictatorship over all China; but as soon as such a theory of government was applied to the whole of the Chinese Empire, it dramatically collapsed within a few years.

Two other drastic reforms were attempted under Emperor Wu of the Han Dynasty and under Wang Mang, in the second century B.C. and the first century A.D. respectively. The first, following the finance theory of state capitalism of Sang Hungyang, successfully enriched the Emperor's treasury for his extensive wars, but was rescinded because it ended in a near rebellion; the second, under the usurper Wang Mang, ended when the usurper was over thrown. That Wang Anshih failed now in the fourth experiment is, therefore, no surprise. But in each of these four great new experiments, the idea started from an original thinker who was willing to make a complete break with the past and who combined the strength of his convictions with great determination of character. It is an interesting fact that Wang Anshih was an admirer of the fascist philosopher Shang Yang and wrote a poem pleading for a better understanding of this man. At the same time it must be noted that never was a totalitarian theory advanced, in ancient or modern days, without the basic appeal that it was for the good of the state and of the common people. How many political crimes have been committed in history in the name of "the people," the modern reader can well appreciate.

Wang Anshih was a curious man, extraordinary in mind and character. He was an industrious student, a good scholar except in his abominable philology, and certainly a major poet. Unfortunately, he combined a Messianic sense of mission with a deplorable lack of tact and inability to get along with anyone but himself. He was at the same time unquestionably an impractical idealist. If by idealist we mean a man who was negligent of his food and appearance, Wang Anshih was certainly one. He achieved a certain notoriety by his dirty dress and his unshaved and unkempt appearance. Su Shun characterized him in a rhetorical flourish as "dressed in a barbarian's robe and eating the food of pigs and dogs," and said that "he discussed history and poetry with a convict's unshaven head and unwashed face." Whether Wang Anshih loved that distinction or not we do not know, but it is easy to believe that a man so absorbed in his ideas was naturally negligent of his external looks. The story is told that he never changed his gown. One day some of his friends went with him to a bathhouse at a temple. The friends stealthily left a clean robe while he was in the bath and wanted to test whether he would find out his dress had been changed. Wang Anshih came out of his bath and put on the new robe, totally unaware of what his friends had done. Anywan, he had put on *a* robe.

Another day, his friends reported to Wang Anshih's fat wife that her husband loved shredded venison.

"I don't believe it," said his wife, greatly surprised. "He never pays any attention to his food. How could he suddenly love shredded venison? What makes you think so?"

"We know because at the dinner he did not take food from the other dishes, but finished all the shredded venison."

"But where did you put that dish?"

"Right in front of him," was the reply.

The wife understood, and said to his friends: "I tell you what. You have some other kind of food put in front of him tomorrow and see what happens."

The friends, therefore, changed the position of the dishes the next day and put the shredded venison away from him and watched him eat. Wang Anshih began to take food from the dish next to him and did not know that the deer meat was upon the table.

The story is also recorded how Wang Anshih studied all night when he was serving on a magistrate's staff at Yangchow. The chief magistrate then was Han Chi, who later became premier. Wang would read all night and doze off in the chair toward dawn. On waking up he would find that he was late and then rush to the office without washing his face or combing his hair. Han Chi noted his appearance and, thinking that he had indulged himself all night with women, gave him a piece of advice.

"Young man," he said, "I should advise you to make the best use of the years of your youth and apply yourself to studies."

Wang Anshih stood there without giving any explanation, and on departing told his friends that Han Chi did not appreciate him. Later, as Wang's fame as a scholar steadily grew, Han changed his poinion of him and accepted him as a follower, which Wang rather resented. As it happened, the year Wang accepted a high office at the capital was the year in which Han Chi quit his office as prime minister. Wang also diligently kept a diary, running to seventy volumes, and in this diary he often put in the remark that "there is nothing to Han except his fine looks."

But there is more to this strange man than his unkempt appearance. For about two decades before his rise to power, what made him most talked about was his repeated refusal to accept promotion to an office at the court. It is hard to believe that he did this for the sole purpose of earning fame, for from his twenty-first year, when he passed the examinations, to his forty-sixth, when he came into power—that is, during the most active years of his manhood, a period of twenty-five years—he steadily declined appointments and always preferred to serve as a minor magistrate in the outlying provinces. It was during the reign of Jentsung, a very good period when all distinguished talents who could do so gathered at the court. The more Wang Anshih refused an offer of a good post, the more his fame grew. Finally it got to the point where all the officials at the court were dying to have a look at this man. For besides distinguishing himself by his literary compositions, he had proved himself an able administrator as a magistrate. He had built dams, reformed schools, established loans for the farmers, and put into practice some of his new social ideas. It was a good administrative record and the people liked him. Enticements for him to come to the capital were without avail, and it was not until he was offered a job on the board of finance that he was attracted to the capital, in 1060. It is clear that this man was primarily interested in economics and finance and felt he could do most for the country along this line. Then his mother died and he had to retire; but even after the mourning period was over, when he was called to the court again, he refused the offer and remained away at Nanking.

This period of his self-imposed obscurity is difficult to understand, for the man certainly believed that he had great things to do for the country when the time came, and it would have been logical for him to have built up his official career during the period of his manhood. Perhaps the competition of great scholars at the capital was too great for him, for there were certainly older, better, and sounder scholars, such as Fan Chungyen, Szema Kuang, Ouyang Shiu, Tseng Kungliang, and others, who were inclined to look askance at any radical reforms and who commanded sufficient popular prestige to discourage any young man with newfangled ideas. Wang Anshih bided his time. But I think psychologically there was another reason. A man of Wang's temperament had to be the boss wherever he was, and when serving as a magistrate in an outlying district, he was the big frog in a little puddle. Again and again, when he was in the capital holding some office for a short time, he quarreled with his colleagues and upset everything. He wanted to change the rules and run things in his own way. Wu Kuei and Chang Fangping both recalled such experiences of difficult co-operation with him as a colleague or even as a junior official.

In 1060, therefore, he had come to the capital as a rather strange phenomenon. He had written good prose and poems. He had original ideas and was a good talker. The high-ranking old officials such as Fu

Pi and Wen Yenpo had the best opinion of him, and even Ouyang Shiu liked him. Here was a singular man beneath whose strange appearance lay talents and character the officials could not quite fathom. Among the few people who saw through Wang Anshih's character and considered him a great danger to the country were Su Shun and his old friend Chang Fangping. The latter had worked with him as a colleague in supervising certain local examinations, had dismissed him and never talked with him again. He must have told Su Shun about his experiences with Wang in his early days. The two, therefore, intensely disliked Wang, the more for what they considered his affectations in dress and habits. Ouyang Shiu had introduced Wang to Tungpo's father, and Wang himself was desirous of making the acquaintance of the Sus, but Su senior refused to see him. When Wang's mother died, of all the invited guests, Su Shun refused to attend the funeral and wrote the famous *Pien Chien Lun*, or "Essay on the Hypocrite," one of the most popular essays for school reading today.

In this essay Su Shun started by pointing out how difficult it was to know a man's character and how often even clever people were deceived. Only the quiet observer could see through a man's character and foretell his future development. He quoted an ancient scholar who was able to foretell about Wang Yen when the latter was a brilliant young man distinguished for his appearance, and another great general who was able to foretell about Lu Chi, who was more or less responsible for bringing an end to the Tang Dynasty. Lu Chi was a scheming person of great ability but so fearfully ugly that, in receiving him, the host had to dismiss all his female entertainers for fear that the women would be shocked or would offend him by ill-concealed titters. But, says Su Shun, each of these separately would not have been enough of a personality to ruin an empire, had it not been for the weak-minded emperors under whom they came into power. Now, however, a man had appeared who combined the ugliness and scheming ability of a Lu Chi and the eloquence of a Wang Yen. "Here is a man who discourses on Confucius and Laotse and lives the life of the famous recluses, who associates himself with disgruntled persons and establishes a group for mutual admiration which declares to the world, A sage has arrived!' His cunning and his dark scheming mind lead him toward strange ways." Such a person could deceive the most discerning ruler and be a great danger to the state if he should ever come into power. "It is natural for a man to want to wash his face when it is dirty and to send his filthy garments to the laundry. Not so with this man! He wears a barbarian's robe and eats the food of pigs and dogs and discusses poetry and history with a convict's unshaved head and unwashed face. Now is this natural? A man who does not act according to common human nature must be a great hypocrite and a scheming intriguer." Su Shun hoped that his prophecy was wrong, that he could be like a good general who defeats an enemy before the battle. But, he said, "if my prophecy goes wrong, people will think that these words are exaggerated and the man himself will complain of his fate. Nobody then will be aware of the calamity he could have brought upon the nation. But if these words come true, the country will be plunged into a dire calamity, and I shall be honored as a wise prophet—a sad consolation indeed!"

Whether Wang's strange habits were an affectation or not it is impossible to decide; but when a person overdoes a thing, people are inclined to suspect there is an element of conscious self-advertisement in it. If we may believe Shao Powen, Emperor Jentsung had the same suspicion. One day, at an imperial dinner given for the ministers, the guests were to catch their own fish for dinner from a pond. Before the dinner, fish bait, in the form of little pills, was laid out on gold plates on the table. Wang was not interested in fishing and began to eat the fish bait from the table and finished the plate. The next day, the Emperor said to the prime minister, "Wang Anshih is a fake. A person may well eat one pill by mistake, but no one will in a state of absent-mindedness finish them all." According to the sotry, that was the reason why Jentsung never liked Wang. In Wang's private diaries, he was also particularly hard against Jentsung.

In view of later developments, Su Shun was right. Somehow in all countries, cranks and crackpots and schizophrenics have always believed that slovenliness is the mark of genius and that the best assurance of immortality is the refusal to dress like a gentleman. There is also a curious notion that filth and squalor imply contempt for material surroundings and therefore high spirituality, the logical conclusion of which is that heaven must reek with stinking angels.

When this essay was written, Su Tungpo said that both he and his brother thought the condemnation too extreme. Only Chang Fangping heartily approved. However, very soon Su Tungpo's contemporaries were to find out how true the prediction was; and the essay survives to this day, revealing the uncanny insight of the old father.[1]

Very soon after he assumed office on the board of finance, Wang Anshih tried to test the political ground under him. Emperor Jentsung was ruling at this time, and Wang submitted to him a long memorial on governmental policies, running to about ten thousand words. In this document he enunciated the basic principles of his financial reform, the principles of "using the nation's power to produce the nation's wealth, and using the nation's wealth to provide for the nation's expenditure." He said

---

[1] Incorporated in a tomb inscription of Su Shun, written by Chang Fangping. Some scholars who wish to defend Wang Anshih try very hard to prove that this piece was a forgery, by pointing out that it was not included in Su Shun's works. Su Tungpo's own testimony, however, confirmed its genuineness.

that since the beginning of the dynasty, the government had suffered from insufficient revenue, and this resulted from the lack of a good financial and economic policy. Such a policy had not been thought of only because there were no men great enough to deal with the problems. The men in power at the time, he said, were not "great" enough for this job, nor did he think that there were other talents in the country who could be called into power. He cleverly pointed out that in making radical reforms, one should connect them with the practices of the ancient kings so that people would not regard them as a radical departure from the past. But then, he said, in following the tradition of the past, one should not copy the methods of the ancient kings, but rather their intentions, which were, after all, only for the good of the people, no matter how the policies differed. On the whole, it was a very well-written and well-organized treatise on political reforms, covering every aspect of government, including finance, civil service, and even education.

If Wang Anshih wanted to test his political ground, he found that the ground yielded under his feet. After reading the long memorandum, Emperor Jentsung laid it aside and let it sleep. During the short four-year reign of the following emperor, Ingtsung, Wang was once recalled, but again he declined office. Historians usually give the reason that he felt uneasy because he had advised against the nomination of Ingtsung as successor to Jentsung, who had died without an heir.

Meanwhile, Ingtsung's son, who was to succeed him, was living at the capital as crown prince; he latter became the Emperor Shentsung, under whose regime Wang Anshih came to power. While he was the crown prince, Han Wei, a great admirer of Wang Anshih, was his secretary. Han would express certain views on government, and whenever the Crown Prince liked them, he would say, "This is not my own opinion, but that of Wang Anshih." The Crown Prince, therefore, developed a very high opinion of Wang, and hoped one day he would be able to utilize his great political talents. In 1067, as soon as he ascended the throne at the age of twenty, he had Wang appointed chief magistrate of Nanking, and in September again promoted him, to the rank of a *hanlin* scholar. Wang was in constant communication with his friend and was convinced that now his opportunity had come. Contrary to his previous practice, he accepted the post at once. But he delayed coming to the capital for seven months.

"This Anshih has always declined an appointment and refused to come to the capital in the previous reigns," said Emperor Shentsung. "Some people thought he was impudent, and now again he does not come, giving illness as his excuse. Is he really ill, or is he fishing for a better post?"

At this time there was great jealousy between two veteran officials, Tseng Kungliang and Han Chi. The latter had served successively as premier and privy councilor under three emperors and was becoming too powerful. In his endeavor to shake Han Chi's position, Tseng Kungliang hoped to find in the person of Wang Anshih a powerful ally for himself. He assured the Emperor that Wang had the true caliber of a prime minister and that His Majesty should believe in him. On the other hand, another high official, Wu Kuei, who had known Wang Anshih intimately, warned the Emperor that if Wang should ever be given power he would plunge the whole country into chaos.

Finally, in April 1068, Wang Anshih, having been assured of the Emperor's attitude, appeared at the capital and was ordered to go into imperial audience with special permission to "speak out of rank;" i.e., without observance of protocol.

"What is the most important thing to do in a government?" asked the Emperor.

"To choose the right policy," answered Wang.

"What do you think of Emperor Taitsung of Tang?" asked the Emperor again, referring to the most beloved emperor of that dynasty.

"Your Majesty should take the emperors Yao and Shun, and not merely Tang Taitsung as your standard. The principles of Yao and Shun are really very easy to put into practice. Because the scholars of the latter days do not really understand them, they think that the standards of such a government are unattainable." (Yao and Shun were the emperors idealized by Confucius, ruling China in the semi-legendary era of the twenty-third and twenty-second centuries B.C.)

The Emperor said with some satisfaction, but modestly, "You are expecting too much of me. I am afraid I cannot live up to your high expectations."

But then there came a time for Wang Anshih to have a private audience with the Emperor alone, when the other officials had been dismissed. Here was a great chance for Wang Anshih.

"Sit down," said the Emperor. "I want to have a long talk with you." His Majesty then began to ask him why two famous emperors, one of them Tang Taitsung, had to secure two famous scholars as their premiers to run the government. One of the two premiers mentioned was none other than Chuko Ling, probably the most renowned and capable administrator in history. Again Wang Anshih brought the discussion around to the topic of the legendary emperors of three thousand years ago. Wang said that he preferred to talk of the able assistants of the emperors Yao and Shun. "Chuko Liang is not worth talking about in the opinion of the best minds." Chuko Ling's political genius consisted in proceeding step by step toward a definite goal, which hardly suited the impatient, self-confident wizard of finance.

"Your Majesty," continued Wang, "is now reigning over a vast empire with a huge population. After a century of peace, with so many scholars all over the land, is it not strange that no worthy men have arisen to assist Your Majesty in the government? The reason must be that Your Majesty has no decided policy and has not shown confidence in men. Though there may be great talents living at present, like those who assisted Emperors Yao and Shun, they will soon lay down their office because of obstruction by petty politicians."

"There are petty politicians in every regime," said the Emperor. "Even in the reigns of Yao and Shun there were the famous Four Evil Monsters."

"Exactly," Wang agreed. "It was because the emperors Yao and Shun knew the four wicked ministers for what they were and had them killed that they were then able to accomplish what they did. If the four evil ministers had remained at court to carry on their machinations and intrigues, the good and able ministers would have left, too."

Shentsung, the "Divine Emperor," was duly impressed. He was only twenty, and like all young men was very ambitious and wanted to make his country strong and prosperous. He was a good and just man and he had a round and well-proportioned face, like those of his imperial ancestors. It was not until after Shentsung that the emperors of the Sung Dynasty began to show distinctly degenerate traits in their physiognomy. His young enthusiasm was fired by the high expectations that Wang Anshih had entertained of him, and from that conversation on, the young emperor was ready to go through fire and water to carry through this man's political doctrines, even if it cost him all the other ministers— which was what happened. Somehow images of the "Four Evil Monsters" appeared in the young emperor's mind whenever the wise old ministers offered counsel and advised caution against Wang Anshih's proposed reforms.

In February 1069, when the Su brothers arrived at the capital, Wang Anshih was appointed a vice-premier. The next two years were to see an exodus of all the old ministers from the courst, the purging of the imperial censorate and the packing of it with Wang Anshih's own underlings. No sooner had Wang assumed office than he began to sweep the whole governmental household with a wide new broom. Protest followed protest and the whole officialdom was thrown into a deep turmoil. There was great and outspoken opposition from all ministers of proved ability and respected character. The young emperor could not understand it. Wang Anshih managed, however, to make him see the turmoil and the uproar in the light of a desperate struggle struggle between the Emperor himself and the wicked ministers who dared to oppose his will.

"Why all this hubbub?" asked the Emperor. "Why is it that all the great ministers, censors, and scholars of the court are lined up against the new reforms?"

"You should understand," said Wang Anshih, "that Your Majesty is trying to follow the great teachings of the ancient emperors, but in order to do this you have to overcome the reactionaries. It is inevitable, therefore, that there will be a struggle for power between Your Majesty and the reactionaries. If they win in the struggle, the government will be in their hands, and if Your Majesty wins, then the power of the government will rest in the hands of Your Majesty. These selfish men are trying to obstruct the will of Your Majesty in carrying out the great teachings of the ancient emperors. That is why there is all this hubbub."

Given the earnest desire of an ambitious young ruler to make his country powerful and strong, and a premier who had an overweening confidence in his own political and financial theories, the stage was set for launching the radical reforms of Wang Anshih. The motives of such reforms cannot be questioned. It is perfectly true that the Sung Dynasty, coming after fifty years of disunity and internecine strife, had never known a strong government. Besides, the Shishias, the Kitans (later called the Liaos), and the Kins had been making constant inroads into China's northern border. Brief wars with these northern tribes were followed by temporary treaties of uneasy peace. The terms of the treaties were humiliating to a Chinese emperor, for while some of these kingdoms acknowledge the emperor, it was not they but the emperor who had to give annual contributions in silver and silks to the northern tribes, running anywhere from a hundred thousand to a quarter of a million dollars a year. This acted as a tremendous drain on the imperial treasury. The domestic administration had always been lax, and the government was constantly running into financial deficits. Wang Anshih believed that he was a great financial wizard who could raise money for the imperial treasury by juggling with the systems of taxation and conscription. I believe that the desire to build China into a powerful state and to increase the prestige of the empire through wars of conquest in the northwest were prime factors in influencing the young emperor Shentsung in Wang Anshih's favor, for Wang's administration was characterized by several wars started by China with the northern tribes, some victories and one disastrous defeat. In order to carry on wars, the Emperor needed money, and in order to have money, the country's financial system had to be reorganized. Yet, without ever questioning the sincere motives of the reformer, we shall see how these reforms, financial and economic in character, produced the most grievous consequences of a different nature.

Soon after Wang Anshih had arrived at the capital, Szema Kuang had an argument with him in the Emperor's presence which seems to sum up the fundamental opposition of the two sides. The imperial treasury was actually impoverished at this time, and during an important ceremony at the worship of Heaven in spring, the Emperor wished to dispense with the customary gifts of silver and silks to the officials, thus saving some money for the imperial household. This started an argument between Szeman Kuang and Wang Anshih. Wang Anshih maintained that the national treasury was impoverished only because the officials did not understand finance.

"What you mean by finance," countered Szema Kuang, "is only increase of taxation and levies from the people."

"No," said Wang Anshih. "A good financier can increase the

government revenue without increasing taxation."

"What nonsense! After all, a nation possesses a definite amount of wealth, and this wealth is either in the hands of the people or in those of the government. No matter what measures you carry out or by what names you call them, they can only mean taking away part of the wealth of the people and giving it to the government."

The Emperor was inclined to agree with Szema Kuang, and for a month or two the measures were held in abeyance.

Without being an economist, one is safe to accept the general thesis that the two factors in a nation's wealth are production and distribution. To increase a nation's wealth, one must increase its productivity or have a better distribution of goods. In Wang Anshih's day, however, increase of production was out of the question, since there was no means of industrialization. Therefore, all that a financial wizard could do would be in the line of distribution. Since Wang was primarily interested in enriching the national treasury, increase of the nation's wealth strictly meant the increase of the government's revenue. Wang saw clearly that the rich merchants and landlords were making money in a system of free enterprise, and he could not see why the government should not take away the profits from free enterprise and run business and make the money itself. The conclusion was inevitable. The terms he used were actually strikingly modern. He wanted to stop "monopoly" (*chienping*)by capital; he wanted to equalize wealth by "taking it away from the rich and giving it to the poor;" he wanted to prevent the peasants from borrowing from landlords at high interest. It would be a great and charitable measure on the part of the government to lend money to the peasants during spring planting and have them return the money when the crops were harvested. Wang Anshih was able to convince the Emperor that all these measures were "for the good of the people;" but history records that after a period of hesitancy, the thing that decided him on launching the loans was the argument of a certain minor official that with an investment of half a million dollars, the government stood to earn a quarter of a million dollars in interest per year, since there were two crops and the twenty or thirty per cent interest could be collected twice a year.

Without going too much into the details of the various reforms, which were started in 1069 and ended disastrously about eight years later when both Wang Anshih himself and the Emperor were thoroughly sick of them and of each other, we may give a brief summary of these measures.

The most important and the best know were nine in number, which I have for the sake of convenience arranged in three groups. There were three state capitalist enterprises, three new taxes, and three systems of registration for a complete regimentation and control of the people. The three state capitalist enterprises were: a government bureau for national trade, a bureau for government stores in retail trade, and the famous loans to the farmers with an official interest of twenty per cent and an actual interest of thirty per cent (i.e., plus application and registration charges). The three new taxes were the draft exemption tax, the excise tax, and the income tax. The systems of registration were the organizing of all citizens into groups of ten families for military draft (the *paochia*), and the re-registration of land and of horses. In general, all these measures suggest the tendency to economic collectivism of modern days.

The state capitalist enterprises began in July 1069 with the establishing of a bureau for national or interprovincial wholesale trade. Convinced of the great profits to accrue to the government, the Emperor allocated a sum of five million dollars in cash and thirty million bushels of rice as capital with which the government would take over the interprovincial trade in goods and raw materials. Immediately this system ran into practical difficulties. In February of the same year a bureau of economic planning was established, charged with the duty of studying the plans and programs before promulgation. Among the staff of the planning bureau was Su Tungpo's brother, Tseyu. In his memorandum Tseyu pointed out that when the government took over the national trade, free enterprise would at once be paralyzed, for local dealers would be handicapped in competition with the government. It was inevitable that the government and the businessmen would be treading on each other's toes. Moreover, he denied that the imperial treasury stood to gain. While private business worked through an established system of credits and other arrangements, the government lacked these facilities. It must first set up a big staff with high salaries and beautiful office buildings. It would not be doing business according to supply and demand but instead would make transactions on the merit of commissions, distributing favors and contracts according to personal connections. Tseyu argued that, short of forcing down the price of its purchases by official pressure, through sheer bureaucratic incompetence the government would buy at a higher price than independent businessmen were able to get. Therefore it stood to lose.

This so-called government wholesale trade was, therefore, stopped for a year's further study; then the government came out with a modified program under a new name. The division between wholesale and retail was not a hard and fast one, and trade bureaus in charge of the large government-run stores were established in big cities such as Chengtu, Canton, and Hangchow. Another government grant of a million dollars from the national treasury and $870,000 in the local currency of the capital was allocated for the development of these trade bureaus. The reasons advanced for their establishment were that "the country's goods had fallen into the hands of capital monopolists" and that "the prices of goods fluctuated from time to time because of capitalist manipulations; in order to rule the country peacefully, one should take away the wealth from the rich and give it to the poor." A very capable official was put at the head, and the more profits he was able to report to the government, the more capable he was considered to be. This Lu Chiawen became a kind of trade dictator of the country, having monopoly control of the small businessmen. The rules of the trade bureau at the capital, for instance, were that the small traders were to become affiliated members of the bureau; that these small traders could pool their goods with the bureau's assets, or that the government would provide the capital for purchasing stocks for the stores run by them; that in case traders wished to liquidate their business and hand over the goods to the government bureau they would be permitted to do so; that they could use part of their goods as security for cash advances from the government for which they were to pay an interest of ten per cent per half year or twenty per cent a year; that others not connected with the bureau would also be permitted to sell their stocks to it at prices fixed by the government; and that, finally, all imperial purchases, by whatever department, would be transacted through the trade bureau.

The government's absorption of small business was one of the worst features of the regime, and private business came almost to a standstill. In a few years trade and commerce actually decreased so that the government revenue was affected to an alarming degree, in spite of the theoretical high profits. The Emperor found himself, to his great disgust, degenerating in the eyes of the people into a petty peddler selling fruits, ice and coal, calendars, and straw mats. In the end it was the scandal connected with the trade bureau at the capital and the excise tax that reached the ears of the imperial household and caused the Emperor to put a stop to the most unpopular features of the reform.

But the most widely known of the new reforms in this regime was the farmers' loans, and to this day when people speak of Wang Anshih's reforms they always think first of these loans. It was a measure that affected every village of the empire and precipitated the biggest political battle among the ministers at the court. In itself the plan was good and sound, suggesting the idea of a farmers' bank. While serving as a young magistrate, Wang Anshih had made loans to the farmers during spring planting and collected them with interest when the harvest was in. He had found that this was a real help to the farmers because in a local administration he could see to it that the farmers come to borrow money only in actual cases of need, and upon proper personal investigation. In Shensi the local authorities also tried this scheme with success, and it was from the practice started in Shensi that the farmers' loans received their Chinese name of "seedling loans."

In a good year, when the authorities were sure of good crops, they made loans to enable the farmers to purchase equipment and seedlings for their wheat fields; and when the harvest came, they were able to collect grains for the army with an advantageous interest. In the words of the bureau of economic planning, "It is proposed that the money and grain from the price equalization granaries be loaned to people upon application, following the example of Shensi province. They may be asked to pay an interest of twenty per cent, which they will pay together with the capital during the collection of the summer and autumn taxes. People who wish to repay the loans in cash in place of grain may be permitted to do so. In case of natural calamities, they may be permitted to delay the repayment until a good year comes. Thus not only will the people be able to tide over famine and drought, but through these loans they will be spared the necessity of borrowing from the rich exploiters at double interest before their harvest is in. Besides, the stocks of wheat and grain are now usually kept in the price equalization granaries for a long time and sold to the people only when the prices have gone up, and this system benefits only the idle rich who live in the cities. It is proposed now that such sales and purchases be organized and unified within each province, so that price stabilization may be better carried out and the farmers enabled to plant their farms without being exploited. All this is for the benefit of the people and without profits to the government. It is in accordance with the principles of the ancient kings in giving money to the people and assisting the farmers."

How such a beautiful and innocent plan turned out to harass and destroy the lives and homes of the farmers for whose benefit it was conceived, we shall see later. It should be explained, however, that this new measure started as a continuation of the old system of the price equalization granaries and gradually replaced it. From the very beginning of this dynasty, such granaries had been maintained in different districts by the government to stabilize the price of grains. In years of good crops, when low prices hit the farmers hard, the government bought up the surplus wheat and rice. Conversely, in bad years, when the prices of grain went up, the agencies poured the grain into the market to force the prices down. It is true that the agencies were not always kept up to their highest efficiency, for many officials did not bother to buy up grain when it was cheap. But even in 1066 the published figures of the price equalization granaries showed that they had bought from the people 5,014,180 bushels of grain and sold 4,711,570 bushels during that year. Now, when the money and stocks of the granaries were used as capital for the farmers' loans, the normal operations of the granaries were naturally stopped.

The heart of the matter was that the subscription of the loans inevitably became compulsory. Intolerant of opposition, Wang Anshih had to succeed. He had to show the Emperor that the loans were a great success and were welcomed by the people. He would not hear of slackness in selling them. He could not understand why the farmers should not want the loans, and when loans were not sold up to the quota, he flew into a rage. He began to promote officials who showed a good record, and to punish the slackers. As each official was looking out for his own career, his most important concern was to make a good report. The incentive for personal competition was very much like the selling of government bonds in modern days. When the officials knew that they would be cashiered and degraded for "blocking reforms" if they did not sell up to their quota, it was inevitable that loans began to be allocated by official pressure, by what Wang was pleased to call the "energetic" officials. Every family had to borrow from the government, and everybody had to pay thirty per cent interest for a period of three months. There were good officials who knew what harm these loans were causing the poor people and the certainty of their being put in jail for failure to repay capital and interest. These took the government at its word and announced to the public that these loans, according to the imperial decree, were strictly "voluntary;" and they were prepared to be degraded for "blocking reforms" when the day of reckoning came.

In the draft exemption tax also, there was a great discrepancy between official intentions and actual practice. This was probably the best reform put through by Wang Anshih, and it was this measure which Su Tungpo alone defended against his own party, when the latter was in power and was determined to wipe out each and every one of Wang Anshih's reforms.

For a long time the people of China had been subjected to conscription for military service. The proposal was that the people should pay a tax in place of the conscription. In other words, in meant replacing a military draft system by a standing army of hired and paid soldiers. However, from a careful study of the rules of this draft exemption, one cannot escape the conclusion that the government was primarily interested in the revenue from the tax, and whatever benefit it had in relieving the people from military draft was nullified entirely by the *paochia* system which was even worse as a form of compulsory draft. After careful deliberation for over a year, the regulations were published. They provided that families which had been exempt from the military draft were also compelled to pay the draft exemption tax; for example, widows, families without children or with only one son or with children not of age, and nuns and monks, were compelled to pay the tax under a different name, called "the draft-aid tax." Moreover, twenty per cent was added to the regular tax over and above district draft quotas, nominally to provide against the bad years when the people might not be able to pay. With the money collected from this tax, soldiers and other employees of the government were to be hired. Just as Su Tseyu had pointed out in the case of the farmers' loans that the people would be put in prison and whipped for default, so Szema Kuang pointed out now exactly what happened later, that people who had no cash to pay this tax in autumn and summer—when all the other taxes came—would be compelled to sell their grain, kill their cows, and cut down trees in order to obtain the cash. Moreover, in the preceding system of military draft, the people took turns serving for a period of years, whereas in the new system the people were compelled to pay for exemption every year, including the years when they would not have to serve.

Together with the new excise tax and the income tax, this draft exemption tax must be viewed principally as a new means to raise revenue from the people, rather than to relieve them of the draft for service, since the people were drafted for military training under another name, the paochia. The excise tax was a tax on the profits of businessmen, based on an examination of their books. The income tax was not an income tax in the modern sense. I call it income tax here because it was a system of compulsory registration of a citizen's income and property as a basis for allocation of the other taxes. It was like the income tax also in the sense that the people had to make returns of their income and property, under pain of defrauding the government. In the fight over this reform it was stated that after the order was issued, there was "not a chicken or a pig on a farm, or an inch of soil, or a beam or rafter in a roof" that was not reported and registered with the government. This last measure, instituted in 1074, was short-lived because Wang soon went out of power; and even before its suspension Su Tungpo refused to enforce it in the district under his control on the ground that it was illegal.

What gave the lie to Wang Anshih's desire to relieve the people from military draft, professed in the preceding draft exemption tax, was the *paochia* system. This is clear because both the new *paochia* system and the draft exemption tax were promulgated in the same month, December 1070. The government took away the burden of military service from the people with one hand by making them pay for the "exemption," and put it back on the people with the other. The *poachia* was a system for collective guarantee under the law of families living in the same neighborhood. Each ten families were organized into a *pao*, and each fifty families formed a great *pao*. The members of a *pao* were to be collectively responsible in cases of harboring criminals and thieves; and in cases of such crimes as murder and rape they were bound to report the circumstances to the court. Able-bodied persons in each great *pao* were to be organized into a company for military drill and training, a family with two able-bodied males contributing one, and a family of more than two males contributing more in proportion. These were to leave their farms for drill every fifth day, the five-day period being the ancient equivalent of the week, dividing a month conveniently into six periods. Thus instead of taking the sons of the families to the army as in the regular draft system, this reform brought the army right into the village. But Wang Anshih was a great propagandist; he knew that by giving a thing a new name, he made it cease to exist. "Conscription was abolished."

Besides this collective registration and regimentation of the people, there was also a new and compulsory registration of the farmers' lands as a basis for the new taxes, and a system of farming out the government's cavalry to be cared for by the farmers. Like all other collectivistic systems, Wang Anshih's administration could not leave the people alone. In its anxiety to take good care of them, the government had to know exactly what the people did and what they possessed. Like all other collectivistic systems also, this regime found it impossible to govern without secret agents, which were instituted in the year 1072, luckily after Su Tungpo had left the capital. Nor was it able to operate without bringing under control the imperial censorate, the equivalent of the modern press, and packing it with the party's underlings who were willing to follow strictly the party line. Again, Wang Anshih considered it necessary to control the thoughts and ideas of the scholars. Like Wang Mang of the ancient days, and like the modern Hitler, he had the idea of one state, one belief, and one leader. Like Hitler, he exploded in fits of temper when he encountered opposition; modern psychiatrists might classify him as a paranoiac.

What showed the "paranoid" character of the man, and what all historians and critics agree to have been his one inexcusable act, was not any of his political or socialistic ventures, but his setting up himself now as the one and only interpreter of the classics. As Wang Mang re-edited and falsified the ancient classics, so now Wang Anshih worte his own interpretation of three Confucian classics and made it the official guide to thinking, to replace all the great commentators of the past. Wang was a fairly good scholar, but not good enough to replace the great masters of the past, such as Cheng Shüan, Ma Yung, Lu Tehming, and others. To do this was both an abuse of his official power and an insult to scholarship. The examination papers were usually upon passages from the classics, and candidates' interpretations had to conform. Setting up this new standard, therefore, meant that every scholar of the land had to study and absorb what Wang Anshih said on every topic, from principles of government and Buddhist-colored Confucianism to the etymology for "quail," "owl," and "pheasant." After leaving the capital, Su Tungpo had once to supervise a local examination, and wrote a poem recording his disgust with the deadening uniformity of thought and ideas expressed by the candidates in the papers.

Like his philology, Wang's New *Commentaries* on the Three Classics, often savoring of Buddhist ideas, showed more originality than sound scholarship. He believed, however, that in the interpretation of the ancient ideas and political systems, whatever he thought was so must therefore be so. These *Commentaries* were so bad that they were soon forgotten after his death, and no copy has been preserved. But while he was in power, they were the bible of the scholar candidates at the examinations; the slightest variation from the interpretation of the premier was enough to disqualify a paper. Particularly it showed offense to scholarship to have the compilation of the *Commentaries* made in only two years; the work was formally started in March 1073, with the help of his young son and a political henchman, and published in June 1075. This hurried piece of work was set up as the orthodox interpretation of Confucianism, and as Wang changed his mind about the interpretations, new versions were published for the benefit of the scholar candidates who knew their lives depended on keeping abreast of the revisions.

This is not the place to discuss Wang Anshih's scholarship, a subject rather painful for Su Tungpo because he was by far the sounder scholar. But it may be mentioned that Wang Anshih's "etymology" was indescribably funny, as all amateurish etymology is. Besides the *Commentaries on the Three Classics*, the great rage among the scholars of the time was the fashion for discussing etymology started by Wang Anshih. This "etymology" was really a study of the structure and origin of the written characters, not by the comparative method, but by the lively use of one's fancy. Wang believed this to be his most original and lasting contribution to learning and continued to work on it in his old age, completing it in twenty-five volumes. Western scholars can understand how easy it is to compose twenty-five volumes on etymology once the scholar lets his imagination go without checking it by scientific methods—the methods used, for instance, by Han and Ching dynasty scholars. For "fanciful etymology" can be spun out of pure fantasy at the rate of a dozen a day. It was easy and it was a great deal of fun to try to read into the composition of a Chinese character all sorts of reasons why a particular combination of certain components should come to be the symbol for a certain meaning. Some fifty items of Wang Anshih's etymology have survived to this day, chiefly as after-dinner pleasantries. Many jokes that passed between Su Tungpo and Wang Anshih hinged on these "etymologies."

Su Tungpo loved to use the method of *reductio ad absurdum*. There is a Chinese world, meaning turtledove. It is composed of two elements, "nine" and "bird." Clearly the element "nine" is phonetic, because both "nine" and "turtledove" are pronounced *chiu*. Wang Anshih, however, ran riot over the phonetics of the elements in his desire to make something interesting out of their meaning. Su Tungpo one day, in the course of a chat, asked Wang Anshih, "By the way, why is the word turtledove written with the elements nine and bird?" Wang was stumped. "I can tell you why," said Su Tungpo. "The Book of Poetry says [in a poem of satire]:

'O turtledove! O turtledove!
He has seven young.'

The seven young plus their two parents, make nine, don't you see?"

The character for "waves" or "ripples" is written with the classifier radical designating water, and a phonetic component which happens to denote skin. It struck Wang's fertile imagination that the character for ripples was so constructed because "ripples were the skin of water." Su Tungpo met him one day and wittily remarked, "If so, then the word for

slippery must be constructed that way because it means the *bones of water.*"
(The phonetic component in this case happens to mean bones). Wang
Anshih violated the very elementary principles of the structure of the
Chinese literary symbols. The way he mutilated a "root," riving it in half
and misconnecting it with another component, as he did in the character
for "rich" (*fu*), would make any philologist weep.

Some Chinese scholars of later days, following Western ideas of
collectivism, have tried to rescue Wang Anshih from historical infamy
and revise his reputation upward by showing that his ideas were
essentially "in conformity with modern socialism."[1] Among those
who took up the defense of Wang Anshih was a great modern scholar,
Liang Chichao. It would be possible to argue the pros and cons of
Wang's socialistic ideas, but Wang's socialistic regime must be judged
by its results. The facts are that in place of "private monopoly" the
state set up its own monopoly; small businessmen were thrown out of
jobs, and farmers, unable to repay the compulsory loans or keep up the
interest, sold their wives and children or fled, an their neighbors who
were made guarantors of the loans fled with them or sold or mortgaged
their properties. The country jails were full, every district government
found thousands of closed mortgages and confiscated properties on its
hands, and lawsuits filled the courts. It was a misrule that would have
ruined any dynasty, even if there were no foreign invaders. In 1074
an imperial edict said that business was at a standstill and people were
thrown out of their jobs; and another edict in 1076, which stopped the
loans, said that many were jailed and flogged for failure to repay them.
In a memorandum sent in June 1090, some twenty years later, when he
was trying to salvage the economic wreckage left of the countryside and
begging for restoration of confiscated properties and forgiveness of all

---

[1] For the argument advanced in defense of Wang,
see brief statement in Section K, Bibliography.

debts of the poor, Su Tungpo wrote:

"Since the order to return the confiscated properties, the people are overjoyed. They have said to me that since they were driven out from their homes and business, parents have been separated from their children and wives from their husbands, living the life of homeless, wandering refugees. Since the establishment of the trade bureaus and government stores, all means of livelihood of the people have been taken over by the government. The small traders, deprived of their normal trade, were forced to join up with the government trade bureaus and compelled to mortgage their goods and properties to obtain immediate cash at a high interest. When the loans matured and they were not able to repay, they were fined double interest. Gradually their debts piled higher and higher, and more and more people were put in jail together with their families."

For the first few years, however, Wang Anshih was able to keep the Emperor in the dark about the terrible conditions by adroit propaganda, insisting he had the "people's support" for his "agrarian program" and painting a totalitarian regime as a "democracy"—a confusion of terms strangely reminiscent of modern days. Then as now, whether a people love a regime or not can be judged only when a despotic regime is no longer in power. Sincere in his desire to learn the truth, the Emperor sent out his own reporters. But knowing that the reforms were popular with the Emperor himself, the eunuchs and dishonest reporters always reported to the Emperor that the people loved the reforms, and that upon the arrival of the tax commissioners, the "people cried with joy," which was literally true, as far as a staged reception was concerned. The terrible conditions of the people after a few years of Wang Anshih's regime were at last revealed to the Emperor in the form of pictures submitted by a curious, obscure palace gatekeeper, a very daring man.

Standing at the gate, this official, Cheng Shia, saw the hordes of refugees who had fled from the northeast and were swarming the streets of the capital. Knowing that pictures spoke louder than words, Cheng Shia conceived the idea of making pictures of these poor farmers and presenting them to the Emperor. Here was a picture of the refugees, half clad and starving, traveling on the highway in a blinding storm. There was a picture of half-naked men and women eating grass roots and tree bark, and others working in chains carrying bricks and firewood to sell to pay the taxes. Upon seeing the pictures, the Emperor shed tears. It was this dramatic presentation, which we shall come to later, coupled with the appearance of a spectacular comet and a landslide on a sacred mountain, that made the Emperor suspend many of the "reforms."

第八章　拗相公

　　一场政治风暴现在刮起来了，就要引起燎原的大火，会把宋室焚毁。这场风暴始于国家资本主义者，人称之为"拗相公"的王安石和他的反对派之间的一次斗争。王安石的反对派包括所有的其他官吏，也就是贤德的仁宗皇帝，在思想自由的气氛中拔擢培养、留作领导国政的一代人才。我们需要了解那次政争的性质，因为那种朋党之争笼罩了苏东坡的一生。

　　中国最早的通俗文学至今尚存在者，其中有一篇预示中国小说的来临，是一个短篇小说，叫《拗相公》。那是宋朝通俗文学的短篇小说集，新近才发现，这足以表示，王安石死后不久，在通俗文学之中，他便以其外号为人所知了。那场政争的悲剧之发生，就由于一个人个性上的缺点，他不能接受忠言，他不愿承认自己犯错。朋友对王安石的反对，只增强了他贯彻他那政策的决心。有人告诉我们，说个性坚强是一种重要的美德，但是却需要予以精确的说明：就是说坚强的个性是用去做什么事。王安石很可能还记得学生时代曾听见一个平常的格言，说"决心"为成功的秘诀，自己却把固执当作那种美德了。王安石在世时，他在文学界是以"三不足"为人所知的。"三不足"就是"天命不足畏，众言不足从，祖宗之法不足用"。这是苏东坡赠予他的标志。

这位"拗相公"不容任何方面有人反对，朋友方面，或是敌人方面。他能言善道，能说动皇帝相信他的强国之策，决心要把他的计划进行到底。这就暗示他要压制一般的反对意见，尤其是谏官的话。谏官的职责本来就是批评朝廷的政策和行动，并充当舆论与朝廷之间的桥梁。中国政治哲学的基础，是好政府必然是"广开言路"，而坏政府则不然。所以开始论到新政之后，自然争论迅即涌向一个更基本的问题，就是批评与异议的自由。这次交战，宰相王安石赢了第一回合；但是此后，全国官员分成了两个阵营，陷于朋党之争，直到宋朝灭亡而后已。几年之后，变法方案即遭修正，或予中止，但是两派的裂痕则演变愈甚，其后果亦更加严重。

在朝廷上此一政争，成了"流俗"与"通变"之争，这两个名称在当代文学里曾多次出现，而王安石亦最喜爱用。凡是王安石所不喜，或与王安石持异议者，王安石皆称之为"流俗"派，而他与其同党则称之为"通变"派。王安石攻击批评者，说恶意阻挠新政。在另一方面，反对派则攻击他，说他"视民间清论为流俗，视异己者为腐败"。刘挚则称："彼以此为流俗，此以彼为乱常。"王安石这位宰相排斥反对他的御史之时，反对派对他更重要攻击的，是他欲"钳天下人之口"，也就是使天下人不得批评政府。

中国政府从来没有发展出一个党治的组织，使之具有大家公认的权力，也没有当政党与反对党大家公认的责任。没有计票、举手、表示是否，或其他确定公众意见的方法。中国人在集会时，只是讨论问题，然后同意某一决定。在原则与实际上，对政府政策之批评，政府不但容许，亦且予以鼓励。敌方可推翻内阁，或申谢而退去。每有朋党之争，习惯上是将反对派放出京都，到外地任职。甚至在仁宗和英宗时，政府颇著盛名的领导人物，如范仲淹与欧阳修，都曾贬谪至外地，暂时退居低位，后来又回京得势。在这种情况之下，一派当权，则另一派退避。

朝内的争论在宋朝演变得越发激烈，是由于宋朝的政府组织制度的特殊所致，因为宋朝对宰相的职权没有明确的规定，内阁很像个国会，由皇帝掌握平衡之权。政府由复杂拙笨的连锁机构组成，功能的界限重复，最后决定的大权仍然在皇帝手中。当时所谓宰相，只是个交际上的称呼而已，实际名称为"同中书门下平章事"。也许有两位副宰相。一般组织如下：

户部（财政）完全独立，直接对皇帝负责。御史台独立，其他各机构，只供做赠予空衔之用。通常，宰相兼中书省侍郎与门下省侍郎。三省各侍郎和枢密院太尉构成知院，称为"知政"。后来，神宗锐予改变，意在简化此一组织制度，权责区划较为分明。门下省司研讨命令，中书省（宰相府）司发布，尚书省司执行。但是纷乱与权责分散，依然如故。

王安石最初只是个参知政事（副宰相），但因受皇帝支持，擅自越权进行变法计划，与吕惠卿、曾布私下决定一切。这自然是在神宗驾前和各知政易于发生争论。主要问题只有两个：一是青苗贷款法，一是御史的言论自由一事。一方面，是元老重臣干练有才之士，人数之众，几乎构成了全体；另一方面，只有一个人，王安石，但有神宗支持，以及另一批默默无名的小人，野心大，精力足，阴险而诡诈。为了便于参考，并免于许多人名的累赘，下一表内列有政争中较重要之人名，以见双方之阵容：

王安石　　（拗相公）

神　宗　　（雄心万丈的皇帝）

曾　布　　（活跃的政客）

吕惠卿　　（声名狼藉，后出卖王安石）

李　定　　（母丧不奔，后弹劾苏东坡）

邓　绾　　（两面人，先后服侍吕惠卿和王安石）

舒　亶　　（与邓绾同弹劾苏东坡）

王　雱　　（王安石之子）

谢景温　　（王安石姻亲）

蔡　卞　　（王安石女婿）

章　惇　　（后为苏东坡敌人）

吕嘉问　　（王安石手下的贸易霸主）

司马光　　（反对派之首，大史学家）

韩　琦　　（元老重臣）

富　弼　　（老臣）

吕　晦　　（第一个发动攻击的人）

曾公亮　　（脆弱人物）

赵　抃

文彦博　　（老好人）

张方平

范　镇　　（元老重臣，苏家"叔伯"辈好友）

欧阳修

苏东坡

苏子由　　（东坡之弟）

范仲淹　（伟人）

孙　觉　（高俊，易怒，东坡密友）

李　察　（矮壮，东坡密友）

刘　恕　（性火爆，东坡至交）

吕公著　（美髯，曾与王安石为友）

韩　维　（出自世家，曾为王安石好友）

王安礼

王安国

刘　挚　（独立批评者，后与东坡为敌）

苏　颂

宋敏求　　　　（熙宁中三学士）

李大临

其他御史

郑　侠　（负重任之宫廷门吏，王安石因他而败）

此一极不平衡的阵容，既令人悲，又令人笑。一看此表，令人不禁纳闷王安石化友为敌的才气，以及神宗宠用王安石所付代价之大，因为所有对新政持异议者皆遭撤职，罢官议罪。最后，神宗又不得不罢斥王安石、吕惠卿、邓绾等诸人。他的强国梦破灭了，只落得统治一群庸才之臣。倘若说知人善任为"神"圣的特性，"神"宗这个谥号，他是当之有愧了。

王安石的悲剧是在于他自己并不任情放纵，也不腐败贪污，他也是迫不得已。要把他主张的国家资本计划那么激进、那么极端的制度付诸实施，必得不顾别人的反对。也许这就是他隐退以待时机如此之久的缘故。他有一个幻象，而他的所作所为，都以实现这个光辉灿烂的幻象为依归。

他之所求，不是太平繁荣的国家，而是富强具有威力的国家，向南向北，都要开拓疆土。他相信天意要使宋朝扩张发展，一如汉唐两代，而他王安石就是上应天命成此大业之人。但是在后世的历史家的沉思默想之中，此等上应天命的人，无一不动人几分感伤——永远是个困于雄心而不能自拔的人，成为自己梦想的牺牲者，自己的美梦发展扩张，而后破裂成了浮光泡影，消失于虚无缥缈之中。

　　王安石轻视所有那些"流俗"之辈，不但与那些忠厚长者大臣一等人疏远起来，就连自己的莫逆之交如韩维、吕公著也断绝了来往。我们还记得神宗尚身为太子之时，是韩维使太子对王安石倾心器重的。等这些朋友对他推行新政的方式表示异议时，他毫不迟疑，立刻把他们贬谪出京。他既陷于孤立无援，就拔升些不相知的"才不胜职"之辈，而这些人只是对他唯唯诺诺毕恭毕敬，实际上利用他以遂其私欲。三个劣迹昭彰的小人是李定、舒亶、邓绾。李定隐瞒母丧不报，以免辞官，退而居丧返里，在儒教社会中这是大逆不道的。李定之为后人所知，是他说了一句名言："笑骂由他笑骂，好官我自为之。"但是王安石的两个巨奸大恶的后盾人物，则是两个极端活跃、富有险谋才干又极具说服能力的小人：曾布和吕惠卿，尤以吕惠卿为甚，最后他想取王安石的地位而代之，又把王安石出卖了。王安石八年政权终于崩溃，可以一言以蔽之曰："吕惠卿出卖了王安石，王安石出卖了皇帝，皇帝出卖了人民。"在吕惠卿以极卑鄙的手段公布王安石的私信，以离间他和皇帝之时，王安石便垮了。王安石晚年每天都写"福建子"三个字数次，用以发泄心中的愤怒，因为出卖他的这个朋友吕惠卿是福建人。王安石失败之后，苏东坡一天在金陵遇见他，斥责他发动战争迫害文人之罪，王安石回答说吕惠卿当负全责。此不足以为借口，因为王安石本人坚持严酷对付反对派，而且在熙宁四年（一〇七一）

四月至六年（一〇七三）七月吕惠卿因父丧去职期间，王安石在京师用以
侦察批评朝政的特务机构成立了。

此外，相反两派的领袖王安石和司马光，虽然政见不同，不能相与，
但皆系真诚虔敬洁身自好之士。在金钱与私德上从未受人指责，欧阳修则
至少在家庭生活上曾传有暧昧情事。

有一次，王安石的妻吴氏为丈夫置一妾。等此女人进见时，王安石惊
问道："怎么回事？"

女人回答说："夫人吩咐奴婢伺候老爷。"

王安石又问："你是谁？"

女人回答道："奴家的丈夫在军中主管一船官麦，不幸沉船，官麦尽
失。我们家产卖尽，不足以还官债，所以奴家丈夫卖掉奴家好凑足钱数。"

王安石又问："把你卖了多少钱？"

"九百缗。"

王安石把她丈夫找到，命妇人随同丈夫回去，告诉她丈夫不必退钱。

这种情形司马光也曾遇见过，因为他在勉强之下纳了一个妾。他年轻
时曾官居通判，而妻子未能生育儿子。太守夫人赠送他一妾，司马光不理
不睬。妻子以为是自己在跟前的缘故。一天她告诉那个侍姬等她自己离家
之后，打扮妥当，夜间到老爷书房去。司马光看见那一女子在他书房中出
现，他惊问道："夫人不在，你胆敢来此？速去！"随即让她离去。王安
石和司马光都志在执行自己的政策，而不在谋取权力地位，而且王安
石对金钱绝不重视。他做宰相时，一领到俸禄，就交给弟兄们，任凭他们
花费。

司马光，道德才智，当代罕见其匹，由始至终是光风霁月胸怀，争理
不争利。他和王安石只是在政策上水火不相容。当代一个批评家曾说："王

安石必行新政始允为相，司马光必除新政始允为枢密副使。"

司马光为宋朝宰相，其为人所崇敬，不仅与范仲淹齐名，他还是包罗万有的一部中国史（至五代）《资治通鉴》的作者。这部书全书二百九十四卷，附录考异三十卷，学富识高，文笔精练，为史书中之北斗，后世史学著作之规范。初稿（长编）多于成书数倍。他写作此书时，一直孜孜不懈，每日抄写，积稿十尺，最后全稿装满两间屋子。此空前巨著费去作者二十五年工夫。

引起最后争论的问题，是青苗贷款法。在制置三司条例司研讨数月之后，青苗法终于在神宗熙宁二年（一〇六九）九月公布。朝廷派出四十一位专使大员，到各省去督导实施新法。不久之后，即分明显示官家款项并不能如预先之估计可由人民自行贷出。专使所面临之问题即是：径行还京陈明使命未能达成，抑或勉强人民将款贷去而回京禀报新政成功。官家愿将款项借予富户，以其抵押较为可靠，但富户并不特别需要借款；贫户急需借款，但官家必须取得抵押，因知其无还债能力。有些特使乃思得办法，按人民之财力，自富至贫，将官款定比分配。但是贫户太贫，实在无力借款，只有富户可借——这正是现代银行财务事业的基本特性。官方要做到贫户确能归还贷款，于是使贫户之富有邻居为之作保。一个特使向京都的报告中说：官方把贷款交与贫户时，贫户"喜极而泣"。另一个特使，不愿强民借贷，回京报告大不相同。御史弹劾放款成功的特使，说他强民借贷，大违朝廷之本意。王安石亲自到御史台对诸御史说："你们意欲何为？你们弹劾推行新政的能吏，却对办事不力者默不作声。"

韩琦那时驻在大名府，官居河北安抚使，亲眼看到了青苗贷款法实行的情形，他向皇帝奏明青苗贷款是如何分配出去的。这若与苏东坡的火爆发作相比，韩琦的奏折可以说是顾虑周详，措辞妥帖，言之有物，真不愧是个极具才干、功在国家的退职宰相的手笔。在奏折上他说，甚至赤贫之民也有分担的款额，富有之家则要求认捐更多。所谓青苗贷款也分配给城市居民负担，也分配给地主和"垄断剥削者"，须知这两种人正是青苗法所要消灭的。不可不知的是，每借进一笔钱，短短数月之后就要付出一分半的利息。不论朝廷如何分辩，说贷款与民不是以营利为目的，百姓都不肯相信。韩琦指出，纵然阻止强迫贷款，要力行自愿贷款，并无实际用处，因为富户不肯借，穷人愿借，但无抵押；最后仍须保人还债。同时，督察贷款的特使急于取悦于朝中当权者，低级官吏又不敢明言，韩琦说，他自思身为国家老臣，势不得不将真相奏明皇帝。他请朝廷中止新法，召回特使，恢复故有的常平仓制。

和王安石讨论韩琦的奏折时，皇帝说："韩琦乃国之忠臣，虽然为官在外，对朝廷仍是念念不忘。我原以为青苗贷款法会有利于百姓，没料到为害如此之烈。再者，青苗贷款只用于乡村，为何也在城市推销？"

王安石立即回奏道："有什么害处？都市的人倘若也需要贷款，为什么不借给他们？"

于是韩琦和朝廷之间，奏批往返甚久，这位退位的宰相，明确指出汉朝所一度实行的国家资本制度的影响，那样榨取民脂民膏以充国库而供皇帝穷兵黩武，并不足以言富国之道。

这就动摇了王安石的地位，皇帝开始有意中止青苗法。王安石知道了，遂请病假。司马光在提到王安石请病假时说："士夫沸腾，黎民骚动。"大臣等讨论此一情势，赵抃当时还拥护王安石，主张等王安石销假再说。那天晚上阁员曾公亮派他儿子把政局有变的情形去告诉王安石，告诉他要赶快销假。得此密告，王安石立即销假，又出现在朝廷之上，劝皇帝说反对派仍然是力图阻挠新政。

皇帝也不知如何是好，乃派出两个太监到外地视察回报。两个太监也深知利害，回报时说青苗法甚得民心，并无强迫销售情事。老臣文彦博反对说："韩琦三朝为相，陛下乃信太监之言而不信韩琦吗？"但是皇帝竟坚信自己亲自派出之使者，决心贯彻新政。几名愚蠢无知毫不负责的查报人员，不知自己说的几句话，竟会对国家大事产生了影响，这种情形何时是了！倘若那几个阉宦还有男子汉的刚强之气，这时肯向皇帝据实回奏，宋朝的国运还会有所改变。他们只是找皇帝爱听的话说，等时局变化，谈论"土地改革"已不再新鲜，他们也羞臊得一言不发了。

司马光、范镇，还有苏东坡三个人并肩作战。司马光原对王安石颇为器重，他自己当然也深得皇帝的信任。皇帝曾问他对王安石的看法，他说："百姓批评王安石虚伪，也许言之过甚，但他确是不切实际，刚愎自用。"不过，他的确和王安石的亲信小人吕惠卿在给皇帝上历史课时，发生了一次激烈的争辩，甚至需要皇帝来打断，要他二人平静下来。司马光既然反对他的政策，王安石开始厌恶他。王安石请病假如此之短一个时期之中，神宗皇帝打算使司马光充任副枢密使。司马光谢绝不就，他说他个人的官位无甚重要，重要的是皇帝是否要废止新政。司马光九次上奏折。皇帝回答说：

"朕曾命卿任枢密使，主管军事，卿为何多次拒不受命，而不断谈论与军事无关之事？"

司马光回奏称："但臣迄未接此军职。臣在门下省一日，即当提醒陛下留意此等事。"

王安石销假之后，他的地位又形巩固，他把司马光降为制诰。范镇拒发新命，皇帝见范镇如此抗命，乃亲手把诏命交与司马光。范镇因此请辞门下省职位，皇帝允准。

王安石既复相位，韩琦乃辞河北安抚使，只留任大名府知府，皇帝照准。苏东坡怒不可遏。他有好多话要说，而且非说不可，正如骨鲠在喉，不吐不快。他之坦白直率，是断然无疑的。那时，他只三十二岁，任职史馆，官卑职小，且只限于执笔为文，与行政毫无关系。他给皇帝上奏折两次，一次是在熙宁三年（一〇七〇）二月，一次是在次年二月。两次奏折都是洋洋洒洒，包罗无限，雄辩滔滔，直言无隐，犹如现代报上偶尔出现的好社论文章一样，立即唤起了全国的注意。在第一篇奏折上，一开首就向青苗法攻击。他告诉皇上全国人已在反对皇上，并说千万不可凭借权力压制人民。文章之中他引用孔夫子的话说：

百姓足，君孰与不足？……臣不知陛下所谓富者富民欤？抑富国欤？是以不论尊卑，不计强弱，理之所在则成，理所不在则不成，可必也。今陛下使农民举息而与商贾争利，岂理也哉，而怪其不成乎？……夫陛下苟诚心乎为民，则虽或谤之而人不信；苟诚心乎为利，则虽自解释而人不服。且事有决不可欺者，吏受贿枉法，人必谓之赃。非其有而取之，人必谓之盗。苟有其实，不敢辞其名。今青苗有二分之息，而不谓之放债取利，可乎？……今天下以为利，陛下以为义；天下以为贪，陛下以为廉，不胜其纷纭也。

他又警告皇帝说：

盖世有好走马者，一为坠伤，则终身徒行……近者青苗之政，助役之法，均输之策，并军搜卒之令，卒然轻发又甚于前日矣……今陛下春秋鼎盛，天赐勇智，此万世一时也。而臣君不能济之以慎重，养之以敦朴。譬如乘轻车、驭骏马，贸然夜行，而仆夫又从后鞭之，岂不殆哉。臣愿陛下解辔秣马，以须东方之明，而徐行于九轨之道，其未晚也。

苏东坡又警告皇帝说，若以为用专断的威权必能压制百姓，则诚属大错。多少官吏已然降级或革职，甚至有恢复肉刑之说。他接着又说：

今朝廷可谓不和矣。其咎安在？陛下不反求其本，而欲以力胜之。力之不能胜众也久矣。古者刀锯在前，鼎镬在后，而士犹犯之。今陛下躬蹈尧舜，未尝诛一无罪。欲弭众言，不过斥逐异议之臣，而更用人尔。必不忍行亡秦偶语之禁，起东汉党锢之狱。多士何畏而不言哉？臣恐逐者不已，而争者益多……陛下将变今之刑，而用其极软，天下几何其不叛也？

今天下有心者怨，有口者谤。古之君臣相与忧勤以营一代之业者，似不如此。古语曰："百人之聚，未有不公。"而况天下乎？今天下非之，而陛下不回，臣不知所税驾矣。诗曰："譬彼舟流，不知所届。心之忧矣，不遑假寐。"区区之忠，惟陛下察之，臣谨昧死上对。

使朝廷文武百官最激动的，莫如王安石之清除御史台。最初，王安石威吓朝廷百官，倒不是以他那极端而广泛的经济政策，而是他对胆敢批评他的御史，凭他狂妄的习惯，一律撤职。于是批评朝政之权受到了摧残，政府组织的基础受到了破坏，这样就触动了政体的最敏感部分。官场全体为之大惊失色，王安石自己的朋友也开始背弃他。

单以排除御史台的异己一事，就足以削弱对他的支持力量，也引起朝廷领袖纷纷萌生退意。在中国，监察机构是朝廷一个历史悠久的制度，其作用就是代表舆论时时对当政的政权予以控制或批评。在一个好政府里，监察机构必须能随时对皇帝进净言，向皇帝反映舆论，这种重要性是不可忽视的。由于其地位如此之重要，监察机构既有重大力量，亦有重大责任，御史如对当权者作强有力的攻击，可以把一个政权推翻。这种监察作用，在政府的人事和政策上可以引起变动，不过其方法并未明确予以规定，其作用与现代的新闻舆论大致相似。古代此种制度之异于今日者，就是此等监察机构及其反对权，并无明文规定受有法律保障，只是传统上认为明主贤君应当宽宏纳谏；至于皇帝重视他那明主贤君的名誉与否，那就是他自己的事了。倘若他不克己自律，他可以降旨把御史降级、惩处、折磨，甚至全家杀害。有些皇帝确是如此。身为御史者在个人毫无法律保障之下，却要尽职责向朝廷与皇帝进谏规劝，处境是既难又险。但是像现代，总有对公众抱有责任感的新闻杂志编辑，不惜冒监禁死亡之险而向极权政权挑战的，在过去也总有御史受皮肉之苦、鞭笞之痛，甚至死亡之威胁，而尽其人民之职责。尤其在东汉与明朝两代，当时有御史，写好弹劾奸相的本章，自料必死无疑，在本章呈递与皇帝之前，先行自缢身死。这些御史正如武士之上战场，前仆后继。好皇帝自己爱惜名誉，对于这等御史的处理颇为慎重，因此甚获美誉而得人望，但是恶人当政则急于塞御史之口，正如现代之专制暴君，总以钳制报章杂志之口为急务。

王安石当政之始，元老重臣对他颇寄厚望。现在御史中丞吕晦向王安石发出了第一弹，说他："执邪见，不通物情。置之宰辅，天下必受其祸。"连司马光都深感意外。在吕晦同司马光去给皇帝讲解经典之时，吕晦向司马光透露那天早晨他打算要做的事，从袖子里把那件弹劾表章给司马光看。

司马光说："吾等焉能为力？他深得人望。"

吕晦大惊道："你也这么说！"

吕晦遭受革职，于是排除异己开始了。

现在星星之火使朝廷政争变成了熊熊之势。有一妇人，企图谋杀丈夫，但仅仅使她丈夫受伤而未克致命。此一妇人曾承认有谋杀之意，当时有个高官对处治之刑罚表示异议。此一案件拖延一年有余，未能定案。司马光要以一种方式判决，王安石要另一种方式，而且坚持己见，皇帝的圣旨对此案的处刑亦有所指示。但是御史刘恕则拒不同意，要求再审，御史如此要求，亦属常事。另一御史对王安石的意见不服，王安石则令他自己的一个亲信弹劾刘恕。这样一来，一场争斗，便化暗为明。

御史台则群情激动。问题现在是仍要在不受限制之下自由尽责呢，还是等候逐一被人清除？几位御史乃联名上书弹劾王安石，请求罢除其相位。王安石大怒，欲将此数人投诸监狱而后快。司马光与范纯仁认为基本上不可如此对待御史，最后六个御史遭贬谪至边远外县充任酒监。一见情形如此，范纯仁起而应战。他要求贬谪御史之成命必须撤回，结果他自己也遭流放。下一个要倒下去的是苏东坡的弟弟苏子由。他一直就反对青苗法和市易法。两个月之后，忠厚长者老臣富弼向朝廷辞职归隐，临去警告说，在任何政治斗争中，正人君子必败，而小人必占上风，因为正人君子为道义而争，而小人则为权力而争，结果双方必各得其所，好人去位，坏人得权。他预言国家大事若如此下去，国家行将大乱矣。

朝廷之上，现在是一片骚乱。神宗熙宁二年（一〇六九）二月，制置三司条例司成立，七月实行市易法，九月实行青苗法。数月之后，众人对当权者的意见，由期待而怀疑，由怀疑而迷惑，由迷惑而愤怒恐惧。

现在情势变化甚速。熙宁三年（一〇七〇）三月与四月，御史台大规模遭受整肃，随即大规模布置上新人。随后倒下的两个御史，都是王安石个人的朋友，都曾助他获得政权，王安石也是倚为声援的。身材顾长、性情暴躁又富有口才的孙觉，他也是苏东坡毕生的友人，曾经向王安石发动论争，因为王安石坚称周朝的钱币机构，曾经以百分之二十五的利息把钱借给人民，他对此说表示反对。王安石仍然希望得到他的支援，派他到外地调查为什么当时盛传朝廷强迫贷款与农人，甚至在京畿一带也传闻如此。孙觉回到京师，老老实实地报告确有强迫销售情事。王安石认为他这是出卖朋友——所以孙觉也被革职。更为重要的案子是"美髯公"吕公著的案子。吕公著是宰相之子，学识渊博，但是沉默寡言。在早年，王安石和吕公著在文学上同享盛名，同为儒林所敬佩。吕公著曾帮助王安石位登权要。作为回报，王安石乃使他官拜御史中丞。现在吕公著上神宗皇帝的奏议中，文字未免过于辛辣，使王安石大为不快，在文中他问："昔日之所谓贤者，今皆以此举为非，岂昔贤而今皆不肖乎？"王安石亲拟罢斥吕公著的诏书，用字措辞正好流露他自己喜怒无常的特性。在二人交好之日，王安石曾向皇帝说："吕公著之才将来必为宰相。"而今他把吕公著比作了尧舜时的"四凶"。

最使曾佩服他的人与之疏远的原因，就是在同一个月内，王安石派了两个劣迹昭彰的小人进入御史台，去填补他排挤出来的空缺。他指派李定为全权御史，在御史台引起了群情激愤。李定既没考中科举，也没有为官的其他必要资格。他叫人知道的反倒是他隐瞒母丧不守丧礼一事。在中国人心目中，这简直是败德下流至于禽兽。王安石把他升到那么崇高的地位，只是因为自乡间来京后，他向皇帝奏明青苗贷款法极受人民欢迎，王安石把他向皇上引荐，好向皇上陈奏。这件事使御史们怒不可遏。同时，王安石又把亲戚谢景温升为御史。谢为求升发，把自己的妹妹嫁与王安石的弟弟。有三个御史反对朝廷的此一任命诏书，三个人一起丢官。其余的御史对此事还照旧坚持。张戬请求将三个御史官复原职，并罢斥王安石的心腹李定与吕惠卿。在张戬到中书省去催办此一案件时，他发现王安石心情古怪，只是听他叙述，自己则一言不发，用扇子掩着嘴，一味大笑。

张戬说："我想你一定正笑我愚蠢。但是你要知道，全国老百姓笑你的正多着呢。"

这时另一位遭到牺牲的御史是程灏，他是宋朝理学家"二程"之中的兄长大程。在新政推行之初，他曾经与王安石合作。现在他也到中书省为那同一个案子向王安石争论。王安石刚看了他的奏折，程灏看到他正怒气难消。这位理学大家以颇有修养的风度对他说："老朋友，你看，我们讨论的不是个人私事或家事，我们讨论的是国事。难道不能平心静气说话吗？"从儒家的道德修养看，王安石觉得很丢脸，很难为情。

一个月的光景，御史台的清除异己便已告完成。连前年所罢黜的那六个御史在内，王安石清除的御史一共达到了十四人，十一名是御史台的人，三名是皇宫中的谏官。司马光向皇帝曾经痛陈利害。只有三个人，就是王安石、曾布、吕惠卿，赞成新政，朝廷百官无不反对他们三个人。"难道皇上就只用这三个人组织朝廷？就用这三个人治理国家吗？"韩琦和张方平已在二月告老还乡，司马光对枢密使一职拒而不受，当月也遭贬降，范镇已经大怒而去。在九月，举棋不定的赵抃，他这位内阁大臣，一度想讨好这群新贵，现在决定辞职。他也指出"青苗使者于体为小，而禁近耳目之臣用舍为大"。数月之后，年老信命毫无火气的曾公亮，把王安石之得势归之于天意，以年老多病为由，在极不愉快之下，请求去职，其实多少也是受批评不过而走的。在神宗熙宁三年（一〇七〇），王安石正式出任相职，在整个政府中其权位凛乎不可侵犯。次年九月，欧阳修辞去朝廷一切职位，退隐林泉。

苏东坡现在写他那上神宗皇帝的万言书，准备罢官而去。他和司马光、范镇曾经并肩作战，但是司马光与范镇已经在愤怒厌恶之下辞去官职。范镇后来和苏东坡有了亲戚关系，他曾在前两朝任职于中书省。其人虽然外貌看来肥胖松软，个性之强，则不让钢铁。在去职之时，他在辞呈上说："陛下有纳谏之资，大臣进拒谏之计；陛下有爱民之性，大臣用残民之术。"在早朝之时，皇帝将此奏折交与王安石看，王安石的脸立刻煞白。当时在附近的几个人说曾看见王安石拿着此奏折在手，手气得发抖。

在熙宁三年九月，司马光被派到外地陕西去做外任官，但是他留恋京都不忍去。他和王安石诚恳但有时很严肃认真地讨论新法，书信来往凡三次之后，才与他完全决裂。皇帝原先仍希望他在朝为官，皇帝数次告诉其他大臣说，只要司马光在身边，他不会犯什么大错。皇帝再三再四召他回朝，司马光都予谢绝。他的话早已说够，皇帝若不肯察纳忠言而中止骑此刚愎的蛮驴奔赴毁灭之途，则他的本分已尽。在他决定辞去一切官职退隐林下之时，他仍然怒不可遏。他写给皇上的奏折上说：

> 安石以为贤则贤，以为愚则愚；以为是则是，以为非则非。诏附安石者，谓之忠良；攻难安石者，谓之谗慝。臣之才识，固安石之所愚；臣之议论，固安石之所非。今日之所言，陛下之所谓谗慝也。伏望圣恩，裁处其罪。若臣罪与范镇同，则乞依范镇例致仕。或罪重于镇，则或窜或诛，所不敢逃。

从现在到十六年后神宗皇帝驾崩这段时间，司马光要避门不出，倾其全力继续九年前即已开始的历史巨著的写作。后来，神宗皇帝罢黜王安石之后，打算重召司马光回朝主政，司马光唯一的回答仍然是：皇帝要立即废除新法吗？由此看来，这两个极端相异的政治思想，一直到最后，都是丝毫不变动而且不可能变动的。可是在随后一位皇帝英宗即位的第一年，王安石已死，司马光也卧床病重，那时他以宰相的地位发出的最后一道命令是："王安石为人并不甚坏。其过端在刚愎自用。死后朝廷应以优礼葬之。"

苏东坡的上神宗皇帝万言书，甚为重要，其中包括他自己的政治哲学，也表示其个人之气质与风格，其机智学问与大无畏的精神，都显然可见。愤怒的争论与冷静清晰的推理，交互出现。有时悲伤讥刺，苛酷的批评，坦白直率，逾乎寻常；有时论辩是非，引证经史，以畅其义。为文工巧而真诚，言出足以动人，深情隐忧，因事而现。在正月蒙皇帝召见之时，皇帝曾称赞那篇《议学校贡举状》，并命他"尽陈得失，无有所隐"。苏东坡即认真遵办。那是他最后一次尽其所能求皇帝改变主意，这时所有高官大臣都已去职，一切情势都呈现不利。苏东坡知道，即便自己不遭大祸，至少将遭罢黜，是必然无疑之事。

对现代读者最重要的两个论点，一是孟子所说的君权民授，一是为政当容清议。他警告皇帝说，君之为君，非由神权而得，乃得自人民之拥护。为帝王者不可不知。他说：

书曰"予临兆民，凛乎若朽索之御六马"，言天下莫危于人主也。聚则为君民，散则为仇雠，聚散之间，不容毫厘。故天下归往谓之王，人各有心谓之独夫。由此观之，人主之所恃者，人心而已。人心之于人主也，如木之有根，如灯之有膏，如鱼之有水，如农夫之有田，如商贾之有财。木无根则槁，灯无膏则灭，鱼无水则死，农夫无田则饥，商贾无财则贫，人主失人心则亡。此理之必然，不可逭之灾也。其为可畏，从古已然。

但是，为人君者若不容许自由表示意见，焉能得到人的支持？苏东坡进而发挥这一点，我认为是这篇奏议中最重要的。就是政治上不同意一事之原则，有御史监察制度，便是具体的做法。根据苏东坡所说，一个好政权之得以保持，大部分在于不同的政见合理地发挥其功用。民主政治体制，系表现于党派间政见之歧异。苏东坡如生于现代，必然反对联合国安理会全体同意原则，在基本上为反民主。他知道，中国自盘古开天辟地以来，还没有两个人事事完全同意，而民主制度的另一途径，唯有暴政制度。我从未发现民主制度的敌人，在家庭，在国内，或是世界政治上而不是暴君的。苏东坡接着说：

孙宝有言："周公上圣，召公大贤，犹不相悦，著于经典。两不相损。"晋之王导，可谓元臣，每与客言，举座称善，而王述不悦，以为人非尧舜，安得每事尽善。导亦敛衽谢之。若使言无不同，意无不合，更唱迭和，何者非贤？万一有小人居其间，则人君何缘得以知觉？

我想，把监察机构存在的理由与其基本原则，说得清楚明白，再无人能比得上苏东坡这篇奏议了。一个发挥自由功用不惧利害的监察机构所代表的，就是真正的公众意见。

夫弹劾积威之后，虽庸人亦可奋扬；风采消委之余，虽豪杰有所不能振起。臣恐自兹以往，习惯成风，尽为执政私人，以致人主孤立。纪纲一废，何事不生？……是以知为国者，平居必有忘躯犯颜之士，则临难庶几有徇义守死之臣。苟平居尚不能一言，则临难何以责其死节？

他把当时的舆论状况与古代相比，说：

> 臣自幼小所记，及闻长老之谈，皆谓台谏所言，常随天下公议。公议
> 所与，台谏亦与之。公议所击，台谏亦击之……今日物议沸腾，怨交至。
> 公议所在，亦可知矣。

苏东坡比较中国历代政府制度的异同，而发挥监察机构其所以存在
之必要。在此他俨然以倡导者出现，其态度博学，其推理有力，其识见
卓绝。

> 古者建国，使内外相制，轻重相权。如周如唐，则外重而内轻。如秦
> 如魏，则外轻而内重。内重之弊，必有奸臣指鹿之患；外重之弊，必有大
> 国问鼎之忧。圣人方盛而虑衰，常先立法以救弊……以古揆今，则似内重。
> 恭惟祖宗所以预图而深计，固非小臣所能臆度而周知。然观其委任台谏之
> 一端，则是圣人过防之至计……自建隆以来，未尝罪一言者……风采所系，
> 不问尊卑，言及乘舆，则天子改容；事关廊庙，则宰相待罪。故仁宗之世，
> 议者讥宰相，但奉行台谏风旨而已。
>
> 圣人深意，流俗岂知？擢用台谏，固未必皆贤，所言亦未必皆是。然
> 须养其锐气，而借之重权者，岂徒然哉！将以折奸臣之萌，而救内重之弊也。
> 夫奸臣之始，以台谏折之而有余；及其既成，以干戈取之而不足……陛下
> 得不上念祖宗设此官之意，下为子孙立万一之防。朝廷纲纪，孰大于此？

苏东坡告诉皇帝，千万不可用威权慑服百姓而使之服从。他又提到有
谣传恢复肉刑之说。数百年以前，有各种砍截人体处罚罪犯之法，包括

墨、劓、剕、宫四刑。这些残忍的刑罚在第二世纪之后，约在隋朝时期，除去宫刑，已然废止。此等酷刑之未曾恢复，当归功于苏东坡上神宗的奏议。当时谣传之甚，与日俱增。

陛下与二三大臣，亦闻其语矣。然而莫之顾者，徒曰我无其事，又无其意，何恤于人言？夫人言虽未必皆然，而疑似则有以致谤。人必贪财也，而后人疑其盗；人必好色也，而后人疑其淫……

苏东坡指出，当时商业萧条，物价飞涨，由京师附近各省，远至四川，谣言漫天飞，黎民怨怒，声如鼎沸，甚至深远至山区，酒亦属于专卖；和尚尼姑亦遭逮捕，没收其财产，官兵的粮饷都遭降低。

夫制置三司条例司，求利之名也。六七少年与使者四十余辈，求利之器也。驱鹰犬而赴林薮，语人曰"我非猎也"，不如放鹰犬而兽自驯；操罔罟而入江湖，语人曰"我非渔也"，不如捐罔罟而人自信。

苏东坡相信皇帝会看得清楚国内的不和与纷争，他从良臣能史之挂冠去职，舆论之背向不难判断。在数度对新政的指责之后，他力言因推行新政，皇帝已失去民心，皇帝本人及当权者已不为清议所容。

苏东坡上书之后，如石沉大海。三月，又上第三书。皇帝已临时下一诏书，严禁强销青苗贷款，但是却没打算废止此等全部措施。苏东坡引用孟子的话说，正如一个偷鸡贼想改过向善，决定每月只偷一只鸡。后来使情形恶化的，是苏东坡在神宗熙宁四年（一〇七一）一月起任告院权开封府推官，在任期内，他出了一道乡试考题《论独断》（全题是：晋武平吴，以独断而亡；齐小白专任管仲而罢；燕哙专任子之而败。事同而功异，何也？），这激怒了王安石。

苏东坡立遭罢黜。正如他所预期，虽然皇帝对他的忠言至为嘉许，王安石的群小之辈会捏造借口，陷他于纠纷之中。王安石的亲戚兼随员谢景温，挟法诬告。当时流传一个谣言，说苏氏兄弟运父灵乘船回四川原籍途中，曾滥用官家的卫兵，并购买家具瓷器，并可能偷运私盐从中牟利。官方乃派人到苏氏兄弟运灵所经各省路途上，从船夫、兵卒、仪官收集资料。苏东坡也许真买了不少家具瓷器，但并不违法。官差回去报称无所搜获，如有所获，必然带回京师了。

苏东坡的内弟，那时住在四川，苏东坡有信给他，信里说："某与二十七娘甚安，小添寄叔并无恙……某为权幸所嫉久矣。然抢拾无获，徒劳掀搅，取笑四方耳。不烦远忧。"

司马光回洛阳之前在京都时，皇帝对他说：

"似乎苏轼人品欠佳，卿对他评价过高。"

司马光回答说："陛下是指有人控告他吗？我对他知之较深。陛下知道谢景温为安石亲戚，控告也是王安石煽动而起。再者，虽然苏东坡并非完美无疵，他不比隐秘母丧不报的畜牲李定好得多吗？"

按苏东坡的政绩说，他而今应当官居太守才是，皇帝也有此意。王安石与谢景温反对，使之任附近一县的判官；但是皇帝予以改动，任命他为杭州太守。苏东坡对御史的弹劾不屑于置理，连修表自辩也不肯，任凭官方调查，自己携眷径赴杭州上任去了。

Chapter Eight
THE BULL-HEADED PREMIER

A political storm now blew and started a conflagration that burned down the house of Sung. It started with a fight between the state capitalist Want Anshih, the "Bullheaded Premier," and the opposition, which comprised the entire officialdom, a generation of men selected and nurtured for government leadership in the atmosphere of intellectual freedom under the wise emperor Jentsung. It is necessary to understand the nature of the political battle because the party strife shadowed Su Tungpo's entire life.

One of the earliest extant copies of Chinese vernacular literature, presaging the advent of the novel in China, was a short story entitled "The Bull-headed Premier" (*Yao Shiangkung*). It is a collection of short stories in the vernacular of Sung Dynasty times, recently discovered, and it shows that soon after Wang Anshih's death he was known by this nickname in folk literature. The tragedies of the political strife arose from the defects of character of a man who was unable to take good advice and unwilling to admit a mistake. Friends' opposition to Wang Anshih only increased his determination to carry through his policy. Determination of character, we are told, is a great virtue, but a qualification is necessary: so much depends upon what a man is determined to do. It is entirely possible that Wang

Anshih, remembering the homely adage he had heard as a schoolboy that determination was a key to success, mistook mulish obstinacy for that desirable virtue. In his lifetime Wang Anshih was known among the *literati* as a man of "three not-worths"—"God's anger is not worth fearing, public opinion is not worth respecting, and the tradition of the ancestors is not worth keeping." It was a label given by Su Tungpo.

The "Bull-headed Premier" brooked no opposition from any quarter, friend or foes. Being a good talker and able to persuade the young emperor of his program for building up a strong state, he was determined to carry his socialistic program through. This implied the silencing of opposition in general, and the silencing in particular of the imperial censors, whose official duty was to criticize the policies and conduct of the government and act as the "channel of public opinion." It was the basis of Chinese political philosophy that a good government "kept the channels of opinion open" and a bad government did not. It was therefore natural that, having begun with questions of the new measures themselves, the fight very soon surged around a more fundamental issue, the issue of freedom of criticism and dissent. It was a fight in which Wang the premier won the first bout; but from then on, all the officials of the country were lined up in two camps, locked in party strife which went on until the end of the dynasty. The reform measures were modified or suspended after only a few years, but the schism which developed had far graver consequences for the country.

In this political battle at court the issue was known as a fight between "reactionaries" and "progressives," terms which appeared again and again in the literature of that period and which Wang Anshih was very fond of using. For him, anybody he disliked or anybody who disagreed with him was a "reactionary" (*liushu*, conservative philistine), while he and his followers were the "progressives" or "reformists" (*tungpien*). The premier charged all critics with malicious intent to block his reforms. On the other hand, the opposition charged that he "regarded the fair criticism of people as reactionary and all who differed from him as corrupt." As Liu Chih formulated it. "One party regards the other as 'reactionary' and the other regards the ruling party as 'rebels against all established values.'" As the premier began to purge all the imperial censors who spoke up against him, the more important charge of the opposition was that he wanted to "shut up the mouths of all people;" i.e., muzzle all free criticism of the government.

The Chinese government had never perfected a machinery of party rule with recognized rights and responsibilities of the party in power and the opposition. There was no counting of votes, show of hands, yeas and nays, or any other form of establishing majority opinion. The Chinese at any meeting merely discussed matters and somehow agreed upon a decision. In principle and practice, criticism of government policy was allowed and encouraged. The opponents might overthrow the cabinet, or might beg to retire. When a bitter factional feud took place, it was the custom to send the opponents away from the court to hold different posts in the country. Even under Jentsung and Ingtsung, famous leaders of government like Fan Chuangyen and Ouyang Shiu had been dismissed to temporary obscurity, and had then returned to power. In this way one party came to power and another went out.

The bickerings and dissensions at the court now were increased by the peculiar Sung system of government, which centered no clear-cut responsibility on one man as prime minister. The cabinet was more like a state council, with the emperor holding the balance of power. The government consisted of a complicated, cumbersome system of interlocking departments with duplicating functions, so that the final decision always rested with the emperor himself. The so-called "premier" (*shiang*), a social term, went by the complicated title of "General Control Head of the Chancellery and the Imperial Secretariat," and there might be two vice-premiers. The general setup was as follows:

Two Councils	Three Departments	Six Ministries
Privy Council (military)(*president* and *vice-president*)		
State Council		
Administrative Council (*premier and vice-premier*)	1. Chancellery, or Premier's Office (*chancellor*)	
	2. Imperial Secretariat (*chancellor*)	1. Civil Service
		2. Interior
	3. Executive Board (*chancellor*)	3. Education
		4. Army
		5. Justice
		6. Public Works

The board of finance was entirely separate, directly responsible to the emperor. There was an independent imperial censorate, besides the censors within the three departments, as well as other various boards and bureaus useful chiefly for conferring nominal titles. Usually the "premier" was concurrently head of the chancellery and of the imperial secretariat. The heads of the three departments and of the military privy council together formed the state council and were called state councilors (*chihcheng*). Later Shentsung tried to simplify the system by drastic changes aiming at better-defined functions: the imperial secretariat was to *deliberate*, the premier's office (chancellery)to *promulgate*, and the executive board to *execute* government orders; but the same confusion and divided responsibility continued to exist.

Wang Anshih was at first only a vice-premier; but, backed by the

Emperor, he went ahead with his program over everybody's head and made all decisions at home with Lu Huiching and Tseng Pu. This seemed an ideal situation for embroiling the state councilors before the Emperor. The issues were mainly two, the farmers' loans and freedom of criticism by the censors. On one side were all the veteran officials, men of tried ability, constituting a majority so overwhelming as to suggest unanimity, and on the other, one man, Wang Anshih, backed by Emperor Shentsung, and a rather curious conglomeration of new and unknown petty, ambitious, energetic but scheming politicians. For convenience of reference, and in order not to encumber the text with too many names, the following table of the more important personages in the conflict, showing the amazing alignment of forces, may be useful:

DRAMATIS PERSONAE

IN POWER	THE OPPOSITION
WANG ANSHIH, "the Bull-headed Premier"	*Elderly Statesmen* (ex-premiers, privy councilors, etc.)
SHENTSUNG, an ambitious emperor	SZEMA KUANG, leader of the opposition, great historian
Two Henchmen	HAN CHI, veteran leader
TSENG PU, energetic politician	FU PI, old minister
LU HUICHING, a notorious character who double-crossed WANG	LU HUEI, fired first shot
	TSENG KUNGLIANG, weak character
Four Rascals	CHAO PIEN
LEEDING, a man who concealed his mother's death; later, court prosecutor of SU TUNGPO	WEN YENPO, friend of everybody
	Su and Close Friends
DUNQUAN, great turncoat, served HUICHING and WANG alternately	CHANGFANGPING ⎤ elderly FAN CHEN ⎥ statesmen, OUYANG SHIU ⎥ like "uncles" SU TUNGPO ⎦ to SU

SUDAN, with DUNQUAN, impeached SU TUNGPO

WANG PANG, son of WANG ANSHIH

Great Horde of Office-Seekers
(As in any other age)

SHIEH CHINGWEN, brother-in-law of WANG ANSHIH

TSAI PIEN, son-in-law of WANG ANSHIH

CHANG CHUN, later enemy of SU TUNGPO

LU CHIAWEN, trade dictator in WANG'S regime

SU TSEYU, Tungpo's brother

FAN CHUNJEN, a great man

SUN CHUEH, tall, fiery

LI CHANG, stocky

LIU SHU, quick-tempered

Wang's Former Friends

LU KUNGCHU, called "Handsome Beard," brilliant scholar

HAN WEI, from powerful Han family

CHENG HAO, neo-Confucianist, elder of the famous "Cheng brothers"

Wang's Two Brothers

WANG ANLI

WANG ANKUO

Independent Critics

LIU CHIH, later enemy of SU

SU SUNG ⎤ "three

SUNG MINCHIU ⎬ secretaries

LI TALIN ⎦ of Shining"

Other Censors

CHENG SHIA, "the little man with the big role," small gatekeeper who overthrew WANGANSHIH

The highly unbalanced alignment of forces is both tragic and amusing. Looking down the list, one cannot help wondering at the unhappy knack of Wang Anshih for alienating his own friends, and the heavy price the Emperor was willing to pay to keep Wang in power, since all those in opposition were cashiered, dismissed, and punished. In the end, Emperor Shentsung had to dismiss Wang Anshih, Lu Huiching, and Dunquan, too. His dream of a strong, powerful state vanished, and he was content to govern in a vacuum of mediocrities. If good judgment of men is an attribute of divinity, it would seem that the posthumous title of the emperor, *Shentsung*, or "Divine Ancestor," was a gross misnomer.

The tragedy of Wang Anshih comes form the fact that he was not in any way self-indulgent or corrupt himself, and that his hand was forced. To carry out anything so radical as his state capitalist program, he knew he had to override all opposition. Perhaps that was why he had bided his time so long. He had a vision, and his wagon was hitched to that starry vision, not of a happy, peaceful and prosperous nation, but of a rich, strong, and powerful state, expanding its borders north and south. God had willed that the Sung Dynasty was to be great and expansionist, like the Hans and the Tangs, and he, Wang Anshih, was the manifest Man of Destiny. But there is not one "Man of Destiny" who does not appear slightly pathetic in the contemplation of future historians—a man caught in the prison of his ambition, a victim of his own dream, which grew and expanded and then burst like a bubble.

Despising all the "conservative philistines," he not only alienated the good old ministers but even lost Han Wei and Lu Kungchu who were his best friends. Han Wei, we remember, was the friend who had turned Shentsung's heart and hopes toward Wang Anshih when the former was crown prince. When these friends disagreed with him on the manner in which he carried out his projects, he had no hesitation in banishing them from the court. Deserted and alone, he took in and promoted unknown and unqualified men who were smart enough to agree with him and use him for their own purposes. To make it easier to distinguish the three notorious characters, I have given them a more familiar spelling: Leeding, Sudan, and Dunquan. Leeding was a man who concealed the news of his mother's death to avoid going out of office, a daring offense in Confucian society. Dunquan is remembered by posterity as the author of the famous saying, "Let them all laugh who want to laugh; a good official post is mine." But the arch supporters of Wang Anshih were two extremely active and persuasive talkers of great scheming ability, Tseng Pu and Lu Huiching, particularly the latter, who eventually double-crossed Wang Anshih in an effort to supersede him. The collapse of this eight-year regime was summarized by a contemporary as follows: "Huiching sold out Wang Anshih, Wang Anshih sold out the Emperor, and the Emperor sold out the people." When Huiching stooped to publishing Wang's private letters to alienate him from the Emperor, Wang was overthrown, and in his old age he used to spend his fury over the turncoat friend by scribbling the word "Fukienite" a few times every day, Fukien being the province from which Huiching came. When Su Tungpo met Wang Anshih in Nanking after the regime was over, and rebuked him for starting wars and persecuting scholars, Wang replied that Huiching was responsible for all the doings. This is hardly a plausible defense, since it was Wang himself who insisted on dealing harshly with all opposition, and since the institution of espionage at the capital against critics of the government was established during the period when Huiching was in retirement in mourning for his father, between April 1071 and July 1073.

Otherwise, the two leaders of the opposite factions, Wang Anshih and Szema Kuang, while uncompromising in their fight over government policies, were both sincere in their convictions and above reproach in their private lives. Neither was ever accused of corruption in money matters or of looseness of morals, while Ouyang Shiu was at least alleged to have had some affairs in his private household.

Once Wang Anshih's wife, Wu, had bought a concubine for her husband. When the woman was presented, Wang asked, in surprise, "What is that thing?"

"The Madame has asked me to serve you," replied the woman.

"But who are you?" asked Wang again.

"My husband," replied the woman, "was working with the army in charge of a boatload of government rice. The boat sank and he lost the whole cargo. We sold all our property to restore the loss still could not make up the amount. And so my husband sold me to pay for the balance."

"How much were you sold for?" asked Wang.

"Nine hundred dollars."

Wang Anshih sent for her husband and bade the woman go back to him, telling him to keep the money.

The same thing happened to Szema Kuang, for he, too, had a concubine against his wish. In his younger days he was serving as a deputy magistrate and his wife had not yet produced a son for him. The chief magistrate's wife presented him with a concubine, but Szema Kuang ignored her. Thinking that it was because of her own presence, his wife one day asked the girl to wait till she was out of the house and then dress up and go into his study at night. When Szema Kuang saw the girl appear in his room, he said in surprise to the girl, "How dare you come here? The Madame is away," and he sent her away. Both men were more interested in carrying out their policies than in personal power, and Wang Anshih certainly had no regard for money. While he was premier, as soon as his salary was received, he turned it over to his brothers to spend it any way they liked.

Szema Kuang, who towered intellectually and morally above his generation, fought a clean-cut battle of principles from the beginning to the end. He and Wang Anshih stood at opposite poles on government policy. In the words of a contemporary, "Wang Anshih refused to be premier unless the new policies were carried out, and Szema Kuang refused to be vice privy councilor unless the new policies were abolished."

Not only did Szema Kuang rank with Fan Chungyen as one of the two most respected prime ministers of Sung Dynasty; he was, besides, author of the monumental comprehensive history of China up to the Sung period, the *Tsechih Tungchien or Mirror of History*, in 294 volumes, with 30 volumes of appendix on sources and comparative material, a work sound in scholarship and masterly in judgment and style, which became the pole star to which all history writing in China after him must be orientated. The first draft (*changpien*)was several times the number of volumes. He used to work at it steadily, filling ten feet of paper copying notes every day, and his manuscripts were said to fill two whole rooms. The gigantic work occupied the author for twenty-five years.

What started the final fight was the issue of the farmers' loans. After months of deliberation by the bureau of economic planning, the "Regulations for Seedling Loans" were promulgated in September 1069. Forty-one high commissioners were sent out to the provinces to push through the new plan. It soon became apparent that the loans could not be voluntarily sold to the people as had been intended. The question for the high commissioners, then, was whether they wanted to come back and report that their mission had been a failure or to force the loans on the people and report a great success. The government preferred to lend money to the rich for better guarantees, but the rich were not in particular need of money. Some poor people were in need of money, but the government had to have guarantees of their ability to repay. Some of the commissioners therefore devised a system of allocating the loans to the people according to their financial standing, down to the poorest farmers. But the poor can be too poor to borrow; only the rich can borrow money, which is the essence of sound modern banking and finance. To make sure that the loans were repaid, the government made their richer neighbors stand guarantors for the poor. One of the commissioners reported that the people "cried for joy " when they were offered the loans. Another commissioner, who was not willing to force the measure on the people, came back with a different report. Censors impeached the successful commissioner for "forcing" the loans on the people, which was clearly against the intention of the original edict. Wang Anshih went to the censorate office and said to the officials, "What are you people trying to do? You impeach one commissioner who is energetic in carrying out the reforms, while you say nothing of the other who is slack in his duties."

Han Chi, who was serving at Tamingfu as governor of Hopei, had seen how the loan plan worked in the country, and he submitted a memorial which gives the best picture of how the loans were being distributed. In contrast to Su Tungpo's vehement outburst, here was a well-considered and well-worded, matter-of-fact report to the Emperor by a retired premier who had served the country in the highest capacities. In the paper he said that even the poor people of the lowest class were assigned a denomination, while the richer classes were asked to subscibe more. The so-called farmers' loans were also enforced among the city people and were sold among the landlords and "monopolist exploiters" whom it was the intention of the new measure to supplant and suppress; the loans were, therefore, defeating their own purpose. For every dollar borrowed, the people had to pay back $ 1.30 after a few months. However energetically the government denied that it was lending money for profit, people would not believe it. Han pointed out that it was impractical to prevent the forcing of loans and depend on voluntary subscription, for the rich would not borrow and the poor, who would, could not offer guarantees; therefore, in time, it would be necessary to make the guarantors pay for the loans. And since the high commissioners were anxious to please the authorities at the court, while the lower officials dared not speak up, so Han said, he found it incumbent upon him as an old faithful servant of the court to bring the facts to the Emperor's attention. He asked for the suspension of the new measure, the recall of the tax commissioners, and the restoration of the price equalization granaries on the old basis.

"Han Chi is a faithful minister," said the Emperor, discussing this memorandum with Wang Anshih. "While serving in the country, he still has not forgotten about the imperial house. I thought the loans were for the benefit of the people and did not realize that they were doing so much harm. Besides, these seedling loans were intended for the farming districts. Why do they sell them in the cities?"

"What's the harm?" replied Wang Anshih quickly. "If the people in the cities want the loans, why not let them have them?"

There was, therefore, a long exchange of letters between Han Chi and the court, and the retired premier specifically pointed out that what the state-capitalist of the Han Dynasty had done in squeezing the life blood of the people in order to fill the emperor's war chest could hardly be considered a measure to "enrich the country."

This shook Wang Anshih's position, and the Emperor began to think of suspending the loans. Wang Anshih heard about it and asked for sick leave. In referring to Wang's request for leave, Szema Kuang used the phrase, "the scholars are in a boiling rage and the people of the country are in an uproar." The high ministers discussed this situation, and Chao Pien, who was still for Wang, said that they had better wait until Wang's leave was over. That very night Tseng Kungliang, a cabinet member, had his son tell Wang Anshih secretly of the impending change, and asked Wang to cancel his leave. Following Tseng's secret tip, Wang did cancel his leave and appeared at the court again, and was able to persuade the Emperor that the opposition was merely trying to "block His Majesty's reforms."

Not knowing what to think, the Emperor now sent two eunuchs to the country to report on the situation. The eunuchs, however, knew on which side their bread was buttered, and came back with the report that the loans were "popular" with the people and that "there was no compulsion." Wen Yenpo, and old official, objected and said to the Emperor, "Do you believe two eunuchs, but will not believe Han Chi, who has served as premier in three successive regimes?" But the Emperor believed his own reporters and was strengthened in his determination to go through with the new measure. How often a few irresponsible or ignorant reporters who do not understand what they are talking about can affect the development of events and influence the national policy of a country! If the castrated men had had the manliness to tell the truth, the course of the Sung Dynasty would have taken a different turn at this time. What happened to those two eunuchs when the truth was revealed to the world we do not know. They had reported what the Emperor wanted to hear. When times changed and it was no longer the fashion to talk about these wonderful "agrarian reformers," they could keep sheepishly quiet.

Szema Kuang, Fan Chen, and Su Tungpo carried on their fight together. Szema Kuang had had a good opinion of Wang Anshih, and he enjoyed the great confidence of the Emperor. When the Emperor asked him about Wang Anshih, he said, "People's criticism of him as a hypocrite is perhaps extreme. But he is impractical and terribly stubborn." However, he had had a hot debate with Wang Anshih's henchman Huiching during a class in history for the Emperor, so much so that the latter had to break up the dispute and tell the parties to calm down. Wang Anshih had therefore begun to dislike Szema Kuang as opposed to his policies. Now while Wang was so briefly on sick leave, the Emperor wanted to make Szema Kuang vice-president of the privy council. Szema Kuang declined the office, saying that his personal positon was of no concern whatsoever, and that the important thing was whether His Majesty was going to stop these new policies. Nine times Szama Kuang submitted these memorandums. The Emperor replied,

"I am asking you to be a privy councilor in charge of military affairs. Why do you keep on declining the office and talking about these things which have nothing to do with the army?"

"But I have not yet accepted the military post," replied Szema Kuang. "So long as I am in the imperial secretariat, I must bring these things to your attention."

When Wang canceled his leave, his position was strengthened and he degraded Szema Kuang into the position of a treasurer in the secretariat. Twice Fan Chen rejected the imperial edict carrying this new appointment, and the Emperor, thus being defied, with his own hand handed the edict to Szema Kuang. Upon this, Fan Chen begged to resign his position in the imperial secretariat and was permitted to do so. With the restoration of Wang Anshih to power, Han Chi also begged to resign as governor of Hopei, retaining only his district office as magistrate at Tamingfu. Naturally, this also was granted.

Su Tungpo was getting hot under the collar. He had so much to say and he had to say it. As may be expected, he was much more forthright than the others. He was then only thirty-two, and his position in the department of history was a low and strictly literary, nonadministrative post. He wrote two letters to the Emperor, in February 1070, and February 1071. The letters were long, exhaustive, eloquent and minced no words. They were like those occasional modern editorials which arouse immediate national attention. He opened his first letter with a direct attack on the farmers' loan. He told the Emperor that the entire nation was turning against him, and warned him not to rely on power to suppress the people. Quoting Confucius, he said:

"If the people of the country are rich, does a ruler ever have to worry about his private wealth?... I do not know, when Your Majesty speaks about enriching the country, whether you are speaking about enriching the people or enriching your own purse.

"In all things, great and small, one should not depend on force, but must observe reason and the nature of things. For in all things done according to reason one is bound to succeed, and in all undertakings against reason one is doomed to fail. Now Your Majesty has compelled the farmers to pay you high interest, and you have entered into competition with businessmen for profits. Is this in accordance with nature, and do you wonder that it has failed?... If Your Majesty has the welfare of the people truly at heart, the people would show confidence in you despite all rumors; but if you are going only after revenue, the people can hardly be convinced by words. If a judge receives presents from a defendant and lets himself be influenced in his decision, people will say that he has been bribed; and if a man takes what does not belong to him people will call him a thief. That would only be calling a thing by its right name. Now, you are receiving twenty per cent interest from the farmers' loans, yet you insist that you are not making these loans for interest. How are the people to believe you?... A man is condemned by his acts and not by what he professes to do... All this commotion is because the whole country is coming to believe that Your Majesty is looking for the revenue, while you maintain that you are working only for their good. While you insist that you are totally disinterested, the whole world thinks that you are avaricious."

He advised the Emperor on a course of caution.

"Sometimes a man falls from a horse in his youth and never dares to ride again all his life... Bent on a mad rush for drastic reforms, you have started the farmers' loans, instituted the draft exemption tax, started the national trade bureau, shifted the army units. You are determined to carry these through against all criticism, but should you find out the error, then when you have good policies to carry out in the future, you will have lost all self-confidence... Your Majesty started the reign with the high hopes of youth, gifted with high intelligence and determination, and if your ministers should fail to advise you now to take the path of steadiness and caution, you would be like a man dashing over dangerous terrain in a light coach on a dark night with the coachman lashing the horse. Might it not be far better if Your Majesty would ease the reins, feed the horse, and wait patiently till the dawn, when you could travel on safe highways in broad daylight?"

The Emperor was greatly mistaken, Su Tungpo warned, if he thought he was going to succeed by reliance on his arbitrary power. Officials had been degraded and dismissed; there was talk of restoring severe punishment by bodily mutilation. He went on:

"Now the court is torn by dissension, for which there must be a cause. Instead of seeking the cause, Your Majesty intends to overcome opposition by force. But since history began, force has never been able to suppress the people. In ancient days, scholars were threatened with knives and saws in front and the boiling pot behind, but that did not stop them from voicing their convictions. Your Majesty has not yet killed any minister. So far you have only dismissed those who oppose your policy. I hardly think Your Majesty will have the heart to imitate the example of the Chin dictator and kill men for gossiping in the streets, or revive the party inquisitions of Han. Do you suppose scholardom will be frightened and silenced? The more men you banish from the court, the more will rise in protest... If Your Majesty intends to change the code of punishment and do the extreme, how will you prevent a rebellion?

"There is not a man in the country whose heart is not turning against the government, and not a tongue which is not talking ill of the regime. Does this sound like the beginning of a great reign when the Emperor and his ministers work in complete harmony for the good of the state? The ancient saying has it, A hundred people cannot be wrong.' Now it is not only a hundred people, but the entire nation which is voicing the same opinion, and yet Your Majesty persists in your course against the opposition of the entire nation. I really do not know what to say. *The Book of Songs* says:

'Like unto a drifting boat,
None knows where it is heading.
Restless I lie upon the pillow,
For my heart is bleeding.'

I hope Your Majesty will consider these humble words of mine, although I know I am courting death by this memorial.

Your humble servant,

Su Shih"

The issue that deeply stirred all officialdom was Wang's purge of the censorate. From the very beginning, Wang Anshih frightened the entire court, not so much by his drastic and extensive economic plans and policies as by his arbitrary habit of cashiering all censors who criticized them. The right to criticism of public policies was challenged. The foundation of the governmental structure was being undermined. A sensitive spot in the body politic had been touched. All officialdom was dismayed, and friends began to desert him.

The issue of the purge of the censorate was in itself enough to cause the withdrawal of support and the resignation of the government leaders. The imperial censorate was an old institution in the Chinese government, whose purpose was to represent public opinion and constantly check and criticize the ruling regime. It was held as essential to a good government that free criticism should be made readily available to the emperor so that the state of public opinion could be properly reflected. In consequence of its position, the censorate had tremendous powers and responsibilities and could overthrow an administration when the censors attacked it hard enough. It was a somewhat lax and not too well defined method for bringing about changes in the government personnel and policies, acting in somewhat the same way as the modern press. The difference in ancient China was that there was no legal protection for the censorate or for the lights of the opposition, but only the established tradition that a "good" emperor should be liberal toward criticism; whether he cared for such a good reputation was up to the emperor himself. If he did not choose to exercise moral restraint, he could constitutionally degrade, punish, torture, or kill the censors and their entire families. Many did so. The censors were placed in the impossible position of having the official duty to admonish both the government and the emperor himself without any constitutional protection of their personal liberties. But as in modern times there are always editors with a sense of responsibility to the public who are brave enough to defy a totalitarian regime at the risk of imprisonment and death, so there were always censors who braved corporal punishment, flogging, and even death to carry out their duties to the people. This is particulary true of the Easern Han and the Ming periods, when there were censors who, having written their protests against a vile premier and knowing that they were only courting death, hanged themselves before they sent in their letters of protest. These censors went up to battle like soldiers; as soon as one fell, another rose to take his place. Good emperors who loved a good name would be careful in their treatment of these censors, earning great fame and popularity for themselves, but bad administrations were anxious to silence the censors just as modern dictators find it necessary to muzzle the press.

Wang Anshih had started his administration with great expectations from the elder statesmen. Now when the chief of the censorate Lu Huei fired the first shot at Wang Anshih, describing him as "a hypocrite and a sinister character destined to bring the country to the brink of catastrophe," even Szema Kuang was surprised. As they walked together to a class in classics to be given to the Emperor, Lu revealed to Szema Kuang what he was going to do that morning, and showed him the memorial concealed in his sleeve.

"But what can we do? He is so popular," said Szema Kuang.

"You, too!" replied Lu Huei, shocked.

Lu Huei was dismissed from his post, and the purge began.

Now a spark set the court politics on fire. There was the case of a woman who had attempted murder of her husband but had only succeeded in wounding him. The woman had confessed her intent of murder, and the highest officials disagreed on the proper punishment. The case had therefore been standing for over a year. Szema Kuang wanted to settle it one way, and Wang Anshih wanted to settle it the other and insisted on carrying it through. The punishment was embodied in an imperial decree, but the censor, Liu Shu, rejected it for reconsideration, as the imperial censors often did. A second censor defied Wang's will, and Wang impeached him through one of his underlings. This then brought the fight into the open.

The imperial censors were aroused. The question was whether they were to be free to prosecute their duties, or whether one by one they were to be politically disposed of. Several of the censors sent a joint impeachment of Wang Anshih and asked for his recall. Wang Anshih was angered and wanted to put them in jail. Szema Kuang and Fan Chunjen opposed this on principle, and eventually six censors were sent out to distant provinces to sell wine at the government stores. Upon this, Fan Chunjen took up the fight. He demanded that the order dismissing the censors be rescinded—and was dismissed himself. The next to fall was Tseyu, Su Tungpo's brother, who had consistently opposed the farmers' loans and the national trade bureau. Two months later the good old premier Fu Pi resigned, warning that in any political fight the good men were bound to lose, while the bad politicians were bound to come out on top. For good men fought for principles and bad men fought for power, and in the end both would get what they wanted, by the good men's quitting and the bad men's staying. He predicted that with this trend of afffairs, the country would soon be plunged into chaos.

The court was now thrown into an uproar. The bureau of economic planning was instituted in February 1069, the national trade bureau in July, and the farmers' loans in September. In the course of a few months public opinion toward the new administration changed from great expectations to doubt, doubt gave place to confusion, and confusion to anger and fear.

Things were happening fast now. The months of March and April 1070 saw a wholesale purge and packing of the censorate. The two censors who fell next were Wang's personal friends, men who had helped him to power and on whom he had depended for support. Tall, fiery, eloquent Sun Chueh, who was also Su's lifelong friend, had challenged Wang on his claim that the currency bureau of the Chou Dynasty, established in the twelfth century B.C., had lent money to people at the rate of twenty-five per cent interest. Still hoping for his support, Wang sent him out on a court investigation, again demanded by the Emperor, into the persistent rumors that the loans were being "forced" on the farmers even in districts close to the capital. Sun came back and honestly reported that there was compulsion, which Wang regarded as a "betrayal" of friendship—so Sun was dismissed. The more important case was that of "Handsome Beard" Lu Kungchu, son of a premier, and a man of great learning but few words. In their earlier days Wang and Lu had divided literary honors and the admiration of scholars. Lu had helped Wang to power, and in return Wang had made him chief of the censorate. Now Lu asked in a petition to the Emperor, somewhat too pointedly for Wang's comfort, "How is it that all public opinion has suddenly become 'reactionary,' and how is it that the great and able ministers of yesterday have suddenly become the 'corrupt' men of today?" Wang drafted the edict of dismissal himself in words which showed something of the temperamental character of the man. In their days of friendship, Wang Anshih had said to the Emperor, "A man of Lu's ability simply has to become a prime minister some day." Now he compared Lu to one of the "Four Evil Monsters" under the ideal emperors Yao and Shun.

What alienated his former admirers more was that in the same month Wang appointed two disreputable characters to replace the censors he had dismissed. The appointment of Leeding as a full-rank censor aroused a great fury in the censorate. Leeding had neither passed the official examinations nor acquired the necessary civil service standing, and he was known to have concealed the news of his mother's death and failed to observe the rites of mourning. In Chinese eyes, this is tantamount to degenerating into a beast. Wang promoted him to this post because Leeding had come up from the country and had reported that the farmers' loans were "extremely popular" with the people; Wang had introduced him to the Emperor to make the report in person. This aroused the ire of the censors. At the same time Wang made Shieh Chingwen, his brother-in-law, also a censor. To secure promotion, Shieh had married his sister to one of Wang Anshih's brothers. Three imperial secretaries rejected the edict of appointment—which brought about the dismissal of these three from their office. The other remaining censors then took up the issue. Chang Chien demanded the recall to power of the dismissed censors and the cashiering of Leeding and Huiching, known as the power behind Wang Anshih. When Chang Chien went up to the premier's office to press his case, he found Wang Anshih in a curious state of mind. The latter listened to him without saying a word, but was laughing behind a fan held before his face.

"I do not doubt," said the censor, "that you are laughing at me for my stupidity. But you should be aware that there are many more people in the country who are laughing at you."

Another important censor to fall at the same time was Cheng Hao, the elder of the two "Cheng brothers," great neo-Confucianist philosophers of the Sung Dynasty. Cheng Hao had co-operated with Wang intimately in the early days of the reforms. Now he also went to the premier's office to fight the case out with Wang personally. The latter had just read his memorandum, and the caller found him in a state of uncontrollable rage. Philosophically, the neo-Confucianist said, "Look here, my friend, we are not fighting over personal or family affairs; we are discussing the affairs of the country. Can we not talk in a calm and dispassionate manner?" By all Confucian standards, Wang lost face and felt ashamed of himself.

Within a few weeks the purge of the censorate was complete. With the six censors who had been cashiered in the previous year, the total of dismissed censors was now fourteen, eleven in the censorate and three in the palace. Szema Kuang warned the Emperor in unmistakable terms. Only three persons, Wang, Tseng Pu, and Lu Huiching, were for the new reform measures, and the entire court was against them. "Is His Imperial Majesty going to make up the government and the nation with these three persons?" Han Chi and Chang Fangping had quit in February; Szema Kuang had refused a post as privy councilor and was degraded in the same month; Fan Chen had left in anger. In September the vacillating Chao Pien, the cabinet minister who had for a time been inclined to favor the new regime, now decided to resign. He too pointed out that "the farmers' loans and the appointment of tax commissioner are by comparison small matters, but the choice of the right men to assist the Emperor in his government is a matter of far greater consequence." A few months later, aged, fatalistic, imperturbable Tseng Kungliang, who had ascribed Wang's rise to power to "God's will," resigned in disgust, giving old age as his excuse, but in reality partly under fire from the critics. By December

1070, Wang Anshih was formally made premier and was placed in an unchallenged position at the head of the whole government. In June of the following year Ouyang Shiu resigned all his posts in the government and went to live in retirement.

Su Tungpo now wrote his famous nine-thousand-word letter to the Emperor, and was prepared to be dismissed. He and Szema Kuang and Fan Chen had carried on the fight together, but Szema and Fan had quit in disgust and anger. Fan Chen, later related to Su Tungpo, had served in the imperial secretariat under the last two emperors. Fat and soft in appearance, he had the strength of steel in his character. When he left, he said in his letter of resignation, "Your Majesty is disposed to take frank criticism, but your minister obstructs it; Your Majesty loves the people at heart, but your minister is oppressing them in practice." The Emperor showed this letter to Wang Anshih during a court audience, and Wang's face blanched. Some of those close by reported that they saw his hands holding the letter shaking with rage.

Szema Kuang had been sent to an outpost in Shensi in September 1070. He had been slow to give up. It was after three exchanges of earnest if bitter letters with Wang that the complete break came. The Emperor was still hoping for him to return to the court, for he had repeatedly told the other ministers that he felt safe from committing bad blunders so long as Szema Kuang was by his side. Again and again the Emperor called him to the capital, and Szema Kuang refused. He had said enough. If the Emperor could not be dissuaded from riding on the stubborn mule to perdition, his duty was done. When he decided to quit altogether and live in retirement, his anger was unrestrained. He wrote to the Emperor, "Whoever agrees with Anshih is right, and whoever disagrees with Anshih is wrong. Those who lick Anshih's spittle are the 'loyal ministers,' and those who oppose his policies are the 'scheming intriguers'... I have disagreed with Anshih, and am therefore both wrong and a 'scheming intriguer' in Your Majesty's opinion. I ask for your decision. If my crimes are like those of Fan Chen, allow me to lay down my office as you allowed Fan Chen to do. If my crimes are worse, exile or sentence me to death, and I will gladly accept my fate."

From now until the Emperor's death sixteen years later, Szema Kuang was to shut himself up completely to devote himself to the monumental history already begun nine years before. Later, when Emperor Shentsung had dismissed Wang Anshih and wanted to call Szema Kuang back to power, his one reply was still, was the Emperor ready to reverse his economic policies? Thus the two poles of political thought stood, each unmoving and immovable to the end. Yet in the first year of the next emperor, when Wang Anshih died and Szema Kuang was on his deathbed, the order he gave as premier then was: "Wang Anshih was not too bad a person. His only fault was his stubbornness. Let him be buried with all the honors the court can give."

Su Tungpo's nine-thousand-word letter to the Emperor is important as embodying his political philosophy, and as indicative of his personal temperament and style, a mixture of wit, learning, and intrepid courage. Angered polemics alternate with cool, lucid reasoning. Now he was despondent, bitter, sharply critical and uncommonly forthright; now he was arguing, citing examples, quoting from Mencius, Confucius, and the histories to bolster his thesis. Adroit, sincere, and convincing, it was written with profound emotion and sorrow at the state of affairs. In his audience with the Emperor in January, His Majesty had praised a memorial by him on educational reforms and asked him for "straight criticism... even of His Majesty himself." Su Tungpo took him at this word. It was his last desperate effort to make the Emperor change his mind, when all high officials had left and all chances were against him. He knew that he would be dismissed, if nothing worse happened.

The two most important points for the modern reader are the

Mencian principle that the ruler derives his power from the people, and the defense of free criticism on the principle of dissent in politics. Su Tungpo warned the Emperor, a ruler is ruler, not by virtue of a mythical "divine right" of kings, but by the support he derives from the people. Let the king beware!

"It is said in the *Book of History*, 'In ruling over the people, I feel as if I were holding six horses with worn-out reins.' This means that no one in the nation is in a more precarious position than the emperor himself. When the emperor and the people come together, they are ruler and subjects; when they detest each other, they become foes. But the line of division, determining whether the people go with the ruler or against him, is extremely tenuous. He who is able to command the support of the millions becomes a king, while he who alienates their support becomes a solitary private individual. The basis of the ruler's power lies, therefore, entirely in the support of the people in their hearts. The relation of the people's support to the ruler may be likened to that of the roots to a tree, oil to the lamp, water to the fish, rice fields to the farmer, and capital to the businessman. A tree dries up when its roots are cut; the lamp goes out when the oil is gone; fish die when they leave the water; farmers starve when deprived of their rice fields, and merchants go bankrupt when they have no more capital. And when an emperor loses the support of the people, it spells his ruin. This is an inexorable law from whose consequences no ruler can hope to escape. From ancient times such has been, always, the danger confronting a rualer."

But how was the ruler to obtain the support of the people unless he permitted the free expression of opinion? Su Tungpo went on to develop what I consider the most important point in the memorandum. This was the principle of disagreement in politics, as embodied in the system of the imperial censorate. For, according to Su Tungpo, the maintenance of a good regime depended very much upon the healthy operation of political opposition. Democracy itself is predicated upon the principle of disagreement among parties. In modern times I am sure Su would have opposed the principle of unanimity in the United Nations Security Council as being essentially antidemocratic. He knew that at least since Chinese Adam no two persons have ever completely agreed, and that the only alternative to democracy is tyranny. I have never yet found an enemy of democracy who is not a tyrant in the home, in the country, or in world politics. Su Tungpo went on:

"Sun Pao has well said, 'The Duke of Chou was a great sage and the Duke of Shao was a great genius, and yet history records they seldom agree with one another at court.' There was, too, Wang Tao of the Chin dynasty, who may be considered truly a great minister. But when at dinner the guests approved of whatever he said, Wang Shu was displeased. 'No one is a sage; you cannot always be right,' said Wang Shu, and the minister thanked him for the advice. If Your Majesty wants everybody to think the same thought and express the same opinion and the whole court to sing the same tune, everybody can do it. But should there be in the government unprincipled men serving along with the rest, how will Your Majesty expect ever to find it out?"

No one, I believe, stated the reasons for the existence of the censorate and the principles underlying it so clearly as Su Tungpo in this letter. The issue of a free, unfettered, fearless censorate was the issue of a free public opinion.

"It appears to me that when the atmosphere for free criticism prevails, even mediocre people will be encouraged to speak up, but when such freedom is destroyed, even the best people will be inclined to hold their tongues. I fear that from now on the pattern may be set and the censors will become no more than the flunkies of the cabinet ministers, with the result that the Emperor will stand in complete isolation from his people. Once the system has been destroyed, anything may happen... One cannot, furthermore, escape the conclusion that when there are no fearless critics of the government in times of peace, there will also be no national heroes willing to die for the country in times of trouble. If you do not permit your people even to put in a word of criticism, how do you expect them to die for the country when trouble comes?"

He compared the state of public opinion of the present with the past.

"I remember hearing in my childhood from the elders that the censors always reflected faithfully the public opinion of the country; what the public praised, the censors also praised, and what the public disliked, the censors condemned... Now the country is in an uproar and grumblings are heard on every side; it should not be difficult for Your Majesty to gauge what the state of public opinion is like."

Su developed the *raison d'être* of the censorate by a comparative study of different systems of government in the different dynasties. Here he showed himself as a great advocate, scholarly in manner, cogent in reasoning, penetrating in insight.

"From a study of the government systems of the ancient times, we see that there was always the question of balance of power between the central and the provincial governments. In the Chou and Tang Dynasties the system inclined toward decentralization, while in the Chin and Wei it inclined toward centralization. The result of overcentralization was that a few corrupt men close to the court were able to make the emperor their tool for power, while the result of over-decentralization was that the provincial governors became too powerful and sometimes raised the banner of rebellion. A great statesman shows foresight by providing against the causes of corruption and decay while a country is yet at its height of prosperity... In comparision with the other dynasties, it [the persent dynasty]may be described as inclining toward a centralized system of government. I do not presume to know what the founders of this dynasty, the Imperial Ancestors, had in mind as the means to check the dangers of overcentralization. But it seems to me the establishment of the Imperial Censorate was meant as such a safeguard... Since the founding of the Sung house, never has an official censor been severely punished... When there was important information concerning the country, everyone was free to speak up, regardless of his rank. If it concerned the personal character and morals of the emperor, he always listened with attentive respect; if it concerned important government policies, the cabinet ministers held themselves ready for questioning. This was carried to such an extent in the regime of Jentsung that it was derisively said of the cabinet ministers of the time that they were merely servants of the censorate carrying out their orders.

"Now there is a deep purpose in the establishment of the system of the censorate, of which people are not usually aware. It is true that what the censors suggest may not be always right, but it is of the greatest importance that these critics should be given complete freedom and great responsibility, not merely as a matter of form, but for the very definite purpose of checking the rise of selfish men to power and of safeguarding against the danger always inherent in a strongly centralized government. Before a bad minister comes into power, it is a comparatively easy thing for the censors to stop him, but after he is entrenched in his position, it may take an army to overthrow him, and then it may not always succeed... I hope Your Majesty will ponder deeply the purpose and meaning of this institution of government critics, and keep it alive for the protection of Your Imperial Descendants. There is in my mind nothing more important for maintaining the proper functioning of the government than this institution."

Su Tungpo warned the Emperor against reliance upon his power to cow the people into submission. Again he referred to the growing rumor of restoration of punishment by bodily mutilation. Hundreds of years earlier, various forms of mutilation had been used in the punishment of criminals, including branding, cutting off noses, cutting off legs, and castration. These inhuman punishments were abolished after the second century B.C., except castration, which was abolished around the year 600 A.D. It is to the credit of Su Tungpo that he prevented the restoration of such cruelties by these two letters. The gossip was increasing.

"Even Your Majesty and the few ministers close to you have heard of these rumors. You have disregarded them by saying, 'Why should I worry about these rumors when there is no basis to them?' While it is true that such rumors may not all be correct yet they must have sprung up for good reasons. A man must be greedy before he is accused of being a thief, and a man must be loose in his morals before he is accused of immorality with women..."

Business had been paralyzed, Su pointed out, and prices had gone up; from the near-by provinces to distant Szechuen, rumors were rife and the people were in an uproar; even deep in the mountainous districts a wine monopoly had been established; monks and nuns had been arrested and deprived of their property, and solders' and officials' pay had been cut.

"You have established the bureau of economic planning which is for the purpose of securing revenue. You have sent out over forty tax commissioners, whose evident objective can only be to raise money for the government. It is useless for a man to ride out to the forests with a pack of greyhounds and announce to the world, 'I am not going hunting,' or for a man to go with a fish net to the lakes and declare, 'I am not going fishing.' It would be much better to stop the rumors by throwing away the fish nets and sending home the hunting dogs."

He trusted that the Emperor would be able to see clearly for himself that there was dissension and strife in the country. He should be able to deduce from the resignation of all the able ministers what the state of public opinion was like. After repeating most of the arguments against the current reforms, he drove home the idea that in carrying out these economic policies, the Emperor had already forfeited the people's support, and public opinion was against him and against the regime.

The letter was received in silence. In March, Su followed up with a third letter. The Emperor had in the interim issued an edict forbidding compulsory allocation of loans, but he was not ready to put a complete stop to these measures. Quoting Mencius, Su said this was like a chicken thief who said he was now ready to reform, and would steal only one chicken per month. What aggravated the situation was that in his capacity as magistrate at the capital, an office he had held since January 1071, he gave out as subject for the local examinations "On Dictatorship," which angered Wang Anshih greatly.

Promptly, Su Tungpo was cashiered. Just as he predicted, although the Emperor might take his advice kindly, the politicians could get him in trouble by some framed-up charge. The brother-in-law and flunkey of Wang Anshih, Shieh Chingwen, set the wheels of the law moving against Su Tungpo. There was now a rumor that while he was carrying his father's coffin home in the long voyage back to Szechuen, he had made unwarranted use of government guards and had bought furniture and porcelain and possibly smuggled salt for profit. Officials were sent out to the different provinces along the route which the Su brothers had traveled to collect data from boatmen, soldiers, and custom officers. Su Tungpo probably did buy a lot of furniture and porcelain, but there was nothing illegal about it. The couriers came back and reported that they could not find anything, and they certainly would have if they could.

In his letter to his wife's brother, who was at this time living back at Szachuen, Su wrote, "Miss Twenty-Seven [Mrs. Su]is doing well and recently a son has been born to us... I have been a thorn in the sides of the authorities for a long time. Let them investigate all they want. I know they will only make fools of themselves. You may have heard of the rumor, but do not worry on my account."

When Szema Kuang was in the capital before proceeding to his home in Loyang, the Emperor said to him:

"It seems to me Su Shih has not a good personal character. Perhaps you have made a mistake in your high opinion of him."

"Are you referring to the charges against Su?" replied Szema Kuang. "I know the man better. Your Majesty is aware that this Shieh Chingwen is a relative of Anshih and the charge was instigated by Wang himself. Besides, though Su Shih may not be perfect, is he not better than Leeding, the beast who concealed his mother's funeral?"

According to his official standing Su should now have been made a full magistrate, which the Emperor had intended to do. Wang Anshih and Shieh Chingwen objected and made him deputy magistrate in a near-by district; however, the Emperor changed it and appointed him deputy magistrate of the beautiful city of Hangchow. Against the charge of the censor Su Tungpo did not even bother to write a defense. He let the investigators do their work, while he proceeded with his family to Hangchow.

第九章　人的恶行

现在朝廷上平静了，死一般的平静。苏东坡携眷离都之时，当年仁宗在位年间的名臣儒吏都已清除净尽，四散于外地。欧阳修正退隐于安徽富阳。苏家世交张方平家正在河南淮阳。

苏子由年前即被神宗任命为淮阳州学教授。苏子由也有其特点，不像兄长子瞻那么倔强任性，但一直洁身自好，使清誉不受玷染，能照顾自己免于危害，所以挑选一个平安卑微的职位，与贤士大儒相往还。后来张方平辞官归隐，迁居河南商邸，或称"南都"，子由请调至商邸为官。次年，苏东坡往返京都之时，总是路宿张宅，向张方平请求指教，如对叔伯长辈。司马光与吕公著现在西都洛阳，过着退隐的生活。吕晦病重将死，死前，他呈给皇帝一个难题求教：

臣本无宿疾，遇值医者用术乖方，妄投汤剂，率情任意，差之指下，祸延四肢，浸成风痹。非只悍螫之苦，又将虞心腹之变。虽一身之微，固不足恤，而九族之托，良以为忧。

贤德的老宰相富弼不能平安度日，已经被降职为博州太守，当道认为他推销青苗贷款，办理不力。并且他还胆敢上奏折称："此法行，则财聚于上，人散于下。"这时王安石的心腹邓绾，突然十分活跃起来，一看有机会可以效忠主子了，他向主子说可以控富弼阻碍新政之罪，于是富弼宰相的显爵全被剥除，调至另一县去任太守。但是王安石于愿未足，对皇帝说富弼所犯之罪，情如尧舜时之"四凶"，倘若只将他的宰相官爵褫除而已，何以遏阻其他奸邪之辈？皇帝对王安石所奏，置之不理，任由富弼去担任那一卑小的职位。富弼在往就新职途中，路过南都，访问老友张方平。

老相国感慨系之，他向张方平说："知人甚难。"

张方平说："你说的是王安石吗？我认为了解他并不难。当年我有一次和他共办乡试，他就把一切老规矩都弄得乱七八糟的，我就把他调离我的部下，再不理他。"老宰相自觉难堪，又起程赶路。在老年，他常常仰望屋顶，默然叹息。

苏东坡离京之前，京中曾发生一次暴乱。在前年冬天，保甲制便已实行，新兵在乡村受军事训练，新兵疑心受训的用意，以为会调离家乡，会开至北方去和外族打仗，于是临近京都的村子里发生了示威抗议。骚乱之发生还另有原因。当时官方命令农人自备武器，其实也只是弓箭而已。父子相拥而泣，村民有断腕以躲避征调者。由于这次暴乱，王安石丢掉了他最后一个朋友韩维。因为韩维正是那一县的太守，他奏明暴乱经过，呈请暂将军训延缓，至深冬举行，因那时农忙已过，空闲较多。就因此一表章，连韩维也遭罢黜了。

要使王安石失势，还须上天显示昭然可见的征兆，需要宫廷门吏的仁行义举。在神宗熙宁六年（一〇七三），南岳华山山崩。皇帝至为慌乱，依照习俗，乃迁居另一宫殿，以示敬仰神祇，并下令以粗粝三餐上进。此外，自此年夏季到次年春季，一直干旱不雨，皇帝至为忧愁，不知如何是好。他问王安石，王安石回答说：

"旱涝乃是天灾，在尧汤之世也曾发生。吾人之所能为者只是力行善政而已。"

皇帝说："我所担心的也是此事，恐怕我们所行的不是善政啊。我听见关于商税法的怨言甚多。宫里人人都听说了，连皇后、太后也听说了。"

另一个阁员大臣冯京也在场，他也说："我也听说了。"

王安石回答说："为什么我没听人说？冯大人之所以听说，是因为所有发怨言不满的人都奔赴你的四周了。"

现在命定要成大事的渺小人物快要出现了。他叫郑侠，就是画难民图的皇宫门吏。他呈给皇帝的难民图上，画的是戴着脚镣的难民在砍树挣钱，用以付还官家的青苗贷款。郑侠还随图附上一篇短文：

窃闻南征北伐者，皆以其胜捷之势、山川之形，为图来献。料无一人以天下之民质妻鬻子、斩桑坏舍、流离逃散、皇皇不给之状，图以上闻者。臣谨按安上门逐日所见，绘成一图，百不及一，但经圣览，亦可流涕。况于千万里之外，有甚于此者哉！陛下观臣之图，行臣之言，十日不雨，即乞斩臣宣德门外，以正欺君之罪。

皇帝把画卷带到寝宫，给皇后和皇家别人看。先说话的是皇帝的祖母：

"我听说百姓为了免役税和青苗贷款，其苦不堪。我觉得我们不应擅改祖制。"

皇帝回答说："但是实行新法也是为民谋福，并无害民之意。"

太后又说："我知道王安石自有大才，但是已然树敌甚众。为了他自己的好处，你还是暂时把他的职务中止吧。"

皇帝说："我发现在满朝大臣之中，只有王安石愿意身当大任。"

皇帝的弟弟歧王这时正立在一旁，他说："我认为你应当听听祖母老人家刚才说的话。"

皇帝突然大怒说："好！好！我不会治国，你来接。"

歧王说："我不是那个意思。"

大家僵住，静了片刻，然后皇太后说："这些乱子都是王安石闯的，你要怎么办呢？"

第二天早晨王安石罢相，但吕惠卿和邓绾仍然在位。皇帝决定把商法、青苗法、免役法、保甲法、土地登记等一共八种新法，中止推行。

天开始下雨。老天爷高兴了。

但是王安石的时刻还未到。弹劾门吏郑侠还得需要技巧。郑侠第一次循正规献画时，宫廷的官吏拒而不受，说官卑职小，无权与皇帝上奏章。郑侠乃到京师城外的官差站，因为此系非法利用官差制度，郑侠要在御史台受审。

审问的结果如何，历史上并无记载。但是次年正月，郑侠又将一画册呈献给皇帝，名为《正人君子邪曲小人事业图》。所绘乃唐代贤臣奸佞图像，虽未指明系宋代当时权要，而前代奸佞之辈所作所为，却与当代奸人有其相似处，一看便知，决不致误，即使容有含混难解之处，画册上的故事也可以祛除心中的疑问。与这本画册同时进献的还有一个奏章，推荐一位贤人出任宰相，因为此时王安石已遭罢黜。现在当政的是吕惠卿，邓绾已然改向吕惠卿效忠。在这两个小人狼狈为奸之下，将郑侠贬谪到偏远的广东去。

在郑侠离京之前，一位御史前去看他，对他说："所有各御史对朝政都钳口不言，独君一人挺立不屈，作此殊死战，殊为可敬！"而今似乎全御史台监察朝政之重任，移到一宫廷门吏的肩上了。那个御史于是交给他包好的两卷名臣奏议，都是弹劾御史台里当权的小人的文章，并且对他说："我把这些资料交托与你，务必妥为保管。"但是吕惠卿由于他那颇有效能的侦察网，获得了这项消息，他派舒亶在路上追到郑侠，搜查他的行李。按照此两册上曾经批评朝政的官名，吕惠卿、邓绾、舒亶乃按部就班地逐一迫害那些人，并予以监禁。吕惠卿打算把郑侠判处死刑，但是皇帝阻止道："郑侠谋国而不谋身，忠诚勇气，颇可嘉许，不可重罚。"所以郑侠仍准径赴流放之地，未予阻挠。

苏东坡去世之后，一黄某获得苏东坡一珍贵的手稿，其中有苏东坡下列的名句："处贫贱易，处富贵难。安劳苦易，安闲散难。忍痛易，忍痒难。人能安闲散，耐富贵，忍痒，真有道之士也。"每一次革命在未得势之前，能表现出最大的力量与团结；但在既已得势，既已清除反对力量之后，则开始由内部的纷争而分裂，终至崩溃。在力图推翻别人时，人性中的精华发挥作用；在企图控制别人时，则人性中之糟粕发挥作用。只要情况顺利，这群小人各有肥缺在手，邓绾、吕惠卿、曾布之间，则忙得无空闲自相争吵；但在王安石一旦失势，情况开始逆转，此一帮派则内部失和了。

在此失和之前，内部腐坏的种子早已播下。王安石的儿子很恨吕惠卿，而吕惠卿很恨曾布，而邓绾是跟着兔子跑，却帮猎狗忙，吃里扒外，所以往后是够忙的。王安石最后只落了一个儿子。这个儿子聪明外露，古怪任性，而又残忍凶暴，王氏集团许多恶行他当负其责任。现在他已长大成人，他已经开始管理家中的钱财，他的叔伯不再能像往常那样乱用王安石的钱。这个权倾一时的宰相的傲慢无理的儿子，以为凭态度恶劣，由他的令人厌恶，便可以显得出人头地。据说，新政初期，一天，道学家程灏正在王安石家开会。这个儿子出现了，头发散乱，赤足无鞋，手拿女人的头巾，一直走到父亲跟前，问他们正在说什么话。

王安石回答说："我正和程先生谈论新政，我们的新政总受到别的大臣批评。"

儿子一下子坐在大人坐的座位上，大笑道："只要把韩琦和富弼的头砍下来就够了。"

王安石自己为他儿子受了什么罪，随后自可看到。王家不是和睦可喜的一家人，因为这一家有两个叔叔，一直不赞成王安石的做法，特别警告王安石提防吕惠卿那个骗子。孔夫子一次说人应当"驱郑声，远佞人"。有一天，王安石正和吕惠卿商讨政事，弟弟安国在外面吹笛子。王安石向外面的弟弟喊道："停此郑声如何？"弟弟应声回敬道："远此佞人如何？"

现在这一帮派很担心他们的前途。但是吕惠卿并没完全失望，而且正好看到自己得势之日已近，取王安石而代之的机会到了。世界上有些人能随意操纵眼泪，吕惠卿和邓绾便是此等人。他俩去见皇帝，以一副极为动人的样子在皇帝面前哭，好像他们想到国家的前途就悲从中来。应用他们动人的口才，又把皇帝拖回了原来那条老道路，而吕惠卿也官拜了宰相之位。

现在争吵真正开始了。全国的市易务官吕嘉问这时遭到弹劾。市易务的滥权枉法的报告，自然传到皇帝耳朵里。皇帝问王安石，那时王安石还在京都。

王安石回奏道："嘉问一向认真守法，自然树敌甚众，所以才受攻击。"

皇帝说:"但是朝廷从商税方面收到的钱的确很少,而且我很不喜欢官家卖水果、卖水、卖煤这等事,对朝廷太不体面。"

王安石回奏道:"陛下不必为这些小事操心,这是低级员司管的事,皇帝只要留心朝廷的主要政策就行了。"

皇帝回答道:"即便如此,可是为何朝廷上人人把这种措施看作暴政呢?"

王安石回答道:"请把那些人的名字交给臣。"

这些肮脏龃龉的口角争吵,不值得详谈。实际上的内幕是,市易务官吕嘉问身居要津,开始公然蔑视条例司,污辱了一个叫薛向的官员,而曾布却偏袒着薛向,攻击吕嘉问,吕嘉问因而免职。吕惠卿和曾布奉命调查此一案件。吕和曾二人一向交恶,二人与王安石的关系,正如斯大林与托洛茨基之与列宁一样。在调查期间,吕惠卿开始攻击曾布,曾布也开始攻击吕惠卿,曾布垮台。

这是纠纷的开端。吕惠卿而今成了朝廷唯一的魁元。他不但抓住郑侠案件的机会罢黜了王安石的弟弟王安国,又借着无处不在的邓绾的帮助,想把王安石牵连在山东省一个谋反案件中,其实那是由一个亲王发动的。王安石被控与叛逆串通,因为他与一逆贼是朋友。还有另一个阁员,也曾名义上做过宰相,他与吕惠卿极不相容,他想使王安石官复原职,用以抑制吕惠卿。他除去请皇帝罢黜吕惠卿,重用王安石之外,又送一密函与王安石。控告谋反自然是极严重,王安石以七日之内,火速进京。

王安石与谋反一案确无干系,在神宗熙宁八年(一○七五)二月,又重任宰相。这使邓绾有几分尴尬,他只好连忙背弃吕惠卿,又投入王安石这边来。为了重获王安石的青睐,他决定出卖吕惠卿。邓绾背着王安石,暗中和王安石的儿子勾结,控告吕惠卿勒索华亭商人五百万缗。朝廷降吕惠卿官，出为太守。邓绾以吕惠卿如此轻易逃过，心有不甘，乃联合吕嘉问请求重新审问，将吕惠卿羁押在京师的御史台监狱中。

一度权势炙手可热的小人权要，一一遭到罢黜，邓绾也非例外。邓绾还依然是精力充沛，他亲眼看到吕惠卿垮台，又看出皇帝对王安石也日形厌倦。他以天纵阴谋之才，洞烛机先，心想下一个身揽大权的人必是王安石的儿子和女婿。他上一表章，请皇帝将此二人升迁重用。但是王安石和皇帝对邓绾的变节背信早已厌腻，不但不心存感激，反将他罢官斥退。邓绾现在对人性应当是失去了信心吧！

吕惠卿在御史台监狱等待审判之时，对王安石发出了最后的一击。原来那些年他保存了王安石的一些私人信件，以备敲诈之用。现在他把这些信都呈交给皇帝，控告王安石在皇帝背后图谋不轨，因为有几封信上有"无令上知此一帖"。皇帝对这些纷乱如麻的事早已厌恶，而今在这些信上的发现，真使皇帝对王安石第一次发了脾气。王安石痛骂自己的儿子，不该背着他胡乱攻击吕惠卿。他儿子显然不知道吕惠卿手中藏有这些信，并且握有他父亲的把柄，深悔自己行动鲁莽。受父亲斥责之后又心中憋气，立刻病倒，不久背上生出了恶疮。王安石一向信佛，他请和尚诵经，请医生开药，但均无法救儿子一命。儿子王雱之死，是对老相国的一个严重的打击。这位相国对政治与人生的虚幻，大彻大悟了，他感觉厌倦，呈请辞官归隐。皇帝允许他在熙宁九年（一〇七六）十月辞去职务，但仍保有若干最高爵位，王安石并非遭受罢黜。数年之后，有人在金陵附近的乡间，看见他骑着驴，嘴里喃喃自语，听不清说些什么。

Chapter Nine
THE EVIL THAT MEN DO

There was peace at the court now, the peace of death. By the time Su Tungpo left the capital with his family, all the brilliant scholars of the famous reign of Jentsung had been disposed of and had dispersed out into the country. Ouyang Shiu was living in retirement at Fouyang in Anhuei. The great friend of the Su family, Chang Fangping, was living at Huaiyang, in Honan.

Tseyu, the year before, had been appointed a teacher in the district college at the same place. There is something curious about Tseyu; less headstrong than his brother, he had always, without compromising his integrity, nevertheless been able to look out for himself and to choose a safe and obscure position, living in the company of some great scholar. Later, when Chang Fangping retired and moved to Shangchiu, then called Nanking, or "Southern Capital," Tseyu had himself appointed to a post there also, and in the following years Su Tungpo always stopped at Chang Fangping's house on his way to and from the capital, asking and getting advice from him as from an uncle. Szema Kuang and Lu Kungchu were now to spend the following years in quiet retirement at the "Western Capital" in Loyang. Lu Huei fell ill and was about to die, but before he died, he sent a conundrum for the Emperor to solve.

"Your Majesty:

"Since my departure from the court I have fallen ill. There was really nothing wrong with me, but I had a bad doctor, and was forced to take all kinds of drastic medicines and strange prescriptions. In time I developed a paralysis of the limbs, and my movements are no longer free. But I suspect there is deeper trouble at the heart of the whole system for I feel a revolt from within. Now the disease has developed to such a point, what can I do? Although my own person is not important and I do not mind dying, still I am mindful of the fact that I am a member of a house, entrusted with the duty toward my ancestors, and I am greatly worried about my descendants."

The good old premier Fu Pi was not yet able to live quite at peace. He had been degraded to a magistracy at Pochow, and had not been dutiful in selling the loans to the farmers. Besides, he had the audacity to write to the Emperor that "if this state of things keeps on, soon wealth will be concentrated at the top and the people will be scattered below." It was a great chance for one of Wang Anshih's men, Dunquan, who now suddenly sprang into great activity, to serve his master. Dunquan proposed prosecuting Fu Pi for blocking reforms, and the old minister was deprived of his high ranks and transferred to another district as magistrate. But Wang was dissatisfied and said to the Emperor that Fu Pi had committed crimes similar to those committed by the Four Evil Monsters, and if he were merely deprived of his ministerial honors, how could other traitors be warned and stopped from following in his footsteps? The Emperor refused to listen to Wang's advice, and permitted Fu Pi to keep his small job. On the way to his new appointment Fu Pi passed the Southern Capital and called on Chang Fangping.

Regretfully the old premier said to Chang, "It is so difficult to know a man's character."

"You mean Wang Anshih?" replied his friend. "I did not think it was so difficult to know *him*. I once served with him on the board of a local examination and he started to upset everything. I dismissed him from my staff and never talked with him again." The old premier felt ashamed of himself. He went on his way, and in his old age he used to gaze at the roof and sigh in silence.

Just before Su Tungpo left, there was a riot at the capital. The *paochia* system had been enforced during the previous winter. Military training of the conscripted men was going on in the villages. Suspicious of this training, and thinking that the conscripts would soon be taken from their homes to fight wars with the northern tribes, the villagers near the capital staged a demonstration. The trouble also arose from the fact that the farmers were asked to provide their own military equipment, which really consisted only of bows and arrows. Fathers and sons wept together, and there were villagers who chopped off their fingers or their wrists in order to evade the draft. Through this riot Wang Anshih was to lose his last remaining friend, Han Wei, for as magistrate of the district he reported the riot and asked that the military traning be delayed till late winter when the farmers would no longer be busy with their crops. For this even Han Wei was dismissed.

It took a visible demonstration of God's anger and the curious gatekeeper of the palace to put Wang Anshih out of power. In 1073 there was a landslide on the sacred mountain Huashan. Thrown into consternation, the Emperor, according to custom, moved to another palace as a sign of respect for God, and ordered poorer food to be served for his dinner. Besides, from the summer of 1073 to the spring of 1074 there had been no rain; the Emperor was deeply worried and did not know what to do. He questioned Wang Anshih about it, and the latter replied:

"Floods and droughts are natural calamities; they occurred even in the regime of the ideal emperors Yao and Tang. All we need to do is to carry on with a good government."

"That is exactly what I am afraid of," replied the Emperor, "that we have not been carrying on a good government. I hear so many complaints about the excise tax. Everybody at the court has heard about it, including the Empress and the Empress Dowager."

Another cabinet minister, Feng Ching, was present, and he said, "So have I heard also."

"Why, I've never heard anything," replied Wang Anshih. "Mr. Feng hears all about these grumblings because all the disgruntled persons flock around him."

Now the little man destined to play the big role appeared. It was Cheng Shia, the gatekeeper who had made paintings of the refugees.[1] Along with these paintings of the victims of the administration working in chains to cut down trees and obtain cash to pay back the government loans, he now sent a brief note to the Emperor.

"Your Majesty:

"It has been the custom after the successful completion of military campaigns to have paintings made to celebrate the victories. No one, however, has submitted to you paintings of the hardships and sufferings of the people, paintings that would show families being separated and refugees roaming over the countryside. Your servant has stood at the Anshang Gate and daily watched these scenes, and has had a panoramic picture made of them. These show only one hundredth part of what I saw, but I know that even you will shed tears when you see them. Imagine, therefore, those who see the reality in the provinces! If Your Majesty will

---

[1] See page 207.

look at these pictures and take my suggestions for abolishing reforms, if it does not rain within ten days, you can behead me on the execution ground outside the Shüanteh Gate as a punishment for lying to Your Majesty.

Your humble servant,

Cheng Shia"

The Emperor took the scroll of paintings to his sleeping quarters. He showed them to the Empress and other members of the royal household. It was the Emperor's grandmother[1] who first spoke:

"I hear that the people are suffering from the draft exemption tax and the farmers' loans. I do not think that we should change the tradition set by the ancestors."

"But these are for the benefit of the people and were never intended to oppress them," replied the Emperor.

"I know that Wang Anshih has great ability," said the Empress Dowager, "but he has made too many enemies. For his own good I think you had better temporarily suspend him from office."

"I find," replied the Emperor, "that among all the courtiers only Wang Anshih is willing to shoulder all the responsibilities."

The Emperor's brother, Prince Chi, was standing by. He said, "I believe you should think over what Grandmother has just said."

His Majesty flew into a rage. "All right, all right!" he cried. "I don't know how to run the government. You take over."

---

[1] It was the rule that when an emperor's grandmother was living, she, rather than the emperor's mother, was the empress dowager. In relation to the emperor's mother, she was mother-in-law, and in relation to the imperial household, she was the eldest. This empress dowager was the wife of Jentsung, not of Ingtsung.

"I didn't mean that," said Prince Chi.

For a moment there was an awkward silence. Then the Empress Dowager said, "Wang Anshih has brought on all this trouble. What are you going to do about it?"

The next morning Wang Anshih was dismissed, although Huiching and Dunquan remained. The Emperor decided to suspend the excise tax, the farmers' loans, the draft exemption tax, the *paochia* system, and the registration of land, a total of eighteen measures in all.

It began to rain. Truly God was pleased!

But Wang Anshih's hour was not yet over. There was a technicality by which the gatekeeper was impeached. When he first submitted the scroll through the regular channels, the palace officials had refused to accept it on the ground that, as a minor official, he had no qualifications to communicate with the Emperor. Cheng, therefore, had gone to an imperial courier station outside the capital and, telling the courier that it contained urgent military business, had asked him to dispatch it immediately on horseback. On this technicality of illegal use of the courier system, Cheng Shia was tried at the censor's court.

History does not record the result of the trial. But we find that in January of the following year Cheng Shia sent up another painting album to the Emperor, entitled *The Story of Righteous and Corrupt Ministers*. It was the story of certain famous good ministers and evil geniuses of the Tang Dynasty, and while no direct reference was made to the men of the present regime, the story of what these evil geniuses did in a previous dynasty bore unmistakable resemblance to the acts of the men in power. If there was any possible ambiguity, the legend in the paintings had provided against it. Along with the album, Cheng also submitted a memorial recommending a good man to be the prime minister, since Wang Anshih had already been dismissed. Huiching was now in power, and Dunquan had already switched his allegiance from Wang Anshih to him. The two, therefore, succeeded in banishing Cheng Shia to remote Kwangtung.

Before his departure a certain censor came to visit him and said, "It is wonderful of you to keep up the fight when all the censors are gagged. It almost appears that the censorate's responsibility for criticizing the government has now devolved upon the shoulders of a palace gatekeeper." Thereupon the censor handed him a package of two volumes of collected reports against those in authority that had accumulated in the office of the imperial censorate, saying, "I consign these data to your care." But Huiching obtained this news through his efficient spy system, and now he sent Sudan to overtake Cheng Shia on the way and search his baggage. With the two volumes of reports which contained all the names of people who had ever criticized the administration, Huiching, Dunquan, and Sudan proceeded systematically to prosecute these critics, one by one, and put them in jail. Huiching wanted to sentence Cheng Shia to death, but was prevented by the Emperor, who said, "Cheng Shia is not thinking of himself but of the country. I admire his courage and honesty. He should not be punished too severely." So Cheng Shia was permitted to go on to his place of exile.

A certain Huang, after Su Tungpo was dead, obtained a wonderful manuscript by Su Tungpo, which contains one of his famous sayings. "It is easier to stand poverty than success, easier to stand hard work than leisure, and easier to stand a pain than an itch. If a man can take success well, be happy in leisure, and stand an itch, he must indeed be a man of great principles." Every revolutionary party shows its best strength and unity before it comes to power, but after achieving power and weeding out opposition, it begins to crumble and split from internal strife. There is no question that the desire to overthrow someone in power brings out some of the best instincts in human nature and the power to rule others brings out the worst. As long as things were going well and everybody had a good job, Dunquan and Huiching and Tseng Pu were too busy to quarrel among themselves. As soon as Wang Anshih was out of power and things began to go wrong, the gang soon fell out with one another.

Long before this happened, the seeds of internal decay had been planted. Wang Anshih's son hated Huiching and Huiching hated Tseng Pu. Dunquan, who ran with the hare and hunted with the hounds, was going to have a very busy time. Wang Anshih was unfortunate in his one remaining son. Brilliant, erratic, and cruel, the son was responsible for many of the mischiefs of this administration.[1] Now that he was grown up, he had taken charge of the family's finances and his uncles could no longer have a free time with Wang Anshih's money. The arrogant son of an-powerful premier, he thought he could achieve distinction by abominable manners. There is a story that once the neo-Confucianist philosopher Cheng Hao was having a conference with Wang Anshih at his home in the early days of the reform. The son appeared with disheveled hair and bare feet and, carrying a woman's scarf in his hand, walked right up to his father and asked what they were talking about.

"Why, I am discussing with Mr. Cheng the new measures which are being criticized by the other ministers," Wang replied.

The son plumped down on the mat where they were sitting and said with a laugh, "All we need to do is to cut off the heads of Han Chi and Fu Pi, and there will be no more opposition."

How much Wang was to suffer for his son we shall see soon. It was not a very pleasant household, for there were the two uncles who had all along disapproved of Wang's doings and who had particularly warned Wang against the double-crosser, Huiching. Confucius once said that one should "banish the lewd music of Cheng and keep away from the fawning flatterer." So one day when Wang Anshih was having a conference with

---

[1] He also suspected his wife and believed that his son was not his own. Wang persecuted his wife and she died very young.

Huiching and his brother Ankuo was playing a flute outside, the premier shouted to his brother, "Will you banish the lewd music of Cheng?" His brother shouted back, "Will you keep away from the fawning flatterer?"

Now the clique was worried about the future. Huiching, however, had not given up all hope, and he now saw his chance to rise to power in Wang's stead. There are certain people in this world who can turn on the tears at will, and Huiching and Dunquan went to the Emperor and "wept before him" in the most touching manner. The thought of what was going to happen to the country gave them great distress. With their gift of persuasion they were able to turn the Emperor back on his old course, and Huiching was made the prime minister.

Now the quarreling really began. The trade dictator of the country, Lu Chiawen, was at this time impeached. Reports of the abuses and extortions of the trade bureau had of course reached the Emperor's ears, and he asked Wang Anshih, who was still in the capital, about the matter.

"Chiawen has always followed the official regulations rigorously, and therefore he has made many enemies. That is why he is being attacked," Wang Anshih replied.

"But," said the Emperor, "the government receives actually very little revenue from the excise tax. Besides, I don't like the idea of selling fruit and ice and coal. It is undignified for Our Imperial Government."

"Your Majesty," said Wang Anshih, "should not bother yourself about such trifles. These are things for the small officials to worry about. You should concern yourself only with the major policies of the government."

"Even so," replied the Emperor, "why is it that everybody at the court regards it as an oppressive measure?"

"Please give me the names of those persons," Wang Anshih replied.

We need not go into all the details of this dirty squabble. What happened was that the trade dictator in his powerful position had begun to defy the board of finance and had insulted one Shüeh. Tseng Pu began to side with the latter and attacked the trade dictator, who was removed from office. Huiching and Tseng Pu were appointed to investigate his case. The two men had always heartily disliked each other, both being in a position relative to Wang Anshih similar to the position of Stalin and Trotsky under Lenin. In the course of the investigation Huiching began to attack Tseng Pu, and Tseng Pu began to attack Huiching, and Tseng Pu was overthrown.

This was only the beginning of the trouble. Huiching was left the sole head of the government. He not only took the occasion of Cheng Shia's case to dismiss Wang Anshih's brother Ankuo, but with the help of the ubiquitous Dunquan tried to implicate Wang Anshih himself in a local rebellion in Shantung, motivated by a prince. Wang Anshih was charged with complicity in the plot because he was a friend of one of the members of the rebellion. There was another cabinet minister, also nominally a premier, who could not get along with Huiching, and he hoped to get Wang Anshih back to the court to check Huiching. He sent a secret message to Wang Anshih, besides asking the Emperor to cashier Huiching and make Wang Anshih prime minister once more. The charge of rebellion was a serious one, and Wang made the trip from Nanking to the capital in seven days.

Wang Anshih had really nothing to do with the plotting of the rebellion, and he was again made premier in February 1075. It was a little awkward for Dunquan, who now lost no time in turning against Huiching and coming over to Wang Anshih's side. In order to bribe himself back into Wang's favor, he decided to sell out Huiching. Without the knowledge of Wang Anshih himself, Dunquan plotted with Wang's son to prosecute Huiching for extortion of 5,000,000 cash from a merchant at Huating; and the court had Huiching dismissed and appointed a magistrate. Dissatisfied with the easy escape of Huiching, Dunquan and the trade dictator, Lu Chiawen, reopened the prosecution and had Huiching detained in the prison of the imperial censorate awaiting trial.

One after another the members of the once powerful administration fell into disgrace. Dunquan was no exception. Still as energetic as ever, he had seen that Huiching had fallen and observed that the Emperor was growing tired of Wang Anshih himself. With his great genius for scheming, he thought the next men to serve would be Wang Anshih's son and son-in-law. He submitted a petition to the Emperor asking for their promotion. But both Wang Anshih and Emperor were tired of Dunquan's turncoat tactics, and instead of being grateful, had him dismissed from the court. Dunquan began now to "lose faith in human nature"!

It was then that Huiching, while awaiting trial, dealt the final blow to Wang Anshih. He had kept all these years some private letters of Wang for blackmail purposes, and now he submitted these to the Emperor, accusing Wang of plotting behind the Emperor's back, for several of the letters contained the words, "do not let His Majesty know about this." The Emperor was thoroughly sick of the whole mess, and now the revelation of these private letters made him really angry with Wang for the first time. Wang scolded his son severely for recklessly attacking Huiching without his knowledge. The son evidently did not know that Huiching had kept these letters and had a secret hold on his father. Regretting his rash step, and mortified at being scolded by his father, the son fell ill and soon developed a malignant ulcer on his back. Wang Anshih had always been a believer in Buddhism. He tried monks as well as doctors but was not able to save his son's life. Fang's death was a deep blow to the old premier. Thoroughly disillusioned politically and about human life in general, he felt tired and begged to resign. The Emperor allowed him to retire from his office in October 1076, but retaining some of his highest ranks. He was by no means in disgrace. Years later, he was seen in the Nanking countryside, riding his donkey and mumbling to himself.

第十章　两兄弟

熙宁四年（一〇七一）七月，苏东坡携眷离京往富有湖山之美的杭州上任。在随后八九年内，他始终在杭州、青岛附近的密州以及江苏的苏州为官，无不政绩斐然。这段时间，他作诗甚多，所写的诗歌很美，或感伤，或诙谐，或愤怒。以天真快活的心情，几乎赤子般的狂放不羁，将心中之所感，尽情歌唱出来。可是这样忧虑愤怒的诗歌触怒了权要，终于给他招惹了灾祸。

他弟弟子由这时在陈州（淮阳）充任教授，淡泊自甘。陈州位于国都东南七八十里，正在苏东坡治下的视察行程之中，他随后几年都常常利用机会到弟弟家盘桓小住，有时会住上七十几天。苏东坡的儿子已经十二岁，还有一个婴儿，才一岁，但是他弟弟则儿女很多。沉默寡言的苏子由，一声不响只顾生儿育女——最后直到生了三个儿子、七个女儿，都是苏东坡帮助婚配的。苏东坡欣然接受弟弟的请求，与他们共度中秋后才走。子由很穷，住的房子又小又矮。东坡常常对弟弟的高大取笑，他写了两句：

常时低头诵经史，

忽然欠伸屋打头。

他们的老朋友，那位退隐的国家元老张方平，也和他们在一个城里住，大家常酒饭相聚。张方平饮酒甚豪，他的酒量是一百杯。据苏东坡自己说，他自己的酒量则小得多，但是他说他并不以自己酒量小而戒酒。欧阳修也是海量，但是张方平却胜过他，因为张方平开始喝酒时，他不向客人说他们要喝多少杯，而是多少天。苏东坡说："对你们海量的人我并不羡慕，我喝完一杯就醉，不是和你们一样得其所哉吗？"

那几个月，兄弟二人和家人悠闲团聚，共度时光。兄弟二人常到柳湖去划船，或是在城郊漫步，谈论政治、家事、前途。一天，二人正在讨论国家情势，子由向哥哥进了些忠言。苏东坡的一个短处就是老向客人谈论自己的心思，写文章也是发挥自己的见解。当时不是什么好年月，子由对哥哥太了解。后来，苏东坡的监禁解除之后，子由用手捂住他的嘴，那是告诉他以后要三缄其口。

兄弟二人，气质不同，形貌各异。子由高大，丰满的圆脸，两颊附近的松肉很多，而东坡则健壮结实，骨肉匀称。由他的画像，我们不难判断，他是五尺七八寸身高，脸大，颧骨高，前额高大，眼睛很长而闪闪发光，下巴端正，胡须长而末端尖细。最能透露他特性的，就是他那敏感活动、强而有力的嘴唇。他的脸色红润，热情洋溢，会由欢天喜地的表情一变而成抑郁沉思的幻想状。

苏东坡对他弟弟说："我知道我一向出言不慎。我一发现什么事情不对，就像在饭菜里找到个苍蝇一样，非要唾弃不可。"

弟弟说："但是你要了解你说话的对方，有的人你可以推心置腹，有的不可以。"

苏东坡点头说："这就是我之所短。也许我生来就太相信人，不管我是跟谁说话，我都是畅所欲言。"

他告诉弟弟，他送出上神宗皇帝书之后，真怕有生命之险。他有一个朋友，也为他担心。那个朋友是晁端彦，正好去看他。晁端彦和他同科考中，正如今之同年毕业的同学一样。

东坡说："但是我告诉晁端彦说，我曾殿试高中，多少高官显宦立刻把我看作朋友。皇帝已然接受我的忠言。我不坦诚进谏，舍我其谁？我告诉晁端彦，我真正怕的是会因此而被杀害。他一言不发，面色极其严肃。于是我又对他说：'没关系。皇帝若想杀我，我死而无怨。但有一件，我不愿一身就戮而使你拍手称快。'我二人都大笑起来。"

子由说："有一件事你知道吗？你留意过没有？一日空闲长似两日。所以人若一生七十年都在空闲中过，他实际上等于活了一百四十年。这是求长寿最容易的办法。"

兄弟二人在政治上虽然看法相似，而且也立场相同，二人个性则迥然相异。子由沉稳、实际、拘谨、寡言，而东坡则轻快、开阔、好辩、天真、不顾后果。在朋友同僚的心目中，子由为人可靠，而东坡之直言无隐，玩笑戏谑，则使人害怕。在亲密朋友之间，东坡谈笑风生夹杂惊人的双关语。天下拘谨实际的人听他说话，都觉得他随时可以吐露真理，仿佛不论何事，只要是真，便值得说出口来，此外不知还有什么禁忌！

在文学风格上，也有一种差异——就犹如亨利·詹姆斯（Henry James）和威廉·詹姆斯（William James）。东坡像威廉，子由像亨利。由各自的才气上看，威廉原应当写小说，而亨利应当写心理与哲学性的论文。可是威廉·詹姆斯却把他的才华和诙谐注入到通常枯燥无味的心理学和哲学教科书，而亨利·詹姆斯则在小说的世界里注入了他人性的思想和观察这样充实的内容，这对世界的文化反倒有益而无损。子由没有哥哥才气的一半，但是他的文章内容充实，具有深度，使他在这一类文章之内，足称大家。

苏东坡知道弟弟的忠言大有道理，倘若他的气质像子由那样恬淡沉静，他必然会乐于接受的。但是问题不是他如何想，而是他如何感，不是理性的问题，而是感性的问题。我们论到苏东坡，我们就不能避免"气"这个字。因为每个文学批评家一综括苏东坡的个性，必用孟子所说的这个"气"字。"气"本是普通字，是空气，是气体，是大气，是精神，是力量，是运动，是闷在心里的恼怒。在《孟子》里，"气"是哲学的概念，类似柏格森所说的"生气勃勃"，是人格上的"元气"。使伟人和匹夫显然不同的，往往是精力元气上的差异。在孟子的哲学上，"气"是伟大的道德动力，更简单说，就是人求善、求正义的高贵精神。这种精神，人人皆有，是与生俱来的。人在世界上生活下去，这个"气"可因得其陶冶营养而增长强大，亦可因消减而衰弱。以苏东坡的情况而言，其意义正同于伟大的精神，一个人高升到无极限的精神，至大至刚，激烈冲动，因其本身充沛的元力必要发之于外而不可抑制。佩服苏东坡的人和批评苏东坡的人，就常说到他这种至大至刚之气。孟子在自己本身觉察到有此力量，这种力量若辅以正义真理，便在天地之间无所畏惧。

孟子的一个弟子问："敢问何谓浩然之气？"

孟子回答道："难言也。其为气也，至大至刚，以直养而无害，则塞于天地之间。其为气也，配道与义，无是，馁也。行有不慊于心，则馁矣。"

苏东坡既然天赋这样生气蓬勃的精神，自然常遭遇到道德的矛盾，一方面要保持英雄本色，不失其与生俱来的大无畏精神；另一面又要顾到同样重要的明哲保身这一人生的本分。在苏东坡一生的官宦生涯中，有某些时期此种冲突特别尖锐，往往他宁愿保持他的英雄本色。所以他内心中的冲突总不会太大的。他那伟大的天才不断自由流露而一发不可抑制。正是：

> 猿吟鹤唳本无意，
> 不知下有行人行。

苏东坡与其弟弟子由及家人共度中秋。这次中秋值得记忆，他后来一直思念不止，也是随后六年中唯一的一次中秋聚会。临别时，二人难分难舍，子由决定送兄长至颍河下游八十里外的颍州（今阜阳）。到颍州在欧阳修相伴之下，又一同过了半个多月。但是终须分手。在苏东坡开船出发的前夜，兄弟二人又在颍河的船上共度一夜，吟诗论政，彻夜未眠。二人论政的结论，后来苏东坡写在一首诗里，到达杭州之后，寄给子由。其中有句为：

> 眼看时事力难任，
> 贪恋君恩退未能。

兄弟二人不觉都想起了孟子的话："责难于君谓之恭，陈善闭邪谓之敬，吾君不能谓之贼。"事实上，二人都明白下面这段话的真理：

> 徒善不足以为政，徒法不能以自行……为高必因丘陵，为下必因川泽。

为政，不因先王之道，可谓智乎？是以惟仁者宜在高位；不仁而在高位，
是播其恶于众也。上无道揆也，下无法守也，朝不信道，工不信度，君子
犯义，小人犯刑，国之所存者幸也。故曰城郭不完，兵甲不多，非国之灾也；
田野不辟，货财不聚，非国之害也。上无礼，下无学，贼民兴，丧无日矣。

那天夜里，苏东坡写了两首诗，足以显示他的心境：

征帆挂西风，别泪滴清颍。

留连知无益，惜此须臾景。

我生三度别，此别尤酸冷。

念子似先君，木讷刚且静。

寡词真吉人，介石乃机警。

至今天下士，去莫如子猛。

嗟我久病狂，意行无坎井。

有如醉且坠，幸未伤辄醒。

第二首诗是：

近别不改容，远别涕沾胸。

咫尺不相见，实与千里同。

人生无离别，谁知恩爱重。

始我来宛丘，牵衣舞儿童。

便知有此恨，留我过秋风。

秋风亦已过，别恨终无穷。

问我何年归，我言岁在东。

离合既循环，忧喜迭相攻。

悟此长太息，我生如飞蓬。

多忧发早白，不见六一翁。

"六一翁"指的是六一居士欧阳修。"飞蓬"一词正足以象征苏东坡的一生，因为从现在起，他就成为政治风暴中的海燕，直到他去世，都不会再在一个地方安安静静度过三年以上的时光。

次日凌晨，兄弟二人分手。苏东坡对子由的深情确是非比寻常，后来，他在写给好友李常的一首诗中说："嗟余寡兄弟，四海一子由。"杭州三年任期届满时，他请调至密州，因为当时子由正任职济南，两地都在山东，相距不远。

Chapter Ten
THE TWO BROTHERS

Su Tungpo left the capital with his family in July 1071, to take up his post in the beautiful city of Hangchow on China's southeast coast. For the next eight or nine years he served successively at Hangchow, Michow near Tsingtao, and Suchow in Kiangsu. This was the period of his great activity as a poet, and he wrote beautiful songs, songs of sadness, of humor, and of anger. Innocently and with a carefree, almost childish abandon he sang of what he felt in his heart, and in the end it was these songs of sadness and of anger against the ruling authorities that brought him into trouble.

His brother Tseyu was working as a poor college professor at Chenchow, then called Huaiyang, a city lying about seventy or eighty miles to the southeast of the capital and on the direct route of Su Tungpo's journey. As he always did later, he took this opportunity to spend as much time as he could with his brother and he stayed over seventy days. His son was twelve years old and he had a baby of one year, but his brother had a big family with many children. The quiet Tseyu just kept on producing children until he had three sons and seven danghters, whom Su Tungpo helped to marry off. Su Tungpo gladly agreed with his brother's plea to stay with them until the mid-autumn festival was over. Tseyu was very poor and they were living in a small low building, and Su Tungpo used to make fun of his brother's height.

"Bending his head, he reads the classics and history,
Straightening, his solid head strikes the roof."

Their old friend Chang Fangping, the retired elderly official, was living in the same city and they had frequent wine dinners together. Chang was a great drinker, his capacity being one hundred cups. According to himself, Tungpo had a much smaller capacity, but he felt that was no reason for his abstaining from wine. Ouyang Shiu, too, was a great drinker—but Chang Fangping was able to outdrink him, for when Chang began to drink, he did not say to his guests how many cups they were going to drink, but how many days. "Yet," says Su Tungpo, "I don't envy the great drinkers. I get drunk after a couple of cups, but don't I enjoy it just as much as you people do?"

Enjoying these months of leisure and family reunion, the two brothers often went boating on Willow Lake or walking in the suburbs of the city, discussing politics, domestic affairs, and their future. One day when they were walking together in the country and discussing the political condition of the country, Tseyu gave his elder brother a piece of advice. Su Tungpo's one great fault was his habit of always speaking his mind before guests or in writing. The times were bad, and Tseyu knew his brother all too well. As he did later after Tungpo's release from confinement, Tseyu put his hand across his mouth, which was to tell him to keep still henceforth.

The two brothers were different in temperament and appearance. Tseyu was taller, and had a plumper, rounder face, with plenty of loose flesh round his cheeks, while Su Tungpo had a more muscular build, with the right proportion of bone and muscle. As far as we can judge from his portraits, he was about five feet seven or eight, had a big face with very prominent cheekbones and an imposing forehead, extremely long, brilliant eyes, a well-proportioned chin, and a beautiful, tapering, long, mandarin beard. The most revealing was his sensitive, mobile, full-powered lips. It was a face which flashed and glowed with human warmth, quickly changing its expression from hearty fun to a pensive look of thought-drunk fantasy.

"I know," said Su Tungpo, to his brother, "that I am always careless of my speech. When I feel something is wrong, it is like finding a fly in my food, and I just have to spit it out."

"But you've got to know the people you are talking to," said his brother. "Some people you can trust, and some you cannot."

"That's my weakness," Su Tungpo agreed. "Perhaps I am too confiding in nature. Regardless of whomever I am talking with, I like to unburden my whole inside."

He told his brother that when he had sent the letter to the Emperor, he was truly afraid for his life. One of his friends, he said, was also worried. This was Chao Tuanyen,[1] who had come to visit him, and who, having passed the examinations in the same year with him, was often referred to as of the "same class," in the same sense as modern college graduates of the same year.

"But I told Chao I had passed the special examination under Emperor Jentsung," Su Tungpo went on, "and that I was at once regarded by the high officials as a friend. And the Emperor had accepted my advice. If I did not speak up now, who would? I told Chao that what I was really afraid of was that I might be killed. Chao remained silent and looked very grave. Then I said to him, 'It's all right. If the Emperor

---

[1] Father of Chao Puchih, who became Tungpo's disciple.

wants to kill me, I shall take it without regret. But there's one thing, I don't want to give you the pleasure of seeing me dead.' And we both laughed."

"Do you know something?" said the younger brother. "Do you notice that when one has a day of leisure, it seems twice as long as other days? Therefore, if a man can spend all his days in leisure during a life of seventy years, he will practically have lived one hundred and forty. That's an easy way of achieving long life."

While the two brothers always agreed in their political viewpoints, and had taken an identical stand in politics, their characters were really different. Tseyu was steady, practical, reserved, and given to few words; Tungpo was volatile, expansive, loquacious, naive and inclined to disregard the consequences of his actions. Tseyu was considered dependable by his friends and associates, while Tungpo often frightened people by his outspoken genius and his fun and frivolity. Among his close associates, Tungpo bubbled, joked, and made atrocious puns. He gave the practical people of the world the nervous feeling that at any moment he might tell the truth—as if a thing's being true were enough reason for telling it!

In literary style, too, there was a difference—the difference suggested by that between Henry and Willam James, Tungpo being William and Tseyu being Henry. By all the indications of their separate genius, William James should have written novels and Henry James treatises on psychology and philosophy. Nevertheless, the world stands to gain by the injection of William James's brilliance and humor into the usually dull textbooks on psychology and philosophy, and by the solid structure of Henry James's thoughts and observations on human nature in the field of fiction. Tseyu had not half the brilliance of his brother, but his writings had enough substance and depth to make him a major writer on his own merit.

Tungpo knew that his brother's advice was right, and if he had had the quieter temperament of his younger brother, he would have followed it. But it was not a question of what he thought, but what he felt. It is difficult to avoid the term *ch 'i* when we discuss the character of Su Tungpo, for every critic of the poet mentions this Mencian word when he comes to summarize Su Tungpo's character. *Ch'i* is a common word meaning gas, air, atmosphere, spirit, force, drive, stored-up anger. In Mencius it was a philosophic notion akin to Bergson's *élan vital*, the vital, impelling force in a human personality. What distinguished greater personalities from lesser people was often the difference in the energy, drive, dash, and vivacity of such men. In Mencian philosophy it means the great moral impetus, or more simply, the noble spirit of man that makes for good and righteousness, a spirit inherent in all men, either nourished and grown strong or weakened as one gets along in life. In the case of Su Tungpo it was synonymous with a great spirit, the spirit of man raised to the nth degree, big and strong and impetuous, demanding expression by its own vitality. It was this something tremendous in his spirit, a big, booming force, that Su's critics and admirers constantly spoke of. Mencius felt this force in himself, and described it as a spirit which, when sustained by justice and truth, fears nothing in the universe.

"What do you mean by the vital spirit?" one of the disciples of Mencius once asked.

"It is very difficult to describe," Mencius replied. "This spirit is tremendous and strong. If unobstructed and properly nourished, it will fill the whole universe. But it requires for its growth the steady pursuit of the sense of justice and truth. For without the sense of justice and truth, the spirit of man withers."

Given this vital, expansive spirit so characteristic of Su Tungpo's bubbling personality, he was constantly confronted with an ethical conflict, the duty to remain himself and keep up the fearless spirit born in man, and the other equally important duty of self-preservation. At different times in Su Tungpo's career the conflict became acute and usually the duty to remain himself won. I do not think it ever was very much of a struggle for Su Tungpo. The vitality of his great genius constantly demanded free and unfettered expression.

> "Beautiful lines come and will not be denied.
> How can I alter them as favors to friends?
> The apes and wild geese cry on mountaintops,
> Unaware of passers-by in the valley below."

So Tungpo spent the mid-autumn festival with his brother's family. It was a memorable mid-autumn, one which he recalled later with fond regret, and the only one which he could spend with his brother for the next six years. The parting was hard and Tseyu decided to accompany his brother as far as Yingchow (modern Fouyang), eighty miles down the river, where they again spent over two weeks together in the company of Ouyang Shiu. Still, the parting had to come. The night before Tungpo was to sail, the two brothers spent together in the boat on the Ying River, sitting up all night discussing politics and writing poems to each other. The conclusion of their discussion on politics was summed up in a poem which Su Tungpo wrote and sent to Tseyu on his arrival at Hangchow.

> "One can see that further opposition is useless,
> And to repay the Emperor's favor is beyond one's power now."

A thought by Mencius came aptly to the brothers' minds: "To expect the highest of the ruler is to show the highest respect; to guide him with good advice and keep unprincipled men away from him is in accordance with duty; but if the ruler will not take the advice, he becomes a thief to his country." In fact, they realized the full truth of what Mencius said in that whole passage:

Goodness of heart alone is not enough to govern a country, and laws alone without good men cannot be properly enforced... Therefore it is said that to reach a high position, one must go up a hill, and to go down a valley, one must follow the stream. In the governance of a nation, it would be foolhardy indeed to depart from the principles of the ancient kings. Therefore only the kindhearted man should be appointed to a high office; for an unkind man to assume a high position is merely to reveal his wicked-ness to the world. When a ruler does not follow the ancient tradition, the ministers upset the law, the court has no respect for truth, and workmen no longer follow the squares and compasses; when educated people violate their own principles, and the common people violate the laws, it will be sheer good luck if such a country can continue to exist. Therefore, I say, it is not a national calamity when the city walls are not fortified and the army is not properly equipped; it is not a national calamity when the farms are not cultivated and there is no financial reserve; but when educated people lose their manners and morals and the common people are not educated, then destroyers of society will arise and the country will soon perish.

That night Su Tungpo wrote two poems which reveal his state of mind:

"The western wind fills the boat sails
And my parting tears drop into the Ying.
I know it is useless to delay the parting;

Let's make the best of the remaining hours.
Three times have we been parted in this life,
Bur this parting is the hardest of all.
You are so much like our deceased father,
Quiet, reticent, but inwardly strong.
To have few words is evidence of the blessed man,
And inward possession [*kai-shek*]gives wisdom and strength.
Among all the scholars of the land,
You were the first and quickest to resign.
Alas, I have been like a crazy man,
Walking straight toward an unfenced well,
Like a drunkard who totters and tumbles,
But luckily wakes before the fatal fall."

In the second poem he writes:

"For a short parting, I can bear it well,
But for a long parting, tears wet my breast.
When we do not see one another,
Distances great and small are all the same.
Without parting in this human life,
Who would guess how much one really cares?
When I first arrived at Huaiyang,
You tossed the children who clung to my gown.
You knew then the sorrow of parting
And asked me to stay until the autumn came.
The autumn wind has now arrived and gone,
But this remembrance will always remain.
You asked when I would be coming back,
And I said, 'It will be three years from now.'

So parting and reunion go in a cycle,
And joys and sorrows pursue our way.
Talking about this I draw a long sigh,
For my life is like a spikelet in the wind.
With many sorrows, my hair turns white early.
Say farewell to the 'Six-One Old Man.'"

"Six-One Old Man" is the literary title of Ouyang Shiu. The image of the reed flower being blown about by the wind is a fit symbol of Su Tungpo's life, for from now on, he was to be the stormy petrel of politics and was never to remain in one place for more than three years till the end of his life.

Early at dawn the next morning the brothers said farewell. Su Tungpo's deep attachment to Tseyu was really extraordinary. Later, in a poem he wrote to one of his best friends, Li Chang, he said, "Alas, I do not have many brothers; in all the world there is only Tseyu." When his three-year term of office at Hangchow was over, he asked to be transferred to Michow, just because Tseyu was then serving at Tsinan, which was close by in the same province of Shantung.

第十一章　诗人、名妓、高僧

杭州，在当年一如今日，是一个美妙难言的都市，谚云："上有天堂，下有苏杭。"杭州后来几乎变成了苏东坡的第二故乡。他初到杭州便写出下面的诗句：

未成小隐聊中隐，可得长闲胜暂闲。

我本无家更安往？故乡无此好湖山。

杭州像是苏东坡的第二故乡，不只是杭州的山林湖海之美，也非只是由于杭州繁华的街道，闳壮的庙宇，也是由于他和杭州人的感情融洽，由于他一生最快活的日子是在杭州度过的。杭州人有南方人的轻松愉快，有诗歌，有美女，他们喜爱苏东坡这位年轻的名诗人，喜爱他的朝气冲力，他那潇洒的神韵，他那不拘小节的胸襟。杭州的美丽赋予他灵感，杭州温柔的魅力浸润他的心神。杭州赢取了苏东坡的心，苏东坡赢取了杭州人的心。在他任杭州通判期间，也无权多为地方人建设，但是他之身为诗人，地方人已经深感满足。他一遭逮捕，地方人沿街设立香案，为他祷告上苍早日获释。他离开杭州之后，南方的秀美与温情，仍然使他梦寐难忘，他知道他还会故地重归。等十八年之后，他又回去任太守之职。他对地方建树良多，遗爱难忘，杭州人爱之不舍，以为与杭州不可分割。今天，去此伟大诗人居住于杭州，歌咏于杭州，已经一千余年，在你泛舟于西湖之上，或攀登上孤山岛或凤凰山上，或品茗于湖滨酒馆中，你会听到杭州本地的主人嘴边常挂着"苏东坡，苏东坡"。你若指出苏东坡是四川人，他会不高兴听。他心里认为苏东坡生于杭州，除去到京都之外，何尝离开过杭州！

在性情，在放浪的风情，在爱与笑等方面，苏东坡与西湖是密不可分的。西湖的诗情画意，非苏东坡的诗思不足以极其妙；苏东坡的诗思，非遇西湖的诗情画意不足尽其才。一个城市，能得诗人发现其生活上复杂的地方性，并不容易；而诗人能在寥寥四行诗句中表现此地的精粹、气象、美丽，也颇不简单。公认为表现西湖最好的诗，就是苏东坡写西湖的一首诗，苏东坡把西湖比作古代的美人西施，清晨在家不施脂粉时也好，施脂粉而盛装时也好；晴天也好，阴天也好，都会显出西湖不朽的美色来。苏东坡描写西湖的那首七言绝句是：

水光潋滟晴方好，山色空濛雨亦奇。
欲把西湖比西子，淡妆浓抹总相宜。

这当然是个譬喻而已。西施若是描画蛾眉，不论何时，总比不画更好看。苏东坡润饰了湖滨，再以至高无上的艺术手法略予点染，使之看来不失其自然。今日苏堤横卧湖上，此一小小仙岛投入水中的影子，构成了"三潭映月"，湖边垂柳成行，足以证明苏东坡在设计风景方面的奇才。杭州的西湖与扬州的小西湖，都表现出中国布置风景的巧思，并且显示人为的技巧与艺术只增加了自然之美，并未破坏自然之美。艺术家首先把握住那个地方大自然的设计，并将其自然的结构与章法作一全盘的估量。他只是略加点染，以求收紧或铺开，或在此处，或在彼处，加强某一些轮廓而已。

苏东坡携带妻儿来杭州，是在神宗熙宁四年（一〇七一）十一月二十八日。公馆位于凤凰山顶，南见钱塘江，出海的大船出没于江面；北望西湖四周环山，山顶隐没于白云中，庙宇与富家别墅点缀于山坡之上；东望钱塘江湾，但见惊涛拍岸。杭州为一大都市，故除去太守一人外，另设二官辅佐之。苏东坡之官邸占公馆之北面，可俯瞰西湖。就在凤凰山下，夹于西湖与钱塘江湾中间，自北而南的，正是杭州城，城外环以高墙，城内有河道，河道上架以桥梁相通。苏夫人清晨起身，打开窗户，看见下面西湖平静的水面，山巅、别墅、飘浮的白云，都映入水中，不觉心旷神怡。离中午甚早，湖面上早已游艇处处。夜晚，由他们的住宅，可以听见吹箫歌唱之声。城内有些街道比别处显得更为明亮，因为有夜市数所，直到次晨两三点始行收市。尤其在女人们看来，总有些令人着迷的货品，如美味食物、绸缎、刺绣、扇子。孩子们则会看到各式各样糖果、玩具、走马灯等东西。宋朝时的糖果商贩都利用特殊广告技巧，以广招徕。有的用赌博，有的装作白胡子老汉，有的戴面具，载歌载舞。有的卖棉花糖，有的卖糖吹的各种小兽，有的做"沙糖"，类似现在的枫糖。有一本书写杭州城的生活情况，写在宋末——在苏东坡以后百年左右，在马可·波罗来中国百年之前，把当时的街道、沟渠、湖泊、食粮、娱乐，写得纤悉无遗，读之令人神往。把当时杭州城的生活描绘得比马可·波罗写的更为详尽。马可·波罗谈到王公贵人的打猎，公主贵妇在西湖边洗浴，富商的游艇往来于杭州、泉州之间，但他对糖果、糕饼、通俗的娱乐等名称，并不熟悉。吴自牧这本《梦粱录》上，像老妪般滔滔不绝地叙述那些精美的各式小食美味，真会使读者观之入迷。

苏东坡有一半相信他前生曾住在杭州。这种想法曾记在他的诗里，他同代人的笔记里也记载过。有一天他去游寿星院，一进门，便觉得所见景物十分熟悉，他告诉同游者走九十二级便到忏堂，结果证明他所言不误。他还可以把寺院后面的建筑、庭院、树木、山石，向同行人描写。我们倒无须乎相信此等前生之事，但是社会上一般人相信有鬼有前生之时，总会有很多此等亲闻亲见的故事，也像鬼故事一样，虽然不能完全证实确有其事，也不能完全证实确无其事。在苏东坡的时代，一般人都相信有前生，此等故事自然不稀奇。有一个关于张方平前生的故事。一天，张方平前去游庙，他告诉别人他记得前生曾在那个庙里当住持。他指着楼上说，他记得曾在楼上抄写经卷，那本经并没抄完。他同一个朋友到楼上一看，果然有一本佛经尚未抄完，字体和张方平的字体一样。他拿起笔来又由前生停下的地方接着往下抄写。还有一个故事，说的是苏东坡的一个好朋友的事。大诗人黄庭坚告诉人说他前生是一个女子，他左夹肢窝有狐臭。一天夜里，那是他在四川涪州做太守时，他梦见一个女子对他说："我是你的前身，现在埋在某处。棺木已经腐朽，左侧有一个大蚂蚁洞。把那个蚂蚁洞给我移开。"黄庭坚照办，左夹肢窝的狐臭就好了。

苏东坡在杭州任判官，除去审问案件，并无重大任务。这种情形他颇为不喜，因为被捕者多为违犯王安石新法的良民，犯的那些法条都是他所反对的。可是那是法律，他无权更改。若一读关于他在新年除夕需要审问因贩私盐而被捕的犯人那首诗，就不难了解他在此一时期的心情。但是杭州湾附近产盐区的盐贩子，都不肯放弃他们原来的生意。当地贩卖私盐的整个情形，苏东坡在给一位阁员的书信中说得十分清楚。我们在此先不管贩卖私盐一事，还是看看东坡这位诗人对同胞的态度吧，因为他觉得他自己和那些他审问的阶下囚，并无不同。

除日当早归，官事乃见留。

执笔对之泣，哀此系中囚。

小人营糇粮，堕网不知羞。

我之恋薄禄，因循失归休。

不须论贤愚，均是为食谋。

谁能暂纵遣，闵默愧前修。

对子由他写的才是肺腑之言：

平生所惭今不耻，坐对疲氓更鞭箠。

道逢阳虎呼与言，心知其非口诺唯。

居高志下真何益，气节消缩今无几。

在另一首诗里，他写百姓在保甲制度下所受的痛苦，描写老百姓在鞭笞之下的哭叫，甚至壮丁的妻子儿女也被关入了监狱。这些诗句累积起来，后来他被捕受审时，竟确立了他企图摧毁人民对新政的信心之罪行。

但是，他仍能随时随地自得其乐。他尽量逃向大自然，而自然美之绝佳处，在杭州随处皆是。他的诗思随时得在杭州附近饱餍风光之美。因为不但杭州城本身、西湖，而且连杭州城四周十里或十五里之内，都成了苏东坡时常出没的所在。游客自杭州西湖出发，可以往各方面走去，或沿北岸到有名的灵隐寺和天竺顶；或由南岸出发到葛岭，在虎跑品尝名泉沏的茶，然后顺着一条蜿蜒的山间小溪归来。西湖和城郊，共有三百六十个寺院，大都在山顶上，在这等地方与山僧闲话，可以消磨一个下午的时光。若去游览这些寺院，往往需要一整天，而且返抵家中时已是暮色昏黄、万家灯火了。穿过灯火通明人群拥挤的夜市，陶然半醉到家，自己头脑里的诗句，已经半记半忘了。

> 睡眼忽惊矍，繁灯闹河塘。
> 市人拍手笑，状如失林獐。
> 始悟山野姿，异趣难自强。
> 人生安为乐，吾策殊未良。

杭州是多彩多姿的，而西湖又引人入胜。江南的天气，一年四季都引人出外游玩。在春秋两季，全杭州人都在湖滨游玩。甚至冬季下雪的日子，还有寻乐的人乘船到湖上玩赏雪景。尤其是重要的节日，比如三月初三、五月初五、中秋节、重阳节、二月十一当地神祇的生日，湖上全是游逛之人，必须前一天预先雇妥游艇。游人无须自带食物，因为一切东西，包括茶杯、茶托、汤勺、筷子，全由游艇供给。还有船夫捕鱼卖与游客放生，这样救生积德，按佛教说，这是在天堂积存财宝。同一条鱼被捕三次，又被放三次，这条鱼说不定就可从阴曹救三条人命了。

苏东坡充分参与西湖上的生活。湖上的游乐分为两种，一种是家庭同乐，一种是挟妓游湖。在湖上这个地方，家庭妇女是望妓而生畏意，而妓女则望家庭妇女而有妒心。妓女们从心眼儿里盼望她们能跳出火坑，自己有家有儿女，就犹如那些家庭妇女一样。苏东坡有时和妻子儿女一起去游湖，有时与好喝酒的同僚同游。他多才多艺，方面最广。他的一支笔运用自如，写出的诗句，巧妙华美，合规中矩，地方文人，对他敬佩万分。他写出的诗句飘逸自然，使人一见难忘。与家人在一起，他唱出下面的诗句：

> 船头斫鲜细缕缕，船尾炊玉香浮浮。

同官衙僚属同游时，大家欢天喜地之中，他就写出这样清新愉快的句子：

> 游翁已妆吴榜稳，舞衫初试越罗新。

他们一到湖畔，船夫便把他们围住，争揽顾客。他们总是挑一只小船，够坐四五人便好，有时人多，便需要一个可摆一张饭桌的，然后吩咐船娘预备饭菜，这种船上的船娘通常都是精于烹调的。这等住家船上都是雕刻精美，船头有笕嘴。湖上也有船贩卖食品与游客。有些船夫卖栗子、瓜子、夹馅藕、糖果、烤鸡、海鲜食品。有的船夫专门卖茶。有的船上载着艺人，按照习俗靠近游客的船，表演歌舞、特技、投掷、射击等游戏。

在船的四周，湖水一碧如染，约有十里之遥，往远处看，白云依偎于山巅，使山峦半隐半显，白云飘忽出没，山容随之而改变；山峦供白云以家乡，使之倦游而归息。有时天阴欲雪，阴霾低垂，丘阜便隐而难见。阴霾之后，游客尚可望见楼塔闪动，东鳞西爪，远山轮廓，依稀在望。晴朗之日，水清见底，游鱼可数。苏东坡在两行七言诗里，描绘船夫的黄头巾，衬托着碧绿的山光，给人以极为鲜明的印象。他的诗句是：

映山黄帽蜒头舫，夹道青烟雀尾炉。

登岸之后，往山中走去，在阒寂无人的树林里，可以听到鸟声此呼彼应。苏东坡本来就性喜游历，现在常常独自一人漫游于山中。在高山之顶，在人迹罕到的水源岩石上，信笔题诗。有些寺庙他常去游历，因而成了庙中和尚的至交。在苏东坡去世后，一个老和尚说出苏东坡的一个故事。他说，他年轻时在寿星院当和尚，常看见苏东坡在夏天一人赤足走上山去。他向和尚借一把躺椅，搬到附近竹林下选好的处所。他全无做官的架子，脱下袍子和小褂，在下午的时光，赤背在躺椅上睡觉。小和尚不敢走近，由远处偷看这位一代大儒，他竟尔看到别人无法看到的情形。他看见，也许他以为他看见，这位大诗人背上有七颗黑痣，排状恰似北斗七星一样。老和尚又说，那就足以证明苏东坡是天上星宿下界，在人间暂时做客而已。

苏东坡在离开杭州之后，曾写了一首诗给晁端彦，概括叙述他出外游历的习惯，那时晁端彦即将出使杭州，苏东坡写诗告诉他当注意的事。诗如下：

西湖天下景，游者无愚贤。
深浅随所得，谁能识其全。
嗟我本狂直，早为世所捐。
独专山水乐，付与宁非天。

三百六十寺，幽寻遂穷年。

所至得其妙，心知口难传。

至今清夜梦，耳目余芳鲜。

君持使者节，风采烁云烟。

清流与碧巘，安肯为君妍。

胡不屏骑从，暂借僧榻眠。

读我壁间诗，清凉洗烦煎。

策杖无道路，直造意所便。

应逢古渔父，苇间自寅缘。

问道若有得，买鱼勿论钱。

由文学掌故上看来，苏东坡在杭州颇与宗教及女人有关，也可以说与和尚和妓女有关，而和尚与妓女关系之深则远超于吾人想象之上。在苏东坡的看法上，感官的生活与精神的生活，是一而二，二而一的，在人生的诗歌与哲学的看法上，是并行而不悖的。因为他爱诗歌，他对人生热爱之强使他不能苦修做和尚；又由于他爱哲学，他的智慧之高，使他不会沉溺而不能自拔。他之不能忘情于女人、诗歌、猪肉、酒，正如他之不能忘情于绿水青山，同时，他的慧根之深，使他不会染上浅薄尖刻、纨绔子弟的习气。

这个年轻耽于玩乐的诗人之态度，若予以最好说明，那就要看他怎样使一个道行高洁的老僧和一个名妓见面的故事了。大通禅师是一个持法甚严、道行甚高的老僧，据说谁要到他的修道处所去见他，必须先依法斋戒。女人当然不能进他的禅堂。有一天，苏东坡和一群人去逛庙，其中有一个妓女。因为知道那位高僧的习惯，大家就停在外面。苏东坡与此老僧相交甚厚，在心中一种淘气的冲动之下，他想把那个妓女带进去破坏老和尚的清规。等他带着那个妓女进去向老方丈敬拜之时，老方丈一见此年轻人如此荒唐，显然是心中不悦。苏东坡说，倘若老方丈肯把诵经时用来打木鱼的木槌借给妓女一用，他就立刻写一首诗向老方丈谢罪。结果苏东坡作了下面的小调给那个妓女唱：

> 师唱谁家曲，宗风嗣阿谁，借君拍板与门槌，我也逢场作戏莫相疑。
>
> 溪女方偷眼，山僧莫皱眉，却愁弥勒下生迟，不见阿婆三五少年时。

这正是戏台上小丑的独白，甚至持法甚严的大通禅师也大笑起来。苏东坡和那个妓女走出禅房向别人夸口，说他俩学了"密宗佛课"。

把女人与和尚分开是不可能的，至少在中国文学上是如此。和尚的故事，往往是女人的故事，而女人的故事也往往是和尚的故事。在东方西方是一样的，在一般世俗人的心里，对那些独身主义者总是暗怀恶感，因为他们向天下宣称他们没有男女之欢的生活，不同于一般人。而对独身主义者暗怀的恶感，就增强了薄伽丘《十日谈》小说的流行。再者，和尚与女人之间的艳闻，比商人与女人之间的艳闻可就使人觉得精彩多了。

苏东坡做杭州通判时，有一次，他曾判决一件与和尚有关的案子。灵隐寺有一个和尚，名叫了然。他常到勾栏院寻花问柳，迷上了一个妓女，名叫秀奴。最后钱财花尽，弄得衣衫褴褛，秀奴便不再见他。一夜，他喝得醉醺醺之下，又去找秀奴，吃了闭门羹。他闯了进去，把秀奴打了一顿之后，竟把她杀死。这个和尚乃因谋杀罪而受审。在检查他时，官员见他的一只胳膊上刺有一副对联："但愿同生极乐国，免如今世苦相思。"全案调查完竣，证据呈给苏东坡。苏东坡不禁把判决词写成下面这个小调儿：

> 这个秃奴，修行戒煞，云山顶空持戒。只因迷恋玉楼人，鹑衣百结浑无奈。
>
> 毒手伤心，花容粉碎，色空空色今安在，臂间刺道苦相思，这回还了相思债。

和尚押赴刑场斩首示众。像以上的这两首小调儿，因为是用当日的口头话写的，大家自然口口相传，对这位天才怪诗人的闲谈趣语又加多了。

在那些名人逸事中，有一本是关于苏东坡和他那喜爱寻欢取乐的朋友佛印的故事。那时节，苏东坡对佛学还没有认真研究，在他四十岁以后，在黄州时，他才精研佛学。黄州的几个和尚成了他最好的朋友，后来他在靖江、金陵、庐山，又交了些和尚朋友。在那些人中，至少有两个——惠勤和参寥，是诗人学者，颇为人所尊敬。由那些随笔逸闻上看，佛印并不算重要。但是佛印是以风流潇洒出名的，而且在一般通俗说部里，佛印比参寥更常为人提到是苏东坡的朋友。

佛印原本并不打算出家为僧，并且他出身富有之家。根据一个荒唐故事，他的生身之母也就是李定的母亲。显然他母亲是个放荡不羁的女人，曾出嫁三次，和三个丈夫各生过一个儿子，在当年是不可多见的。在皇帝对佛教徒赐予接见，以示对佛教抱有好感时，苏东坡就把此人推荐上去。佛印在皇帝驾前力陈对佛教的虔诚信仰。皇帝一看，此人颀长英俊，面容不俗，说他若肯出家为僧，慨允赐他一个度牒。佛印当时进退两难，只好答应出家。他在黄州时，常在一队仆从侍奉之下，乘骡出游，与出家苦修的生活相去十万八千里了。

佛印富有机智捷才。在他和苏东坡有点儿哲理味道的故事中，有一个是这样的。一天苏东坡和佛印去游一座寺院，进了前殿，他俩看见两个面貌狰狞可怕的巨大金刚像—— 一般认为能伏怪降魔，放在门口当然是把守大门的。

苏东坡问："这两尊佛，哪一个重要？"

佛印回答："当然是拳头大的那个。"

到了内殿，他俩看见观音像，手持一串念珠。

苏东坡问："观音自己是佛，还数手里那些念珠何用？"

佛印回答："噢，她也是像普通人一样祷告求佛呀。"

苏东坡又问："她向谁祷告？"

"向她自己祷告。"

东坡又问："这是何故？她是观音菩萨，为什么向自己祷告？"

佛印说："你知道，求人难，求人不如求己呀！"

他俩又看见佛桌上有一本祷告用的佛经。苏东坡看见有一条祷告文句：

咒咀诸毒药，愿借观音力，

存心害人者，自己遭毒毙。

苏东坡说："这荒唐！佛心慈悲，怎肯移害某甲之心去害某乙，若真如此，佛便不慈悲了。"

他请准改正此一祷告文句，提笔删改如下：

咒咀诸毒药，愿借观音力。

害人与对方，两家都无事。

在苏东坡与佛印富有讥讽妙语的对话中，大多是双关语，难以译成另一国文字，不过下面有一条。

"鸟"这个字有一个意思，在中国俚语中颇为不雅。苏东坡想用此一字开佛印的玩笑。苏东坡说："古代诗人常将'僧'与'鸟'在诗中相对。举例说吧：'时闻啄木鸟，疑是叩门僧。'还有：'鸟宿池边树，僧敲月下门。'我佩服古人以'僧'对'鸟'的聪明。"

佛印说："这就是我为何以'僧'的身份与汝相对而坐的理由了。"

这些逸事中总是说这位和尚斗智胜过了苏东坡这位诗人。我疑心这些故事都是佛印自己编的。

根据现在可知的记载，中国的娼妓制度，创始于战国的管仲，他订这种办法作为士兵的康乐活动。甚至在苏东坡时代，还有官妓，当然另有私娼。但是中国却有一种特殊的传统发展出来，就是出现了一种高级的"名妓"，与普通的娼妓大为不同，她们在中国文学史上崭露头角，有些自己本人就是诗人，有些与文人的生活密切相关。她们这一阶层，与中国歌曲音乐史的发展，以及诗歌形式的变化，密不可分。中国诗歌经文人亦步亦趋呆板生硬地模仿一段时期之后，已成了一连串的陈词滥调，这时往往是这种名妓创一种新形式，再赋予诗蓬勃的新生命，可以说音乐与诗歌是她们的特殊领域。因为演奏乐器与歌唱都受闺阃良家女子所歧视，原因是那些歌词都离不开爱与情，认为对情窦初开的少女有害，结果音乐歌舞便完全由歌伎保存流传下来。

在苏东坡时代的生活里，酒筵公务之间与歌伎相往还，是官场生活的一部分。和苏格拉底时代名女人阿西巴西亚参加男人的宴会相比，也没有什么丢脸的。歌伎在酒席间招待，为客人斟酒，为大家唱歌。她们之中有不少颇有天赋，那些会读书写作擅长歌舞的，多为文人学者所罗致。因为当时女人不得参与男人的社交活动，男人需求女人相陪伴，男人只好向那些职业性的才女群中去寻求快乐。有时，那种调情挑逗却是纯真无邪，也不过是戏谑而已，倒有几分像现在的夜总会的气氛。歌伎唱的都是谈情说爱的歌曲，或轻松，或世故，或系痴情苦恋，或系假意虚情，或暗示云雨之情，或明言鱼水之欢。高等名妓也颇似现代夜总会的歌女艺人，因为芳心谁属，可以自由选择，有些竟有不寻常的成就。宋徽宗微服出宫，夜访名妓李师师家。总之，当时对妓女的看法，远较今日轻松。美国曼哈顿的诗人今日不为歌女写诗，至少不肯公然出版，可是当日杭州的诗人则为歌女公然写诗。即使是颇负众望的正人君子，为某名妓写诗相赠也是寻常事。在那个时代，不但韩琦、欧阳修曾留下有关妓女的诗，甚至端肃严谨的宰相如范仲淹、司马光诸先贤，也曾写有此类情诗。再甚至精忠爱国的民族英雄岳飞，也曾在一次宴席上写诗赠予歌伎。

只有严以律己的道学家，立身之道完全在一"敬"字，同于基督教的"敬畏上帝"，只有这等人才特别反对。他们有一套更为严厉的道德规范，对淫邪特别敬而远之。道学家程颐——苏东坡的政敌，在哲宗皇帝才十二岁时，就警告皇帝提防女人淫邪的诱惑。这位年轻皇帝竟那么厌恶这种警告，到他十八岁时，只有一个女人就把他说服了，使他相信那个女人是对的，而那位道学家是错的。有一次，程颐的一个学生写了两行诗，论"梦魂出窍"，在梦中去找女人，程颐大慌，喊道："鬼话！鬼话！"大儒朱熹也是深深畏惧女人的诱惑，正人君子胡铨十年放逐，遇赦归来，写了两行诗："君恩许归此一醉，傍有梨颊生微涡。"朱熹在感叹之下写出了一首七绝：

> 十年江海一身轻，归对梨涡却有情。
> 世路无如人欲险，几人到此误平生。

正相反，苏东坡对性持较为诙谐的看法。在他著的《东坡志林》里，他在黄州时曾写有下列文字：

> 昨日太守唐君来，通判张公规邀余出游安国寺。座中论调气养生之事。余云："皆不足道，难在去欲。"张云："苏子卿吃雪啖毡，蹈背出血，无一语稍屈，可谓了生死之际矣，然不免为胡妇生子，穷居海上。而况洞房绮疏之下乎？乃知此事不易消除。"众客皆大笑。余爱其语有理，故为录之。

苏东坡一生，遇有歌伎酒筵，欣然参与，决不躲避。十之八九歌伎求诗之时，他毫不迟疑，即提笔写在披肩上或纨扇上。下面即是一例：

> 停杯且听琵琶语，细捻轻拢，醉脸春融，斜照江天一抹红。

苏东坡写了有关女人的抒情诗，但从来不写像他朋友黄庭坚写的那种艳诗。

宋朝的歌伎使一种诗的新形式流行起来，那就是词。苏东坡不但精通此道，而且把前此专供谈情说爱的词，变成表达胸怀感想的文学形式。他的词中最好的是《赤壁怀古》（调寄"念奴娇"），对三国英雄人物发思古之幽情。李白、杜甫早于苏东坡三百余年，使绝句和律诗成为诗体之正宗，多少杰出的诗人竞相模仿。但是律诗，每句五言或七言，中间两副对子，已经陈腐，诗人都想有所创新。但是观瀑、白鹭、柳荫等的情调早已发现用厌，唐代诗人淋漓的元气与强烈的感情也已不复存在。更可怕的是，甚至诗的辞藻都是陈旧比喻的重复，那些比喻一用就令人生厌。苏东坡在他的一首咏雪诗前面的小序里说，决不用"盐"这个字指雪，"雪"这个字总是胜过"盐"。唐诗的主题已经用滥，在文字上，有些作者总喜欢蹈袭前人的诗句，也有些博学的读者，一看便知道诗中思想与辞藻的来源，因此有会心的微笑。评注家的努力只限于寻出某些生僻词语的出处，得到机会以博学自炫。结果，作诗集评注的人并不以阐述判断诗的含义为要务，而以指出某些词语之出处为已足。

从诗的衰微沉滞状态解救出来，一定有待于一种新的诗体的发展，而这种发展却有待于歌伎使之普及流行。宋词的文字清新活泼，比唐诗更近于口语，后来的元曲比宋词则又更近于口语。词只是根据乐谱填出的歌曲，所以不说"写词"，而说"填词"。在词里，不像唐朝绝句律诗每行字数固定，行的长短有了变化，完全配合歌曲的需求。

在苏东坡时代，词这种诗的新形式正在盛极一时。由于苏东坡、秦少游、黄庭坚，以及宋代别的词人如晏幾道、周邦彦等的创作，词这一体的诗成了宋朝诗的正宗。苏东坡在黄州时才发现了词，极其喜爱，从在黄州的第二年开始大量填词。但是词只是一种抒情诗，内容歌咏的总是"香汗""罗幕""乱发""春夜""暖玉""削肩""柳腰""纤指"等。这种艳词与淫词从何处何时划分开，完全在于词人对素材处理的手法。情欲和纯爱在诗中之难划分，正如在现实人生中之难划分一样。不可避免的是，诗人，也像现代有歌舞助兴的餐馆的艺人一样，偏爱歌唱伤心断肠的悲痛、爱的痛苦、单恋的思念。他们歌咏的是闺中的少妇怨女，怅然怀念难得一见的情郎，默然自揽腰围，悄然与烛影相对。其实，女人的魅力全在她的娇弱无依无靠，她的芳容憔悴，她那沉默无言的泪珠儿，她那睡昏昏的情思，她的长宵不寐，她的肝肠寸断，她的茶饭不思，她的精神不振，以及一切身心两方面的楚楚可怜——这一切，和穷苦一样，都显得有诗意美感。这些文辞都与"苏慵"一词相似，而含有色欲淫荡的意思。苏东坡不但成为有宋一代的大词家，而宋词之得以脱离柔靡伤感的滥调儿，要归功于苏东坡，至少他个人是做到了。

根据记载，苏东坡没有迷恋上哪个歌伎，他只是喜爱酒筵征逐，和女人逢场作戏，十分随和而已。他并没有纳妾藏娇，倒是有两个女人与他特别亲密。才女琴操听从了他的规劝，自己赎身之后，出家为尼；朝云，后来成了他的妾，当时才十二岁，我们以后再提她。

现在有一份宋拓苏字帖，上面记有一个妓女的一首诗，叫作《天际乌云帖》，是从第一句诗得名的。帖里说的是营妓周韶的故事，周韶曾赴宴席侑酒。她常和书家兼品茶名家蔡襄比赛喝茶，都曾获胜。苏东坡经过杭州，太守陈襄邀宴，周韶也在座。宴席上，周韶请求脱除妓籍，客人命她写一首绝句。周韶提笔立成，自比为笼中白鹦鹉"雪衣女"。诗曰：

陇上巢空岁月惊，
忍看回首自梳翎。
开笼若放雪衣女，
长念观音般若经。

席上其他诗人也写诗为念。苏东坡补言当时周韶正在居丧，着白衣。

众人都受感动，周韶遂脱籍。

过这样的官场生活，自然需要做妻子的信任和了解。要做一个好妻子，主要是如何物色一个好丈夫；从反面说，要做一个好丈夫，主要就是如何物色一个好妻子。有一个好妻子，则男儿不违法犯纪，不遭横祸。苏东坡的妻子知道她嫁的是一个人人喜爱的诗人，也是个天才，她当然不会和丈夫去比文才和文学的荣誉。她早已打定主意，她所要做的就是做个妻子，一个贤妻。她现在已生了两个孩子。做一个判官的妻子，她有一个舒服的家，享有社交上的地位。她还依然年轻，二十四岁左右。丈夫才气焕发，胸襟开阔，喜爱追欢寻乐，还有——是个多么渊博的学者呀！但是佩服丈夫的人太多了——有男的，也有女的！难道她没看见公馆南边那些女人吗？还有在望湖楼和有美堂那些宴会里的。新到的太守陈襄，是个饱学之士，在他们到差之后一年来的，这位太守把对外界的应酬做得很周到，官妓自然全听他们召唤。另外还有周邠、鲁少卿等人，并不是丈夫的真正好朋友。歌伎们都有才艺，会唱歌曲、会弹奏乐器，她们之中还有会作诗填词的。她自己不会作诗填词，但是她懂那些文句。那些诗词她也觉得熟悉，因为她常听见丈夫低声吟唱。她若出口吟唱，那可羞死人！高贵的夫人怎么可以唱词呢？她丈夫去访那些赤足的高僧——惠勤、辩才，还有那些年高有德的长胡子的老翁，她反倒觉得心里自在点儿。

苏夫人用了好几年的工夫才摸清楚丈夫性格，那是多方面的个性，既是乐天达观随遇而安，可是有时又激烈而固执。到现在她倒了解一方面，就是他不会受别人影响，而且你无法和他辩论。另一方面，倘若他给歌伎题诗，那又何妨？那是当然的。他对那些职业性的女艺人，决不迷恋。而且她还听说他曾把一个歌伎琴操劝服去遁入空门修道为尼呢！琴操真有很高的宿慧，诗与佛学一触即通。苏东坡不应当把白居易写歌伎末路生活的诗句念给琴操听。苏夫人聪明解事，办事圆通，她不会把丈夫反倒推入歌伎的怀抱。而且，她知道丈夫这个男人是妻子管不住的，连皇帝也没用。她做得最漂亮——信任他。

她是进士的女儿，能读能写，但是并非一个"士"。她只为丈夫做眉州家乡菜，做丈夫爱喝的姜茶。他生病时，多么需人照顾啊！若丈夫是诗人，因而有些异乎寻常之处，那是应当的。丈夫知道有书要读，上千上百卷的书，做妻子的也知道要管家事，要抚养孩子，要过日子。因此，她愿忍受丈夫睡觉时有名的雷鸣般的鼾声——尤其是酩酊大醉之时。

这些先不说，与这样的人同床共寝，真得承认这个床头人是够怪的。妻子在床上躺着难以入睡，听着丈夫打鼾，却不能惊醒他。在他入睡之前，他要不厌其烦地把被褥塞好。他要翻来覆去把躯干四肢安放妥帖，手拍被褥，直到把自己摆放适当又自在又舒服为止。他身上倘若有地方发僵发痒，他要轻轻扣，轻轻揉。这些完毕，这才算一切大定。他要睡了，闭上眼，细听气血的运行，要确待呼吸得缓慢均匀而后可。他自言自语道："现在我已安卧。身上即使尚有发痒之处，我不再丝毫移动，而要以毅力精神克服之。这样，再过片刻，我浑身轻松安和直到足尖。睡意已至，吾入睡矣。"

苏东坡承认，这与宗教有关系。灵魂之自在确与身体之自在有关联。人若不能控制身心，便不能控制灵魂。这以后是苏东坡一件重要的事。苏东坡在把自己睡眠的方法向两个弟子讲解之后，他又说："二君试用吾法，必识其趣，慎无以语人也。天下之理，戒然后能慧，盖慧性圆通，必从戒谨中入。未有天君不严而能圆通觉悟也。"

后来，苏夫人还发现夜里和黎明时，丈夫习惯上要有更多的改变。用细梳子拢头发和沐浴是这位诗人生活中的重要大事。因为在那一个时代，若有人细心观察人的身体及其内部的功能，并注意草药及茶叶的研究，再无别人，只有苏东坡。

苏夫人头脑清爽而稳定，而诗人往往不能。丈夫往往急躁，灰心丧气，喜怒无常。苏夫人有一次在一个春天的月夜，作了一个比照说："我对春天的月亮更为喜爱。秋月使人悲，春月使人喜。"数年后，在密州，他们正过苦日子，苏东坡对新所得税至为愤怒，孩子揪着他的衣裳对他哓哓不休。

他说："孩子们真傻！"

苏夫人说："你才傻。你一天闷坐，有什么好处？好了。我给弄点儿酒喝吧。"

在一首诗里记这件事时，苏东坡觉得自己很丢脸，这时妻子洗杯子给他热酒。这当然使他很欢喜，他说他妻子比诗人刘伶的妻子贤德。因为刘伶的妻子不许丈夫喝酒。

但是在苏东坡的心灵深处有一件事，人大都不知道，苏东坡的妻子一定知道，那就是他初恋的堂妹，不幸的是我们无法知道她的名字。因为苏东坡是无事不肯对人言的人，他一定告诉过他妻子。他对堂妹的深情后来隐藏在两首诗里，读苏诗的人都略而未察。

苏东坡并没常年住在杭州，而是常到杭州的西南、西部、北部去。由神宗熙宁六年（一〇七三）十一月到次年三月，他到过附近的上海、嘉兴、常州、靖江，这些地方在宋朝时都属于浙江省。他的堂妹现在嫁给了柳仲远，住在靖江附近。他在堂妹家住了三个月，他虽然写了大量的旅游诗记述这次旅行，并且常和堂妹的公公柳瑾一同写作游历，却一次也没提到堂妹丈夫的名字，也没写过一首诗给他。他写过一首诗记堂妹家的一次家宴，还写过两首诗论书法，那是堂妹的两个儿子请他题字时写的。苏东坡对柳瑾这个诗人和书法家的成就颇为器重，对堂妹的孩子也很顾念。但是到堂妹家的盘桓却对堂妹的丈夫一字不提，实在令人难以理解。

此行写的两首诗，暗含有对堂妹的特别关系。一首诗是他写给刁景纯的，主题是回忆皇宫内的一株花。其中有下面的句子：

> 厌从年少追新赏，
> 闲对宫花识旧香。

那时他并没坐对宫花，因为他并不是正置身于皇宫之内。他说"厌从年少"的伴侣时，他显然是描写自己；而"花"照例是女人的象征，"旧香"可能指一段旧情。

这个暗指在另一首诗里更为清楚。那是给杭州太守陈襄的。题目中说春归太迟，误了牡丹的开花时节（诗前叙言颇长）诚然不虚，他回到杭州时，牡丹的花季已过，这是暗示少女已嫁，今已生儿育女，则极明显，并且在咏牡丹的一首诗里也没有理由用两次求爱已迟那么明显的典故。为明白这两个典故，要说明一下。在唐朝有一个少女杜秋娘，在十五岁时写了下面一首诗：

> 劝君莫惜金缕衣，劝君惜取少年时。
> 花开堪折直须折，莫待无花空折枝。

"空折枝"便表示误了求爱时期。唐朝杜牧与杜秋娘同时，也写出了

下面的一首诗:

> 自是寻春去较迟，不须惆怅怨芳时。
> 狂风落尽深红蕊，绿叶成阴子满枝。

自从杜牧写了这首诗，"绿叶成阴子满枝"就用来表示少女成了母亲之意，更因为中文的"子"既代表"果子"，又代表"儿子"。

在苏东坡那首诗里，思想似乎并不连贯，并且特别用"金缕""成阴结子""空折枝"这些字眼儿。他的诗如下:

> 羞归应为负花期，已是成阴结子时。
> 与物寡情怜我老，遣春无恨赖君诗。
> 玉台不见朝酣酒，金缕犹歌空折枝。
> 从此年年定相见，欲师老圃问樊迟。

这首诗给陈襄，或是赋牡丹，都不相宜，仔细一看，连与诗题都漠不相干，"成阴结子"与牡丹更无关系。他也没有理由要太守陈襄"怜我老"。"从此年年定相见"是分别时的语句，并且用于归见同僚，而且苏东坡心中绝无心在陈太守邻近安居务农的打算。倘若说这首诗确是写给陈太守的，用"绿叶成阴"喻求爱已迟，必然是够古怪的。诚然，在唐朝这类诗里，中间两联里字的词性要同类相对，中间两联有时只做点缀之用，前后两联才真用以表达作者的情思;不过唐律之上品仍然全首有整体性的。苏东坡写的诗里用几行空洞无物的句子充数儿的坏诗，可少见得很。若从另一角度观之，看作是他写给堂妹的，则这首诗在主题和思想上便很完整了。第一行说此次归来实感羞愧，因自己误了花时，也可以说误了堂妹的青春时期。第二行分明说她已儿女成行。第三行求她同情，又表示自己的孤独寂寞。第四行说因有她相伴，今春过得快活。第五和第六句分明是他对求婚已迟感到歉疚。第四联自不难解。苏东坡这时写了一首诗，表示愿在常州安居下来，这样离堂妹家不远。他后来的确按照计划在常州买了房子田地，后来也是在常州去世的。

我知道敬爱苏东坡的人会不同意我的说法，怪我说苏东坡暗恋堂妹。这是否在苏东坡的品格上算个瑕疵，看法或因人而异。这事如果属实，并且传到人耳朵里，那些道学家必会谴责苏东坡。不过自古至今，堂兄妹、表兄妹不断相恋，但苏东坡不能违背礼俗娶自己的堂妹，因为她也姓苏。

苏东坡游靖江时，他在焦山一个寺院的墙上题了一首诗，西方的读者对此最感兴趣。苏东坡料必知道唐朝段成式在《酉阳杂俎》中所写"叶限"那篇短故事，述说小姑娘叶限受继母和后妹折磨，丢了鞋，后来嫁给国王的经过。但是据我所知，苏东坡是第一个记载老翁睡眠时怎么安排自己须子的人。他用一首简易的韵语说一个有长须的人，从来没想过在床上怎么安排自己的胡子。一天，有人问他睡觉时胡子放在什么地方。那天夜里他开始惦记他的胡子，他先把胡子放在被子外面，后来又放在被子里面，又放回外面，折腾了一夜没合眼。第二天早晨，他一直感觉坐立不安，心想最好的办法是把胡子剪掉。由那首诗看来，那只是通俗故事，不是苏东坡创作的。

在这里我们不妨提一下《盲者不识日》的故事，这倒是苏东坡第一个想到的，这篇寓言写在密州。爱因斯坦似乎在什么地方引用过这篇故事，来说明一般人对相对论的看法。

日 喻

生而眇者不识日，问之有目者。或告之曰："日之状如铜盘。"扣盘而得其声，他日闻钟以为日也。或告之曰"光如烛"。扪烛而得其形，他日揣籥以为日也。日之与钟、籥亦远矣，而眇者不知其异，以其未尝见而求之人也。道之难见也甚于日，而人之未达也无以异于眇。达者告之，虽有巧譬善导，亦无以过于槃与烛也。自槃而之钟，自烛而之籥。转而相之，岂有既乎。故世之言道者，或即其所见而名之，或莫之见而意之，皆求道之过也。

说也奇怪，这篇寓言是苏东坡在殿试时写的。他用以讽刺当时学者盲从王安石的《三经新论》。

苏东坡这个人物个性太复杂，方面太多，了解不易。因为他精通哲理，所以不能做道学家；同样，也因为他深究儒学，故也不能为醉汉。他对人生了解得太透彻，也对生活太珍惜，自然不愿把生活完全消耗于醇酒妇人之间。他是爱自然的诗人，对人生抱有一种健康的神秘看法。这个看法永远与深刻精确的了解自然密不可分。我相信，没有人与大自然、春夏秋冬、雨雪、山峦谷壑亲密相处，并接受大自然赐予人的健康治疗的力量后，而同时对大自然还会抱有一种歪曲偏颇的看法。

在熙宁六年九月九日，他拒绝去参加重阳节的宴会。他躲开了朋友，自己去泛舟为乐。按照重九的风俗，他破晓之前起身，到西湖上访孤山的两位僧人。那天晚上，他一人独坐舟中，凝视山顶有美堂窗内射出的灯光，那时他的同僚正在那里一间大厅里欢呼畅饮。他给一个同事周邠写出下面的一首七律：

蔼蔼君诗似岭云，从来不许醉红裙。

不知野屐穿山翠，惟见轻桡破浪纹。

颇忆呼卢袁彦道，难邀骂座灌将军。

晚风落日原无主，不惜清凉与子分。

Chapter Eleven

POETS, COURTESANS, AND MONKS

Hangchow, then as now, was a magic city, sometimes called "Paradise on Earth." It was to be almost like a second home to Su Tungpo, who wrote upon his arrival:

"Come, take from time the leisure's share you will.
Semi-retirement is retirement still.
Where better could I settle and find a home
Than such a place with peerless lake and hill?"

It was like a second home to him not only because of the beauty of its hills and forests and lake and sea and its busy streets and magnificent temples, but also because he was very popular with the people and spent some of his happiest days there. The people had the gaiety of the south, with its songs and its women, and they loved this young famous poet just as poet, with all his desh and verve and insouciance. His mind was inspired by the beauty of the place, and his heart was soothed by its pliant charm. Hangchow won his heart and he won the hearts of the people of Hangchow. During his term of office as an assistant magistrate he was not able to do much for the people, but for them it was enough that he was poet; when he was arrested, the common people of the city set up altars in the streets to pray for his release. After he left, the soft beauty and warmth of the south continued to haunt him in his dreams. He knew he would go back. When he went back eighteen years later as governor of the province, he did so much for the city that he left a permanent halo around his memory at Hangchow, and it claimed him as its own. Today, almost a thousand years after the poet lived and sang there, as you go on the lake or mount the top of the Kushan Island or the Phoenix Hill or have a sip at one of the lakeshore restaurants, you hear your host, who is a native of Hangchow, repeating frequently the name "Su Tungpo—Su Tungpo." If you point out that the poet came from Szechuen, he will not like it. Why, he thought Su was born here and never went anywhere else in China except to the capital!

Su Tungpo and West Lake make a perfect combination in mood, vagrant charm and love and laughter. The poetry of the region and the poetry of the poet found in each other a perfect expression. It is not an easy thing for a town to find its poet, who can discover the living, changing, complex individuality of the locality and in a verse of four lines compress and express the essence, the spirit, and the beauty of the region. In what is justly considered the best poem on West Lake, Su compared it to the beauty of the days of Mencius; a "Miss West," who was just as beautiful when she was in a morning negligée, at home and familiar, as she was in full make-up. Both clear and rainy days added their charm to the immortal lake:

> "The light of water sparkles on a sunny day;
> And misty mountains lend excitement to the rain.
> I like to compare the West Lake to 'Miss West,'
> Pretty in a gay dress, and pretty in simple again."

That was of course merely a figure of speech. "Miss West" looked at any time prettier with painted eyebrows than without them. It was Su Tungpo who embellished the fringes of the lake and gave them little touches with consummate art to make them natural. Today the Su Embankment stretching across the lake, the reflections in water of the enchanted isle, called "Three Ponds Reflecting the Same Moon," and the willow-fringed shore line, bear testimony to his skill as a landscape architect. The West Lake of Hangchow and the "Little West Lake" of Yangchow are two places where the profound landscaping genius of China found perfect expression, where human art and skill improve but do not spoil. The artist first seized the natural design of the locality and saw it as a whole in its natural structure and composition. He merely added a few touches to tighten or smooth out, or to emphasize a contour here and there, and nothing more.

Su Tungpo arrived at Hangchow with his wife and children on November 28, 1071. The residences of the magistrates were situated on top of the Phoenix Hill, enjoying a full view of the Chientang River with its great fleet of seafaring ships on the south, and the West Lake, surrounded by cloud-capped mountains, dotted with temples and rich men's villas, on the north, while the waves of the bay lashed its shores on its east. There were two deputy magistrates at Hangchow besides the chief magistrate, for Hangchow was a big metropolitan city. The Su family occupied a building on the north side of the compound, which was the lake side. Immediately below the Phoenix Hill, and lying on a strip running north and south between West Lake and the Chientang Bay, was the city itself with its high walls, its bridges and canals. Mrs. Su was transported when she opened the window in the morning and saw beneath her the beautiful placid surface of the lake reflecting moving clouds and mountaintops and villas. Before the day was well advanced, pleasure-seekers' boats filled the lake, and at night from their house on the hill she could hear the sound of flutes and songs. Certain sections of the city were more brilliantly illuminated than others, for there were fairs open every night until two or three in the morning. For the wife, particularly, there was an exciting variety of fancy foods, silks, embroideries, and fans, and for the children, a great variety of candies and toys and rotating lanterns. The candy sellers of Hangchow in Sung times resorted to strange advertising tactics to attract the attention of the public. There were candy sellers who sold their wares on the roulette principle, others who dressed as white-bearded old men, and those who wore masks and danced and sang. Some sold candy floss, some blew candies into shapes of different animals, and some made "sand sugar," which is like maple candy. There is a book about the city life of Hangchow written at the end of the Sung Dynasty about a hundred years after Su Tungpo and a hundred years before Marco Polo visited it, giving fascinating details of the streets, canals, the lake, the foodstuffs and popular amusements, and providing a more detailed picture of the city life of those times than is made in Marco Polo's description of the city. While Marco Polo mentioned the hunting of princes and the bathing of princesses on the lake shore and the great merchant fleets that plied between Hangchow ("Kinsai")and Chuanchow ("Zayton"), he was not familiar with the names of the sweetmeats, fancy bakery, and popular amusements. The long and almost old-womanish lists of fancy delicatessen food recounted again and again on the pages of this book by Wu Tsemu can drive any reader crazy.

Su Tungpo half believed that he had lived here in his previous incarnation. This is recorded in his own poems and in the journals of contemporaries. One day he was visiting the Shoushing Temple, and the moment he entered the gate he felt the scene was very familiar. He told his companions that he knew there were ninety-two steps leading up to the Penance Hall, which they found to be correct. He could also describe to his companions the buildings, courtyards, and trees and rocks at the back of the temple. We do not have to believe these stories of reincarnation, but when society believes in ghosts or in reincarnation, there are always many such firsthand stories, and like ghost stories, they cannot be conclusively proved or disproved. In Su Tungpo's time the belief in a person's previous existence was general and such stories were not uncommon. There was a story about the previous existence of Chang Fangping. One day he was visiting a temple and told people that he remembered he had been abbot at this place in a previous life. Pointing upstairs, he said that he recalled being occupied in copying a certain Buddhist classic in the attic, a work which was left unfinished. He and his friends went upstairs and found indeed an unfinished manuscript in a handwriting bearing a striking resemblance to Chang's writing. He took up his brush and began to copy from where he was supposed to have left off in his previous life. There was also the story told of one of Su Tungpo's best friends. Huang Tingchien, the great poet, told people that in his previous life he had been a girl. He suffered from body odor in one of his armpits. One night when he was magistrate at Fouchow, a little below Chungking in Szechuen, a girl appeared in his dream and said to him, "I am your previous self and I am buried in a certain place. The coffin is decayed and on the left side there is a big ant nest. Please have it removed for me." Huang did so, and the body odor in his left armpit disappeared thereafter.

As an assistant magistrate Su had no great responsibilities except presiding at court trials. This was something he heartily disliked, knowing that the people who had been arrested were chiefly those who had violated laws of the new regime, laws that he disapproved. Yet there was the law and he could not alter it. It is perhaps easiest to understand the mind and heart of Su Tungpo at this period by reading the poem he wrote on New Year's Eve when he had to try prisoners arrested for salt smuggling. The government monopoly had taken over the trade in salt, but the traders in the salt-producing area around Hangchow Bay refused to be driven out of business. The complete situation of salt smuggling was embodied in a letter by Su Tungpo to a cabinet minister. We are not concerned here with the objective conditions, but rather with the poet's attitude toward his fellow men, for he saw no difference between himself and those on trial.

"On New Year's Eve, I should go home early,
But am by official duties detained.
With tears in my eyes I hold my brush,
And feel sorry for those in chains.
The poor are trying to make their living,
But fall into the clutches of the law.
I, too, cling to an official job,
And carry on against my wish for rest.
What difference is there between myself
And those more ignorant than I?
Who can set them free for the time being?
Silently I bow my head in shame."[1]

To Tseyu he wrote more intimately: "There are certain things which used to shame me, but of which I am no longer ashamed now. I sit facing the ragged prisoners and witness their flogging. When I talked with my superiors, my mouth said 'yes' but my heart said 'no.' What is the use of occupying a high position, while degrading one's character? My vital spirit has shrunk and withered, no longer what it used to be."

In another poem he spoke about the sufferings of the people under the *paochia* system, and described how the people screamed when they were whipped, and how even men's wives and children were put in jail. It was the steady accumulation of lines like these which later, when he was arrested and tried, established his guilt as one trying to destroy confidence in the regime.

Meanwhile he enjoyed himself when and where he could. He tried to escape to nature, and nature was there at its best at his feet. His poetic spirit feasted upon the beauties of the neighborhood. For not only the city itself and West Lake, but all the mountains within ten or fifteen

[1] A facsimile of the original of this poem in the poet's own handwriting is reproduced in the beginning of this book.

miles of Hangchow became his favorite haunts. Starting from West Lake, the traveler could go in all directions, either following the north bank to the famous Lingyin Temple and reaching the top of Tienchu, or starting from the south bank, he could go to Kehling, stop over at Hupao, famous for its spring water, have his tea there, and return by following a beautiful winding mountain brook. In the city and the suburbs there were three hundred and sixty temples, usually on mountaintops, where he could while away a whole afternoon chatting with the monks. An outing to these hills usually took a whole day, and he reached home late at twilight, when the street lights were already on. Passing the crowded and illuminated night fair at Shahotang, he would come home drowsy and half drunk, thinking up poetic lines and forgetting half of them.

> "Suddenly rubbing my sleepy eyes,
> I saw the brilliant lights of Hotang.
> The milling people were clapping their hands,
> And frolicking like young deer in the wilds.
> I realized then that the simple joys of life
> Could be enjoyed only by the simple men.
> What is happiness in human life?
> My ways, I fear, are all wrong."

Hangchow was gay and West Lake was enticing. The southern climate invited one to spend one's time outdoors in all seasons. In spring and autumn all Hangchow played on the lake. Even in winter on a snowy day there were pleasure seekers who went out in boats to enjoy the landscape in snow. Particularly on great festivals, like the third day of the third moon, the fifth day of the fifth moon, the mid-autumn festival, the ninth day of the ninth moon and the birthday of a local god, the eleventh day of the second moon, the lake was filled with holiday makers, and one had to engage a boat on the previous day. It was not necessary to bring food along because everything, including cups, saucers, spoons, and chopsticks, was provided by the boatmen. There were also boatmen who caught fish and sold them to people who could put them into the water again as a way of "accumulating merit" or laying up treasure in heaven for having saved living creatures, according to Buddhist teachings. It was quite possible that one and the same fish could save three lives from Hell, if he were caught three times and loosed three times.

Su Tungpo participated fully in the life on the lake. There were two kinds of parties, families enjoying themselves and others with sing-song women. The lake was a place where the wives looked at the sing-song women with fear, and the sing-song women looked at the wives with envy. The sing-song women wished from the bottom of their hearts that they could be "liberated" and have homes of their own with growing children around them, like those wives. Su Tungpo sometimes went with his wife and children, and sometimes with his drinking official friends. He was versatile. He had at his command a pen which could produce such skillful, ornate, and technically excellent lines that they compelled admiration from fellow scholars, and he could write simple effortless lines that stuck in one's memory. With his family, he could sing:

"The sound of chopping fish comes from the bow,
And the fragrance of cooking rice issues from the stern."

With his fellow officials he wrote lines that delighted them in their gaiety:

"The pleasure boats with oars of Wu have been painted,
The dancing dress of new Yueh gauze is first being tried."

As soon as they arrived at the lake shore, the boatmen crowded around them and each asked them to take his boat. They would choose a small one, seating four or five people, or sometimes when there was a bigger party, one large enough to set a dinner table in, and have food prepared by the boatwoman, who was usually an expert cook. There houseboats were elaborately carved and had gargoyles at the bows. On the lake there were other boats catering to the holiday makers. Some boatmen sold chestnuts, melon seeds, stuffed lotus roots, sweetmeats, roast chicken, and fresh seafood. Other boatwomen specialized in serving tea. Some boats carried entertainers who customarily drew up to the tourists' boats and entertained them with songs, light acrobatics, and provided slings and other shooting games.

Around them all lay the clear blue waters of the lake with a circumference of about ten miles, and in the distance beyond, clouds nestled against the mountaintops, half concealing and half revealing them. The clouds gave variety to the mountains by lending them a changing shape, and the mountains housed the clouds by providing them a home of rest. Sometimes the air felt as if it were going to snow, and a low haze covered the foothills. Behind the haze, the pleasure seekers could see here and there glimpses of pagodas and towers and catch the faint outlines of the distant hills. Or on a sunny day, the water was so clear they could count the fish in the water. In two delightful lines Su Tungpo gave an impressionistic color picture of the boatmen's yellow turbans moving against the background of the green hills.

"Against the hills yellows turbans bob on gargoyle-head boats.
Along the streets blue smoke rises from sparrow-tail lamps."

Going ashore toward the mountains, they could hear the birds calling to one another in the deserted woods. A lover of travel, Su often roamed alone over the mountains, and scribbled poems on the rocks at the highest mountaintops or near the head streams seldom visited by other tourists.

He became a great friend of the monks in the temples which he frequently visited. An old monk told the story after Su Tungpo's death that when he was a young boy serving at Shoushing Temple, he used to see Su come up the hill on foot alone on a summer day. There he would borrow a monk's couch and move it to a selected place under the near-by bamboo grove. Totally devoid of any sense of official dignity, he took off his jacket and shirt and slept bare-backed on the couch during an afternoon. The young acolyte peeped at the great scholar from a respectful distance, and saw something that nobody had been privileged to see. He saw, or thought he saw, seven black moles on the poet's back, arranged like the constellation of the Dipper. And that, the old monk said, was an evidence that he was a spirit sent down from the heavenly sphere to live merely as a temporary guest in this human world.

In a poem which he sent to Chao Tuanyen after he left Hangchow, Su Tungpo made a good summary of his habit of travel. Chao was going then to Hangchow as a commissioner, and Su Tungpo advised him what to do.

"The landscape of West Lake tops the world.
Tourists of all classes, intelligent and otherwise,
Find and appreciate each what he wants.
But who is there that can comprehend the whole?
Alas, in my stupid honesty,
I have long been left behind by the world.
I gave myself completely to the joys of hills and water—
Is it not all determined by God's Will?
Around the three hundred sixty temples,
I roamed throughout the year.
I knew the beauty of each particular spot,
Felt it in my heart but could not say it in my mouth.
Even now in my sweet sleep,
Its charm and beauty remain in my eyes and ears.

Now you come as a commissioner;
Your official pomp will insult the clouds and haze.
How can the clear streams and the purple cliffs
Reveal their beauties to you?
Why not dismiss your retinue
And borrow a couch from the monk,
Read the poems I inscribed on the rocks,
And let the cool mountain air soothe your troubled soul?
Carry a cane and go where you like,
And stop wherever seems to you best.
You'll find some ancient fishermen
Somewhere among the reeds. Talk with them,
And if they say wise things to you,
Buy fish from them and argue not about the price."

It seems from the literary records that Su Tungpo's preoccupation at Hangchow was with religion and women, or rather with monks and courtesans, and the two are more closely related than we think. In Su Tungpo the life of the senses and the life of the spirit were one, coexisting without conflict in a poetic-philosophical view of human life. With his poetry, he loved this life too passionately to become an ascetic or a monk, and with his philosophy, he was too wise to give himself up to the "devil." He could no more renounce women and song and pork and wine than he could renounce the blue waters and the purple mountainsides, and at the same time he was far too profound to put on the garb of a shallow, cynical fop.

The best illustration of the attitude of the young and fun-loving poet is the story of how he tried to bring an austere priest and a courtesan together. Abbot Tatung was a severe old man of saintly character, and it was said that people who wanted to see him in his retreat had to take a ceremonial bath. Women were of course forbidden his chamber. Su Tungpo was one day visiting the temple with a party in the company of a showgirl. Knowing the priest's habits, the party stopped outside. Su knew the old priest well and felt a devilish urge to bring the woman in and break his monastic rules. When he went in with the showgirl to pay their respects to the old abbot, the latter was visibly displeased at the young man's impudence. Su said he would write a song of apology and make the showgirl Miaochi sing it, if the abbot would permit her to borrow the clapper used for beating time during the singing of litany. So Tungpo gave the girl these lines to sing:

> "Holy Father, I do not know what to say,
> Being not conversant with your way.
> May I borrow the door rapper and litany clapper?
> Kindly take this in a spirit of fun.
> A maiden's stolen glance should cast no blemish,
> Please, Your Reverence, be not so squeamish.
> For if you were my age, I might be all your rage.
> As it is, no harm is done."

It was strictly a one-man comic opera, and even the austere Tatung laughed. Su Tungpo came out with the girl and boasted to the others that they had learned a great "lesson in the mysteries."

It is not possible to separate monks from women, at least not in Chinese literature. The stories of monks are often stories of women and the stories of women are often stories of monks. For East and West, there is a secret grudge among lay people against a special class of celibates who announce to the world that they have no sex life and are different from the generality of mankind, and it is this secret grudge against celibates that underlies the popularity of the stories of Boccaccio. Besides, a monk's affairs with women make a better story than a businessman's.

As a judge, Su Tungpo had once to adjudicate a case involving a monk. There was a monastic brother at the Lingyin Temple, by the name of Liaojan, who frequented the red-light district and fell madly in love with a girl named Shiunu. In time he spent all his money and was reduced to rags, and Shiunu refused to see him any more. One night in a drunken fit he went to call on the girl again, and being refused admittance, he forced his way in, beat the girl, and killed her. The monk was therefore being tried for murder. In examining him the officers found on his arm a tattooed couplet: "May we be born together in Paradise, and not suffer the love pangs of this life!" After the completion of the investigation the evidence was submitted to Su Tungpo. Su could not resist writing the sentence in the form of a light verse:

"Away from here, you bald-head daisy!
In vain you took the vow of celibacy,
Reduced yourself to this ragged shape
By your unmonkish profligacy.
By your cruel fists you killed your love.
What's illusion now, and what reality?
Your arm bears witness to love's longing,
This time you shall pay love's penalty."

The monk was sent to the execution ground and beheaded. Comic poems, such as the two above, written in the language of the day, quickly passed from mouth to mouth and added to the current gossip about this eccentric genius.

Among such stories there was a small collection of tales about Su Tungpo and his friend the pleasure-loving monk Foyin. At this period Su Tungpo had not taken up Buddhism seriously; it was only after he was forty, during his period at Huangchow, that he began an intensive study of Buddhist philosophy. But some of the monks of Hangchow became his best friends, and in time he gathered more and more friends among the monks of Chinkiang, Nanking, and Lushan as well. Among them, two at least, Huichin and Tsanliao, were poets and scholars worthy of respect. From the literary records, Foyin was not important. But he cut a romantic figure, and in popular literature he, rather than Tsanliao, became most frequently talked about as the friend of Su Tungpo.

Foyin had never intended to be a monk. Furthermore, he came from a wealthy family. According to one curious story, he was born of the same mother as Leeding. Apparently the woman was a loose character and had married three times, having three sons by three different husbands—quite a record in those days. When the Emperor gave an audience to Buddhist believers as a gesture toward Buddhism, Su Tungpo presented this man at court. Foyin tried to impress the Emperor with his ardent conviction in the Buddhist faith. The Emperor looked at him and saw a tall, handsome man with an unusual face, and graciously said that he would be glad to give a monetary grant, the so-called *tutieh*, to endow him in a monastery if he would join the church. Finding himself in a quandary, he could not but accept the Emperor's suggestion, and thus he had to enter a religious order. While he was living in Hangchow, legend says he used to travel with a whole retinue of servants and pack mules, in a far from ascetic way of life.

Foyin was quite a wit. One of the better stories with a philosophic point told about these two men runs as follows. Su Tungpo was one day visiting a temple with Foyin. Entering the front temple, they saw two fierce-looking giant idols who were conceived as conquerors of the evil spirits and were placed there to guard the entrance.

"Of these two Buddhas," asked Su Tungpo, "which is the more important?"

"The one who has a big fist, of course," replied Foyin.

Going into the inner temple, they saw the image of the Goddess of Mercy holding a rosary in her hand.

"Since the Goddess of Mercy is a buddha herself, what is she doing there telling the beads?" asked Su Tungpo.

"Oh," replied Foyin, "she is only praying to buddha like all the others."

"But which buddha?" asked Su Tungpo again.

"Why, the buddha, the Goddess of Mercy herself."

"Now what's the meaning of that? She is the Goddess of Mercy; why does she pray to herself?"

"Well," said Foyin, "you know it's always troublesome to beg from others—it is always easier to depend on oneself."[1]

They saw then a Buddhist prayer book lying open on the altar. Su Tungpo found that a prayer read thus:

"A curse upon all poisons!
By the help of the Goddess of Mercy,
May those who use poison on others
Take the poison themselves."

"This is utterly unreasonable," said Su Tungpo. "Buddha is kind. How can she be expected to avert trouble from one person in order to give it to another?

If that is so, then Buddha is not Love."

Asking permission to have the prayer corrected, he took up a brush and crossed out some of the lines to make it read:

"A curse upon all poisons!
By the help of the Goddess of Mercy,
May both the users of poison
And the intended victims be spared."

Many of the stories of clever repartee between Su Tungpo and Foyin

---

[1] The original word *chiu* means both "to beg" and "to depend."

were based on puns and are untranslatable. There is, however, the following.

The word "bird" had a dirty meaning in Chinese slang, and Su Tungpo thought to make fun of his friend with it. "The ancient poets," said Su Tungpo, "often placed *monks* opposite *birds* in a couplet. For instance, there is a couplet, 'Hearing a *bird* pecking at a tree, I thought it was a *monk* knocking at the door.' Again, another couplet says, '*Birds* perch on trees beside the pond, and a *monk* knocks at the gate under the moon.' I always admire the wisdom of the ancient poets in placing monks against birds."

"That is why," said Foyin, "I, as a monk, am sitting opposite you."

These stories always show the monk as outwitting the poet. I have a suspicion that Foyin himself was the author of the stories.

The institution of courtesans in China dated back, according to known records, to Kuan Chung in the seventh century B.C., who regularized it in order to entertain soldiers. Even in Su Tungpo's time, there were state-owned courtesans, who continued to be known as "barracks entertainers," and others who were independent. But a peculiar tradition had developed so that the higher-class courtesans, as distinguished from the common prostitutes, made their mark on literary history, some by being poets themselves, and some by being closely associated with the lives of the literary men. As a class, they were closely connected with the history of song and music and therefore with the changing forms of poetry. After a period of servile imitation at the hands of the scholars, when poetry had become no more than a string of outworn chichés, it was always the courtesans who introduced new forms and gave poetry a new lease on life. Music and song were their special domain. Inasmuch as the playing of musical instruments and singing were deprecated among family girls, the songs also tended to concentrate almost entirely on love and passion, which in turn was considered detrimental to the virtue of adolescent girls. The result was, the tradition of music and dance was carried through the centuries almost entirely by the courtesans.

In the life of the times of Su Tungpo, mixing with courtesans at wine dinners and official functions was a part of an official's life. No more opprobrium was attached to it than to the presence of Aspasia at men's parties in the time of Socrates. The courtesans were entertainers who poured wine for the guests and sang for the company. Many of them were gifted, and those who understood reading and writing and were accomplished in music and song were very much sought after by the scholars. Because women were excluded from the social parties of men, the desire for female company made the men seek gaiety in the company of the professional artists. Sometimes the flirtations were innocent, carried on in the teasing, suggestive atmosphere of a modern night club, with the courtesans singing light, sophisticated, and genuine or fake songs of love, and making concealed or brazen insinuations about sex. The higher-class courtesans resembled the modern night club artist also in that they had complete freedom to choose their men friends, and some had fabulous establishments of their own. Emperor Huitsung was known to leave his palace and woo such a courtesan at her home. However, the attitude toward courtesans was much more lax than it is today. The poets of Manhattan do not write love poems to chorus girls, at least do not publish them, but the poets of Hangchow did. The practice of writing poems in honor of certain courtesans was quite common even among highly respected gentlemen. In this period we find that not only Han Chi and Ouyang Shiu left poems about courtesans, but even the austere premiers Fan Chungyen and Szema Kuang wrote this type of sentimental poetry. The great patriot general, Yo Fei, also wrote a poem concerning female singers at a certain dinner.

Only the strict, puritanical neo-Confucianists, whose code of life was summed up in the one word *ching* ("reverence," an equivalent of "fear of God"), highly disapproved. They had a more stringent code of morals, and a greater respect for the devil. Cheng Yi, who was Su Tungpo's political enemy, used to warn Emperor Tsehtsung, when the latter was only a child of twelve, about the lascivious charm of women. The young child was so sick of such warnings that when he reached eighteen, one woman alone convinced him that she was right and the puritan was wrong. Once one of Cheng Yi's disciples wrote two lines on his "dreaming soul going out of bounds" and visiting a woman in his sleep, and Cheng Yi cried in horror, "Devil's talk! Devil's talk!" Chu Shi, the great neo-Confucianist of the twelfth century, had the same horror of the seductive power of women. Once a good man, Hu Chuan, wrote two lines on the occasion of his pardon after ten years of exile, "For once let me get drunk to celebrate the pardon, with a girl's sweet dimpled face by my side." Chu Shi was moved to express himself as follows:

"Despite ten years' exile and tribulation,
The sight of a dimple caught him unaware.
Nothing should be more feared than this damnation.
How many lives are wrecked by woman's snare!"

In contrast, Su Tungpo took a more humorous view of sex. In his *Journal* he wrote, later, at Huangchow:

"Yesterday I went to Ankuo Temple with chief magistrate Tang Chuntsai and deputy magistrate Chang Kungkwei, and in the conversation we talked about the art of prolonging life. I said, 'All is easy except continence.' Mr. Chang said, 'Su Wu was a great man. He went to Mongolia, lived like a Mongolian, and went through all hardships without a grumble. He was quite a philosopher, wasn't he? Yet he could not help marrying a Mongolian woman and having children by her. It must be, therefore, more difficult to practice continence even in marriage. This thing is really difficult to overcome.' We all laughed at the remark. I am putting this down because there is a lot of sense in it."

All his life Su Tungpo took part at courtesans' dinners, and nine times out of ten had to write poems on shawls or fans by request of the entertainers.

"Oh, hush the night, each minute an ounce of gold,
While faintly floats the music of flute and song.
So fragrant the air, so cool the moonlit courtyard,
While darkly glides the silent night along."

Su wrote many sentimental poems about women, but he never wrote erotic poetry as his friend Huang Tingchien did.

The Sung courtesans had popularized a new form of poetry, the *tse*, and Su Tungpo mastered it and transformed it from a meter for sentimental poetry of the lovelorn into a vehicle fit to express any thought or sentiment in his breast. One of his best *tse* was on the "Red Cliff," whose theme was the passing of great ancient warriors. Li Po and Tu Fu had sung three centuries earlier, and by their genius had made the Tang quatrain and double quatrain the regular verse patterns for a distinguished host of imitators. But these quatrain forms, uniformly of five or seven words to the line, with the inevitable two couplets in the middle, had become stereotyped. Every poet tried to evolve a new style. But the last nuance in observation of a waterfall or an egret or the shadows of willow trees had been discovered, and somehow the richness and emotional intensity of the Tang poets were gone. What was more serious, even poetic diction had become a repetition of hackneyed metaphors. Some of them were bad in themselves to begin with. Su Tungpo wrote in a preface to one of his poems on snow that he was determined not to use the word salt. After all, snow was a better word. The themes of Tang poetry had been overplayed, and the language too often deliberately harked back to lines by other poets, giving a secret delight to the learned reader who knew where that particular twist of thought and expression came from. It was the tracing of the expressions to their obscure sources that gave the greatest opportunity for the "commentators" to display their pedantry. As a rule, writers of the so-called commentaries on collected poems did not consider it part of their duty to elucidate the meaning or judge the quality of the poem, but contented themselves with pointing out the source of a particular expression.

The liberation of poetry from decadent inertia always came from the growth of a new form of poems popularized by the courtesans. The language was fresh and new, the Sung *tse* was closer to the vernacular than Tang poems, and the later Yuan drama was still closer to the vernacular than Sung *tse*. The *tse* was nothing but a song written to a given piece of music. People did not "write" *tse*, they "filled in" the words to a known melody. Instead of lines of a uniform number of syllables of Tang "regulated verse," there was a rich variety of long and short lines, strictly conforming to the requirements of the song.

In the time of Su Tungpo this new form of poetry was at the height of its popularity. Through Su Tungpo, Chin Kuan, Huang Tingchien and others of his generation, like Yen Chitao and Chou Pangyen, it became *the* poetry of the dynasty. Su Tungpo discovered it in Hangchow, fell in love with it, and from his second year in Hangchow began to write a great number of verses in the meters of the songs. But the *tse* had been strictly a form for sentimental love verse. Such poems invariably sang of "fragrant perspiration," "gauze curtains," "disordered hair," the "spring night," "warm jade," "sloping shoulders," a "willowy waist," "tapering fingers," etc. When and where such sentimental poetry bordered on the licentious depended entirely on the poet's handling of the material. The difference between passion and love is as difficult to establish in poetry as in real life. Invariably also, like modern cabaret artists, the poets preferred to sing of heartbreak and the pangs of love and the longing of the unrequited lover. They sang of a woman secluded in her chamber, sadly longing for the absent one, fondling her belt silently, or keeping lone company with the candlelight. In fact, the whole feminine appeal was built around woman's helplessness, her sallow cheeks, her silent tears, her *ennui*, insomnia, "broken intestines," lost appetite, general lassitude, and every form of physical and mental misery, which, like poverty, sounds poetic. It would seem the word *suyung*, "lassitude," was almost voluptuous. Su Tungpo not only became one of the acknowledged few great *tse* masters of this dynasty; it was to his credit that he freed it, in his own practice at least, from sentimental drivel.

There is no record that Su Tungpo became enamored of any of the courtesans. He enjoyed the gay parties and "fooled around" with women enough to be a "good fellow," not enough to take a mistress. Two of the women were especially close to the poet. Chintsao, a gifted courtesan, was persuaded by him to free herself and become a nun. Chaoyun, who became later his concubine, was then a girl of twelve. We shall come to her later.

Today there is a Sung rubbing of a stone inscription in the handwriting of Su Tungpo which records a poem written by a courtesan. It is called "The Dark Clouds Script" from the first words of a poem. It tells the story that once a state-owned courtesan, Chou Shao, was present at a dinner. She used to hold tea contests with the great tea connoisseur and calligraphist Tsai Shiang, and won them. When Su Sung passed through the town, the chief magistrate Chen Shiang gave him a party with Chou Shao present. During the party Miss Chou begged to be released from her profession, and the guest asked her to write a quatrain. The courtesan wrote the following, comparing herself to a caged parrot (the "snow-dress maiden").

"See her turn her head and her sad feathers preen,
Dreaming of her old nest where a home had been.
Open the cage and set the snow-dress maiden free!

She will say her whole life, 'Blessed be Kuanyin!' "

The other scholars also wrote poems about the occasion. Su Tungpo adds that the woman was then wearing white in mourning. Everybody was touched and she was released.

An official life such as this demanded a great deal of trust and understanding from the wives of the officials. However, the problem of being a good wife is principally the problem of finding a good husband, and conversely the problem of being a good husband is principally the problem of finding a good wife. Having a good wife is the best guarantee against a husband's going wrong. Mrs. Su knew she had married a popular poet and a genius, and she certainly did not try to compete with him in literary honors. She had made up her mind that her best job was to be a wife, a good one. She had now two babies of her own, and as wife of a deputy magistrate she had a comfortable home and enjoyed certain social honors. She was still very young, between twenty-three and twenty-five. Her husband was brilliant, bighearted, fun-loving, and—what a scholar! But he had so many admirers—men *and* women! Did she not see those women on the south side of the compound and those dinners at Wanghulou (Lakeview House)and Yumeitang? The new chief magistrate, Chen Shiang, a good scholar who arrived the year after them, certainly attended to a magistrate's social duties well, and the state courtesans were at their beck and call. There were Chou (Pin)and Lu (Shaoching), not really desirable company for her husband. The courtesans were accomplished, could sing and play stringed instruments, and some of them could write verse. She herself could not versify, but she understood these songs. They were growing familiar to her, for she heard her husband humming them. She would die of shame to sing them, for no respectable lady would. She felt really much more comfortable when her husband went to see the barefooted monks, Huichin, Pientsai, and others, those old men with their adorable long beards.

It took her some years to know the depth of his character, a character with so many facets, so easygoing and yet at times so intense and strong-willed. She had learned by now one thing, that he could not be influenced, and certainly there was no way of arguing with him. On the other hand, if he wrote poems to courtesans, what of it? He was expected to. He had not taken fancy to any of the professional artists, and she had heard he had even converted one of the most famous courtesans, Chintsao, to become a nun. Chintsao had really remarkable intelligence, and from poetry to religion was only a short step. He really should not have quoted Po Chuyi's lines about the end of a courtesan's life to Chintsao. With her good sense and tact, Mrs. Su was not going to push her husband into a courtesan's lap the wrong way. Besides, she knew her husband was a man not to be stopped by wife or emperor. She did the smart thing—she trusted him.

As daughter of a *chinshih* scholar, she could read and write, but she was not an "intellectual." Instead she cooked the Meichow dishes and ginger tea that he loved. And how he needed attention when he was ill! If poet husbands sometimes were unusual, that was their privilege. The husband knew there were books to be read, thousands of them, and the wife knew there was a home to be built, children to be brought up, a life to be lived. For that, she was willing to put up with his famous snore in bed—especially when he was drunk.

Apart from that, he was certainly a curious man for a bedfellow. She must not disturb him in bed when she lay awake listening to his snoring. Before he fell asleep, he was fussy about tucking himself in properly. He would turn about and arrange his body and limbs and pat the sheet until he was well-placed and nice and cozy. If any part of his body was stiff or itchy, he would gently rub and massage it. But after that, order was established. He was going to sleep. He closed his eyes and "listened" to his respiration, making sure that it was slow and even. "And then I lie perfectly still," he said of himself. "Even when some part of my body itches, I do not make the slightest move, but overcome it by will power and concentration. Thus, after a short while, I feel relaxed and comfortable down to the toes. A state of drowsiness sets in and I fall into sound sleep."

This really had something to do with religion, Su claims. The freedom of the soul does depend so much upon the freedom of the body. Unless one controls one's mind and body, one cannot control one's soul. This was to be a great part of Su Tungpo's occupation. After describing his way of sleeping to his two disciples, he continued, "Try my method, and you will find how good it is, but don't tell it to everybody. Remember this, wisdom comes from self-control. The awakening of the divine spark in men and knowledge of buddhahood begin with self-discipline. No one who does not achieve control of his mind can ever understand God."

Later Mrs. Su was to discover more variations of the husband's habits at night and dawn. Combing his hair with a fine comb and taking a bath were among the important occupations of the poet's life. For if there was one man in that period thoroughly devoted to speculation about the body and its internal functions and the study of medicinal herbs and teas, it was Su Tungpo.

She was sane and she was steady, which a poet usually is not. Her husband was often impatient, despondent, and moody. In contrast, Mrs. Su once said on a moonlight night in spring, "I like the spring moon much better. The autumn moon makes one too sad, while the spring moon makes everybody happy and contented." A few years later, at Michow, when they were very poor and Su Tungpo was greatly angered at the introduction of the new income tax, he was once annoyed by his children tugging at his gown and bothering him.

"The children are so silly," said Su.

"You are the silly one," replied his wife. "What good will it do you to sit around and brood the whole day? Come, I will make you a drink."

In a poem recording this incident, the poet said that he felt ashamed of himself, and the wife began to clean the cups and prepare warm wine for him. This, of course, made him very happy and he said that she was much better than the wife of the poet Liu Ling, who asked her husband not to drink.

But there was one corner of Su's heart, hidden from most, which Mrs. Su must have known about. This was his first love for his cousin, who to us, unfortunately, is nameless. Being the confiding soul be always was, Su Tungpo must have told his wife about it. His deep affection for the cousin afterward lay buried in two poems that passed unnoticed by all students of the poet's works.

Su Tungpo did not stay all the time at Hangchow but took frequent trips southwest, west, and north. From November 1073 to March 1074 he went up to the neighborhood of Shanghai, Kiashing, Changchow, and Chinkiang, which in the Sung Dynasty were parts of the province of Chekiang. His cousin-sister was now married to Liu Chungyuan and living in the neighborhood of Chinkiang. He remained in his cousin's home for three months, and although he versified a tremendous lot on this trip and wrote and traveled constantly in the company of his cousin's father-in-law, Liu Chin, he never once mentioned his cousin's husband or wrote a poem to him. He also wrote a poem about a family dinner at his cousin's home, and two poems on calligraphy to his cousin's two boys when they came to ask for his autograph. Su Tungpo had great respect for Liu Chin as a poet and as a calligraphist, and also thought a lot of his cousin's children. But the complete silence about the cousin's husband during this trip is hard to explain.

Two poems, written during this trip, suggest this special relationship with his cousin. One was a poem he wrote to Tiao Yueh, and the subject was declared to be reminiscence of a certain flower he had seen at the palace. It contained the following two lines:

"Tired of seeking new beauties in the company of youth,
I sit facing the palace flower and recognize its old fragrance."

He was not exactly sitting opposite that flower at that moment, for he was not in the palace. He was obviously describing himself when he said he was tired of youth's company; and as "flower" was the regular symbol for woman, the "old fragrance" could be a reference to an old love.

The reference is clearer in another poem, one he wrote to the chief magistrate of Hangchow, Chen Shiang. The subject stated was that by returning so late in spring, he had missed the flowering season of the peony. (Titles of poems indicating the occasions were sometimes quite long.)It was true that by the time of his return to Hangchow the peony season would be over. Nevertheless, the references to a girl now married and become a mother are unmistakable, and there was no reason why in a poem on peonies he should make two clear references to belated courtship. In order to understand the references, it must be explained that there was a girl in the ninth century who wrote the following poem at the age of fifteen:

"Spare not, my friend, the gold-embroidered gown,
Miss not the years of youth—enjoy them now.
Come, pluck the flower while to pluck is good,
Wait not until you pluck the empty bough."

To "pluck the empty bough" was therefore to miss the courtship of youth. Furthermore, Tu Mu, a contemporary of this girl, wrote as follows:

"It is my fault I should have missed the spring,
Yet shall I fret because the flowers are gone?
Late storms have blown the petals far away,
On leafy bending boughs rich fruits are borne."

Ever since Tu Mu wrote this poem, "On leafy bending boughs rich fruits are borne" has become a common expression for a woman become a mother of many children, particularly because in the Chinese language the same word (*tse*)is used for "fruit" and "sons."

In his poem, where the thoughts seem to be disconnected, Su Tungpo specifically used the phrases, the *gold-embroidered gown*, the *leafy boughs bearing fruit* and *plucking an empty bough*.

"I'm ashamed to come home for I missed the spring bloom;
See the generous green of the fruit-laden tree.
If I'm lonely and changed, think kindly of my age;
With your poems, I have passed this year's spring happily.
I am now no more drunk in the morn in jade halls;
But in gold-braid dress celebrate still the bare bough.
From now on every year let us meet without fail,
While I learn the fine art of the spade and the plough."

The song was neither appropriate to Chen Shiang nor to the peony, and on close examination bears no relation to the subject. A fruitladen bough is hardly appropriate for the peony. There was no reason why he should ask Chen Shiang to "think kindly" (*lien*)of his age. The pledge to see each other "from now on" was written for parting, not for one returning to see a colleague; and Su certainly had no idea of settling on a farm to live as Chen's neighbor. Above all, the reference to belated courtship of a mother of children must be considered strange, if it was really meant for Chen Shiang. It is true that in a Tang poem of this kind, where the middle two pairs are always couplets with nouns, adjectives, etc. in one line balanced by the same class of word in the other, sometimes such pairs in the middle are decorations for the verse, with the first and last couplets bearing the poetic message; nevertheless, a skillfully constructed Tang poem should have complete unity. Rarely would

Su Tungpo write such a badly constructed poem with lines made merely to fill a vacuum. On the other hand, read as a message composed for his cousin, the poem has a unified thought and theme. The first line says he was ashamed to come home because he had missed the spring bloom, or the girl's youth. The second line makes a clear reference to her having children now. The third line asks for her sympathy and expresses his feeling of loneliness. The fourth line expresses the thought that he has had a happy spring this year, in her company. The third couplet then clearly expresses his regret at the belated courtship. The fourth couplet becomes easily intelligible. Su Tungpo at this time wrote a poem expressing his desire to settle at Changchow, which was not very far from the Lius' home. He did carry out his plans to buy a house and farm at Changchow, and it was here that he died.

I know that admirers of Su Tungpo will take issue with me for thus suggesting that he had a secret love for his cousin. Whether it casts a slur on his character or not, however, is a matter of opinion. Su Tungpo would have been condemned by the neo-Confucianists if it had been true and known. Bur cousins have often fallen in love since time began. Su Tungpo did not and could not defy the conventions by marrying his first cousin on the father's side who bore the same clan name, Su.

One poem which he scribbled on the wall of the monastery at Chiaoshan, during the trip to Chinkiang, is of particular interest to Western readers. Su Tungpo should have known of the Cinderella story, with the stepmother, step-sisters, missing slipper and all, which was contained in the writings of a ninth-century Chinese author. But as far as I know, he was the first to put in writing the story of how an old man arranged his beard when he went to bed.

In a simple thyme he told of a man with a long beard who never gave a thought to how he should arrange his beard in bed. One day someone asked him where he put his beard during sleep. That night in bed he became conscious of his beard. He first put it outside his quilt and then inside, and then outside again, and lost sleep the whole night. The next morning he got so restless that he thought the best way would be to cut it off. From the text of the poem, this seems to be a popular tale, not an invention of the poet himself.

It may be appropriate to mention here that Su was the originator of the parable of "The Blind Man's Idea of the Sun," written at Michow. Albert Einstein somewhere quoted this parable to illustrate the average man's idea of the theory of relativity.

"There was a man born blind. He had never seen the sun and asked about it of people who could see. Someone told him, 'The sun's shape is like a brass tray.' The blind man struck the brass tray and heard its sound. Later when he heard the sound of a bell, he thought it was the sun. Again someone told him, 'The sunlight is like that of a candle,' and the blind man felt the candle, and thought that was the sun's shape. Later he felt a [big]key and thought it was a sun. The sun is different from a bell or a key, but the blind man cannot tell their difference because he has never seen it. The truth (*Tao*)is harder to see than the sun, and when people do not know it they are exactly like the blind man. Even if you do your best to explain by analogies and examples, it still appears like the analogy of the brass tray and the candle. From what is said of the brass tray, one imagines a bell, and from what is said about a candle, one imagines a key. In this way, one gets ever further and further away from the truth. Those who speak about *Tao* sometimes give it a name according to what they happen to see, or imagine what it is like without seeing it. These are mistakes in the effort to under-stand *Tao*. "

Curiously, this fable was used as testimony at his court trial. The charge was that he was ridiculing the scholars of the time for following blindly the commentaries of Wang Anshih on the classics.

Su Tungpo was too complex a character, too many-sided, to be understood easily. While he was too good a philosopher to be a puritan, he was also too good a Confucianist to be just a drunk. He understood life too well and valued it too highly just to squander it with wine and women. He was a poet of nature, with that peculiar wholesome mystic view of life which is always associated with a deep and true understanding of nature. No one, I believe, can live in close touch with nature and its seasons, its snows and rains, its hills and dales, receiving its healing powers, and have a warped mind or a warped view of life.

On the ninth day of the ninth moon, 1073, he refused to go to the drinking parties usually held on such a festival. Running away from his friends, he took a boat all by himself. Getting up before dawn, as was the custom on this festival, he went out to the lake and called on the two priests at Kushan. That night he sat alone in a boat on the lake, watching the lights from the windows of Yumeitang on the top of the hill, where his colleagues were enjoying themselves at one of those usually boisterous wine dinners. Writing to a colleague, Chou Pin, he said:

"The high note of your poems suggests the mountain clouds.
You would not fall drunk on a woman's breast!
If you won't pierce the country green with your sandals,
Why not watch the boat cut ripples on the blue?
I remember the gambling and shouting of Yuan Yentao;
But where is the angry, cursing General Kuan[1]
The sunset and the breeze are nature's free gifts,
Come to the lake, and share the cool evening air!"

---

[1] Allusions, not to contemporaries, but to historic characters.

第十二章 抗暴诗

我们最好记住，即便是在天堂般的杭州，也不是遍地荷花牡丹的。苏东坡也不能一直放声大笑纵情高歌，一直演独角丑儿戏，一直月夜泛舟湖上，因为还有一万七千囚犯，因无力还债、因贩卖私盐正待审判，有蝗灾尚待扑灭，有盐渠尚待疏浚，有饥馑尚待调查。在苏东坡这一段生活中写的数百首诗里，很难找到何者是主要的情调。他写戏谑讽刺诗、启人灵思的山水诗、荡气回肠的爱情诗，有的诗轻松愉快惹人大笑，有的诗辛酸凄苦令人落泪。可是在表面的嬉笑欢乐之下，在筵席上的戏谑打趣之下，却是一片不安、失望、忧伤，甚至恐惧的气氛。再没有别人把人民的心情反映得更充分，别的作家要表达的，现在苏东坡都用美妙的诗歌表达出来：表达得更为清楚而深刻。可是要知道，苏东坡是离京在外，内心还有以前的创伤。对现时政局演变的方向，他感到不安，感到了隐忧。这种忧伤，他灵魂感受的比别人更敏锐。看他用多么美妙的诗句表达出来：

天静伤鸿犹戢翼，月明惊鹊未安枝。

他在密州写的一首诗，是寄给乔太傅的，综括熙宁四年（一〇七一）
至九年，他在杭州、后来在密州那段写作多产时期他的一般态度：

> 百年三万日，老病常居半。
> 其间互忧乐，歌笑杂悲叹。
> 颠倒不自知，直为神所玩。
> 须史便堪笑，万事风雨散。
> 自从识此理，久谢少年伴。

在另一首给孔文仲的诗里，他流露出对声势煊赫的官场气派的蔑视：

> 我本麋鹿性，谅非伏辕姿。
> 闻声自觉聚，那复受絷维。
> 金鞍冒翠锦，玉勒垂金丝。
> 旁观信美矣，自揣良厌之。
> 人生各有志，此论我久持。
> 他人闻定笑，聊与吾子期。

跟着他朗朗笑声的歌，我们也听到怒吼和叹息；在鹭鸶的鸣声之外，
我们又听见监狱中的呻吟声；在水车上潺湲的水声之外，我们又听到农村
老妪的悲叹声；湖滨楼头的庆祝喧哗声里，我们也听到稀疏灰发人绝望的
幽怨声。

苏东坡此人，是不可以预测的。他在诗的开端，习惯上总是出之以轻
松自然，随之用一两个历史上的典故，再往后，谁也不知道会有什么出

现，诗人他自己更不知道。有时，他笔下写出虽不相连贯的东西，却构成了惊人的妙文；一首毫无用意的歌，记载刹那之间奇特的印象，然后忽然一变为苛酷、为讽刺、为寓有深意的讥评。他不愧为诗文大家，动起笔来，真是"如行云流水，常行于所当行，常止于不可不止"。他的风格是属于那全任自然一发不能自己的一类。在朝廷上最厌恶清议之时，他这种风格是必然会给自己招致麻烦的。

苏东坡不知道他下一行写什么，而且也并不在意。在他那天才横溢之下，他往往抓住一个题目就接连写四五首诗，而且用同样的韵。有一首诗，开始就写天欲雪的气氛，他这样开始：

天欲雪，云满湖，楼台明灭山有无。

接到他诗的朋友寄和诗回来，苏东坡又答以诗寄回去，诗的开头如下：

兽在薮，鱼在湖，一入池槛归期无。

朋友再和，他又寄第三首如下：

东望海，西望湖，山平水远细欲无。

第四首开头如下：

君不见，钱塘湖，钱王壮观今已无。

他的第二首诗惹出了麻烦，因为他的思路一直顺着鱼和兽失去了自由的方向发展下去。从此处一步就会跳到在监狱中被鞭打的囚犯，还有那些囚犯的妻子儿女也被关入监狱的事。在这些长诗里，他必须押前面字句的韵，而思想也自然要顺着那些同韵的字发展。这诗里有两个要押的韵脚，一个是"逋"，一个是"摹"。在一首诗里他说"作诗火急追亡逋"，在另外一首诗里自然写出"岁荒无街归亡逋"。在押"摹"字韵时，他写出"孤烟落日不可摹"；但在另一首诗写囚犯时，他又说"鹄则易画虎难摹"——这分明是指暴政了。

苏东坡这个人，快乐时很难说不快乐，不快乐时也难做快乐状。好多朋友和他通信，彼此作诗相酬唱。这时刘恕和李常都在九江，孙觉在湖州，在杭州北不远。这些都是反对王安石新政的一批朋友，现在都在东南各地为官。他们都对时局感到厌恶，因为当时王安石仍未失势，他们不像以前那么激烈，意见姑且放在心头。韩琦和欧阳修已死，富弼和范镇退隐林下，司马光潜心治学，张方平纵情饮酒，东坡之弟子由则明哲保身，闭口不言时事。只有苏东坡不够圆滑。在看见人民陷于水深火热之中，这时应当不应当不顾后果，坦率表示自己的感慨，这是一个问题。也许苏东坡从来没想过这个问题。所以，他一边写令人心旷神怡可惊可喜的田园诗，同时也写乡间并不那么美丽的诗。他若不是疯狂得不顾利害，便是义愤填膺不能自制。他知道他的诗很快就会传到京师，但是他却毫不在乎。

苏东坡写的这些诗，渐渐累积成卷，若认真看看某些行是否足以证明他蔑视当政者的威信，倒也有趣。单独看，那些句子只是偶一置评；但合起来看，则是些动人的抗暴诗。少数几个例子，便已足够。他用平易的文字写被征调的人民挖通运河以通盐船。他以官员之身监督工人，他亲眼看见黎明之时，工人闻号声而聚集开工，用寥寥几个字便写出"人如鸭与猪，投泥相溅惊"。

在到杭州西南的富阳之行时，他写出天放晴时清新可喜的诗句，开始如下：

东风知我欲山行，吹断檐间积雨声。
岭上晴云披絮帽，树头初日挂铜钲。

但是他还是对其他情形闭目不见，他在歌咏"春入深山处处花"时，也写农民的食粮。农民正在吃竹笋，他说竹笋好吃，但是没有咸味，因为"尔来三月食无盐"，原因是朝廷的专卖食盐扼杀了盐业。他若一放手写去，就无法节制，他会写出农民的儿子私用农民的贷款，停留在城内把钱挥霍净尽，回家时两手空空，只学到一口京腔而已，因为官家很精明，在放款处附近就开设了酒馆娱乐场所。

他往北游到太湖地区，看见好友，高大长须的孙觉。他这位书画名家，在友人的名家书法集上题了一首诗。在诗里他说的也是："嗟余与子久离群，耳冷心灰百不闻。"他写了一首极美的诗描写水车泻出的水流，他起的题目是"吴中田妇叹"：

今年粳稻熟苦迟，庶见霜风来几时。
霜风来时雨如泻，杷头出菌镰生衣。
眼枯泪尽雨不尽，忍见黄穗卧青泥。
茅苫一月垅上宿，天晴获稻随车归。
汗流肩赪载入市，价贱乞与如糠粃。
卖牛纳税拆屋炊，虑浅不及明年饥。

官今要钱不要米，西北万里招羌儿。

龚黄满朝人更苦，不如却作河伯妇。

　　他也写快乐的诗歌，给杭州钱塘江潮时的"弄潮儿"。每年八月中秋，各地人都自老远跑到钱塘江岸边观看潮水自海外奔腾而至，不停高涨，涌入狭窄的钱塘江口。在高潮来临之前，总是举行水上特技表演。现在我们还不清楚当年是如何在波涛上漂浮的。在水上表演的人名叫"打浪儿"，似乎那些深识水性的人乘小舟出海，船上饰以红绿旗帜，出去迎接涌来的高潮。苏东坡给那些"打浪儿"编出通俗的歌曲唱。歌曲里说雪白的浪花吞没了"打浪儿"的红旗帜，浪潮遮蔽住半个越山的景色。但是他也写出早晨酒醒后内心的感触：

众人事纷扰，志士独悄悄。

何异琵琶弦，常遭腰鼓闹。

三杯忘万虑，醒后还皎皎。

……

忧来不自寐，起视天汉渺。

阑干玉绳低，耿耿太白晓。

　　在日后引起是非的一首诗里，他挖苦了当权派，把他们暗比作夜枭。他那时正同周邠游历岭南。根据记载，后来在审问苏东坡时，岭南的一个太守草拟了一篇呈文，请求简化免役税的征收。这位太守曾经带着呈文经过杭州到京都，现今南返，他在杭州告诉苏东坡说："我被夜枭逐回矣。"

　　苏东坡问他："你的话什么意思？"那位太守说他曾携带呈文到京都，

将呈文递交一个税吏，税吏命武装侍卫送他出城。苏东坡要看那篇文字，发现所提的是一个很好的简化征收办法。

苏东坡又问："你说夜鸮是什么意思？"

太守回答说："这是一个很通俗的寓言。一天，一只燕子和一只蝙蝠争吵起来。燕子认为日出是一天之始，而蝙蝠则认为日落是一天之始。两鸟相持不下，它们去请教凤凰。在路上，它俩遇见一只鸟，那个鸟儿向它们说：'近来我们没有看见凤凰。有的鸟说它请假不在，有的说它正在睡一大觉。现在夜鸮正在代替它的职位。你们去问它也没有用。'"

苏东坡写的那首诗，是给周邠的，诗里显出消沉失望，大有退隐之意：

年来战纷华，渐觉夫子胜。

欲求五亩宅，洒扫乐清净。

……

独游吾未果，觅伴谁复听。

吾宗古遗直，穷达付前定。

……

奈何效燕蝠，屡欲争晨暝。

后来，这些诗都被当权派收集去仔细研究。内容并无煽动叛乱，没有公开批评，没有公然反对当局。但是这些诗却如蚊叮虫咬，令人觉得刺痛、烦扰、不安；这种刺激若是过多，也会扰人通宵，难以入睡。再加上苏东坡的一位好友王诜驸马把这些诗刊印出来，可就更使人烦恼。在诗是表情达意最通俗的文学形式的时代，两行巧妙的诗，比长篇大论的表章更有力量。而苏东坡当时是家喻户晓的；他的诗在文人雅集时是要歌诵的。

对苏东坡的呼声不能再置之不理了。

在神宗熙宁七年（一〇七四）九月，苏东坡在杭州的任期届满。他弟弟子由那时正在山东济州任职，苏东坡已经呈请调到山东去。他所请照准，这次他是升任密州太守，密州离青岛很近。他在密州只有两年，然后又调到徐州任太守，在徐州是从熙宁十年（一〇七七）到元丰二年（一〇七九）三月。

苏东坡在向杭州南山、北山上寺院的方丈至交告别之后，携眷起程北上。他妻子已经买了一个非常聪明的丫鬟，才十二岁，名叫朝云，她以后在苏东坡的生活里非常重要。

密州是一个很穷的县份，主要只长麻、枣、桑树，此地的生活和杭州有天渊之别。当时官员的薪俸已经减低。苏东坡在他《杞菊赋》的序言中说："余仕宦十有九年，家日益贫，衣食之俸，殆不如昔。及移守胶西，意且一饱，而斋厨索然，不堪其忧。日与通守刘君廷式循古城废圃，求杞菊食之，扪腹而笑。"

王安石已去职，现由吕惠卿当权，创行了新所得税法。免役税的分派远非县中人民所能负担。这一时期苏东坡写的诗中曾说绕城而走，孩童死于道边葬埋尸体，热泪盈眶。几年后，他在一封信里曾提起他救了三四十个饥饿的孤儿，在自己家里抚养。

这是苏东坡最难过、最沮丧的一段时光；说也奇怪，这位大诗人在最难过的日子却写出了最好的诗歌。按照中国的标准说，到了这一时期，他的诗才达到完全成熟的地步。这时愤怒与苛酷的火气已无，只剩下安详平和与顺时知命的心境。甚至他对大自然之美的喜悦与生活中的乐事的享受，也比以前更洒脱而不执着。显然和他在杭州年轻时之富有火气大为不同了。他对陶渊明的诗越发爱好，他那首《西斋》诗和陶诗相比，简直可以乱真。在这首诗里，不但可以看到真正的宁静满足，还有与自然的浑然一体，以及对大自然本身的声音色彩显示出静谧的喜悦。原诗如下：

> 西斋深且明，中有六尺床。
> 病夫朝睡足，危坐觉日长。
> 昏昏既非醉，蜗蜗亦非狂。
> 褰衣竹风下，穆然濯微凉。
> 起行西园中，草木含幽香。
> 榴花开一枝，桑枣沃以光。
> 鸣鸠得美荫，因立忘飞翔。
> 黄鸟亦自喜，新音变圆吭。
> 杖藜观物化，亦以观我生。
> 万物各得时，我生日皇皇。

只有诗人达到这种与自然浑融为一体时，他才能写出下面《吏隐亭》这样的诗句：

> 纵横忧患满人间，颇怪先生日日闲。
> 昨夜清风眠北牖，朝来爽气在西山。

从这种神秘观中，他获得了精神上的解脱，这种解脱正仿佛白云无心飘浮在山峰之上一般。他的《望云楼》诗如下：

> 阴晴朝暮几回新，已向虚空付此身。

出本无心归亦好，白云还似望云人。

说来也颇有趣，往往为了子由，苏东坡会写出最好的诗。苏东坡在由杭州到密州时，心中思念子由，他写了一首词，调寄《沁园春》：

孤馆灯青，野店鸡号，旅枕梦残。渐月华收练，晨霜耿耿，云山摛锦，朝露。世路无穷，劳生有限，似此区区长鲜欢。微吟罢，凭征鞍无语，往事千端。

当时共客长安，似二陆初来俱少年。有笔头千字，胸中万卷。致君尧舜，此事何难。用舍由时，行藏在我，袖手何妨闲处看。身长健，但优游卒岁，且斗樽前。

又在密州时，想起不能见面的弟弟，他写出了公认最好的中秋词。批评家说这首词写出之后，其他以中秋为题的词都可弃之不足惜了。这首词调寄《水调歌头》：

明月几时有？把酒问青天。不知天上宫阙，今夕是何年。我欲乘风归去，又恐琼楼玉宇，高处不胜寒。起舞弄清影，何似在人间？

转朱阁，低绮户，照无眠。不应有恨，何事长向别时圆？人有悲欢离合，月有阴晴圆缺，此事古难全。但愿人长久，千里共婵娟。

上面这首《水调歌头》是熙宁九年（一〇七六）在密州时作的。

Chapter Twelve
POETRY OF PROTEST

It is well to remember that even Hangchow was not all lotus and peonies. Su Tungpo could not always laugh and sing and stage one-man comic operas and go boating on the lake in the moonlight, for there were seventeen thousand prisoners in jail to be tried for debt and for salt smuggling, locust pests to be fought, the salt canal to be dredged, a famine to be investigated. In the hundreds of poems written by the poet at this time of his life, it is hard to find any dominant mood. He wrote comic and satiric verse, inspiring descriptions of landscape, sentimental poems of love, songs gay with laughter, and other songs bitter with tears. But underlying all his superficial frivolities and gaieties and cracking of jokes at the wine feasts, there was a spirit of restlessness, of despondency, of sorrow and even of fear. No one man reflected the feelings of his people more fully than Su Tungpo, and it was given to him to put into songs and words of beauty more richly and more fully what the other writers were trying to express. Yet, it is well to remember that Su Tungpo had come away from the capital to his post with a wound in his heart. There was a feeling of insecurity and of hidden grief over the trend of political events, a grief which touched his soul more deeply than others. As he beautifully expressed it:

"The wounded mallard folds its wings e'en though the wind is quiet,
The frightened rook sleeps lightly when the moon is clear."

One poem he wrote at Michow, addressed to Chiao Shu, sums up his general attitude in this time of prolific writing, between the years 1071 and 1076, at Hangchow and then Michow.

"Thirty-six thousand days comprise a human life.
Of this, old age and sickness occupy half.
And in this life, joy is attended by sorrow,
Laughter and song keep company with tears.
Without a why or wherefore, madly we plunge
Headlong like puppets or playthings of the gods.
Then in a while we laugh about the past,
All things blow over like a thunderstorm.
—Since I perceived this truth some time ago,
I have forsaken my merrymaking friends."

In another poem, addressed to Kung Wenchung, he revealed his inner contempt for the pomp of office.

"By nature I am like a forest deer,
With hardly the temper of the harnessed breed.
Look at these gilded accoutrements,
The jadeite buckles and the silken reins!
Compelling admiration from onlookers,
But meriting well my inner contempt...
Every man has his goal and aim in life,
And I have always held to my belief.
Others will laugh at what I am saying,
But I expect the highest of you and me."

And so along with his songs of laughter we hear a voice of outcry and a sigh. We hear beyond the boom of the bittern the moaning of those in jail, and beyond the gurgle of water on the waterwheel the sad plaint of an old farmer's wife. Mixed with the noise of celebrations overlooking the lake, we hear a resigned voice complaining of his thin and graying hair.

Su Tungpo was unpredictable. He had the habit of beginning his poems in the most natural, simple and effortless manner, he would put in an allusion or two recalling ancient history, and from then on nobody knew what was going to happen, least of all the poet himself. Sometimes he gives us an amazing piece of contented inconsequentialities, a song without purpose, recording the curious impression of a moment, and then he may burst into bitterness, satire, or profound irony. There is no question that he was a master of both prose and poetry, written in the stly of "sailing clouds and winding waters, going whither it wants to go and stopping whenever it is right to stop." It also may be said to be the style of an author who cannot help himself. At a time when free criticism was most resented at the court, it was a style definitely calculated to land the poet in trouble.

But Su Tungpo did not know what lines he was going to write next, and he did not care. With the prodigality of his genius, he would often write three or four or five poems in succession on the same theme and using the same thyme words. There was a poem which started by describing the atmosphere of a day when it felt as if it were going to snow. And so he began:

"It is going to snow,
Clouds cover the loch,

Towers and hills seem to be there, and seem not."

The friend to whom he sent it wrote back, and he replied with a second poem which begins like this:

"Beasts are in the lair,
Fish are in the loch,
Once in the traps and snares, they return not."

The friend replied and he sent a third, which begins:

"Eastwards lies the sea,
Westwards lies the loch.
Distant hills appear so dim, they appear not."

And in the fourth poem he began:

"Don't you see
The Chientang loch?
Today King Chien's palaces exist not."

In the second poem, he got into trouble, for then he was carried away by the thought of the fish and the beasts losing their freedom. From then on it was only a step in thought to go on and speak about the prisoners who were being flogged in prison and whose wives and children were sent to jail. These were long poems, and he had to start with the end rhyme words and build his thoughts around them. Two of the thyme words were "fugitive" and "describe." Which in one poem he said, "I write this poem in a hurry, like a fugitive," it was natural for him to say in the other poem, "In a famine year there is no way of sending the fugitives home." In using the thyme word "describe," he said in one poem, "The setting sun and cottage smoke are difficult to describe;" but in the other poem about the prisoners, he also said, "It is easy to paint a stork, difficult to describe a tiger"—a clear reference to a rapacious government.

Su Tungpo was hardly the kind of man to deny that he was happy when he was, or to pretend that he was happy when he was not. Many of his friends kept up correspondence with him and they wrote poems to each other. Liu Shu was now at Kiukiang and so was Li Chang. Sun Chueh was at Huchow, only a short distance north of Hangchow. These were friends who had fought together against Wang Anshih's administration and were now serving in various capacities in the southeast. All of them felt disgust with the state of things, for at this time Wang Anshih was still in power, but being less headstrong, they kept their opinions to themselves. Han Chi and Ouyang Shiu were dead. Fu Pi and Fan Chen were living in retirement. Szema Kuang devoted himself to authorship, Chang Fangping gave himself to drink, while Tungpo's own brother was wise enough to keep his mouth shut. Tungpo was less tactful. It was just a question whether, when one actually saw the people suffering, one should express his feelings regardless of consequences for himself. Perhaps he never considered the question. And so along with poems of delight and wonder at pastoral beauty, he kept on writing about what was not so beautiful in the countryside. The poet was either mad or terribly in earnest. He knew that his lines traveled fast to the capital, and he did not care.

It would be interesting to take a close look at some of these lines which, as time went along, accumulated in sufficient volume to convict him of disrespect for the ruling regime. Taken separately, they were merely occasional comments, but together they were impressive as a collection of poetry of protest. A few examples will suffice. He wrote in the simplest language of the horrible scenes of people conscripted to dredge a canal for salt boats. As an official supervising the work, he saw the workmen gather together at the sounding of the horn at dawn, and he said in so many words that "the men were like ducks and pigs, splashing about in the mud."

On his trip to Fuyang, southwest of Hangchow, he wrote a fresh and delightful poem on the clearing up of the sky, beginning as follows:

"The east wind knows that I am going home,
It stopped the sound of raindrops from the eaves.
The cloud-lined blue peaks lift their cotton caps,
And the morning sun hangs like a gong atop the trees."

But he could not help seeing things, and while he sang about how "the spring brought flowers into very village," he also wrote about the food of the farmers. They were eating bamboo shoots, and the bamboo shoots were good, he said, but they were not salted, for "they have not tasted salt for three months," because the government monopoly had killed the salt trade. Once he let himself go, he could not help telling how the young sons of the farmers took advantage of the farmers' loans, borrowed the money, stayed in the city and spent it all, and came home bringing no more than a city accent, for the government was clever enough to open wine shops and amusement places right next to the loan bureaus.

On his trip north, near the Taihu Lake district he saw his good friend, the tall, bearded Sun Chueh. As a connoisseur of painting and calligraphy, he wrote a piece on his friend's collection of famous handwritings; but in his poem he also said, "Alas, you and I stand alone in this world, Stuffing our ears and steeling our hearts against all current affairs." While he wrote a beautiful poem on the gushing current of water coming up the water wheels, he also wrote a poem called "The Sigh of a Peasant Woman."

"This year the rice crop ripens late,
Waiting for the sharp, dry winter wind to come.
But the rains came when the frost was due,
The sickle rusted and the rake was covered with mold.
I cried my tears out, but the rains continued.
How could I bear to see the ears lying in the mud?
After waiting for a month living in a shack,
The skies having cleared, I carted the crop home.
With sweat on my red shoulders I carried it to town,
The price was low and I begged to sell it like chaff.
Careless of next year's hunger, I sold the cow
To pay the tax and chopped the doors for fuel.
The government wants tax in cash and not in kind;
For wars in the northwest across a thousand miles,
My sons are drafted."

Again, he was writing joyous songs for the surf riders during the period of the Hangchow bore. It was the custom at mid-autumn every year at Hangchow for people to come from great distances and line up on the bank of the Chientang River and watch the coming of the bore, which steadily rose in height as it came in from the sea and entered the narrowing bay. Before the bore came, there was usually a marine display. It is not clear how they rode on the surf. While they were called by the name of "riders on the surf," *ta-lang-erb*, the impression was that good swimmers rode out in small boats with red and green flags on them to meet the oncoming bore. Su Tungpo wrote rousing popular songs for these surf riders to sing, and spoke of the white foam swallowing up the red flags of the riders and the height of the surfs covering half the view of the Yueh hills. But he also wrote of his inner feelings after waking up from a drink in the early hours of the morning.

"The affairs of men are in a turmoil.
The lonely scholar's spirit is vexed.
Why should the melody of the lute
Be drowned in the noise of the kettle drum?
Three cups can drown then thousand worries,
And after waking up my spirit is cleansed...
Sleepless with the burden of my thoughts,
I rise to see the lambent Milky Way.
Over the railings the Dipper has turned low,
And the bright Venus shimmers in the east."

One of the poems that got him into trouble was a subtle crack he made at the ruling authorities, by implication comparing them to owls. He was visiting the district of Linan in the company of Chou Pin. According to the story told later at Su's trial, a magistrate of Linan had drafted a proposal for simplifying the collection of the draft exemption tax. This magistrate had come up to Hangchow with his proposal, and now, returned home, told Su Tungpo his story.

"I was driven out by the owl," the magistrate said.

"What do you mean?" asked Su Tungpo, and the magistrate told him how he had gone to the city with the plan and submitted it to a deputy tax commissioner, and how the latter had him escorted out of the city under armed guards. Su Tungpo asked to see his proposal and found that he had suggested a good simple system of collection.

"What do you mean by the owl?" asked Su Tungpo, and the magistrate replied:

"Well, this is a popular fable. One day a swallow and a bat were having a dispute. The swallow held that the sunrise was the beginning of the day, while the bat argued that sundown was the beginning. As they could not decide the matter, they went to ask the opinion of the wise phoenix. On the way, however, they met a bird who said to them, 'We haven't seen the phoenix lately. Some say he is on leave and some say he is taking a long nap. At present the owl is taking over the position in his stead. So there is no use your going to consult that third.'"

In this poem written on this occasion, addressed to his companion Chou Pin, he said in a tone of resignation and great despondency:

"For years I have been going through a struggle,
And now I gradually feel the Master prevails.
I want to find a farm of five acres,
And clear all vexations from my breast...
I have not yet been able to go my way,
But who will listen when I try to persuade?
I have always admired the upright ancients,
And I shall leave the rest to heaven's will...
Why follow the example of the swallow and the bat,
And argue about the beginning of the day? "

In time, lines like these were carefully collected and scrutinized by those in power. There was no preaching of rebellion, no overt criticism, no declamation against those in authority. But such lines have the power of mosquito bites. They sting, they irritate, and they annoy; and if there are too many bites, they can thoroughly ruin one's sleep for the night. It was particularly annoying to have these poems published by one of Su's close friends, Prince Wang Shien, who was married to the Emperor's sister. At a time when verse was the popular form of communication of ideas, two clever lines of verse made better "quotes" than a windy memorandum. And Su Tungpo was enormously popular; his verse was repeated at scholars' parties. The day was coming when it was no longer possible to ignore Su Tungpo's voice.

In September 1074 his term of office at Hangchow was up. His brother was now serving only as a secretary at Tsichow, modern Tsinan, in Shantung province, and Tungpo had begged to be transferred to that province. His wish was granted, and this time he was appointed chief magistrate of Michow, which is near Tsingtao. He served at Michow only for two years, then was again appointed a chief magistrate, of Suchow, where he served from April 1077 to March 1079.

After saying goodbye to his friends in the monasteries on the northern and southern hills of Hangchow, Su started with his family on the way north. His wife had bought a very intelligent maid of twelve, by the name of Chaoyuan, who was to become most important in the life of Su Tungpo.

Michow was a very poor district, growing principally hemp, dates, and mulberries, and the life here offered a striking contrast to that of Hangchow. The officials' salaries had been cut at this time, and in his preface to a descriptive poem, "Medlar and Chrysanthemum," Su Tungpo said, "After being in the service for nineteen years, I am becoming poorer every day and can no longer live as I used to. When I came over to be magistrate of Kiaochow, I thought at least that I would not have to starve, but the pantry is bare, and we have to live frugally. I often go out with a fellow magistrate, Liu Tingshih, along the ancient city walls, and pick the medlar and the chrysanthemum in the abandoned gardens and eat them. Then we feel our bellies and laugh."

With Wang Anshih out of office, Huiching was now in power and a new income tax was instituted. The allocation of the draft exemption tax was far beyond the ability of the people of the district to pay. Children were dying on the roadsides. One line in a poem Su wrote at this period spoke of his "going along the city wall with tears in my eyes" to bury the exposed corpses. In a letter he wrote years later, he mentioned the fact that he was able to save thirty or forty starving orphans and put them in homes.

It was a period when Su Tungpo was feeling sad and despondent, and strange to say, it was when the poet was saddest that the wrote his best poems. That is, judged by Chinese standards, it was in this period that he reached complete maturity as a poet. The anger and the bitterness were gone, and there was only peace and resignation. Even his joys in the beauties of nature and the pleasures of the day were more mellow, indicating a clear difference from the youthful gusto and effervescence of his Hangchow days. He had steadily grown in his admiration for Tao Chien, the one great harmonious poetic spirit of China, and in the poem "On the Western Garden" his work cannot be distinguished from that of Tao. In this poem we see not only true peace and contentment but also a complete union with nature and a quiet delight in the sounds and colors of nature itself.

"In the deep western room, I recline on a bed,
Quite awake from a nap, yet the day seems so long.
I feel tired for no reason and dazed though not drunk,
But the wind from the grove sets right all that was wrong.
Then I stroll in the garden, catch the sweet smell of grass,
A pomegranate has burgeoned, the dates are so strong!
The dove rests in the shade, idly folding its wings,
And the oriole's gay golden throat trills a new song.
On a cane, I observe the world's course and myself.

All things prosper in turn; why should I hustle along?"

It was when the poet had reached this state of complete harmony with nature that he could write a poem like the following, "The Recluse Pavilion."

"'How can you pass such days of quiet and calm,
While human life is sore beset with ills?'
Last night I slept by the breezy northern window;
This morn the crisp air fills the western hills."

From such a mystic view, he obtained a sense of spiritual freedom, a freedom which equaled that of the clouds traveling without aim and purpose over the mountain peaks. The poem "Cloud Gazing Tower" reads as follows:

"Through rain and shine, alternate night and day,
Drifting at will and stopping as it may,
The cloud has made the universe its home,
And like the cloud's so is the gazer's way."

It is striking that Tseyu always made the occasion for Su Tungpo to write some of his best poetry. On his journey from Hangchow to Michow, thinking of his brother, Tungpo wrote a beautiful song in the meter of a tse, in this case set to the tune of *Shinyuanchun*:

"A lone dim lamp in a quiet room;
At the wayside inn a cock crows.
On a traveler's pillow lie unfinished dreams.
Declining moon gathers up its beams.
The morning frost covers the hills like a brocade,
Which sparkles with the pearly dew.
Human toil fills life's endless journey,

Freshened now and then with moments of joy.
Holding the reins in silence,
I thought of the myriad things that had gone by.
"I look back upon those days
When we stopped together at Changan,
Like the two Lus,
Both inspired by the high hopes of youth.
With a thousand words from our pens
And ten thousand volumes in our breasts,
We thought it not difficult to make our Emperor the best.
Whether to serve or to retire
Depends entirely now upon ourselves.
Why not fold our hands in our sleeves and leisurely watch?
May we remain forever in good health
And spend the last years of our lives at ease—
Over a contest of wine!"

It was in Michow, thinking of his absent brother, that he wrote what is considered the best poem on the mid-autumn by any poet. Critics say that after this poem was written, all the other poems on the harvest moon could be well forgotten.

" How rare the moon, so round and clear!
    With cup in hand, I ask of the blue sky,
'I do not know in the celestial sphere
    What name this festive night goes by?'
I want to fly home, riding the air,
But fear the ethereal cold up there,
    The jade and crystal mansions are so high!
Dancing to my shadow,
    I feel no longer the mortal tie.

"She rounds the vermilion tower,
Stoops to silk-pad doors,
   Shines on those who sleepless lie.
Why does she, bearing us no grudge,
   Shine upon our parting, reunion deny?
But rare is perfect happiness—
The moon does wax, the moon does wane,
   And so men meet and say goodbye.
I only pray our life be long,
   And our souls together heavenward fly!"

The above poem, "Mid-Autumn Moon," composed in 1076 at Michow, was a *tse*, a song written to music, as has been explained. It may be interesting to analyze the tonal pattern and formal structure of such a poem. Like all Chinese poems, the *tse* uses word tones instead of accent as the basis of rhythm. The word tones are divided into two classes: First, the even and sustained tone, corresponding to English open syllables or syllables ending in liquid consonants (*l, m, n*)and second, the shifting (rising or dropping)and abrupt tones, corresponding in tonal quality to English syllables ending in stop consonants (*p, t,k*). The difference in tone between the two is roughly seen in that between *song* and *sock*, or between *seen* and *sick*, or very roughly between the end of a question and the end of a period. It is necessary to understand this tonal basis of Chinese poetry, which gives rise to its musical character. The Chinese language is essentially monosyllabic; moreover, most of the time, auxiliary particles like *be, should, and, to, of, the, a*, which furnish a great part of the unaccented syllables in English poetry, are omitted. This brevity of the word gives a marked syllabic weight, convenient for the development of a feeling of the tonal scheme. The music of a Chinese poem therefore, whether in the loose "ancient style," or in the precise "Tang poem," or in the still more precisely regulated "*tse*," may be said to consist entirely in the subtle and varied contrast and counterplay of word tones. A basic rule, for instance, is that when a rhyme word is in a sustained tone, all the unrhymed lines must end in the opposite tones, and vice versa.

Taking "Mid-Autumn Moon" as an example, one may let "o" stand for the sustained tone and "x" for the shifting or abrupt tones. It is quite possible to get the tonal pattern as shown below by clinking a glass for an "o" and tapping the table for an "x," letting each letter represent one musical note in the pattern:

First Stanza		*Second Stanza*	
1. ox/oox/		1. ( )xox/o	
xx/xoo/	R	xx/xoo/	R
2. oo/xx/ox/		2. oo/xx/ox/	
xx/xoo/	R	xx/xoo/	R
3. xx/oo/xx		3. xx/oo/xx/	
xx/oo/ox/		xx/oo/ox/	
xx/xoo/	R	xx/xoo/	R
4. xx/xox/		4. xx/oox/	
ox/xoo/	R	ox/xoo/	R

It will be seen that all the rhymed lines ("R")at the end of each long phrase or sentence (four long phrases in each stanza), have essentially the same pattern (x x / x o o /), which is therefore the dominant musical phrase. The variations at the beginning of each long phrase and leading to the dominant phrase are arranged to give contrast to each other. The accent, contrary to that in the musical bar, is always on the last note of the bar; therefore, differentiation in tone on the last note of a bar is absolute, while some slight laxity is allowable in the first note of some bars. In this sense, the fourth long phrase is really a repetition of the first. Also, with the exception of the first long phrase, the second stanza is identical with the first in tonal arrangement. The first long phrase of the second stanza is quickened in pace and shortened into three bars with three notes to each bar, but on examination it discloses the same final dominant phrase.

第十三章　黄楼

甚至才高如苏东坡，真正的生活也是由四十岁才开始的。他现在就要进入他的徐州时期，也就是他的"黄楼"时期。苏东坡现在突然露出了他的本来面目。因为这是他人生中首次以行动为人所知，做事，兴建工程，忙于公众活动，从今以后他的生活都是具有这些特色的。过去在杭州，他始终充任辅佐官员，始终不能从事具有建设性的重要工作，在密州虽然身为太守，但是地方贫穷而偏远，也无由一展其行政才能。后来，他在被迫之下，暂时退隐，在政坛上韬光养晦，此后，一个充实、完满、练达、活跃、忠贞的苏东坡出现了，这才是我们所知道、百姓所爱戴的苏东坡，也是温和诙谐、百姓的友人兼战士的苏东坡—— 一个具有伟大人格的伟大人物。但是在他被捕遭受流放之前，他以徐州太守所表现的政绩，已经证明了苏东坡这个行动人物作为行政官员，也是个干练之才。

在熙宁九年（一〇七六）年底，苏东坡又调离了密州，改派至山西省西南端的河中府任职。次年正月，他路经济南入京，当时子由及其家室正在济南。子由不在，因为政局正在酝酿变化。这时，王安石、吕惠卿、曾布、邓绾，已先后失势，王安石复相后，又再度罢相，无人预知下一步会出现何等局面。

子由为人沉静而果断。苏东坡过去一直不断上书论税政，论征兵法，请皇帝废止所得税。但是子由过去一直沉默，现在大概认为时机已至，可以放手一击，以求根本改变国策。王安石在十月已然最后失势，子由这时来不及等待兄长，已经携带改革政治的重要表章先行入京了。他的家眷仍住在济南，苏东坡到时，只有三个侄子站在城中雪地里迎接。那天晚上，大开盛宴，两家久别重聚，格外欢喜。济南为一大城市，比起密州，新鲜有趣，东坡停留了约一个月光景，直到熙宁十年（一〇七七）二月十日，两家才到黄河岸，离开封不远了。子由出城到离北岸三十里处迎接，兄弟二人在雪地途中亲热相处了好几天。子由告诉兄长调到河中府的任命已经取消，改任徐州太守。

他们到达京都时，遇到一件怪事。他们到了陈桥门，门吏告诉苏东坡不许他进城。这件事他弟弟子由曾经记录下来，只是始终没有令人满意的解释。我不相信这是皇帝的意思。也许是时局酝酿巨变，某些官员不愿让苏东坡见到皇帝；据我所知，皇帝也许根本不知道有这样一条命令。兄弟二人只好折回，住在好友范镇家，是在东外城。

这时，苏东坡的长子苏迈，已经十八岁，到了成家的年龄。钻研历史的学者，始终考证不出那位小姐是谁。我猜想他娶的是范镇的一个孙女。在苏东坡和范镇父子的通信里，他屡次称范家为姻亲。苏范两家到底是何等姻亲关系，尚待解释。范镇也是四川人，那时苏东坡正住在范家。随后两年，苏东坡帮助子由物色了两个佳婿，把子由的两个女儿嫁出去。一个是王适——"仙妻"传说主角王（字子高）的弟弟，另一个是画竹名家文与可的儿子。

儿子苏迈成婚后，苏东坡携眷东行，到徐州上任。子由也携眷到商丘任通判。他把家眷在张方平家安顿好之后，又与兄长东赴徐州，在徐州和兄长同住了三个月，才回到眷属那里。

徐州不仅是个大城市，地控鲁南，一向为军事要冲。在过去各朝代，徐州四面皆有战事，今日仍位于津浦陇海两铁路交会之处。徐州离一个地区近在咫尺，此地区即在此后数十年内因为一个盗匪巢穴受《水浒传》的渲染而出名。徐州位于河畔，南部高山耸立，下有深水急流，在城边流过。当地出产上等花岗岩、煤、铁，苏东坡时已开始开采。因此徐州也以产刀剑著称。苏东坡喜爱此地的自然风光，鱼与螃蟹也种类繁多，因称之为"小住胜地"。

在八月二十一日，苏东坡到任三个月之后，洪水到了徐州。王安石以前曾设法疏浚过黄河水道，但是空花了五百万缗，工程竟归失败，负责工程的人畏罪自尽。黄河现在是在徐州以北约五十里处向东方决口，水势开始漫延，淹没了几百方里。水到徐州城边时，被城南的高山所阻，于是继续高涨，到了九月，水深达到两丈九尺。水高一度超过了徐州城内的街道。苏东坡奋不顾身，抢救城池，有几十天不回家过夜，住在城墙上的棚子里，监督加强外圈的城墙。富有之家纷纷逃难，苏东坡在城门口劝阻他们，以免引起人心惊惶。他说："我不走，你们最好也不要走。"这样把大家劝回去。此处不是细谈苏东坡建筑工程天才之所，不过也得说他是亲自参与了防堵工程的数字计算。在盘旋滚转的洪水势将越过东南外城墙时，他正在忙于加强城基和增加城高。防水工程长九千八百四十尺，十尺高，二十尺厚。完成这项工程，需要数千人之众。扑哧扑哧在泥里跋涉，他亲身到军营去见指挥官。因为禁卫军直接受皇帝命令，苏东坡恳求他们协助。指挥官欣然应允，他说："大人都亲自监工，我们自然应当尽力。"同时在徐州北方也正在准备把洪水引入以前的黄河旧水道，黄河在中国历史上曾改道多次。洪水威胁徐州城四十五天。在十月初五，黄河又回到旧水道，往东在靠近海州处入海，洪水才开始撤退。

百姓欢天喜地，感谢全城得救。但是苏东坡对临时的堤防感到不满，附以详细数字说明，修表呈奏朝廷，请求拨款，重建石头城墙，以防患于未然。空等好久之后，苏东坡修改了原定的计划，建议改用坚强的木材加强堤防，不再用石头。皇帝对他的成就特颁圣旨嘉许，在次年二月，朝廷拨给苏东坡三万贯，一千八百石米粮，七千二百个员工，在城东南建筑了一条木坝。在外围城墙上，由于苏东坡喜爱建筑，他兴工建筑了一座楼，一百尺高，名之为黄楼。后来"黄楼"一词成了苏东坡在徐州所作诗歌总集的名称，正如他在密州建筑的超然台，成了他在密州所写诗集的名称一样。

黄楼之所以如此命名，是因为对古老中国的宇宙论的信念而起。根据中国的宇宙论，宇宙中万物由金、木、水、火、土五行所构成。五行中每一行都代表一种性质，如同坚硬、生长、流动、热、重等，这些性质都具有一种宇宙的意义，不但用以指物质的宇宙，也用以指生命的功能与人的个性行为，也可以用于男女的婚配。生命离不开五行的交互作用，比如相生相克。每一行皆有其颜色，正好象征那种元素的性质。说也奇怪，黄代表土，黑代表水，黄土因具有吸水力量，所以可以克服水。黄楼之命名即含有防水之意。

神宗元丰元年（一○七八）九月初九，黄楼举行盛大落成典礼。苏东坡是由衷的欢喜。老百姓得免于水灾，建堤建楼费了半年工。黄楼属于全城的居民，分明是将来防洪的保障。落成仪式举行时，全城万人空巷，前来参加。一看黄楼耸立于东门之上，高一百尺，下面立有五十五尺高的旗竿。楼的形状犹如一座宽广的佛塔。大家一起登楼，一览四周的景物。那天早晨，偏偏浓雾笼罩。他们往窗外瞭望时，只听见下面过往船只桨橹摇动碾轧作响的声音，大家觉得犹如置身于海船之上。不久，雾散日出，可以看见远处渔村错落，在巉岩嵯峨的山峰之下，有六七个庙宇罗列其间。老人觉得寒冷，苏东坡请他们先喝几杯热酒。往近处看，在南方，看见一个高台，以往用为赛马之地，今已建成一座寺院。由那座庙起，一道一里长的新堤防，顺着东城墙向北伸展。他们可以听到远处陆洪和百步洪波涛澎湃之声，与近处下面的鹅鸭之声相错杂。最后，摆设盛筵，款待来宾，有大乐队奏乐。

苏东坡写了一篇文章记此盛事，刻之于石，以垂久远。那块石碑，也经历非凡。后来苏东坡遭朝廷流放，所有带苏东坡名字的石碑都奉命毁坏，当时徐州太守只把这块石碑投在附近的护城河里。约十年之后，老百姓已然忘记了禁令，而皇家也在搜集苏东坡的墨迹手稿，当地另一位太守把此石碑打捞上来，在夜里暗中把那碑文拓了几千份。此事过后，那个太守突然向诸同僚宣布道："为何我竟会忘记！禁止苏东坡的碑文法令尚未取消，这个碑文还在，应当毁坏才是。"自然在石碑毁坏之后，那碑的拓本的价钱立刻高涨，那位太守名叫苗仲先，发了一笔大财。

苏东坡现在名气甚大，受人欢迎，不仅是因为治河成功，也因为他十分关心囚犯的健康和福利，这是当时为太守者所绝无仅有的。他亲身视察监狱，并指定医生为囚犯治病。当时有一条法律，凡太守鞭打犯人致死者，太守受罚，但是苏东坡指出，犯人因病致死或照顾不善而死，则无人过问。因为犯人并非别人，也是一般的老百姓，因此犯人的家属对苏东坡非常感激。

有些小事，很容易做，只要人想到去做，但是只有苏东坡肯去做。比如说，他看见很多逃兵沦落为盗匪，因为有一条荒谬的法令，凡是低级军士因公出差，官家不发给旅费，等于是逼良为盗。他自己改革这项陋规。他只要每年节省下几百缗钱，就可以够用。他严禁军中赌博饮酒。在上皇帝书中他指出当地军队"熟练技艺为诸郡之冠，陛下遣使按阅所具见也"。

苏东坡今名日大，以中土鸿儒之冠为远近所知。欧阳修去世之后，文坛盟主之名即降到苏东坡头上。文人儒生皆以"夫子"呼之。他以前曾遇见他那"苏门四学士"之中的两个，在淮扬与张耒相识，在杭州附近结识晁补之。另外那两个是秦观和黄庭坚，秦黄二人后来成为宋代有名的诗人、词人，而今请求列在苏东坡的门下。五短身材的李常，春天曾去拜访苏东坡，屡次谈到秦观，并拿秦观的词给东坡看。由于李常的介绍，秦观那年夏天曾去拜谒过苏东坡。秦观这位风流潇洒的词人，据野史说曾娶过苏东坡的小妹。秦观尚未应科举考试，还没有功名，但是年轻，文采风流，有不少的女友。后来秦观死时，曾有一歌伎为爱他寻了短见。他的词清新柔媚，如春日的黄鹂。秦观见苏东坡时说："生不愿封万户侯，但愿一识苏徐州。"他把苏东坡比作"天上麒麟"，又向苏东坡说："不将俗物碍天真，北斗以南能几人？"

黄庭坚日后成了江西诗派的鼻祖，他与秦观又不相同，他沉默寡言，有学者风，他没去拜访苏东坡，但是写了两首诗，以万分谦逊的语气毛遂自荐，将苏东坡比之为高崖的青松，自己则比为深谷里的小草，希望将来能和青松比高。苏东坡以前曾看过黄庭坚的诗，他说黄庭坚的诗内容充实而深厚，诗思高旷，"数百年来未之见也"。他回黄庭坚的信说："今者辱书，执礼甚恭，如见所畏者，何哉？轼方以此求交于足下，而惧其不可得。"苏门四学士中，庭坚年最长，在当时人常以苏黄并称。苏东坡去世后，黄山谷遂成为当代最伟大的诗人，人们也是把他和苏东坡相提并论的。但是黄庭坚终身以苏门弟子自居。黄庭坚后来还是由苏东坡最亲近的朋友引荐的，因为黄庭坚是李常的外甥，孙觉的女婿。

九月间，另一个人后来在宫廷上审问苏东坡的案件时，也深受牵连，现在来看苏东坡。他就是王巩，为人又是另一型。他是宰相之孙，出游之时，携一整车家酿美酒相随，因为他不肯饮酒肆所沽之酒。他随身有三个爱妾：英英、盼盼、卿卿，一起来到徐州。苏东坡对他的爱妾开玩笑，在他那"百步洪涛"前的序言中，描写王巩携带梨窝美女下险滩，自己则身披羽氅立身黄楼高处，俯瞰她们漂浮水面，自己望之若神仙，或如李太白再临人世。

这时，有第四个重要人物在苏东坡生活中出现，就是诗僧参寥，大概是由秦观介绍的。奇怪的是，苏东坡在杭州的三年内，参寥住在附近一个城市，居然苏东坡从未听说过他。参寥为一大诗人，道德崇高，不慕虚名。他只是在遥远之处观察苏东坡而心怀羡慕。由现在起，参寥便成为苏东坡一生的密友了。

在那年的中秋节，我们也许可以把苏东坡看得更近，更清楚一些。八月十二，他得了一个孙子。中秋之夜，他微感不适，稍感寂寞。过了六天，他接到子由写的中秋诗，他也写了一首诗，叙述如何度的中秋节：

明月未出群山高，瑞光千丈生白毫。

一杯未尽银阙涌，乱云脱坏如崩涛。

谁为天公洗眸子，应费明河千斛水。

遂令冷看世间人，昭我湛然心不起。

西南火星如弹丸，角尾奕奕苍龙蟠。

今宵注眼看不见，更许萤火争清寒。

何人舣舟临古汴，千灯夜竹鱼龙变。

曲折无心逐浪花，低昂赴节随歌板。

青荧灭没转前山，浪飐风回岂复坚。

明月易低人易散，归来呼酒更重看。

堂前月色愈清好，咽咽寒螀鸟露草。

卷帘推户寂无人，窗下咿哑惟楚老。

南部从事莫羞贫，对月题诗有几人。

明朝人事随日出，恍然一梦瑶台客。

那时，苏东坡为整个学术界所爱戴，所尊敬，所景仰。那年九月底，在黄楼有一个盛大的集会，苏东坡坦然谈笑，轻松愉快，极为众人所喜爱。只因为他深得众望，他之被捕与审判才轰动一时。

Chapter Thirteen
THE YELLOW TOWER

Even for a genius like Su Tungpo, life began at forty. Su was now to enter his Suchow period, the period of the "Yellow Tower." Suddenly Su Tungpo found himself. For the first time in his life, he is revealed as a man of action, doing things and building things and occupied in the public activities which characterized his life from now on. So far, as an assistant magistrate at Hangchow, he had not been able to do anything constructive and important, and although he was given a full magistracy at Michow, it was a poor, remote district, giving no opportunity for the full expression of his administrative talent. He was later to be forced into a period of temporary retirement and political eclipse, after which emerged the full, round, mature, active, patriotic Su Tungpo that we know and people in China love, the Su Tungpo with a mellow humor, a friend and champion of the people and a great human spirit. But before his arrest and banishment, the magistracy at Suchow already gave proof of what Su Tungpo, the man of action, could do as an able administrator.

At the end of 1076 Tungpo was recalled from Michow, with an appointment to office at Hochungfu, at the southwestern tip of Shansi Province; and in January of the following year he set out for the capital by way of Tsinan, where his brother's family lived. Tseyu was not there, for great political changes were in the air. By now Wang Anshih, Huiching,

Tseng Pu, Dunquan, and again Wang, had all fallen, one after the other, and nobody knew what was going to happen next.

Tseyu was a quiet but determined man. Su Tungpo had kept on sending memorandums on tax and draft reforms and had advised the Emperor against the income tax; but Tseyu, silent before, thought perhaps the time had come to strike hard for a complete change of government policy. Wang Anshih had seen on his final way out in October, and Tseyu, without waiting for his brother, had gone right ahead to the capital with an important memorandum for complete reforms. His family had remained at Tsinan, and there Su Tungpo was greeted by his three nephews standing in the snow outside the gate. That night they had a great feast and the two brothers' families were happily reunited. Tsinan, a large city, provided a great change from Michow, and Su Tungpo remained there for about a month. It was not till about the tenth of February 1077 that the two brothers' families reached the bank of the Yellow River near the capital. Tseyu had come out to meet them some thirty miles north of the bank, and the two brothers spent some good days together during the journey in the snow. Tseyu brought the news that Su Tungpo's new appointment to Hochungfu had been canceled, and that he was appointed chief magistrate of Suchow.

A mysterious incident happened when they reached the capital. Coming to the Chenchiao Gate, Su Tungpo was informed by the gatekeeper that he was not to be admitted to the capital city. This incident, recorded by his brother, has never been satisfactorily explained. I do not think it was the Emperor's will, but with the impending political uncertainty, some of officials probably wanted to make sure that he had no chance to see the Emperor; and so far as we know, the Emperor may not have known of this order himself. The brothers turned back and put up at the home of their great good friend Fan Chen, in the eastern outer city.

By this time Su Tungpo's eldest son, Mai, was eighteen and therefore ready to marry. Research students have never been able to verify who the girl was. My opinion is that he married one of Fan Chen's granddaughters. In Su Tungpo's correspondence with Fan Chen and his son, he referred to them repeatedly as relatives connected by marriage. What that marriage was between the Su and Fan family waits to be explained. Fan Chen was also from Szechuen, and Su was staying at the time in Fan Chen's home. In the next two years Su Tungpo also helped to marry off two of Tseyu's grown-up daughters by selecting husbands for them. One was Wang Shih, brother of the famous Wang Chiung (Tsekao)who, according to legend, actually "married a fairy,"[1] and the other was a son of the famous bamboo painter, Wen Tung.

After his son's wedding Su Tungpo went east with his family to his post at Suchow, in modern Kiangsu. Tseyu, too, was going with his family as a deputy magistrate to Shangchiu, the Southern Capital; and after leaving his family there with Chang Fangping, he continued the journey with his brother to Suchow, where he remained three months before returning to his family.

Suchow was not only a big city, it was a place of the greatest strategic importance, holding control of the mountainous regions in southern Shantung. In past dynasties wars had always been fought around Suchow, which today stands at the junction of the Tsinpu and Lunghai Railways. It was also near a region to be made famous in the next decades as the robbers' lair celebrated in the romance *All Men Are Brothers*. The city lay on a river, surrounded by two high mountains on the south, with deep, rapid currents flowing past the city below. It produced very fine granite,

---

[1] Wang Chiung personally confirmed the story to Su Tungpo. This became so embarrassing to the man that later he changed his name. Wang first met his wife in a supernatural vision, during his affair with a strange unknown woman, but the wife denied that she was a fairy, or at least was totally unaware of her previous existence.

iron, and coal, which were exploited in Su Tungpo's days. Consequently the place was also famous for its knives and swords. He was delighted with the natural scenery and the variety of fish and crabs available, and called it a good place for a "temporary stay."

On August 21, three months after his arrival, a big flood reached Suchow. Wang Anshih had previously tried to dredge the Yellow River; but after spending over half a million dollars he had failed, and the chief engineer had committed suicide. The Yellow River now broke out eastward at a point some fifty miles north of Suchow and began to spread, flooding several hundred square miles. When the flood reached the city, it was held back by the tall mountains south of the city; and the water rose higher and higher until in September it reached 28.9 Chinese feet. At one time the level of the water was higher than the city streets. Su Tungpo plunged into the work of saving the city. For weeks he did not go home, but stayed in a shack on top of the city wall supervising the strengthening of the outer wall. Well-to-do families were fleeing from the city, and Su Tungpo stopped them at the gate, begging them to remain for fear of starting a panic. "I am going to stay, so you had better, too," he said to them, and forced them back. This is not the place to go into Su Tungpo's architectural and engineering genius, but let it be said that he always worked with exact figures in all his engineering projects. While the swirling waters were threatening to overrun the southeastern walls of the outer city, he was strengthening the base and increasing the height of the walls. The defense works that were thrown up against the flood were 9,840 feet long, 10 feet high, and 20 feet wide. For this he needed thousands of workmen. Splashing about in the mud, he went straight to the army camp and spoke to the commander. As this was the so-called Palace Army, under the direct control of the Emperor, he asked for their co-operation. The officers gladly responded, and said, "Since Your Honor has come out personally to supervise the work, certainly we should do our part." Meanwhile, preparations were made in the north to turn the water into an

old abandoned course of the Yellow River, which had already changed its
route many times in history. The waters threatened the city for forty-five
days, but on the fifth of October the flood began to subside as the river
found its old course and drained eastward toward the sea near Haichow.

The people were overjoyed and grateful for the saving of the city. But
dissatisfied with the temporary dams, Su Tungpo sent a letter with detailed
figures to the court, asking for money to build a stone city wall against
future calamities. Waiting in vain for a reply, he modified his proposal and
recommended the building of dams not with rock, but with strong timber
reinforcements. In an official letter the Emperor then congratulated him on
his great work, and in February of the following year, Tungpo was accorded
a grant of over $30,000 and 18,000 bushels of rice, and provision for hiring
7,200 men to build a wooden dam along the southeast side of the city. On
top of this outer city wall, following his love for architecture, Su Tungpo had
a tower built a hundred feet high, which was called the Yellow Tower. Later
this became the name of the collection of poems that he wrote during his
term at Suchow, just as the Chaojan Terrace he built at Michow was used as
the title of the collection of his poems written there.

The Yellow Tower was so called because of a belief in the old
Chinese cosmogony. According to this system, all things in the universe
are composed of five elements, gold, wood, water, fire, and earth. Each
of these stands for a principle, such as hardness, growth, fluidity, heat,
gravity, etc., principles which have a universal meaning and are supposed
to apply not only to the physical universe but also to life functions and
human character and conduct, applicable, for instance, to a matrimonial
match. All life consists of the interplay of these five principles which
overcome or reinforce one another, and each of the elements has a color
which is symbolic of that element. Curiously, yellow stands for the earth
and black stands for water, and the yellow earth is supposed to overcome
the black water by its power of absorption. The name given the Yellow

Tower was, therefore, symbolic of the power to resist water.

On the ninth day of the ninth moon, 1078, there was a grand opening ceremony of the Yellow Tower. Su Tungpo was truly happy. The people had been saved from a flood, they had worked for over half a year at the building of the dam and the tower; and the tower belonged to the people of the city as a visible symbol of their security against future inundations. The whole town was present to witness the opening ceremony. There stood the Yellow Tower, a hundred feet high, on top of the East Gate, with flag poles fifty feet high below. It was in the style of a broad pagoda, and the party went up to the top to get a view of the surrounding country. There was a heavy fog that morning, and as they looked out the window and heard the squeaking oars of the boats passing below, they had the feeling of being on a ship at sea. Soon the sky cleared and they could see fishing villages in the distance and half a dozen temples scattered on the hillsides below the jagged mountain peaks. The old people felt cold, and Su Tungpo asked them to have a drink of warm wine first. In the foreground, on the south, they saw the raised terrace that used to be the race course but was now the site of a Buddhist temple. From this temple stretched the mile-long new embankment northward along the east city wall. They could hear in the distance the roaring torrents of the Lu Rapids and the Hundred-Yard Rapids, amidst the cackling of ducks and geese below. The ceremony ended with a grand dinner, with a full orchestra, for the invited guests.

Su Tungpo wrote a piece to commemorate the occasion and had it inscribed on stone. This tablet had a curious history. Later, when he was exiled and all tablets containing his handwriting were ordered to be destroyed, the magistrate of Suchow at that time merely dropped it into a moat near by. After about ten years had passed, when the people had forgotten about the ban and the imperial household itself began to collect the poet's manuscripts, another magistrate at this place had the tablet hauled out of the moat again. Secretly at night he had several thousand copies of rubbings from the inscription made. After this had been done, the magistrate suddenly announced to his colleagues, "Why, I forget! The law prohibiting Su's incription has not yet been suspended and this inscription is still lying here. Let's have it destroyed." Naturally, the price of the rubbings shot up after the stone was destroyed, and the magistrate, Miao Chungshien, made a lot of money.

Su Tungpo was now very popular, not only because of his successful fight against the flood but also because he had taken a personal interest in the health and welfare of the prisoners, something which was rarely, if ever, done by magistrates at the time. He had personally visited the prisons and for the first time had appointed prison physicians to attend to the sick. While there was a law punishing magistrates who had flogged prisoners to death, Su pointed out that there was nothing being done about prisoners who died of disease and bad care. As the prisoners were no other than the common people, he earned the deep gratitude of their relatives.

There were many small things that could be easily done if a man thought about doing them, but only Su Tungpo cared. He saw, for example, that there were many soldiers who deserted the army and became bandits, because of a preposterous system practically compelling corporals to go into debt when they were sent out on a distant journey on official business without fees for travel. He had this corrected, and he was able to do this by setting aside only a few hundred dollars each year. He had forbidden gambling and drinking in the army, and in his letter to the Emperor was able to point out that the local army there was "the best disciplined of all those in that region, as the court inspectors have seen."

Su Tungpo's fame as poet had steadily risen, until he was now the acknowledged first scholar of the land. After Ouyang Shiu's death the mantle had passed to him. Scholars came to acknowledge him as "Master." He had met two of his four famous disciples before, Chang Lei at Huaiyang and Chao Puchih near Hangchow. The other two, Chin

Kuan and Huang Tingchien, who later became major poets of the Sung Dynasty, now asked to be considered his disciples. The short, stocky Li Chang had come to visit Su in the spring and had constantly spoken of Chin Kuan and shown him Chin's verse. With Li Chang's introduction, Chin Kuan had come to see him that summer. This was the romantic poet who, according to legend, was married to Su Tungpo's younger sister. Not yet having a degree, but young, romantic, and carefree, Chin had many women friends. Later, when he died, a courtesan committed suicide for love of him. Here was a new voice in poetry, singing like a lark in spring. In his presentation to Su Tungpo, Chin said that "rather than be a magistrate ruling over ten thousand families, he would make the acquaintance of Su Suchow [Tungpo]." He compared him to a "unicorn in heaven," and asked, "Of all those born this side of the pole star, how many men are like him?"

Huang Tingchien, who later became the father of the Kiangse school of poetry, was a different type of man, scholarly and quiet. He did not come to visit Su, but wrote two poems in a tone of great humility to introduce himself, comparing Su Tungpo to a towering pine tree standing on top of a cliff, and himself to a tender plant growing at the bottom of a canyon and aspiring to grow to the same height. Su had seen Huang's verse before, which he said had a solid content and depth and an elevation of poetic feeling "not seen for quite a few centuries." In his letter to Huang he said, "Why do you write such a humble letter as if you were afraid of me? I was wanting to have your friendship and was afraid that you might not accept me." Of the four disciples of Su Tungpo, Huang was the eldest, and in the talk of the time the names of Su and Huang were always coupled together. After Su Tungpo died, Huang became the greatest poet of his time, and people always spoke of him in the same breath with Su Tungpo. But to the end, Huang considered himself Su Tungpo's pupil. Huang, also, was introduced through Su Tungpo's closest friends, for he was a nephew of Li Chang and the son-in-law of Sun Chueh.

In September, another man who became closely implicated in the court trial of Su Tungpo's case came to visit him. Wang Kung was again another type. The grandson of a premier, he traveled with a whole cartload of the best wine from his own cellar because he would not touch wine bought from the shops. He also brought to Suchow his three concubines, Inging, Panpan, and Chingching. Su Tungpo joked about his concubines, and in the introduction to his poem on the Hundred-Yard Rapids he described Wang's exciting trip down the rapids in the company of women with dimpled cheeks, while Su himself stood in a feathered coat at the top of the Yellow Tower, watching them sailing below, looking like a fairy or like a Li Po reborn.

A fourth very important person came into Su Tungpo's life at this time, the great poet-monk Tsanliao, who was probably introduced to him by Chin Kuan. Curiously, throughout Su Tungpo's three-year stay at Hangchow, Tsanliao—living at a neighboring town—had remained unknown to him. Tsanliao was too great a poet himself and had too much moral elevation to be a celebrity hunter. He had only watched and admired Su Tungpo from a great distance. From now on Tsanliao was to become one of his closest and lifelong friends.

It is possible to get a close glimpse of Su Tungpo at the mid-autumn festival that year. On August twelfth, a grandson had been born to him, and on this mid-autumn night he was feeling unwell and lonely. Six days after the festival, receiving a poem on the mid-autumn moon from his brother, he wrote one describing how the spent the night.

"Before the moon came up the mountain peaks were high,
A sheet of luminous white then blazed forth in the sky.
Before I finished a cup, the silver gate was opened,
Cloud clusters billowed in retreat like falling waves.
Who could wash the sparkling eyes of Father Heaven

But with a thousand lotions from the Silver Stream?
The moon now so serenely looks upon this earth,
And finds me cool, resigned, like an unruffled well.
In the southwest, meteors shoot across like bullets,
The white Spica used to shimmer bright in the east,
But scanning the eastern heaven, I cannot see it tonight.
Only roaming glow-worms vie in their fluorescent glow.
Who are there sitting on a boat on the ancient Pien?
A thousand lanterns scare the dragons in their lairs.
Out and in, the boats weave glistening chains of ripples,
Up and down, they float to the rhythm of the songs.
The fireflies flit and float against the distant hillside,
And the autumn wind sends up sparkles in the stream.
Too rapidly the moon declines and people disperse,
Coming home I ask for wine to have a look again.
The moon over the courtyard seems even more serene,
While crickets chirp among the grass covered with dew.
Lifting the beaded screen I find the inside silent,
Only my grandson is cooing before the window light.
At the Southern Capital be proud of your poverty;
How many men can sing about this autumn night?
Tomorrow at sunrise comes the usual round of work,
And this night will seem a dream flight to the moon."

By this time Su Tungpo was loved and honored and admired by all scholardom. At a grand gathering at the end of September that year at the Yellow Tower, Su Tungpo, openhearted and fun-loving and carefree, was warmly loved by them all. It was because of his popularity and prestige that his arrest and trial became a national sensation.

第十四章　逮捕与审判

苏东坡，我们用他自己的话说，他过去生活的态度，一向是疾恶如仇，遇有邪恶，则"如蝇在食，吐之乃已"。不过到目前为止，还幸而安然无事。可是在他吐到第一百次时，他就被人抓住了，在神宗元丰二年（一〇七九）三月，他调任江苏太湖滨的湖州。在他到任后的谢恩奏章上，他说了几句朝廷当权派觉得有点儿过分的话。只要他单歌咏人民的疾苦贫穷、捐税、征兵，那派小人还能装聋作哑，置之不顾。现在他直接指明那些小人，其中有在王安石势力下蹿升起来的李定和舒亶。朝政是在无以名之的第三流人才的掌握中，这类人是唯利是图随风转舵，既无所谓东，也无所谓西。苏东坡过去曾不断给皇帝上表，每次皇帝看了他的表章，就向侍臣赞美苏东坡。现在我们想起来，这些小人以前曾经阻挡苏东坡进京城。万一苏东坡蒙召当权，可就真有危险，因为新政的领导人物那时不是已经失势，便是已然退隐。

苏东坡到任呈谢恩表只是例行公事，譬如略叙为臣者过去无政绩可言，再叙皇恩浩荡，以此美缺相赐。但是苏东坡说："伏念臣性资顽鄙……知其愚不适时，难以追陪新进。察其老不生事，或能牧养小民。""新进"

一词，在王安石口中是指突然升迁的无能后辈。在过去为新政的朋党之争里，这一名词是固定代表那种含义的。李定和舒亶心想苏东坡为什么会自信能逃得出他们的手心呢？并且他说在他那个年纪，担任地方官是因为他不可能再惹是生非。他是不是暗示那些在朝为官的必然会惹是生非呢？古之文人学者，因为没有民权的保障，在措辞造句上，便发明出一种极其微妙难以捉摸的表现法，而阅读的学者也养成一种习惯，乐于于字里行间之中寻求含义。在中国古代，朝廷的公报是固定按期出版的，可以说是中国最早的报纸。苏东坡所写的文字，照例惹人注意，这次谢恩表，使那些"新进"成了读者心目中的笑柄。

在神宗元丰二年六月，一个御史把苏东坡谢恩表中的四句挑出来，说他蔑视朝廷而开始弹劾他。数日之后，舒亶，当时尚在御史台，找了几首苏东坡的诗，内容关于农人青苗贷款，农人三个月无盐吃，还有燕子与蝙蝠争论的寓言。他说写的那种诗，显示苏东坡不但考虑欠周，也是不忠于君。舒亶随同弹劾表章，附呈上苏东坡印出的诗集。李定，现今升为御史中丞，也随后跟上一表，陈述有四个理由，苏东坡必须因其无礼于朝廷而斩首。一共有四份弹劾苏东坡的表章。这件案子交与了御史台。李定，当年因隐瞒母丧，司马光骂他禽兽不如，现在担任检察官。他挑选了一个极其能干的官吏到湖州去，免去苏东坡的官职，再押解入京受审。御史请求，一路之上苏东坡必须关入监狱过夜，皇帝不许。神宗皇帝从无意杀害苏东坡，不过这个案子既然依法控告，他也愿予以充分调查一番。

苏东坡的一个好友王诜，是他印了苏东坡的诗集，听到这个消息，赶紧派人去给南部的苏子由送信，子由立刻派人去告诉苏东坡。这可以说是使者之间的大竞赛。朝廷使者偕同他的儿子和两个御史台的兵丁火速出发，但是他儿子在靖江忽然生病，于是耽误了半天的行程，结果苏子由派的使者先到。

这个消息到达时，苏东坡是何等心情，我们必须要知道。他到达湖州不久，也很喜欢这个新职位。他常和长子去山林间漫游，同游的还有子由的女婿、女婿的弟弟。在苏东坡记游飞英寺的诗里，他说自己"莫作使君看，外似中已非"。他最好的朋友画竹名家文与可已在二月去世，他一直哭了三天。在朝廷的差官正趱程前去逮捕他时，他正再度浏览他搜集的名画，那是七月七日，正拿出来到院子去晾。他的眼光正好看到文与可送给他的一幅绝妙的竹子，不觉流下泪来。那天他写的那一段笔记特别表现他的奇思幻想，记述他与文与可的友情。

与可画竹，初不自贵重，四方之人，持缣素而请者，足相蹑于其门。与可厌之，投诸地而骂曰："吾将以为袜材。"士大夫传之，以为口实。及与可自洋州（今陕西洋县）还，而余为徐州。与可以书遗余曰："近语士大夫，吾墨竹一派，近在彭城，可往求之。袜材当萃于子矣。"书尾复写一诗，其略云："拟将一段鹅溪绢，扫取寒梢万尺长。"予谓："与可竹长万尺，当用绢二百五十匹，知公倦于笔砚，愿得此绢而已。"与可无以答，则曰："吾言妄矣，世岂有万尺竹哉！"余因而实之，答其诗曰："世间亦有千寻竹，月落庭空影许长。"与可笑曰："苏子辩则辩矣，然二百五十匹，吾将买田而归老焉。"因以所画筼筜谷偃竹遗予，曰："此竹数尺耳，而有万尺之势。"

根据孔平仲的记载——孔平仲是苏东坡的朋友，他是听湖州祖通判所说，苏东坡遭逮捕时，那位通判正好在场——苏东坡已经先得到子由给他的消息。他可不知道控告的罪名之轻重。使臣一到，苏东坡就正式请假，由祖通判代行太守职务。

官差到时，正式身穿官袍，足蹬高靴，站在庭院中，手执笏板，御史台的两个士兵分立两旁，身穿白衣，头缠黑巾，眼睛里凶光闪动。太守官衙的人慌作一团，不知会有何事发生。苏东坡不敢出来，与通判商量，通判说躲避朝廷使者也无济于事，最好还是依礼迎接他。东坡与通判商量应当怎样出来，因为苏东坡心想自己既然被控，就不应当穿着官衣出来。祖通判认为他还没正式被控，应当以正式官阶出现。于是东坡穿上官衣官靴，手执笏板，立于庭中，面向官差而立。祖通判与官衙人员则头戴小帽，排立于苏东坡身后。两个士兵手执御史台的公文，紧握一个包裹，似乎其中藏有刀剑。官差面目狰狞，默不作声，气氛紧张万分。苏东坡首先说话：

"臣知多方开罪朝廷，必属死罪无疑。死不足惜，但请容臣归与家人一别。"

皇差皇甫遵淡然道："并不如此严重。"

这时，通判迈一步向前道："相信必有公文。"

皇甫遵问："他是何人？"通判回禀自己的身份。士兵乃正式递交公文予通判。打开一看，原来只是一份普通公文，免去苏东坡的太守官位传唤进京而已。皇差要苏东坡立即起程。

官差允许苏东坡出发前归看家人。根据苏东坡在笔记上记载，他到家时，全家正在大哭。苏东坡向他们笑着说出下面一个故事，安慰他们：

在宋真宗时代，皇帝要在林泉之间访求真正大儒。有人推荐杨朴出来。

杨朴实在不愿意，但是仍然在护卫之下起程前往京师，晋见皇帝。

皇帝问道："我听说你会作诗？"

杨朴回答道:"臣不会。"他想掩饰自己的才学,他是抵死不愿做官的。

皇帝又说:"朋友们送你时,赠给你几首诗没有?"

杨朴回答道:"没有。只有拙荆作了一首。"

皇帝又问:"是什么诗,可以告诉我吗?"

于是杨朴把临行时太太作的诗念出来:

更休落魄贪杯酒,亦莫猖狂爱咏诗。

今日捉将官里去,这回断送老头皮。

苏夫人听见这首诗,不由得破涕为笑。这故事曾记在苏东坡的笔记里,但不知是不是他当时现编的。

家中决定由长子迈陪同前往。王适,他一向充任苏家的塾师,现在同他弟弟留在家中,后来才偕同苏东坡全家入京。太守官衙的人全吓得不知如何是好,个个躲躲藏藏。但是老百姓都出来看太守起程。根据县志记载,老百姓都泪下如雨。官差与士兵的态度与办事的要求,都蛮横无礼,后来苏东坡在上哲宗皇帝书中,说他们逮捕太守犹如捕盗。官衙中只有王氏兄弟和陈师锡设酒筵钱别。

有人说途中苏东坡曾想自杀。根据他自己给皇帝上的奏章上说,在扬州渡江时,他想跳入江中。但按孔平仲的记载,开船之后不久,船停在太湖上修理船桨时,他想跳水自杀。那天夜里,月色皎洁,湖上风高浪大。苏东坡不知道他要判什么罪,并且怕他的案子会牵连好多朋友。他想把眼一闭跳入水中,反倒省事。等再一想,倘若如此,必给弟弟招致麻烦。在给文彦博的信里,叙述家里烧了他大部分与友人的通信和手稿。家里人到了安徽宿县,御史台又派人搜查他们的行李,找他的诗、书信和别的文件。有些兵把船包围起来时，女人和孩子们怕得很，那些兵把他们的东西胡乱扔，就如一般兵士执行勤务时一样。兵丁走后，女人们气冲冲地说："这都是写书招惹的。他乱写东西有什么好处？把人都吓死了。"然后焚烧他的手稿，后来东坡发现残存者不过三分之一而已。

苏东坡是七月二十八日由官家逮捕，八月十八日送进御史台的皇家监狱。审问期间很长，前后四十几天。在监里，那个狱卒心肠非常好，大概知道他是谁，对他十分恭敬，每天晚上给他热水洗澡，直到现在每晚上洗热水澡，还是四川人的习惯。

苏东坡在监狱中，发生了一件有趣的事，结果审问时反倒对他大有益处。他儿子每天到监狱去看他，为父亲送饭当然是儿子分内的事。苏东坡和儿子暗中约好，就是儿子只许送蔬菜和肉食，倘若听到坏消息，他才送鱼去。有几天，苏迈要离开京城到别处去借钱，他把送饭这件事交给朋友办，但是忘了告诉朋友那件暗号。那朋友送去熏鱼，苏东坡大惊。他心想事情已然恶化，大概凶多吉少了。他和狱卒商量，给弟弟写了两首诀别诗，措辞极为悲惨，说他一家十口全赖弟弟照顾，自己的孤魂野鬼独卧荒山听雨泣风号，他表示愿世世为手足。在诗里他又细心地表示以前皇恩浩荡，蒙受已多，无法感激图报，实在惭愧。又说这次别无可怨，只是自己之过。子由接到，感动万分，竟伏案而泣，狱卒随后把此诗携走。到后来苏东坡开释时，狱卒才将此诗退回，说他弟弟不肯收。我相信子由根本知道这条计，故意把诗交还狱卒。因为有这两首诗在狱卒手中，会有很大用处。因为狱卒按规矩必须把犯人写的片纸只字呈交监狱最高当局查阅。这个故事里说，苏东坡坚信这些诗会传到皇帝手中。结果正如他所料，皇帝看了，十分感动。这就是何以苏东坡的案子虽有御史强大的压力，最后却判得很轻的缘故。

　　幸亏诗人陆游曾编有一本历史，其中包括所有审问苏东坡的亲笔文件。现在我们还有一本书叫"乌台诗案"，"乌台"是御史台监狱的名称。此书包括四件弹劾本章、审问记录全部，苏东坡的口供、证物和最后的判词。陆游勤于写日记，对苏东坡留在身后的手稿和拓片特别爱好，这些遗物是苏东坡死后六七十年他才见到的。他曾说出这本书的经过。北宋在靖康元年（一一二六）灭亡时，朝廷官员都向杭州逃难，尽量携带珍贵的文件。在扬州，一个名叫张全真的政府官员看到这一份手稿，从朝廷档案里抽出来。后来，张全真死后，一位姓张的宰相，受张全真的后人请求为先人作一篇墓志铭。这位宰相要以那份手稿为代价。那家后人只答应交出一半，另一半作为传家之宝。陆游记载说，他看见全部手稿都是苏东坡手写的，还有改正之处，都由苏东坡签名，再盖上御史台的官印。我们不敢确言今日流传下来的这本书是完全根据陆游所见的那本手稿，不过内容却记载了朝廷公报的细节，包括苏东坡对自己那些诗句的解释。

　　我认为对此案件的判断，完全要看我们对苏东坡的批评朝政如何解释。张方平和范镇正设法营救苏东坡，总括起来，他认为坦诚的批评与恶意的中伤显然有别。我们今天不能不认为那些诗是坦诚的批评，而御史们则认为是对朝廷和皇帝恶意的中伤。张方平指出，《诗经》是由孔子删订的，但是其中有很多对当时当政者的讽刺，而且邦有道，则坦诚的批评完全合法。在另一方面，倘若我们能以君子之心度小人之腹，相信那些御史是由义愤而发，是深恨亲爱的君王受辱而弹劾，这也是一种看法。

　　舒亶在表章中说："臣伏见知湖州苏轼近谢上表，有讥切时事之言。流俗翕然，争相传诵，忠义之士无不愤惋。陛下自新美法度以来，异论之人固不为少……然包藏祸心，怨望其上，讪渎谩骂而无人臣之节者，未有如轼也。应口所言，无一不以讥谤为主。……陛下躬履道德，立政造士，以幸天下后世，可谓尧舜之用心矣。轼在此时以苟得之虚名、无用之曲学，官为省郎，职在文馆。臣独不知陛下何负于天下与轼辈，而轼敢为悖慢无所畏忌以至如是。且人道所立者、以有义而无逃于天地之间者，莫如君臣。轼之所为忍出于此，其能知有君臣之义乎？为人臣者苟能充无义之心往之以为利，则其恶无所不至矣……轼万死不足以谢圣时，岂特在不赦不宥而已。伏望陛下付轼有司论如大不恭，以戒天下之为人臣子者。不胜忠愤恳切之至。"

另一御史的弹劾表里，完全是强词夺理的指责。在苏东坡到湖州上任途中，曾为张氏园写了一篇记。在此一篇文章里，苏东坡说："古之君子不必仕，不必不仕。必仕则忘其身，必不仕则忘其君。"这是孟子对孔夫子参政态度的概要结语。那位御史在他忠君报国的热情之下，极力想劝服皇帝相信苏轼正倡邪说异端，实在大逆不道，他说："天下之人，仕与不仕，不敢忘其君。而独苏轼有不仕则忘其君之意，是废为臣之道尔。"

李定举了四项理由说明为什么应当处苏东坡死刑。在奏章前面序言中，他说："苏轼初无学术，滥得时名，偶中异科，遂叨儒馆。"他又接着说苏东坡急于获得高位，在心中不满之下，乃讥讪权要。其当杀理由之一是，皇帝对他宽容已久，冀其改过自新，但是苏东坡拒不从命。另一个当杀的理由是，虽然苏东坡所写诗之荒谬浅薄，但对全国影响甚大。"臣叨预执法，职在纠奸，罪有不容，岂敢苟止？伏望陛下断自天衷，特行典宪，非特沮乖慝之气，抑亦奋忠良之心，好恶既明，风俗自革。"

审问在八月二十日开始，被告自称年四十四岁（按西方计算法为四十二岁），然后叙述世系、籍贯、科举考中的年月，再叙历任的官职。又把由他推荐为官的列出姓名，因为大臣为国家举荐人才充任公职之贤与不贤，与其本人之贤德大有关系，自然甚属重要。据说，他自为官始，曾有两次记过记录。一次是他任职凤翔为通判时,因与上官不和而未出席秋季官方仪典,被罚红铜八斤。另一次是在杭州任内,因小吏挪用公款,他未报呈,也被罚红铜八斤。"此外,别无不良记录。"

最初,苏东坡承认他游杭州附近村庄时所作的那首诗,对农民食无盐、青苗贷款之弊端,曾出怨言,以及弹劾表章中之其他若干情节。他想不起曾写过其他与时政有关的诗文。有好几天内,他否认给朋友写过讽刺诗,一直声称无罪。至于何者应视为毁谤朝廷,何者不应视为毁谤朝廷,颇难断言。还有,何者构成"毁谤",亦复如此。但是在九月十三日,他决定服罪。他承认曾写讽刺诗讥刺当政,且与朋友以此等诗互相投寄。不过他"并未隐瞒",至于内容如何,解释容有不同而已。在审讯期间,他奉命在下列一道供词上签字:"入馆多年,未甚擢进,兼朝廷用人多是少年,所见与轼不同,以此撰作诗赋文字讥讽。意图众人传看,以轼所言为当。"苏东坡的朋友当中,有三十九人受到牵连,有一百多首诗在审问时呈阅,每一首都由作者自行解释。因为苏轼措辞精练,用典甚多,幸而有此审问记录,我们得见作者自己对好多文句的阐述分析。只有读者完全了解那些典故,才能把握文内的含义。我读诗一向对那类诗避而不观,因为那些隐喻、史实,都需要单独解释,读来甚感吃力,作者自己卖弄学问,为读者加重负担,殊为无谓。其实这样炫耀也并不困难,因为数百年来,苏诗的评注家一直忙着在历史和唐诗里发掘苏诗用典的出处。

对苏东坡的指控,有的十分牵强。最有趣的指控中,有一条是写两株老柏的七律。诗里说柏树"根到九泉无曲处,世间惟有蛰龙知"。这两句诗认为是对皇帝大不敬,因为龙是皇帝的象征,而今皇帝正在位,作者应当说有龙在天,不应当说在九泉地下。另外还有一首牡丹诗,在诗内作者叹造物之巧，能创造出牡丹种类如此之繁多。御史解释此诗为讽刺新当政者能制定如此多之种种捐税。《杞菊赋》的序言里曾提到吃杞菊的苦种子，御史认为作者是在直接讽刺全境百姓的贫陋，尤其是指朝廷对官吏薪俸的微薄。"生而眇者不识日"是讽刺科举考生的浅陋无知，讽刺考生不通儒学，只知道王安石在《三经新义》里对经书的注释。

苏东坡在对方大部分指控上，都坦白承认在诗中批评新政，自然有愤怒之感、失望之声，足以表明自己对当道的苛酷批评，罪有应得。

在给朋友驸马王诜的若干首诗里，有一行诗是坐听"鞭笞环呻呼"。又说，"救荒无术归亡逋"。他也提到"虎难摩"，是为政贪婪的象征。在给朋友李常的诗里，他确是说在密州"洒涕循城拾弃孩"。那些男尸、女尸、婴尸都饿死于路也，当时确是"为郡鲜欢"。关于他给朋友孙觉的诗里，有一行说二人相约不谈政治，是真在一次宴席上约定，谁谈政治，罚酒一杯。在给曾巩的一首诗里（曾巩官位不高，但是一代古文大家），他说厌恶那些"聒耳如蜩蝉"的小政客。在他给张方平的诗里，他把朝廷比为"荒林蜩蚻乱"和"废沼蛙蝈淫"，又说自己"遂欲掩两耳"。在给范镇的诗里，他直言"小人"，我们也知道在给周邠的诗里，他把当权者暗比作夜枭。在写杭州观潮时，他说东海若知君王意，"应教斥卤变桑田"。

在他一个好友刘恕罢官出京时，他写了两首诗给他，把那诗仔细看一下，也颇有趣，并且可以了解官吏的愤怒，也可略知苏诗字里行间的含义。其中一首说：

敢向清时怨不容，直嗟吾道与君东。
坐谈足使淮南惧，归向方知冀北空。

独鹤不须惊夜旦，群乌未可辨雌雄。

庐山自古不到处，得与幽人子细穷。

　　苏东坡承认他很佩服这位朋友，所以用孔子的不怨不容这种说法把他
比孔子。第二行指东汉大经学家派弟子东行的典故。第三行指西汉萧何以
智勇在朝敉平淮南王之乱于无形。第四行指良马出于冀北，又进而指韩愈
《马说》中的伯乐过冀北之野，而冀北骏马遂空一事，亦指满朝已无真才
贤士。第五行指鹤立鸡群，亦即贤人与小人之比，隐含之义即在朝之庸庸
碌碌者，皆鸡鸭之辈，于是午夜长鸣非鹤莫属。第六行更易令人致怒，因
为诗经上有两行"俱曰予圣，谁识乌之雌雄"，等于说朝廷上只有一群乌
鸦，好坏难辨。

　　他给那位朋友的第二首讽刺诗如下：

仁义大捷径，诗书一旅亭。

相夸绶若若，犹诵麦青青。

腐鼠何劳吓，高鸿本自冥。

颠狂不用唤，酒尽渐须醒。

　　这首诗的前三行指的是虚伪的读书人侈谈仁义，实则以此为求取功名
富贵的阶梯，并对官场荣耀表示鄙夷之意。"麦青青"一典，按苏东坡的
意思，是由庄子论追求利禄官爵的人而来，那些人一生迷恋官爵，埋葬时
口中含有珍珠，但是他们的坟墓早晚会夷为青青的麦田。第四行包含另一
个《庄子》上的典故。楚王愿以高位请庄子去做官，庄子谢绝，并且告诉
国王的使者一个故事：有一个专吃腐肉的乌鸦，找到了一只腐烂的老鼠，

正在一棵树上大享其美味，这时一只仙鹤赶巧从旁飞过，乌鸦以为仙鹤来抢它的美味，就发出尖叫的声音想把仙鹤吓走，但是仙鹤高飞到白云中去了。这个故事的含义就是苏东坡对小人的争权争位不屑一顾。

我有一种想法，我觉得苏东坡会以为因写诗而被捕、受审为有趣，他一定以在法庭上讲解文学上的典故为乐事。

当时大家深信苏东坡对朝廷至为不敬，他曾把当政者比为鸣蛙，比为鸣蝉，比为夜枭，比为吃腐鼠的乌鸦，比为禽场中的鸡鸭。最使人不能忍受的是骂他们为"沐猴而冠"，不是人而装人。总之，苏东坡是看不起舒亶、李定那等人，那么舒亶、李定为什么要对苏东坡有好感呢？

审问终结，大概是十月初，证据呈给皇帝。牵连的人很多，尤其是驸马王诜，在审问时牵扯到他，因为他曾和苏东坡交换过各种礼物赠品。皇帝下令凡与苏东坡交换过诗文的人，都得把手中的诗文呈上备查。

仁宗的皇后，她一向支持苏东坡，这时染病而死。她死前曾对皇帝说："我记得苏东坡弟兄二人中进士时，先帝很高兴，曾对家人说，他那天为子孙物色到两个宰相之才。现在我听说苏东坡因为写诗正受审问。这都是小人跟他作对。他们没法子在他的政绩上找毛病，现在想由他的诗入他于罪。这样控告他不也太无谓了吗？我是不中用了，你可别冤屈好人，老天爷是不容的。"这些话实际上等于遗言。

在十月十三日，御史们将案子作了个提要，送呈给皇帝御览。由于太后之丧，案子拖延了些日子。苏东坡在狱中等待案子的结果和自己的命运吉凶之际，发生了一件神秘的事情。

数年之后，苏东坡告诉朋友说："审问完毕之后，一天晚上，暮鼓已然敲过，我正要睡觉，忽然看一个人走进我的屋子。一句话也没说，他往地上扔下一个小箱子做枕头，躺在地上就睡了。我以为他是个囚犯，不去管他，我自己躺下也睡了。大概四更时分，我觉得有人推我的头。那个人向我说：'恭喜！恭喜！'我翻过身子问他什么意思。他说，'安心睡，别发愁。'说完带着小箱子又神秘地走了。

"事情是这样的，我刚受弹劾时，舒亶和另外几个人，想尽方法劝皇帝杀我，可是皇帝根本无杀我之意，所以暗中派宫中一个太监到监狱里去观察我。那个人到了我的屋子之后，我就睡着了，而且鼻息如雷。他回去立即回奏皇帝说我睡得很沉，很安静。皇帝就对侍臣说：'我知道苏东坡于心无愧！'这就是后来我被宽恕贬谪到黄州的缘故。"

遇有国丧，国家总要大赦，所以依照法律和风俗，苏东坡是应当获赦的。那些御史本打算把反对派乘此机会一网打尽，如今倘若一大赦，他们的心血岂不完全白费！李定和舒亶十分忧闷。这时，李定奏上一本，对可能合乎赦罪的那些犯人，力请一律不得赦免。舒亶并进而奏请将司马光、范镇、张方平、李常和苏东坡另外的五个朋友，一律处死。

副相王珪在诸御史的逼促之下，一天突然向皇帝说："苏轼内心有谋反之意。"

皇帝大感意外，回答说："他容有其他过错，但决无谋反之意，你为何这么说？"

王珪于是提起在苏东坡的柏树诗里说龙在九泉一事，那含义是将来某人命定要成天子，要自暗中出现，此人出身寒微。但是皇帝只说："你不能这样看诗。他吟哦的是柏树，与我何干？"

王珪于是沉默无言。章惇，当时还是苏东坡的朋友，为苏东坡向皇帝辩解说，龙不仅是天子的象征，也可以指大臣，于是从文学上引出例句，用以支持自己的理论。

苏东坡的朋友呈上的证物都审查完毕，皇帝指定自己近人重行查阅。

根据御史的案子提要，此种毁谤朝廷要判流放，或是两年劳役，在苏东坡这样的案子，比较严重，应当是削官两级。自法律上看，理当如此。因案情重大，尚待皇帝亲自决定。

在十一月二十九日，使舒亶、李定大失所望，宫廷官员发出了圣谕，把苏东坡贬往黄州，官位降低，充团练副使，但不准擅离该地区，并无权签署公文。

在受到牵连的人之中，三人受的处罚较重。驸马王诜因泄露机密与苏东坡，并时常与他交换礼物，并且身为皇亲，竟不能将此等毁谤朝廷的诗文早日交出，削除一切官爵。第二个是王巩，他并没从苏东坡手中得到什么毁谤诗，他显然是无辜受累，也许是为了私人仇恨的缘故，御史们要处置他。随后几年，苏东坡不断提起王巩因他受累。我们知道王巩的奢侈生活习惯，这次发配到遥远的西北去，日子是够他消受的。

第三个是子由。他曾奏请朝廷赦免兄长，自己愿纳还一切官位为兄长赎罪。在证据上看，子由并不曾被控收到什么严重的毁谤诗，但是因为家庭关系，他遭受降职的处分，调到高安，离兄长被拘留的黄州约有一百六十里，任筠州酒监。

其他人，张方平与其他大官都是罚红铜三十斤，司马光、范镇和苏东坡的十八个别的朋友，都各罚红铜二十斤。

在旧年除夕，苏东坡被释出狱，在监中共度过四个月又二十天。出了东城街北面的监狱大门，他停了一会儿，用鼻子嗅了嗅空气，感觉到微风吹到脸上的快乐，在喜鹊叽喳啼叫声中，看见行人在街上骑马而过。

他真是积习难改，当天又写了两首诗。诗里说："却对酒杯浑似梦，试拈诗笔已如神。"一首诗是：

平生文字为吾累，此去声名不厌低。

塞上纵归他日马，城东不斗少年鸡。

　　他又诗如涌泉了。即在这两首诗里，至少有两句，若由那些御史仔细检查起来，他又犯了对帝王大不敬之罪。塞翁失马还罢了，因为以失马表示并非恶运，重新寻获也并非即是好运，换言之，人总不知道何者为好运，何者为恶运的。但是"少年鸡"则指的是贾昌。贾昌老年时，他告诉人他在少年时曾因斗鸡而获得唐天子的宠爱，而任宫廷的弄臣和伶人，这一点仍可引申而指朝廷当政那批小人，是宫廷中的弄臣和优伶，又是诽谤。另有一行里他自称"窃禄"，意为自己无才为官。但是"窃禄"一词却是从三国时一位大儒给曹操的一封信中摘下来的，而曹操普遍认为是一大奸臣、一霸主。写完这首诗，苏东坡掷笔笑道："我真是不可救药！"

Chapter Fourteen
ARREST AND TRIAL

Su Tungpo, to use the poet's own expression, had gone on "spitting out flies found in one's food," and had so far escaped scot-free. But the hundredth time he "spat," he was caught. In March 1079 he was transferred to Huchow in the lake district of Kiangsu. In his letter of thanks to the Emperor on assumption of the new office he said something that proved too much for the politicians at court. So long as he had sung about the poverty of the people, the tax, and the draft, it was quite possible for the petty men to ignore it. Now he made a direct reference to these men, among them Leeding and Sudan, who had risen to power as Wang Anshih's protégés. The government was in the hands of nondescript, third-rate men who merely temporized and stood for neither one thing nor the other. Su Tungpo had been sending letters to the Emperor, and every time the Emperor read them he had expressed his admiration to his courtiers. It will be recalled that these men had before prevented Su's entry into the capital. There was a real danger that he might be recalled to power, since all the leaders of the new economic policy had been dismissed or retired.

There letter of thanks was written according to the routine formula, briefly stating the official's past unworthy record and continuing with praise of the Emperor's great generosity in giving him such a splendid new post. However, Su Tungpo said, "Your Majesty knows that I am stupid and behind the times, unable to keep up with the young upstarts; seeing that in my middle age I am not likely to cause trouble, Your Majesty has entrusted me with the shepherding of the people." The phrase which I have translated as "young upstarts" did not sound so bad in Chinese; literally it referred to "those unqualified young men who have been suddenly promoted" by Wang Anshih. In the past fight over Wang's regime, this had become a fixed phrase with that definite meaning. Why, Leeding and Sudan thought, did he think he could get away with that? Moreover, he said that he was appointed to a local administration because at his age he was not likely to cause trouble. Did he imply that those remaining at the court were necessarily men who liked to cause trouble? Ancient scholars, in the absence of protection of civil rights, had developed an extreme subtlety in phrasing, saying more than was apparent, and scholar readers had developed the habit of hunting with delight for what was said between the lines. Court bulletins were regularly published, being the earliest form of Chinese printed newspapers. Whatever Su wrote attracted wide attention, and the letter of thanks made the "young upstarts" the laughingstock of the reading public.

In June 1079 a censor took up the four sentences in Su Tungpo's letter of thanks and impeached him for casting a slur on the government. A few days later Sudan, who was still in the imperial censorate, took up some of the poems about the farmers' loans, the reference to farmers eating for three months without salt, and the parable about the argument between the swallow and the bat. To write such lines showed that Su Tungpo was not only impudent but disloyal to the Emperor. Sudan submitted with the impeachment four volumes of Su's published poems. Leeding, who was now promoted to a post in the premier's office, followed with another impeachment showing four reasons why Su Tungpo should pay with his life for such impertinence. Altogether, there were four impeachments. The case was handed over to the imperial censorate. Leeding, whom Szema Kuang had compared to a beast for neglecting his mother's mourning, was made court prosecutor of the case. He selected a very able man to go down to Huchow, relieve Su Tungpo of his office, and bring him to the capital for trial. The censors asked that on the way Su Tungpo be put in prison for the night at every stopping place, but the Emperor forbade this. Emperor Shentsung never meant to kill Su Tungpo, but since the case was officially put up, he was willing to have it fully examined.

One of Su Tungpo's best friends, Prince Wang Shien, who himself had published Su's poems, heard the news and hurriedly sent a messenger to the Southern Capital to Su's brother, who immediately dispatched a messenger to inform Su Tungpo. It was a race between the messengers. The official envoy traveled very fast with his son and two soldiers of the imperial censorate, but his son fell ill at Chinkiang and there was a delay of half a day, and the story goes that Tseyu's messenger arrived first.

It is important to understand Su Tungpo's state of mind when the news came. He had only recently arrived at Huchow and was very happy at his new post. He used to go wandering about the mountains with his eldest son, and Tseyu's son-in-law, and the latter's younger brother. In one of the poems recording their visit to the Temple of Flying Petals, he said, "Do not look upon me as an official. In my appearance I am one, but in my heart already I am not." His best friend, Wen Tung, the bamboo painter, had died in February, and he had wept over his death for three days. While the official messengers were on their way to make his arrest, he was, on July seventh, re-examining some of his collection of paintings, and taking them out to sun them in the courtyard. His eyes fell upon a wonderful painting of bamboos that Wen Tung had given to him, and he broke into tears again. He wrote on that day in his journal an entry typical of his whimsy, describing his friendship with Yuko, which is the courtesy name of Wen Tung.

"When Yuko started to paint bamboos, he did not think highly of it himself, but people from all places came with their silks and crowded his doorstep to beg for his paintings. Yuko was quite annoyed and, throwing the silks to the floor, said angrily, 'I am going to cut these up and have them made into stockings.' When Yuko returned from Yangchow [modern Yangshien in Shensi]and I was at Suchow, he wrote to me, 'Recently I have been telling scholars that my school of bamboo painting in ink has moved over to Suchow, and that collectors should all go there. I am sure all the material for stockings will come to you now.' He added two lines in postscript saying that he wished to paint a bamboo grove ten thousand feet high on a piece of Goose Valley silk, I said to him that for painting a bamboo grove ten thousand feet high one would require two hundred and fifty pieces of silk, and that I knew he was tired of painting but only wanted to get the silk. Yuko could not reply and only said that I was talking nonsense, and there were no bamboo groves ten thousand feet high anyway. I replied in a poem with the two lines 'There are bamboos ten thousand feet high, when you look at their shadows cast by the moonlight.' Yuko laughed and said, 'Su always knows how to argue, but if I had two hundred and fifty pieces of silk I would buy a farm in the country and retire.' He gave me this painting of the Valley of Yuntang [tall bamboos], and said to me, 'This painting is only several feet high, but the bamboos appear to be ten thousand feet in height . . .' "

If we are to believe an eyewitness story recorded by Kung Pingchung, a friend who had the story from the deputy magistrate at the time of the arrest, Su Tungpo was forewarned by his brother's messenger. He did not know, however, how serious the charge and punishment would be. When the messenger arrived, he was officially on leave of absence, and the deputy magistrate, Mr. Tsu, was acting for him.

The officer came, dressed formally in his gown and high boots, and stood with the ceremonial tablet in his hand in the middle of the courtyard. The two soldiers from the censorate stood by his side in white jackets and black turbans, glowering ominously. The people in the office were greatly disturbed, not knowing what was going to happen. Su Tungpo dared not come out, and consulted the deputy magistrate, who advised him that there was no use evading the messenger and that he might just as well receive him. They discussed how he should appear, because Su Tungpo believed that, being the accused, he should not appear in his official gown. Mr. Tsu was of the opinion, however, that before he was formally accused he should still appear according to his rank. Tungpo therefore also put on his gown and boots and stood with the ceremonial tablet in the middle of the courtyard, facing the official, while Mr. Tsu and the staff lined up behind him with small turbans on their heads. The two soldiers who held the message of the censorate in their hands hugged the package as if it contained a sword. The grim silence of the official messenger caused an unbearable suspense. It was Su who spoke first.

"I know I have done many things to anger the court. I am sure this is a sentence for my death. I don't mind dying, but please allow me to go home to say farewell to my family."

The official, Huangfu Chun, replied curtly, "It is not so bad as that."

Then the deputy magistrate advanced a step. "I am sure there is an official message."

"Who is he?" asked Huangfu Chun, and the deputy magistrate told him who he was. The soldiers then formally handed over the message to the deputy magistrate. On opening it, he found that it was only an ordinary message depriving Su Tungpo of his office as magistrate and summoning him to the capital. The official messenger asked him to start at once.

Su Tungpo was permitted to go home and see his family before he started. According to the record in his own journal, the whole family was weeping. Su Tungpo laughingly told them the following story to cheer them up:

In the reign of Chentsung, the Emperor was looking for great scholars living in retirement. Somebody recommended a scholar by the name of Yang Pu. Greatly against his own wish, Yang Pu was escorted to the court and presented to the Emperor.

"I hear you write poetry," said the Emperor.

"No, I don't," said Yang Pu, who was trying to conceal his talent and desperately trying to keep out of politics.

"Didn't some of your friends give you some poems when they were sending you off?" asked the Emperor again.

"No," replied Yang Pu. "Only my wife wrote one."

"What is that poem, may I ask?" said His Majesty.

So Yang Pu recited for the Emperor the poem that his wife had given him on his departure. The poem was:

"Don't be too greedy for the cup.
Please stop fussing over poetry.
Today you are arrested under guard,
This time you'll lose your upper story."

When Mrs. Su heard this, she laughed through her tears, in spite of herself. This story comes from Su's own journal, but we do not know whether he had invented it on the spot or not.

It was decided that his eldest son, Mai, would accompany him to the capital. Wang Shih, who had been tutoring Tungpo's children, and his younger brother were to stay behind and later bring the whole family to the capital. The officials were all scared out of their wits and in hiding, but the common people went out to see the departure of the magistrate, and according to the official history of the district they "shed tears like rain." The manner and procedure of the official messenger and the soldiers were very high-handed, and later Su Tungpo, in a letter to the succeeding emperor, said that they arrested a chief magistrate and laid hands on him like a robber. Only the two Wang brothers and a secretary on the staff of the magistrate's office went out and gave him a little wine dinner to send him off.

There are several stories that Su Tungpo thought of committing suicide while on the way. According to his own letter to the Emperor, he thought of jumping into the Yangtse River while crossing at Yangchow, but according to the record of Kung Pingchung, it was at the beginning of the voyage, when the boat was anchored on Taihu Lake for repair of the oars. That night the moon was very bright and there was a high wind over the lake. Su Tungpo had no idea how he was going to be punished, and his case might implicate many of his friends. He thought it would be a simple matter to close his eyes and jump into the lake, but on second thought he realized that if he did this it would be sure to bring his younger brother into trouble. In his letter to Wen Yenpo he described how his family had destroyed much of his correspondence and many of his manuscripts. When the family reached Sushien in Anhuei, the censorate again sent messengers to search their luggage for further poems, letters, and other possible documents. The womenfolk and children had a great scare when a number of soldiers surrounded the boat, ransacked their trunks, and threw their contents about, as all soldiers on such duties do. After the soldiers had gone, the women said angrily, "This all comes of writing books! What does he get by it? It scared us to death." Then they burned his manuscripts, and later the poet found that only about a third of them survived.

Su Tungpo was arrested on July 28 and was thrown into the imperial censorate prison on August 18. It was a long trial, lasting six or seven weeks. While in the prison he had a very kind warden who evidently knew who he was. This warden treated him with great respect, and every night prepared hot water for his footbath, which even today is the regular custom of people from Szechuen.

There was an amusing incident while Su Tungpo was in jail, which turned out a help to him at the trial. His son saw him in prison every day. It was his duty to send food to his father, and Su Tungpo had a secret agreement with him that he was only to send vegetables and meat, but that if he heard of any bad news, he should send fish. During a few days when Mai was forced to be away from the city to borrow money, he entrusted the sending of food to one of his friends, but forgot to tell him about the secret agreement. The friend sent in some smoked fish and Su Tungpo had a scare. He thought that affairs had taken a turn for the worse and perhaps he was doomed. He entered into a plot with the warden. He wrote two poems of farewell to his brother, couched in very sad language, saying that his family of ten mouths would have to be fed by his brother, while his spirit lying on an abandoned hillside would be listening to the moaning winds and dripping rains. He expressed the hope that for generations and generations they might be born brothers again. In the poems he also took care to express gratitude to His Majesty for his previous kindness, and took all the blame on himself. Tseyu, on reading the poems, was so overcome that he fell weeping on his desk, and the warden took them away. It was only upon Su Tungpo's release that the warden returned the poems, saying that his brother just would not receive them. It is my belief that Tseyu knew all along what the plot was and purposely returned the poems to the warden. For, meanwhile, the two poems in the hands of the warden served a very useful purpose. It was his duty to hand over any writings by the prisoners for examination by the prison authorities. The story goes that Su Tungpo had felt sure these poems would reach the Emperor himself. And so it fell out. The Emperor was greatly moved by them, and that was one reason why later Su was let off with a comparatively easy sentence in spite of the high pressure of the censors.

We are indebted to the poet Lu Yu for the history of a manuscript in Su Tungpo's own handwriting containing all the documents of the trial. Today we have a book called *The Case of Poetry at the Black Terrace*, the Black Terrace being the name of the censorate prison. The book contains the four impeachments, a complete record of the trial, Su Tungpo's affidavit, the summing up of the testimony, and the sentence. Lu Yu, who was industrious in keeping his diary and took a special interest in all the manuscripts and inscriptions left by Su Tungpo, which he saw about sixty or seventy years after Su's death, told the following story about this book. When the Northern Sung Dynasty fell in 1126, the whole government staff fled south in the direction of Hangchow, taking all the precious documents they could. While at Yangchow, an official by the name of Chang Chuanchen got hold of this manuscript and removed it from the government files. Later, when this Chang died, a premier, also by the name of Chang, was asked by the family to write the tomb inscription for him. As a price, the premier asked for this manuscript, but it was decided that the family would give the premier only half of it, keeping the other half in the family. Lu Yu recorded that he saw the manuscript all in Su Tungpo's own handwriting, and that in case of corrections they were always initialed by Su himself and marked with the stamp of the censorate. We cannot be sure today that the book which has survived to this day was based on the manuscript which Lu Yu saw, but it does give full details of the court report, including Su Tungpo's own interpretations of his verse.

Judgment of the trial seems to me to depend entirely on our interpretation of the justness of Su Tungpo's criticism of the administration. Chang Fangping, who along with Fan Chen was trying to save Su Tungpo, summed up the case best by drawing a distinction between honest criticism and malicious slander. While we today cannot but regard these poems as expressions of honest criticism, the censors interpreted them as malicious and willful slander of the government and of the Emperor. Chang Fangping pointed out that the *Book of Songs*, edited by Confucius himself, was full of satire of the rulers of those days, and that in a good government frank criticism was perfectly legitimate. On the other hand, the censors, if was can believe them, were bursting with righteous indignation and deep distress at this impudence and insult to their most beloved Emperor.

As Sudan says in his impeachment, "I have read Su Shih's recent letter of thanks on his assumption of office at Huchow, containing satire on current affairs. While the common people pass it from mouth to mouth in admiration, all the loyal and righteous scholars are angered and distressed. Since Your Majesty instituted the new and beautiful laws, there have been many critics who disagreed with your policy. ...But there is none like Su Shih, who with malicious intent and a disgruntled heart slanders Your Majesty beyond the rules of propriety of a subject." Sudan went on to mention Su's poems of satire. "These lines are aimed at the person of Your Majesty, and are the height of impudence. ...Your Majesty walks in the path of virtue, guides the government, and raises scholars to benefit the world. Your heart is truly that of Yao and Shun. At such a time appears Su Shih, backed by a false, fortuitous reputation and useless abstruse learning. Yet he was given the post of a chief magistrate. I do not understand how Su Shih could have conducted himself with such ungrateful insolence. Besides," Sudan went on in his righteous anger, "the first principle in human relationships in a sense of duty, and among the various relationships none is more important than the duty of a subject toward his ruler. That Su Shih could have the heart to say such things against Your Majesty shows that he has forgotten the duty of a subject to his sovereign. Now," Sudan pointed the moral finger, "when a minister loses his sense of duty and follows his selfish interests, there is nothing that such a person will stop at. What may he not do next? ...Su Shih's crimes are more than unpardonable; even ten thousand deaths will not suffice to make amends for his insult to Your Majesty. I hope Your Majesty will hand him over to the court for criminal effrontery to the throne, as a warning to all Your Majesty's subjects. I am bursting with a spirit of loyal indignation."

There was a bit of curious casuistry in another censor's impeachment. When Su Tungpo was on his way to assume office at Huchow, he had written an inscription for a certain Chang's garden. In this inscription Su had said, "The gentlemen of ancient days did not insist on going into office, nor did they insist on keeping out of office. If a scholar insists on being an official, he is likely to forget his soul; *if he insists on not becoming an official he is likely to forget his Emperor.*" This was a summing up by Mencius of Confucius' attitude toward joining a government. The censor, however, in his great loyalty to the Emperor, tried to persuade the latter that Su Shih was preaching a dangerous doctrine. "A scholar," he said, "should never forget his Emperor whether he is in or out of office. Now Su Shih is preaching that one should not forget his Emperor only when he is out of office!"

It was left to Leeding to show four reasons why Su Tungpo should pay with his life. He prefaced his memorandum by the remark that "Su Tungpo is a shallow scholar and won a reputation only by chance; by an accident he passed the special examinations and was favored with a government post." Leeding went on to say that Su was sour because he had hoped to get a higher post, and to give expression to his petty disgruntled heart slandered those in authority. One of the reasons why he should be killed was that the Emperor had tolerated him long enough hoping for him to reform, but that Su could not take a warning. Another reason why he should be killed was that although Su's writings were nonsensical, they had an important influence on the country. "In my office as guardian of the law, I cannot allow such crimes to go unpunished. I hope Your Majesty will exercise your enlightened judgment and carry out the law, not only to put a stop to this demoralizing influence but to give encouragement to those who are loyal and sincere in their service to the country. Thus good and evil men may be sharply distinguished and the moral atmosphere of society will be purified."

The trial began on August 20. The defendant deposed that he was forty-four years of age (forty-two in the Western reckoning), and gave an account of his ancestry, his place of nativity, the years in which he passed the imperial examinations, and the different official posts he had held. Then followed a long list of the persons he had recommended for office, for it was usually considered an important measure of an official's worthiness whether he had put forward good or bad men for public duty. It was stated that during his official career he had received two demerits. Once he was fined eight catties of copper for failing to attend the official autumn ceremony when he was deputy magistrate at Fengshiang at the time when he had a quarrel with his superior. He was also fined eight catties of copper during his term at Hangchow for failing to report the embezzlement of public funds by a certain minor official. "Outside these two cases, he has a clear official record."

At first Su Tungpo acknowledged responsibility only for those poems he had written when he was visiting the villages near Hangchow, those in which he complained of the farmers eating without salt and the abuse of the farmers' loans, and certain others mentioned in the impeachment. He could not recall having written anything else that had any bearing on current politics. For some days he denied having written satirical poems to his friends, and continued to plead not guilty. It was a question of what should and what should not be considered "slander of the government," and what constituted "slanderous attacks." But on the thirtieth of August he decided to plead guilty; he then admitted that he had written satirical poems about the regime and had exchanged such poems with his friends. He said, however, that he "had not tried to conceal them," since it was a question of interpretation. In the course of the trial he was made to sign an affidavit admitting, "Since I joined the different ministries, I have not received rapid promotions. Besides, the people promoted during the new regime were mostly young men and differed in opinion from myself. Therefore I composed poems and other writings of protest and criticism, in the hope that many people would read these poems and be brought around to my point of view." There were altogether thirty-nine persons among the friends of Su Tungpo who were implicated in the case, and over a hundred poems were brought up in the trial for examination, each of which the author was required to explain. As Su Tungpo had in all his poetry used the choicest phrases and a great number of literary and historical allusions, we are indebted to this record of the trial for the author's own elucidations of many passages in his texts. Some of these poems were highly deceptive and had hidden points to be appreciated only when one understood the historical references. I have so far avoided these poems with learned allusions, because they would require a separate explanation for each literary metaphor or historical reference, and would make difficult reading, besides burdening the reader with pedantry. Such an exhibition of pedantry would not be at all difficult because for centuries Su's commentators have been busy unearthing the original passages in history and Tang poetry to which his lines referred.

Some of the accusations were far-fetched. One of the most interesting cases was a poem about two old cypress trees. It said that the winding roots of these trees reached the underground springs where only the "hidden dragon" would know what they were like. This was considered an insult to the Emperor because the dragon was the symbol of the ruler who was presently reigning over the empire, and therefore one should only refer to a "dragon in the skies," and not a dragon hidden in the underground springs. There was also a poem about peonies in which the poet admired the incredible ingenuity of nature in creating such a great variety of the same species. This was taken by the judges to be intended as a sly reference to the ingenuity of those in power in devising new forms of taxation. The preface to the descriptive poem "The Medlar and the Chrysanthemum," where he spoke of eating these bitter seeds, was considered a direct satire on the poverty of the district in general and on the poor pay of the government officials in particular. The parable of the blind man's idea of the sun was considered a reference to the ignorance of the scholar candidates, who knew nothing about Confucian philosophy except what was in Wang Anshih's commentaries.

However, in most of the cases the defendant frankly admitted criticism of the various new government measures in his poems, and certainly there was enough feeling of anger and disappointment in the tone of his poems to justify the verdict that he was voicing a sharp criticism of the regime.

Among the different poems that he had sent to his friend Prince Wang Shien, there was a line where he said that he had to sit and "listen to the screams of the prisoners being flogged." He did say that "in a famine year there was no way of sending the fugitives home," fugitives compelled to flee their villages because of debt. He did refer to the "difficulty of painting a tiger," which was a symbol of the rapacious government. In his poem to his friend Li Chang, he did say that he "had gone along the city wall" of Michow and "buried the exposed corpses with tears in my eyes," corpses of men, women, and children who had died of starvation and fallen on the wayside, and that "there was no joy in being a magistrate" at that time. Concerning his poem to his friend Sun Chueh, containing a line saying that they would not talk politics, he confessed that at a dinner together they had agreed that whoever mentioned politics was to be penalized with a cup of wine. In a poem to Tseng Kung, an obscure official but a major prose write, he mentioned that he was annoyed by all the hubbub of the politicians who "sounded to him like the every-crying cicadas." In his poem to Chang Fangping he had compared the court to "a deserted forest where cicadas are dinning the air," and "an abandoned pond where croaking frogs are making so much noise" that he wanted "to close both my ears with my hands." In his poem to Fan Chen he made a direct reference to the "petty politicians" and we already know that in the one to Chou Pin he made an implied comparison of the ruling authorities to the owl. In a poem on the Hangchow bore he had said that if the China Sea had known of the good Emperor's intentions, it would "change the salt-producing areas into mulberry fields."

It is interesting to take a closer look at two poems he wrote to one of his best friends, Liu Shu, when the latter was dismissed from the capital. We shall understand better the officials' resentment and also get an idea of the hidden meanings in most of Su Tungpo's lines. Incidentally, it will be seen that a literal translation of some of the poems would be meaningless to an English reader unless properly supported with footnotes. One of the poems says:

"How dare I express discontent in a time of peace?
I only sigh that my teachings are following you east.
By your conversation, you can frighten the south of Huai River,
And after your departure stripped bare will be the north of Chi.
A lone stork does not have to sound alarm at midnight,
It is difficult to tell the sex of black crows..."

Su Tungpo confessed that he was a great admirer of this friend, and that he had therefore compared him to Confucius by the phrase about not expressing discontent. The second line refers to the great commentator of the eastern Han Dynasty, who was sending his disciple to the east. The third line refers to a great, courageous official who quelled a plot for rebellion by the Prince of Huainan ("south of Huai River")by his presence at the court. The fourth line refers to a passage in the ancient classics saying that the best horses were produced in the north of Chi district (modern Hopei), and furthermore, to a line by a Tang poet, Han Yu, who on sending a friend off said that after his departure no good horses were left in the countryside of the north of Chi. It therefore meant that the whole court was now empty of good men. The fifth line about the "lone stork" refers to an ancient passage where a distinguished man in a company of petty men was compared to a stork standing alone in a poultry yard of ducks and chickens. The implied meaning was that those at the court were just common fowl; and crying at midnight was supposed to be a function of the stork. The last line was even more offensive, because there are two lines in the *Book of Poetry* which assert, "Everybody is saying I am a saint, but who can distinguish a male from a female crow?" The court consisted, therefore, of no more than a pack of black crows in which there was no way of telling which was good and which was had.

In a second satirical poem to the same friend he had written:

"Benevolence and righteousness are the great avenues,
Poetry and history are the steppingstones.
They show off their flowing belts to each other
And sing of the wheat's shining green.
Thanks for your exhibition of rotten mice,
But the high-flying crane dives into the clouds.
You don't have to wake me up from my madness;
I shall be sober when I wake up from the drink."

The first three lines refer to the scholar hypocrites who talk of benevolence and righteousness as avenues of official promotion and deride them for being proud of their official pomp. The reference to the "wheat's shining green" is, according to Su Tungpo, a reference to a poem in the *Book of Chuangtse* about officials who sought honor in their lifetime and were buried with pearls in their mouths, but in time their graveyards became wheat fields. The fifth line contains another reference to Chuangtse. On being offered a high post by the king of his country, Chuangtse declined it and told the official messenger the following story: There were some carrion crows who had caught dead rotten mice and were making a feast on a tree. A crane (symbol of the pure and retired scholar) happened to fly by, and thinking that the crane was going to deprive them of the feast of mice, the crows screeched to frighten it away, but the noble bird flew on up to the clouds. The moral of this story was that Su had a haughty contempt for the petty squabbles for power among the politicians.

I have the feeling that Su Tungpo thought it rather wonderful to be arrested and tried for writing poetry. He must have enjoyed lecturing the court on the literary references.

It was, therefore, well established that Su Tungpo had been highly disrespectful to the government. He had compared those in power to croaking frogs, to chirping cicadas, to owls, to black crows feeding on rotten mice, and to common fowl in a poultry yard. More unbearable was his reference to "monkeys who were given baths and caps" to look like human beings. It all amounted to this: Su Tungpo did not think very much of people like Sudan and Leeding, so why should Sudan and Leeding think well of Su Tungpo?

The trial was concluded, probably, at the beginning of October, and the testimony submitted to the Emperor. A great many persons were involved, particularly Prince Wang Shien, who had, as was brought out in the course of the trial, exchanged various gifts and presents with the poet. The Emperor ordered that all those who had exchanged poems with Su Tungpo should submit poems in their possession for examination by the court.

Meanwhile, Emperor Jentsung's wife, who had always stood up for Su

Tungpo, fell ill and died. Before her death she had said to the Emperor, "I remember that when the Su brothers passed the examinations, our ancestor Jentsung told members of the family that he was greatly pleased for he had that day discovered two future premiers for his royal descendants. I hear now that Su Shih is on trial for writing poems. It's the little fellows who want to destroy him. They couldn't find any fault with his official record, and now they try to convict him on his poetry. Is not the charge rather trivial? I do not think I can recover, but you must not condemn the innocent. It will anger the gods." This practically amounted to her dying wish.

On the thirtieth of October the judges made a summary of the case, which was submitted to the Emperor. On account of the funeral for the Empress Dowager, the case hung fire for a long time. While Su Tungpo was waiting in jail for the outcome of the trial and the determination of his fate, something mysterious happened.

"One night after the completion of the trial," Su Tungpo told his friends years later, "the night drum had been struck and just as I was going to bed I suddenly saw a man come into my room. Without saying a word, he threw a small box to the floor and, using it as his pillow, lay down to sleep on the ground. Taking him for another prisoner, I let him alone and fell asleep. About the time of the fourth watch [about 3 A.M.] I felt someone shaking me in my bed, and the man said to me, 'Congratulations!' I turned and asked him what this was all about. 'Sleep well and don't worry,' said the man and mysteriously left the room with his little box.

"What happened was that when I was first impeached, Sudan and the others tried their best to persuade the Emperor to put me to death. But His Majesty had never intended to kill me, so he secretly sent a small palace servant to the prison to watch me. Soon after this little fellow came, I fell asleep, snoring like thunder. He immediately rushed back to report to His Majesty that I was sleeping very soundly and peacefully, and His

Majesty said to the courtiers, 'I know that Su Shih's conscience is clear!' That was how later I was forgiven and sent to Huangchow."

It was the usual custom to grant a general amnesty on the occasion of an imperial funeral, and by law and custom Su Tungpo should have been pardoned. To the censors, who had hoped to involve the whole opposition by this case, this would have meant that all the trouble they had taken had come to naught. Leeding and Sudan were greatly worried. At this point, Leeding submitted a strong protest against any possible pardon of the accused that might be under consideration. Sudan went further and demanded that Szema Kuang, Fang Chen, Chang Fangping, Li Chang, Sun Chueh, and five others of Su Tungpo's friends be killed.

One of the vice-premiers at the time, Wang Kuei, under pressure of the censors, suddenly said to the Emperor one day:

"Su Shih is at heart a rebel against Your Majesty."

"He may have committed some offense," replied the Emperor with an expression of surprise, "but he is not thinking of rebellion. What makes you say so?"

Wang Kuei then mentioned the poem on the two cypresses with a reference to the dragon hidden in the underground springs, which could mean that someone destined to become emperor in the future would arise from his present obscurity. But the Emperor only said,

"You cannot read poetry that way. He was singing about the cypress. What has that to do with me?"

Wang Kuei therefore kept quiet, and Chang Chun, who was still Su Tungpo's friend at this time, defended Su by explaining to the Emperor that the dragon was not only the symbol of the ruler but could refer to ministers as well, and quoted examples from literary history in support of his argument.

When the examination of further evidence handed in by Su Tungpo's friends was completed, the Emperor appointed his own man to review the case. According to the iudge's summary a slander of this kind against the government was punishable by exile and hard labor for two years, and furthermore, in the case of Su Tungpo, whose offense was considered serious, the punishment should also deprive him of two of his official ranks. That was the legal view of the case. The power of decision, however, lay entirely with the Emperor himself in a case of such serious nature.

On December 29, to the great disappointment of Leeding and Sudan, a palace official handed out an order sending Su Tungpo to Huangchow near Hankow. He was given a low rank, with the nominal office of a lieutenant in an army training corps, but the terms of the order were that he was to be "kept" or "confined" there within that district; that is, he was not free to leave that district, and had no right to sign official documents.

Among those implicated in the case, three were dealt with severely. Prince Wang Shien was deprived of all his ranks on the ground that he had betrayed official secrets to Su Tungpo and had constantly exchanged gifts with him, and that, moreover, as a member of the royal household he had failed to report such slanderous poems as were in his possession. The second was Wang Kung, who had not received any particularly slanderous poems, but who was evidently being victimized in this case, perhaps because for private reasons the censors wanted to dispose of him. In the years after, Su kept referring to Wang Kung as one who suffered on his account. We know Wang Kung's luxurious habits, and his banishment to the remote southwest was hard for him.

The third was Tseyu, who had written to the Emperor begging for his brother's pardon and offering to surrender all his own official ranks and office to redeem him. In the testimony, Tseyu had not been charged with receiving any seriously slanderous poems from his brother, but on account of the family connection he was degraded and sent to Kao-an, about a hundred and sixty miles from the detention place of his brother, to sell wine at a government bureau.

Of the others, Chang Fangping and another high official were fined thirty catties of copper, while Szema Kuang, Fan Chen, and eighteen other friends of Su Tungpo were fined twenty catties of copper each.

Su Tungpo was let out of prison on New Year's Eve, after detention for four months and twelve days. Coming out of the prison gate on the north of the Tungcheng Street, he stopped for a while, sniffed the air, and felt pleasure in the breeze blowing on his face, in the noise of the magpies, and in watching the people passing by on horseback in the streets.

Incorrigible as he was, that very day he wrote two poems again wherein he said that "facing the wine cup" he "felt like coming out of a dream," and trying his poetic pen, he "found it was already inspired."

"In all my life, writing has brought me into trouble.
From now on the lesser my fame, the better it is for me.
I feel like the old man's horse that has returned to the fort,
And will no longer have youth's cock fights in the east city."

His lines began to flow again, and in these two poems there were certainly at least two lines that under the scrutiny of the same prosecutors could equally convict him of disrespect for the Emperor. The reference to an old man at the fort losing his horse was harmless enough, since it referred to a parable that losing one's horse did not mean bad luck and finding it again did not mean good luck; in other words, one never knew what was good luck or bad. But the phrase "youth's cock fights" refers to a certain Chia Chang. In his old age Chia told people that when he was a boy, he had obtained the Tang emperor's favor with his fighting cocks and the emperor had treated him as court jester and an actor. The point could be stretched that once more he was referring to those at court as "jesters and actors"—a term of abuse. In another line he said that he had "stolen an office," that is, occupied a post without qualifications; but again, the phrase used was taken from a letter written by a great scholar and addressed to Tsao Tsao, a man popularly considered a great hypocrite and a wicked ruler. On completing the poem, Su threw down his pen and said, "I am really incorrigible."